LEVEL 1 PRACTICE EXAMS – VOLUME 2

Online Resources 3

How to Use This Book 4

Exam 1
    Morning Session 5
    Afternoon Session 45

Exam 2
    Morning Session 83
    Afternoon Session 119

Exam 3
    Morning Session 157
    Afternoon Session 197

Exam 1 Answers
    Morning Session 235
    Afternoon Session 254

Exam 2 Answers
    Morning Session 273
    Afternoon Session 292

Exam 3 Answers
    Morning Session 309
    Afternoon Session 327

CFA® LEVEL 1 PRACTICE EXAMS – VOLUME 2

©2008 Kaplan Schweser. All rights reserved.

Published in 2008 by Kaplan Schweser.

Printed in the United States of America.

ISBN: 1-60373-243-8 / 978-1-60373-243-7

PPN: 45593CFA

USE YOUR SCHWESER ONLINE ACCESS ACCOUNT

All purchasers of this book are sent login information for Online Access in an e-mail. This is your login to use Performance Tracker and access other Schweser online resources. Simply log in at www.schweser.com and select "Online Access" to use any of these features. If you need password help, go to www.schweser.com/password or use the "Password Help" link that appears if your login is unsuccessful.

VOLUME 2 ONLINE FEATURES AT A GLANCE

Links to Curriculum

Within the online answer explanations, we have included page references to the relevant text in both the SchweserNotes and the CFA Institute program texts as well as the primary Learning Outcome Statement supporting the question.

Exam Diagnostics

When you enter your answers in our Performance Tracker utility, you can request a breakdown of your overall score on any one-half (120 question) exam. See how you performed by topic area, study session, or reading. You can also get the Learning Outcome Statement references for just those questions you answered incorrectly to help you focus your review efforts.

Performance Comparison

When you enter your answers on the page for Performance Tracker, you can find out how your score on each half-exam compares to the scores of others who entered their answers.

Log in today and enjoy the benefits of Performance Tracker and the other online resources in your account.

HOW TO USE THIS BOOK

Practice Exams are a very important part of the Schweser Study Program. **Don't neglect them.**

You shouldn't take the 2009 Level 1 CFA® Exam without lots of practice answering exam-like questions. Test yourself with these Practice Exams only after you have completed all the assigned readings.

The purpose of these questions is to make sure that you know all the concepts and ideas that are in the assigned readings. If you truly know the material you will do well on the actual exam. While our practice questions cover all the material, **they are not actual exam questions.** Our practice exams are not designed to predict your score on the actual CFA exam, although we try to match the level of difficulty on the exam. Use them to practice and identify those areas in which you need additional work.

Remember though, that CFA Institute® tries very hard every year to come up with new and innovative ways to test you. Your only defense against a good exam writer is to actually know the material. Learning the material and how to pace yourself on the exam is what our practice questions are designed to help you do.

The CFA exam is structured so that the morning and afternoon exams are each independent exams covering all topic areas. So, the three 6-hour practice exams here in Volume 2 really are six 3-hour practice exams. This gives you several opportunities to test your progress.

Our recommendations for using this book are:

- After you have finished your first complete review of the assigned reading material, take the morning portion of Practice Exam 1, paying strict attention to the time constraint. Enter your answers online. Performance Tracker will identify your weak spots and point you toward the material you need to review. Go back and study the material related to your weak areas.
- After you have reviewed that material, take the afternoon portion of Practice Exam 1. Again, pay strict attention to the allotted time and review the material related to your weak areas identified by Performance Tracker.
- During the two weeks prior to the exam, set aside two days to take Exams 2 and 3. Complete each of these 6-hour exams on one day with only a lunch break between the two halves. This will get you used to doing what you must do on exam day. Again review your weak areas but also look at the explanation for every problem you missed, so it won't happen again.
- Finally, review all of Study Session 1 on the day before the exam. Ethical and Professional Standards and Global Investment Performance Standards will be approximately 15% of the Level 1 exam. A final review of this material, including all the text and all the examples in the *Standards of Practice Handbook,* will serve you well on exam day.

Don't plan on passing the exam by memorizing questions and answers. Instead, learn the logic behind each of the questions. CFA Institute® isn't going to ask you our questions, but they will ask you questions that address the same concepts, logic, and definitions necessary to answer the practice exam questions.

Exam 1
Morning Session

Topic	Questions	Points
Ethical and Professional Standards	1–18	27
Quantitative Analysis	19–32	21
Economics	33–44	18
Financial Reporting and Analysis	45–77	51
Portfolio Management	79–84	9
Asset Valuation	85–120	54
Total		**180**

Test Answers

1.	Ⓐ	Ⓑ	Ⓒ		41.	Ⓐ	Ⓑ	Ⓒ		81.	Ⓐ	Ⓑ	Ⓒ
2.	Ⓐ	Ⓑ	Ⓒ		42.	Ⓐ	Ⓑ	Ⓒ		82.	Ⓐ	Ⓑ	Ⓒ
3.	Ⓐ	Ⓑ	Ⓒ		43.	Ⓐ	Ⓑ	Ⓒ		83.	Ⓐ	Ⓑ	Ⓒ
4.	Ⓐ	Ⓑ	Ⓒ		44.	Ⓐ	Ⓑ	Ⓒ		84.	Ⓐ	Ⓑ	Ⓒ
5.	Ⓐ	Ⓑ	Ⓒ		45.	Ⓐ	Ⓑ	Ⓒ		85.	Ⓐ	Ⓑ	Ⓒ
6.	Ⓐ	Ⓑ	Ⓒ		46.	Ⓐ	Ⓑ	Ⓒ		86.	Ⓐ	Ⓑ	Ⓒ
7.	Ⓐ	Ⓑ	Ⓒ		47.	Ⓐ	Ⓑ	Ⓒ		87.	Ⓐ	Ⓑ	Ⓒ
8.	Ⓐ	Ⓑ	Ⓒ		48.	Ⓐ	Ⓑ	Ⓒ		88.	Ⓐ	Ⓑ	Ⓒ
9.	Ⓐ	Ⓑ	Ⓒ		49.	Ⓐ	Ⓑ	Ⓒ		89.	Ⓐ	Ⓑ	Ⓒ
10.	Ⓐ	Ⓑ	Ⓒ		50.	Ⓐ	Ⓑ	Ⓒ		90.	Ⓐ	Ⓑ	Ⓒ
11.	Ⓐ	Ⓑ	Ⓒ		51.	Ⓐ	Ⓑ	Ⓒ		91.	Ⓐ	Ⓑ	Ⓒ
12.	Ⓐ	Ⓑ	Ⓒ		52.	Ⓐ	Ⓑ	Ⓒ		92.	Ⓐ	Ⓑ	Ⓒ
13.	Ⓐ	Ⓑ	Ⓒ		53.	Ⓐ	Ⓑ	Ⓒ		93.	Ⓐ	Ⓑ	Ⓒ
14.	Ⓐ	Ⓑ	Ⓒ		54.	Ⓐ	Ⓑ	Ⓒ		94.	Ⓐ	Ⓑ	Ⓒ
15.	Ⓐ	Ⓑ	Ⓒ		55.	Ⓐ	Ⓑ	Ⓒ		95.	Ⓐ	Ⓑ	Ⓒ
16.	Ⓐ	Ⓑ	Ⓒ		56.	Ⓐ	Ⓑ	Ⓒ		96.	Ⓐ	Ⓑ	Ⓒ
17.	Ⓐ	Ⓑ	Ⓒ		57.	Ⓐ	Ⓑ	Ⓒ		97.	Ⓐ	Ⓑ	Ⓒ
18.	Ⓐ	Ⓑ	Ⓒ		58.	Ⓐ	Ⓑ	Ⓒ		98.	Ⓐ	Ⓑ	Ⓒ
19.	Ⓐ	Ⓑ	Ⓒ		59.	Ⓐ	Ⓑ	Ⓒ		99.	Ⓐ	Ⓑ	Ⓒ
20.	Ⓐ	Ⓑ	Ⓒ		60.	Ⓐ	Ⓑ	Ⓒ		100.	Ⓐ	Ⓑ	Ⓒ
21.	Ⓐ	Ⓑ	Ⓒ		61.	Ⓐ	Ⓑ	Ⓒ		101.	Ⓐ	Ⓑ	Ⓒ
22.	Ⓐ	Ⓑ	Ⓒ		62.	Ⓐ	Ⓑ	Ⓒ		102.	Ⓐ	Ⓑ	Ⓒ
23.	Ⓐ	Ⓑ	Ⓒ		63.	Ⓐ	Ⓑ	Ⓒ		103.	Ⓐ	Ⓑ	Ⓒ
24.	Ⓐ	Ⓑ	Ⓒ		64.	Ⓐ	Ⓑ	Ⓒ		104.	Ⓐ	Ⓑ	Ⓒ
25.	Ⓐ	Ⓑ	Ⓒ		65.	Ⓐ	Ⓑ	Ⓒ		105.	Ⓐ	Ⓑ	Ⓒ
26.	Ⓐ	Ⓑ	Ⓒ		66.	Ⓐ	Ⓑ	Ⓒ		106.	Ⓐ	Ⓑ	Ⓒ
27.	Ⓐ	Ⓑ	Ⓒ		67.	Ⓐ	Ⓑ	Ⓒ		107.	Ⓐ	Ⓑ	Ⓒ
28.	Ⓐ	Ⓑ	Ⓒ		68.	Ⓐ	Ⓑ	Ⓒ		108.	Ⓐ	Ⓑ	Ⓒ
29.	Ⓐ	Ⓑ	Ⓒ		69.	Ⓐ	Ⓑ	Ⓒ		109.	Ⓐ	Ⓑ	Ⓒ
30.	Ⓐ	Ⓑ	Ⓒ		70.	Ⓐ	Ⓑ	Ⓒ		110.	Ⓐ	Ⓑ	Ⓒ
31.	Ⓐ	Ⓑ	Ⓒ		71.	Ⓐ	Ⓑ	Ⓒ		111.	Ⓐ	Ⓑ	Ⓒ
32.	Ⓐ	Ⓑ	Ⓒ		72.	Ⓐ	Ⓑ	Ⓒ		112.	Ⓐ	Ⓑ	Ⓒ
33.	Ⓐ	Ⓑ	Ⓒ		73.	Ⓐ	Ⓑ	Ⓒ		113.	Ⓐ	Ⓑ	Ⓒ
34.	Ⓐ	Ⓑ	Ⓒ		74.	Ⓐ	Ⓑ	Ⓒ		114.	Ⓐ	Ⓑ	Ⓒ
35.	Ⓐ	Ⓑ	Ⓒ		75.	Ⓐ	Ⓑ	Ⓒ		115.	Ⓐ	Ⓑ	Ⓒ
36.	Ⓐ	Ⓑ	Ⓒ		76.	Ⓐ	Ⓑ	Ⓒ		116.	Ⓐ	Ⓑ	Ⓒ
37.	Ⓐ	Ⓑ	Ⓒ		77.	Ⓐ	Ⓑ	Ⓒ		117.	Ⓐ	Ⓑ	Ⓒ
38.	Ⓐ	Ⓑ	Ⓒ		78.	Ⓐ	Ⓑ	Ⓒ		118.	Ⓐ	Ⓑ	Ⓒ
39.	Ⓐ	Ⓑ	Ⓒ		79.	Ⓐ	Ⓑ	Ⓒ		119.	Ⓐ	Ⓑ	Ⓒ
40.	Ⓐ	Ⓑ	Ⓒ		80.	Ⓐ	Ⓑ	Ⓒ		120.	Ⓐ	Ⓑ	Ⓒ

Exam 1
Morning Session

Ethical and Professional Standards

1. Ronnie Smith is registered to sit for the CFA Level 2 exam. Unfortunately, Smith has failed the exam the past two years. In his frustration, Smith posted the following comment on a popular internet bulletin board: "I believe that CFA Institute is intentionally limiting the number of charterholders in order to increase its cash flow by continuing to fail candidates. Just look at the pass rates."

    Chester Burkett is a CFA Level 3 candidate living in New York. Burkett's best friend, Jim Jones, is a Level 3 candidate living in London. Because of the time difference between London and New York, Burkett suggests that Jones call Burkett during the London exam lunch break to discuss what topics were emphasized in the morning session. Jones agrees and makes the call on exam day.

    Which of the following statements regarding Standard VII(A), Conduct as Members and Candidates in the CFA Program, is *most likely* **TRUE**?
    A. Smith, Jones, and Burkett are all in violation of Standard VII(A).
    B. Smith is in violation of Standard VII(A), but Jones and Burkett are not.
    C. Jones and Burkett are in violation of Standard VII(A), but Smith is not.

2. Which of the following is *least likely* to be a misleading practice that the GIPS standards were created to minimize?
    A. Suitability—presenting a portfolio to appear to fit all clients' objectives, mandates and constraints.
    B. Varying time periods—presenting performance for a selected time period which highlights the firm's very best returns.
    C. Survivorship bias—presenting an "average" performance history that excludes accounts that were discontinued for poor performance.

3. Jack Wilson, CFA, a hedge fund manager, takes a large short position in BNR stock. After Wilson establishes his short position, BNR shares trade down 1.15%. One week later, BNR shares are trading 3.84% below the initial short price, and Wilson reverses the short position and establishes a short position in shares of the company's competitor, HTC. On a well-known investor message board, Wilson posts a highly critical message about HTC, which grossly exaggerates problems with a crucial supplier to HTC. The day after Wilson's message post, HTC shares fall 0.97% and Wilson reverses the short position. Did Wilson's actions related to BNR stock and/or HTC stock violate the CFA Institute Standards of Professional Conduct?
   A. Yes, in both cases.
   B. Only in the case of HTC.
   C. Only in the case of BNR.

4. After working 20 years on Wall Street, Jim Gentry, CFA, decides to open his own investment firm on Turtle Island, located in the Caribbean. Turtle Island has securities laws that are much less stringent than U.S. laws or the CFA Institute Standards of Professional Conduct. Many of his U.S.-based clients have agreed to keep Gentry as their portfolio manager and move their assets to his new firm. After a few months of operations, Gentry has encountered several instances in which Turtle Island regulations relieve him of disclosing information to investors that he had been required to disclose while working in New York. According to the CFA Institute Code and Standards, Gentry must adhere to the:
   A. Code and Standards because they are more strict than the applicable laws in Turtle Island.
   B. laws of Turtle Island, but disclose any discrepancies to U.S.-based clients.
   C. Code and Standards because as a charterholder, he need only adhere to the Code and Standards under all circumstances.

5. All analysts at MK Investments, including Rene Green, CFA, use a statistical model to determine the fair market value of potential investments. Clients are aware of the general model but not its details. MK recently changed the model in an attempt to more accurately price assets. In an e-mail to all of his prospects and clients, Green includes the exact specification of the new model, and states that more accurate asset valuations are expected from the new model. Has Green violated the CFA Institute Standards of Professional Conduct?
   A. No, Green's actions are consistent with CFA Institute Standards.
   B. Yes, because he should have notified existing clients before notifying prospects.
   C. Yes, because he suggested that the new model will generate more accurate asset valuations.

6. Brett Havens, CFA, the Chief Compliance Officer for Westland Investments, is asked by his supervisor to verify that Westland has satisfied all of the requirements of GIPS and can claim that it is in compliance. Havens notes that the firm has released its most recent eight years of performance history in a GIPS- compliant manner, as well as non-compliant history for the two years prior to that. The firm has been in existence for ten years. Which of the following actions must Westland take in order to ensure full compliance with GIPS? Westland must:
   A. utilize the services of an independent third party in order to claim full compliance with the GIPS standards.
   B. disclose the periods of noncompliance and explain how the presentation is not in compliance with the GIPS standards.
   C. present all ten years of its investment performance in a GIPS- compliant manner.

7. Roger Smith, CFA, is a retail broker for a small brokerage firm that caters to high net worth individuals. Smith manages a retirement account for his father-in-law and notices that a stock that his father-in-law owns has been downgraded by the firm's research department. He places a "sell" order for the entire position in that particular stock for three clients' accounts, one of which belongs to his father-in-law. According to the CFA Institute Standards of Professional Conduct, Smith:
   A. has violated the Standards because he has beneficial ownership in the account.
   B. has not violated any Standard because his father-in-law's account should be treated like any other firm account.
   C. has violated the Standards by entering a transaction before all clients have had adequate opportunity to act on the recommendation.

8. Giselle Holt, CFA, is a portfolio manager in the trust department of State Bank. Holt recently inherited a substantial amount of stock of Brown & Company and accepted a position on the board of directors for TVC Plastics Inc. Many of the trust clients at the bank hold positions in Brown & Company and in TVC Plastics. According to CFA Institute Standards of Professional Conduct, which of the following *best* describes the disclosures that Holt must make?
   A. Holt must disclose the stock ownership and board position to her clients.
   B. Holt must disclose the stock ownership to her clients and State Bank.
   C. Holt must disclose the stock ownership and board position to her clients and State Bank.

9. Nancy McCoy, CFA, is an analyst covering the grocery store industry and is currently preparing to update and issue a report on Gourmet Food Mart. As part of her routine research, she contacts the company's contractors, suppliers and competitors. She is told by the CEO of a major produce vendor that he is about to file a lawsuit against Gourmet Food Mart, seeking significant damages for alleged discriminatory practices. The CEO has already notified Gourmet Food Mart of the lawsuit. McCoy incorporates this information into her research report, which projects a decline in profitability for Gourmet Food Mart due to the impending litigation. According to the CFA Institute Standards of Professional Conduct, McCoy:
   A. has not violated any Standard in accordance with the mosaic theory.
   B. has violated the Standards by utilizing material nonpublic information.
   C. has violated the Standards by disseminating confidential information.

10. Ron Welch, CFA, manages trust accounts at a regional U.S. bank. Welch was hired four years ago to manage the Craig Family Trust, which specifies a passive investment strategy of mirroring the S&P 500 Index risk and return. Over the past year, Welch over-weighted technology stocks, which allowed the trust portfolio to earn a return 200 basis points above the S&P 500 return with only slightly higher risk. With respect to Standard III(A) Loyalty, Prudence and Care, and Standard III(C) Suitability, Welch violated:
   A. both of these Standards.
   B. neither of these Standards.
   C. only one of these Standards.

11.	SARS Corporation for the past several weeks has publicly indicated to investment analysts that it is "OK" with an EPS projection of $2.10 to $2.14 for the quarter. Among all analysts who cover SARS, the consensus earnings estimate is $2.14. Lee Rutherford, an analyst at Cleaver Investments, is convinced that SARS is deliberately going along with the consensus earnings estimate and will soon release earnings substantially above what is anticipated. Rutherford goes along with the consensus earnings estimate in Cleaver Investments' research report, including an earnings estimate of $2.13 per share. However, he has a few conversations with selected clients in which he mentions his reasons for expecting an announcement of higher earnings. Which of the following statements *most accurately* describes Rutherford's behavior?

A.	"A few conversations" does not constitute a violation of the Standards. The research report is the official document, and that is what Rutherford is supporting.

B.	Rutherford is in violation of the Standards by failing to deal with clients fairly in disseminating material changes in investment recommendations.

C.	SARS Corporation is in violation of the Standards by not disclosing material earnings information to the public.

12.	Carlos Mendez, CFA, is beginning an investment advisory relationship with a new client and plans to formulate an investment policy statement (IPS) for the client. According to Standard III(C) Suitability, which of the following is Mendez *least likely* to consider in writing an IPS?

A.	Regulatory and legal circumstances.

B.	Conflicts of interest.

C.	Performance measurement benchmarks.

13. Chuck Hill, CFA, the CFO of Niseron Corp., has just learned that Niseron's quarterly net income will fall well short of consensus analyst expectations. Hill decides that he should immediately notify analysts covering Niseron Corp. of this negative development. He feels a certain obligation to call two analysts in particular—these individuals have followed Niseron stock for several years and have from time to time alerted Hill to important developments at competing firms. Failure to notify these analysts might damage Hill's ability to monitor his competition, to the detriment of his own shareholders. Which of the following actions is *most* appropriate under CFA Institute's Code and Standards?
     A. Hill should notify no analysts until he is ready to issue the final numbers for the quarter.
     B. Because their information adds value to Niseron's shareholders, it is acceptable for Hill to notify the two analysts first, so long as his remarks are general in nature and "off the record."
     C. Hill should issue a press release prior to calling analysts.

14. Jim Gordon, CFA, is long 20,000 shares of ABC stock. The stock has recently declined below his original cost and Gordon would like to utilize the loss in calculating his income taxes for the current year. Gordon believes the stock will recover quickly, but he must sell the stock to realize the loss. Repurchasing the stock immediately would be considered a wash sale under income tax law and would negate the recognition of the loss. Gordon decides to sell ABC and use derivative instruments to create a synthetic long position.

     George Turpin, a CFA Level 1 candidate, has decided to enter into a sizeable long position of DEF stock. Since DEF is thinly traded, Turpin is concerned the order will overwhelm the liquidity of DEF and the price will surge. Turpin engages in a series of block trades to accomplish the purchase.

     According to CFA Institute Standards of Professional Conduct, which of the following statements is **TRUE**?
     A. Gordon is in violation of the Standards, but Turpin is not in violation.
     B. Both Gordon and Turpin are in violation of the Standards.
     C. Neither Gordon nor Turpin is in violation of the Standards.

15. Jenny Pickler is a Level 2 CFA Candidate, and is a junior analyst at a regional investment firm. She writes an economic forecast containing several interest rate projections. The firm's investment committee reviews Pickler's report and changes several of the interest rates Pickler had forecast. Which of the following is Pickler's preferred course of action, to properly comply with CFA Institute Standards?
   A. There is no violation of the Code and Standards.
   B. Pickler should go along with the changes, but ask that her name be removed from the report.
   C. Pickler should not concur with the committee and agree to change the report without independently reviewing supporting data.

16. John Malone, CFA, manages pension funds at NBA Trust Company. Malone's wife is on the board of directors of Barley Corporation and owns 3% of its outstanding stock. Barley completed a public offering to finance plant expansion several months ago. Mrs. Malone's stock holdings subsequently have risen in value from $125,000 initially to over $4,500,000. NBA Trust's research division has recently recommended the Barley stock to its trust officers and pension fund portfolio managers. Based on the CFA Institute Standards, which of the following is Malone's *most* appropriate course of action for the accounts under his management?
   A. Malone may purchase the stock after disclosing his spouse's ownership interest to his supervisor and to the trustees of the pension funds he manages.
   B. Malone may not purchase the stock because he is not able to be unbiased and objective, given his spouse's affiliation with Barley.
   C. Malone is free to act as he chooses with no restrictions because he is not a beneficial owner of the Barley stock.

17. Denise Chavez is the senior energy analyst for a major brokerage firm, specializing in power plants. Chavez is also a social and environmental activist, and is much opposed to coal-fired power plants. She has been arrested twice for trespassing during organized pickets at some of these power plants on the weekends. Chavez has recently accepted a volunteer position as Board member of Greensleeves, a foundation that actively lobbies federal and local governments on environmental issues. She does not believe it will interfere with her brokerage firm position, although the position will involve significant volunteer hours, including some travel. Are Chavez's activities consistent with CFA Institute Standards?
    A. Chavez violated the Standards by being arrested as an environmental activist, but the Greensleeves volunteer work is not a violation.
    B. The environmental activism and the Greensleeves Board position are not violations.
    C. The activism and subsequent arrests are not a violation, but Chavez must disclose the Greensleeves Board position to her employer.

18. Peter Potts is a portfolio manager for a small partnership that caters exclusively to high net worth individuals. One of Potts' clients invites him to an extravagant party in Las Vegas. The client is chartering jets to fly his guests to Las Vegas and is hosting them at a high-end hotel. Potts would like to attend the celebration since he has worked with this client for several years. Potts decides to go on the trip, but does not inform his employer of his intentions. Potts' actions are *most likely* in violation of the Standards because:
    A. this benefit may impair his ability to deal fairly with all clients.
    B. his actions could reflect adversely on his professional reputation and integrity.
    C. he must receive the consent of his employer to accept supplemental benefits.

Quantitative Analysis

19. Valeri Kogan analyzes a company and makes the following projection for the possible earnings for the company:

EPS estimates	Probability of occurrence
$5.20/sh	10%
$2.50/sh	40%
$1.00/sh	30%
–$1.00/sh	20%

    The standard deviation for the company's earnings is *closest* to:
    A. $1.75
    B. $1.95
    C. $2.45

20.   Jeff Spider, CFA, is a consultant for SPA Consulting. He has been engaged by Limbo Company to select an equity investment manager for their defined benefit pension plan. Spider is considering Cutter Investments. The money management firm's 10 year performance is as follows: 35.1%, 15.6%, 12.0%, 22.2%, 50.3%, –20.0%, –33.4%, –30.6%, 30.8%, 13.0%. From the data provided, Spider calculated the following statistics:
•   Mean   9.5%
•   Median   14.3%
•   Excess Kurtosis –0.9761

Which of the following *best* describes the shape of the returns distribution for Limbo Company?
A. Positively skewed.
B. Negatively skewed.
C. Not skewed.

21.   Jack Smith, CFA, is the chief economist for Gable Investments. He believes that, in general, a recession is the direct result of higher energy prices. Smith has estimated that in his home country the probability of a recession given higher oil prices is 40%. Smith also believes that there is a 70% probability oil prices will fall from current levels. Calculate the probability of observing rising oil prices and a recession.
A. 12%
B. 18%
C. 28%

22.   After repeatedly sampling the 1-year returns on the common stock of Bernouli Inc., a semiconductor manufacturer, an analyst notices that the returns conform to a normal probability distribution. Which of the following statements *correctly* describes the returns on Bernouli's common stock?
A. The mean value is greater than the median.
B. Large deviations from the mean are less likely than small deviations.
C. The distributions can be completely described by the residual value and the standard deviation.

23.   Frank Jones is considering three separate investments. Investment 1 pays a stated annual interest rate of 6.1%, compounded annually. Investment 2 pays a stated annual interest rate of 6.0%, compounded monthly. Investment 3 pays a stated annual interest rate of 5.9%, compounded quarterly. Which investment should Smith choose?
A. Investment 1.
B. Investment 2.
C. Investment 3.

24. Sean Dahib, a quantitative analyst, has been given the assignment of tallying the P/Es of the companies in the S&P 500 index. He constructed the following table:

P/Es	# of Companies
0 up to 10	25
10 up to 20	100
20 up to 30	150
30 up to 40	145
40 up to 50	35
50 up to 60	25
60 up to 70	10
70 up to 80	10

    What is the relative class frequency for the class of companies with the *smallest* P/Es?
    A. 12.5%.
    B. 5.0%.
    C. 2.0%.

25. Curt Harf, CFA, sold Pride Mining for $80 per share. Harf bought Pride Mining for $20 per share five years ago. Calculate the investment's approximate continuously compounded return.
    A. 25%.
    B. 28%.
    C. 32%.

26. Edward Murray and William Ripken recently examined the accumulated interest, paid in increments of $0.01, that are possible on a 5-year floating-rate bond with a stated floor (minimum interest rate) and cap (maximum interest rate). Murray states that the accumulated interest payments are "an example of a discrete random variable." Ripken states that the graph of the probability distribution for the accumulated interest payments will be a "series of disconnected points." Determine whether the statements made by Murray and Ripken are correct.
    A. Only Murray is correct.
    B. Only Ripken is correct.
    C. Both Murray and Ripken are correct.

27. Gloria Brown, CFA, calculated the intrinsic value of RTN Company and expects the stock to generate a 25% annual return over the foreseeable future. However, Brown is concerned that her price forecast may be too high. She conducted a hypothesis test and concluded that at a 5% significance level, the null hypothesis can be rejected that RTN Company's investment return would be equal to or less than 25% per year. The one-tailed test utilized a z-test. Indicate the meaning of the significance level chosen by Brown.
    A. Brown will reject a true null hypothesis 5% of the time.
    B. Brown will reject a false null hypothesis 95% of the time.
    C. Brown will reject a true null hypothesis 95% of the time.

28. Burle Weaver and James Palmer, analysts for Growthmore Managers, are assigned the task of examining the mean return for growth stocks. After sorting 10,000 stocks based on price-to-earnings ratios, Weaver and Palmer classify the stocks with price-to earnings ratios above the median as growth stocks. They then use a random number generator to select a sample of 100 stocks from the growth stocks. Their sample consists of last year's rate of return for each of the 100 sampled growth stocks. In his meeting with the Growthmore board, Weaver states that his sampling procedure is an example of stratified random sampling. Palmer explains that the distribution of the 100 sampled returns is called a sampling distribution. Determine whether the statements made by Weaver and Palmer are correct.
    A. Only Weaver is incorrect.
    B. Only Palmer is incorrect.
    C. Both Weaver and Palmer are incorrect.

29. Tammy John, CFA, uses contrary opinion technical trading rules to predict trends in the stock market. Based on the most recent month's data, John is extremely bullish and believes the S&P 500 index will rise by 15% or more over the next year. Which of the following indicators is *least likely* to support John's belief?
    A. 65% of investment advisory opinions are bearish.
    B. Low mutual fund cash positions.
    C. High put-call ratio on the Chicago Board Options Exchange.

30. Jon Pelker plans to retire in six years and will require $950,000. Today, Pelker will deposit $100,000 into an interest bearing account and will set aside an additional $100,000 at the end of each of the next six years. What percentage return must Pelker earn to achieve his goal of $950,000 for his retirement?
    A. 8%.
    B. 10%.
    C. 18%.

31. Gus Hayden is evaluating the performance of the portfolio manager in charge of his retirement account. The account started with $5,000,000 and over the past two years has generated a 15% return in the first year and a –5% return in the second year. Hayden has complete discretionary control over the timing and amount of withdrawals and additions to the portfolio. Hayden adds $2,000,000 at the beginning of year 2. Calculate the appropriate annualized return.
    A. 2.98%.
    B. 4.52%.
    C. 9.25%.

32. Kidra Rao ranks and classifies firms into ten groups based on their interest coverage ratios, lowest to highest. Determine what type of ranking system is used by Rao.
    A. Ratio scale.
    B. Nominal scale.
    C. Ordinal scale.

Economics

33. The Screenplex Company operates a chain of multi-screen movie theaters across the U.S. Competition in the industry is intense, but managers have discovered that weekend moviegoers have lower price elasticity of demand than weekday moviegoers. The pricing strategy *most likely* to allow Screenplex to increase its revenue would be to:
    A. raise prices to take advantage of the high elasticity of weekday moviegoers.
    B. lower prices to take advantage of the low elasticity of weekend moviegoers.
    C. charge different prices to weekday and weekend customers.

34. A consumer is willing to pay $4 per gallon for 10 gallons of gasoline, $3 per gallon for 20 gallons, $2 per gallon for 30 gallons, and $1 per gallon for 40 gallons. The consumer is unwilling to pay more than $5 per gallon for gasoline. Which of the following is *most likely* correct?
    A. At a market price of $2 per gallon, the marginal benefit to the consumer is greatest for the 40th gallon consumed.
    B. At a market price of $2 per gallon, the consumer surplus is greater than at a market price of $3 per gallon.
    C. As the market price increases from $2 to $3 per gallon, the marginal benefit to the consumer increases.

35. Sean Quillan, a staff economist at a large investment firm, is discussing the cost structure of firms in the automobile industry. Quillan makes the following point:

    "Based on the law of diminishing returns, the firms' short term marginal cost curve will cross BOTH the average variable cost (AVC) curve and the average total cost (ATC) curve at their minimum points."

    Is Quillan's statement correct?
    A. Yes.
    B. No, because marginal cost should equal marginal revenue.
    C. No, because this will happen only if fixed costs are equal to zero.

36. One month ago, the U.S. Federal Reserve began purchasing Treasury securities in the open market. Which of the following *best* describes the rationale for the Fed's actions?
    A. The Fed believes interest rates are too low to achieve its primary goal of price level stability.
    B. The Fed believes lower interest rates will reduce the M1 measure to its intermediate target level.
    C. The federal funds rate is higher than the Fed's target rate.

37. Country Beta has experienced stagnant real GDP for the past three years. The new Minister of Finance (MOF) of Country Beta wants to increase Beta's potential real GDP. The MOF has decided to focus on economic policies that would increase long-run aggregate supply within Country Beta. Which of the following strategies under consideration by the MOF would offer the *best* potential for increasing the long-run aggregate supply of Country Beta?
    A. Increase both the price level and the money wage rate of the citizens of Country Beta at the same time and by the same percentage.
    B. Increase the price level of Country Beta, but keep money wage rates the same.
    C. Liberalize Country Beta's labor immigration laws to allow less expensive Country Delta workers to enter Beta in greater numbers.

38. As a result of the decline in small scale cucumber production, the U.S. government has decided to provide assistance to cucumber growers by paying them $0.05 per pound produced. Which of the following is the *most likely* result of this policy?
    A. The marginal benefit of cucumbers will exceed the marginal cost, causing a deadweight loss.
    B. The marginal cost of cucumbers will exceed the marginal benefit, causing a deadweight loss.
    C. The marginal cost of cucumbers will exceed the marginal benefit, but the market will still be in equilibrium.

39. Rick Watson, CFA, is evaluating the relative concentration of the international cement industry, which comprises ten international competitors. The market share breakdown is as follows: two firms control 20% of the market each, three firms control 10% of the market each, and five firms control 6% of the market each. Calculate the Herfindahl-Hirschman index for the cement industry.
    A. 1,280.
    B. 1,440.
    C. 5,600.

40. Richard White, CFA, has been analyzing the price elasticity of demand for gasoline. The gasoline demand curve is steep, but does slope normally. White has measured the elasticity of demand at several different price levels, and has concluded that the price elasticity is higher when demand is low, and lower when demand is high. The *most likely* justification for this result is that:
    A. gasoline retailers practice price discrimination.
    B. elasticity changes at different points along a straight-line demand curve.
    C. consumers alter their behavior when price increases endure for longer periods of time.

41. Tetra Corporation holds the exclusive production rights to a wireless cellular phone technology. Tetra's production rights will remain exclusive for 15 years, effectively eliminating any competition while the technology is viable. If their marginal revenue, marginal cost, and average total cost equal $50, $43, and $57, respectively, Tetra Corporation can maximize profits by:
    A. expanding output until marginal revenue equals marginal cost.
    B. reducing output until marginal revenue equals average total cost.
    C. expanding output until marginal revenue equals average total cost.

42. Wilmer Jones owns several restaurants in different cities. His restaurants compete on quality of food and service, price, and marketing. Competitors can enter and exit his markets, and there are usually several competitors in each market. His market structure can best be characterized as:
    A. perfect competition.
    B. monopolistic competition.
    C. oligopoly.

43. Assume a bank currently has $105 million in outstanding deposits, with actual reserves of $30 million. The required reserve ratio is 20%. Based on the information provided, calculate the maximum potential increase in the money supply if this bank lends all of its excess reserves.
    A. $6 million.
    B. $9 million.
    C. $45 million.

44. An increase in oil and commodity prices reduces short-run aggregate supply. Real GDP falls and price levels rise. The central bank responds by lowering interest rates to restore full employment, but prices rise further as a result of the increase in aggregate demand. This is an example of:
    A. cost-push inflation.
    B. demand-pull inflation.
    C. short-run inflation that will be reversed in the long run.

Financial Reporting and Analysis

45. Information about any conflicts of interest between management, the board of directors and shareholders can *most likely* be found in the:
    A. proxy statement.
    B. footnotes.
    C. auditor's report.

46. Which one of the following accounts *least likely* describes a current asset?
    A. Trade receivables.
    B. Prepaid expenses.
    C. Strategic company investments.

47. The following statements are based on the financial reporting standards of the International Accounting Standards Board (IASB) outlined in the Framework for the Preparation and Presentation of Financial Statements (IFRS). Indicate whether each of the statements is true.

    Statement 1: The central objective of the Framework is to provide a fair presentation of information that is useful to investors.

    Statement 2: The level of detail presented is driven by materiality.

    A. Only Statement 1 is true.
    B. Only Statement 2 is true.
    C. Both Statements 1 and 2 are true.

48. Water White Land Corp. sells land along the Arkansas River to low income buyers, who might eventually use the land to build retirement homes. The land requires a low down payment and small monthly payments over the course of 20 years. Water White has experienced a 28% default rate on its contracts over time. Sales commissions are expensed as incurred. The revenue recognition method that Water White should use is *best* described as:
   A. percentage of completion method.
   B. completed contract method.
   C. cost recovery method.

49. Cuban Inc. recently purchased a Gulfstream business jet for $45 million. Cuban expects the jet to make two flights per week. Cuban will depreciate the jet over twenty years and expects maintenance costs to rise sharply over its life. Which of the following is the *most appropriate* depreciation method?
   A. Straight line method.
   B. Production method.
   C. Declining balance method.

50. A company reports the following unusual events:
   • Gain on sale of discontinued operations.
   • Loss on discontinued operations.
   • Restructuring and severance costs applicable to asset sales.
   • Plant shutdown costs.

   Which of these items would be considered nonrecurring and included in operating income?
   A. Restructuring and severance costs applicable to asset sales and plant shutdown costs.
   B. Loss on discontinued operations and restructuring and severance costs applicable to asset sales.
   C. Loss on discontinued operations, restructuring and severance costs applicable to asset sales, and plant shutdown costs.

51.   Upton Corporation has the following capital structure:

Upton Capital Structure	Shares
Cumulative Preferred Stock $100 par value pays $6.50 per share	20,000
Common stock	500,000

Upton's 2008 net income was $830,000 and company's tax rate was 35%.

The 2008 basic earnings per share for Upton Corporation is *closest* to:
A. $1.40.
B. $1.60.
C. $1.66.

52.   At the beginning of the year, Weatherford Corporation had 2,000,000 shares of common stock outstanding. In addition, Weatherford had 150,000 stock options outstanding to purchase common shares at $10 per share. No stock options were exercised during the year. Assuming the average market price of the stock was $15, how many shares should Weatherford use in computing diluted earnings per share for the year?
A. 2,000,000.
B. 2,050,000.
C. 2,150,000.

53.   Product sales reported for the month ended December 31 were $3 million. Collections totaled $1 million in December and $2 million in January. Under accrual accounting, what would be the effect on the balance sheet at December 31?
A. Increase in cash of $1 million and $1 million decrease in Accounts Receivable.
B. Increase in cash of $1 million and $2 million increase in Accounts Receivable.
C. Increase of $3 million in Accounts Receivable.

54.   Jansen Co., a manufacturer of high-end sports equipment, earned $45 million in net income for the year. The company paid out $1.30 per share in dividends. Jansen issued 500,000 shares at the beginning of the year at $20 (1 million shares were outstanding before the issuance). The market value of Jansen's short term investments decreased by $2.4 million. The increase in Jansen's stockholders' equity is *closest* to:
A. $43 million.
B. $51 million.
C. $53 million.

55. Over the course of last year, GatesSoft Inc., which follows U.S. GAAP, sold $100 million of common stock, paid $15 million in interest, recorded $23 million of depreciation, acquired a German software company for $175 million, sold one of their product lines for $86 million, paid $13 million in dividends, and contributed $50 million to a joint venture with AllenSoft Inc. Which of the following is *closest* to the Investing Cash Flow for GatesSoft Inc. for last year?
   A. −$139 million.
   B. −$152 million.
   C. −$167 million.

56. Joplin Corporation reported the following in its year-end financial statements:
   - Net income of $43.7 million.
   - Depreciation expense of $4.2 million.
   - Increase in accounts receivable of $1.5 million.
   - Decrease in accounts payable of $2.3 million.
   - Increase in capital stock of $50 million.
   - Sold equipment with a book value of $7 million for $15 million after-tax.
   - Purchased equipment for $35 million.
   Calculate Joplin's free cash flow.
   A. $16.1 million.
   B. $24.1 million.
   C. $66.1 million.

57. Stanley Electronics is analyzing the effects of different accounting methods on its financial statements. Traditionally, Stanley has used FIFO to account for inventories but is considering transitioning to the average cost method. Use the following information to compute cost of goods sold (COGS) using the average cost inventory method.

Beginning inventory	100 units	$15
Purchases	200 units	$21
	100 units	$18
	300 units	$24
Ending inventory	150 units	

   A. $11,100.
   B. $11,550.
   C. $12,150.

58.   James Lane is analyzing the impacts of various accounting choices for MNB Corporation. In particular, he is interested in assessing the liquidity effects of MNB Corp.'s inventory accounting method. Assume the following for MNB Corp:
    •   LIFO reserve is equal to $600.
    •   Tax rate is 40%.
    •   Sales are $1,500.
    •   Deferred taxes are $50.

Determine the *increase* in working capital if MNB had been a FIFO firm.
    A. $310.
    B. $360.
    C. $600.

59.   Tommy Carter, CFA, is analyzing SDX Company, an auto parts manufacturer that recently went public. The company is generating solid sales growth of 23% per year, which is expected to continue over the next five years. SDX is capitalizing interest costs on its long-lived assets. To complete his analysis, Carter adjusts SDX's financials to reverse the capitalized interest. After Carter's adjustments, SDX's interest coverage ratio will be:
    A.   higher.
    B.   lower.
    C.   unchanged.

60.   BOX Packaging purchases equipment for $75 million with an estimated useful life of 15 years and a salvage value of $5 million. BOX records depreciation expense of $10 million for the first year. After the first year of use, management decides to change to the straight-line depreciation method. As compared to BOX's financial results had it not changed depreciation methods, which of the following statements is *most correct* over the next few years?
    A.   Fixed asset turnover will be higher.
    B.   Return on equity will be lower.
    C.   Return on assets will be higher.

61. Three years ago, JGC acquired an asset to be used in the manufacture of its products. Recently, JGC determined that the future undiscounted cash flows associated with the asset exceed the asset's carrying value. In addition, it is determined that the carrying value of the asset exceeds its fair value. According to U.S. GAAP, what is the effect on the return on equity ratio and the total asset turnover ratio?
    A. The return on equity ratio is overstated, and the total asset turnover ratio is understated.
    B. The return on equity ratio and the total asset turnover ratio are both overstated.
    C. The return on equity ratio and the total asset turnover ratio are both correctly stated.

62. Which of the following statements about deferred tax assets and deferred tax liabilities is *most accurate*? Deferred tax assets result from:
    A. gains that are recognized in the income statement before they are taxable, while deferred tax liabilities result from gains that are taxable before they are recognized in the income statement.
    B. gains that are taxable before they are recognized in the income statement, while deferred tax liabilities result from gains that are recognized in the income statement before they are taxable.
    C. losses that are tax deductible before they are recognized in the income statement, while deferred tax liabilities result from losses that are recognized in the income statement before they are tax deductible.

63. XYZ Company has decided to issue $10 million of unsecured bonds. If issued today, the 4% semi-annual coupon bonds would require a market interest rate of 12%. Under U.S. GAAP, which of the following statements about the cash flow statement impact is *most correct*?
    A. The coupon payments will decrease operating cash flow and the discount, when paid, will decrease financing cash flow.
    B. The periodic interest expense will decrease operating cash flow and the discount, when paid, will decrease financing cash flow.
    C. The coupon payments and the discount, when paid, will decrease financing cash flow.

64. Emma Smith, CFA, is analyzing Golden Co.'s capital structure and is determining what adjustments she should make to the balance sheet to properly reflect the economic reality of the company's convertible debt. Golden reports under U.S. GAAP. The convertible debt has the following features:

Number of bonds outstanding	100,000
Par Value	$1,000
Convertible to	40 shares
Maturity date	20 years
Market price per share of Golden common stock	$50.00

Which of the following *best describes* the result of Smith's adjustments, if any?
A. Increase in the current ratio.
B. Decrease in the debt-to-equity ratio.
C. No adjustment is necessary for analytical purposes.

65. Sanders Company recently leased equipment used in its manufacturing operation. For financial reporting purposes, Sanders treated the transaction as an operating lease. George Batter, CFA, believes that Sanders should have capitalized the lease. Assuming Batter is correct, which of the following *best describes* the effects of Batter's adjustments?
A. The debt-to-capital ratio will be lower.
B. ROE will be higher in the early years of the lease and lower in the later years.
C. The interest coverage ratio will be lower.

66. Earlier this year, Rosa Company sold $40 million worth of receivables, with recourse. Lauren Mode, CFA, is analyzing Rosa's year-end financial statements and decides to treat the sale as a collateralized borrowing at an interest rate of 8%. Which of the following *best describes* adjustments Mode should make for analytical purposes?
A. Decrease operating cash flow by $40 million and increase investing cash flow by $40 million.
B. Increase accounts receivable by $40 million and increase current liabilities by $40 million.
C. Decrease sales revenue by $40 million and increase interest expense by $3.2 million.

67. Keller Company is an apparel manufacturer. The following information is provided:

Partial Common Sized Balance Sheet

	2007	2008
Cash	10%	5%
Accounts Receivable	20%	15%
Inventory	25%	35%
Total Current Assets	55%	55%

Keller's liquidity position has:
A. increased.
B. decreased.
C. remained unchanged.

68. Operating cash flow inflated by inappropriate classification of activities, inappropriate mark-to-market accounting, and high management turnover were all warning signs analysts could have noted with respect to:
A. Enron.
B. Sunbeam.
C. WorldCom.

69. Over the past year, Ardmore Company reported sales of $5.1 million and cost of goods sold of $3.65 million. On average, inventory was sold in 65 days and receivables were collected in 43 days. If the cash conversion cycle was 58 days, calculate Ardmore's average accounts payable.
A. $500,000.
B. $580,000.
C. $650,000.

70. An analyst makes the following statements on international standards convergence. Indicate whether these statements are accurate.

Statement 1: IFRS standards require all borrowing costs to be expensed immediately.

Statement 2: IFRS standards define expenses to include losses, while GAAP standards do not.

A. Both of these statements are accurate.
B. Neither of these statements is accurate.
C. Only one of these statements is accurate.

71. A hockey club is considering purchase of a new Freeze II ice resurfacing machine, to replace an aging machine. The current Freeze I machine being used has a book value of zero and a market value of zero, but *is* in good working order and will last for at least an additional ten years. The proposed *new* machine is anticipated to operate more efficiently, and the club's engineering staff has estimated that it will produce after-tax cash flows (labor savings and depreciation) of $5,000 per year. The new machine will cost $25,000 delivered, and its economic life is estimated at ten years. Freeze II's salvage value will be zero. If the club's cost of capital is 12%, and its marginal tax rate is 40%, should the club buy the new Freeze II machine?
    A. NPV = –2,351. Do not buy the new machine.
    B. NPV = 3,251. Buy the new machine.
    C. NPV = 0. No decision.

72. Jeff Oberweis, CFA, is an international analyst covering European companies. Oberweis is evaluating the capital spending program of Schmidt Manufacturing, a small industrial supplier. Which of Oberweis's observations is *most likely* correct?

    Observation 1: Schmidt Manufacturing uses the payback period method to evaluate potential capital projects, which is uncommon among peers within its region.

    Observation 2: Schmidt's capital budgeting process will likely indicate whether management is concerned about shareholder wealth maximization.

    A. Only Observation 1 is correct.
    B. Only Observation 2 is correct.
    C. Both Observations are correct.

73. Over the next year, Thatherton Co. is expecting their marginal tax rate to increase by 5%. Also, over the course of the next 12 months, Thatherton plans to undertake several expansion projects significantly more risky than previous projects. Thatherton Co.'s current capital structure includes 40% debt and 60% equity. Which of the following statements *correctly* summarizes the effect these changes will have on the company's marginal cost of capital?
    A. The increasing tax rate will increase the MCC.
    B. The riskier projects will increase the MCC.
    C. Both the increasing tax rate and the riskier projects will increase the MCC.

74. An analyst has assembled the following information regarding Net-Zone Incorporated and the market in general:

Net-Zone expected ROE	16.2%
Net-Zone beta	1.8
Expected return on S&P 500 Index	10.7%
30-day Treasury bill yield	3.5%
10-year Treasury bond yield	4.8%

The analyst wants to determine the cost of common equity for Net-Zone's planned upgrade to its manufacturing facilities, which should affect the firm's cash flows for the next twelve years. The appropriate cost of equity using the CAPM approach is *closest* to:
A. 14.2%.
B. 15.4%.
C. 16.5%.

75. YHM Corporation just issued $12 million in debt and $25 million in common equity. The cost of issuing debt was 1.1%. YHM received $22.95 million in net proceeds from the equity issuance. Which of the following *best* describes how analysts at YHM should account for flotation costs when analyzing the project associated with the recent financing?
A. Reduce the NPV of the project by $2.18 million.
B. Increase the cost of debt using flotation costs of 1.1% and reduce the NPV of the project by $2.05 million.
C. Increase the cost of equity using flotation costs of 8.2% and reduce the NPV of the project by $0.13 million.

76. An analyst has discovered that over the last three years GTS Company has experienced a decrease in its net operating cycle, while over the same time period the average net operating cycle for the industry (excluding GTS) has increased. Which of the following *best* explains this trend?
A. GTS has decreased its liquidity position by increasing the amount of time inventory spends in its warehouses.
B. GTS has increased its liquidity position by decreasing the amount of time spent collecting cash from its customers.
C. The industry has decreased its liquidity position by increasing the average amount of time to pay suppliers.

©2008 Kaplan Schweser

77. An analyst is reviewing the working capital portfolio investment policy of a publicly traded firm. Which of the following components of the policy is the analyst *least likely* to find acceptable?
    A. Investments must have an A-1 rating from S&P or an equivalent rating from another agency.
    B. Authority for selecting and managing short-term investments rests with the firm's treasurer and any designees selected by the treasurer.
    C. Investments in U.S. T-bills, commercial paper, and bank CDs are acceptable unless issued by Stratford Bank.

78. George Ross, CFA, is being considered for a board member position with Grambling Incorporated, a multinational food processing company. Which of the following situations would *likely* call into question Ross's independence as a potential Board Member of Grambling?
    A. Ross's wife has a non-controlling equity interest in Grambling through a mutual fund in her retirement account.
    B. Ross's son is one of several mid-level managers of Grow Company, a major supplier to Grambling.
    C. Ross's sister is a partner with Grambling's external auditors, but does not work on the Grambling account.

Portfolio Management

79. Mitra Choudra is considering how to invest her $100,000 investment portfolio. Choudra's investment advisor has recommended that she invest 60% in the S&P 500 stock market index and 40% in the risk-free asset. The advisor has derived the following forecasts for the S&P 500:

Economic Scenario	Probability	Return on the S&P 500
Recession	20%	−10%
Stable growth	50%	10%
High growth	30%	20%

    Assuming a risk-free rate of 5%, the expected return on Choudra's portfolio is *closest* to:
    A. 6.6%.
    B. 7.4%.
    C. 9.0%.

80. Carl Vandenburg has been asked to explain the security market line (SML), including its slope. Which of the following is equal to the slope of the SML?
    A. Beta.
    B. Alpha.
    C. Market risk premium.

81. An analyst is interested in the relationship between the stock prices of two companies. After downloading a time series of stock prices for each company, the analyst concludes that Company A has a variance equal to 0.25 and Company B has a variance equal to 0.20, and the covariance between the two stocks is –0.10. Calculate the correlation coefficient between the two stocks.
    A. –0.45.
    B. –0.50.
    C. –1.00.

82. The standard deviation of a two-stock portfolio *least likely:*
    A. must be less than or equal to the weighted-average standard deviation.
    B. can be reduced by increasing the relative weight of the stock with lower standard deviation.
    C. will be the lowest when the correlation between the two stocks equals zero.

83. An analyst predicts that the return on Royal Company stock will be 15%. The analyst is provided with the following data for Royal and the broad market:
    • Royal Company beta   1.5
    • Risk-free rate   5%
    • Expected market return 11%

    From the data, determine if Royal Company stock is undervalued, overvalued, or correctly valued.
    A. Overvalued.
    B. Undervalued.
    C. Correctly valued.

84. Consider two individuals, David Lywie and Julio Stromek who have requested advice on their investment policy statements. Lywie is mid-career, has very little insurance coverage, and has fairly low job-related income expectations. In contrast, Stromek has fairly high net worth and long-term job-related earning potential. Which of the following statements is *most likely* correct?
    A. Lywie has higher risk tolerance than Stromek.
    B. Stromek has higher risk tolerance than Lywie.
    C. Stromek and Lywie have equivalent levels of risk tolerance.

Asset Valuation

85. Rocky Johnson, CFA, manages a large capitalization equity mutual fund. His superiors have requested that he provide them the appropriate benchmarks to compare future performance against. Johnson makes the following statements:

    Statement 1: We should use an unweighted index because it would best reflect the large company bias in the portfolio.

    Statement 2: Stocks in the portfolio frequently split the number of shares outstanding. Therefore, in the long run, the Dow Jones Industrial Average would best reflect these events.

    Are Johnson's two statements correct?
    A. No. Both statements are incorrect.
    B. Statement 1 is correct and Statement 2 is incorrect.
    C. Statement 1 is incorrect and Statement 2 is correct.

86. Which of the following assumptions is *least likely* to be consistent with the concept of efficient capital markets?
    A. Expected returns implicitly include risk in the price of the security.
    B. Market participants correctly adjust prices based on new information.
    C. New information about securities comes to the market in a random fashion.

87. Sal Nunn, CFA, is a portfolio manager at Walker Investments. Nunn sold 300,000 shares of a NASDAQ listed stock on an electronic crossing network in after hours trading because the company announced a significant negative earnings surprise. Indicate whether the third or fourth market *best* describes the Nunn trade and state whether the NASDAQ market is a call or continuous market.
    A. Nunn's trade is in the third market and NASDAQ is a call market.
    B. Nunn's trade is in the fourth market and NASDAQ is a call market.
    C. Nunn's trade is in the fourth market and NASDAQ is a continuous market.

88. An investor purchased 100 shares of a stock two years ago for $50 per share after deciding the stock would be a good value investment. Since the initial purchase, the stock price has fallen to $35 per share after several of the company's major customers canceled contracts. The investor has decided to purchase another 50 shares at the lower price. Which of the following behavioral biases *best* characterizes the investor's actions?
   A. Escalation bias.
   B. Momentum bias.
   C. Overconfidence bias.

89. Ian Lance, CFA, is discussing short selling with a client and states, "The short seller must pay any dividend of the issuer to the lender of the stock. In addition, the short seller must provide some collateral to the brokerage house." Is Lance correct about the short seller's obligations?
   A. Yes.
   B. Lance is correct about paying the dividend, and incorrect about providing collateral.
   C. Lance is incorrect about paying the dividend, and correct about providing collateral.

90. An analyst is using the following information to value AGF Company's common shares. AGF paid a dividend of $1.90 per share last year. Dividends are expected to grow at 6% forever. The risk-free rate is 5%, the market risk premium is 7%, and the beta of the common shares is 1.3. The value of the AGF Company's common shares is *closest* to:
   A. $23.46.
   B. $24.86.
   C. $33.57.

91. In valuing the stock of Evergreen Enterprises, an analyst compiles the following information about the firm:
   • Expected constant growth rate of dividends = 6%.
   • Next year's expected earnings per share = $4.24.
   • Expected retention ratio = 62.5%.
   • Required rate of return = 11%.
   The value of the firm's stock today is *closest* to:
   A. $31.80.
   B. $38.55.
   C. $53.00.

92. Radio Corp. owns a leading radio network with 200 million weekly listeners. To combat a declining radio audience, the company has implemented a strategy of targeting the Hispanic audience. After careful analysis, Radio Corp. makes the decision to acquire a Hispanic radio station, rather than convert existing radio stations. The acquisition strategy benefits from rules that allow clustering of ownership of local radio stations. The basis of the strategic initiative and the basis of the acquisition strategy, respectively, are:
    A. market timing and geography.
    B. lifestyles and technology.
    C. demographics and regulation.

93. An analyst develops the following information to value a common stock.
    - Last year's earnings per share (E_0) = \$4.00
    - Real risk-free rate (RFR_{real}) = 4%
    - Inflation premium (IP) = 5%
    - Return on equity (ROE), expected to remain constant in the future = 10%
    - Dividend payout, expected to remain stable in the future = 30%
    - Stock's beta = 1.4
    - Expected market return = 14%

    The analyst estimates the required rate of return and uses a DDM to value the shares. The value per share is *closest* to:
    A. \$14.39.
    B. \$21.28.
    C. \$31.39.

94. Jack Saunders is analyzing Barco Incorporated, an industrial conglomerate company. Saunders is estimating the intrinsic value for Barco Incorporated by forecasting the company's earnings per share and earnings multiplier. Which of the following attributes of Barco is *least likely* to increase the company's earnings multiplier?
    A. Barco Incorporated has never had a restructuring charge in its history.
    B. Barco Incorporated's earnings move in tandem with overall economic growth.
    C. Barco Incorporated's dividend has been increasing for the last 30 years.

95. Brad Kit, CFA, is analyzing the broadcasting industry. Kit has narrowed his analysis to Willow Corp. and Vision Inc.

    Willow Corp. is a media company with a diversified group of leading TV, newspaper, and cable news operations. Revenues and earnings have grown slightly over the past ten years. The company's long-term debt to capital ratio is 40%. During the last recession, the company's earnings remained flat with the prior year. Still, Kit believes that Willow Corp. will have positive earnings surprises over the next several quarters, due to several new programs that have been hugely successful.

    Vision Inc.'s operations are located in emerging markets with a high degree of political and regulatory risk. However, the TV, radio, and internet operations have the potential for extraordinary returns. Vision's stock is trading at 30 times next year's earnings and five times book value.

    A client asks Kit whether Willow Corp. is a growth company or growth stock and whether Vision Inc. is a speculative company or speculative stock. Kit's *most appropriate* response would be that:
    A. Willow Corp. is a growth stock and Vision Inc. is a speculative stock.
    B. Willow Corp. is a growth company and Vision Inc. is a speculative stock.
    C. Willow Corp. is a growth stock and Vision Inc. is a speculative company.

96. The following information is provided about Jacko Industries.
    - Jacko's stock is trading at $50 per share.
    - Jacko reported earnings of negative $2.50 per share.
    - Jacko reported a $2.00 per share nonrecurring loss.
    - Jacko's total assets equal $5 billion.
    - Jacko's total liabilities equal $4 billion.
    - Jacko's long run return on equity has been 25%.
    - Jacko has 50 million outstanding shares.
    Using the method of average return on equity, Jacko's P/E ratio is *closest* to:
    A. 10.0.
    B. 16.67.
    C. 20.0.

97.   An analyst has stated that, holding all else constant, an increase in the maturity of a coupon bond will increase its interest rate risk, and that a decrease in the coupon rate of a coupon bond will decrease its interest rate risk. The analyst is correct:
    A. only with respect to the effect of the increase in the maturity.
    B. only with respect to the effect of the decrease in the coupon rate.
    C. with respect to both the effect of the increase in maturity and the effect of the decrease in the coupon rate.

98.   An analyst has been researching a possible investment in collateralized debt obligations (CDOs). Identify the statement which is *most likely* correct.
    A. The underlying securities for a CDO are typically issued only by U.S.-based entities.
    B. A CDO with corporate bonds as the underlying security is known as a collateralized loan obligation (CLO).
    C. A CDO is typically structured into tranches, similar to a collateralized mortgage obligation (CMO).

99.   Chris South owns $25,000 face value of Bradco bonds, which have a 7% coupon, pay interest semiannually, and have six years remaining until maturity. The bonds are callable at par. The bonds were rated A when Chris bought them at par two years ago, and they are currently worth $26,225, with a rating of AA. Which of the following statements *most accurately* describes the change in the risk of the Bradco bonds?
    A. Call risk has decreased.
    B. Liquidity risk has increased.
    C. Credit risk has decreased.

100.   Ned Jameson, CFA, is considering the purchase of a newly issued asset-backed security (ABS) for his fixed income portfolio. According to the broker/dealer offering the bond, the OAS for the issue is 75 basis points (bps). Based on the OAS value, which of the following assumptions can Jameson make about this particular ABS?
    A. The OAS represents the investor's compensation for credit risk, liquidity risk, and option risk.
    B. The bond is trading at a yield that is more than 75 bps higher than a Treasury security with a comparable maturity.
    C. The implied cost of an option embedded in the security is always equal to the difference between the OAS and the Treasury spread.

101. With regard to a theoretical Treasury yield curve constructed with the bootstrapping method:
    A. every point on the curve is constructed by utilizing current on-the-run Treasury yields of various maturities.
    B. the yield for most maturities used to construct the Treasury yield curve are observed yields rather than interpolated yields.
    C. any yield on the Treasury yield curve that is not one of the on-the-run maturities is only an approximation for that maturity.

102. Bond X is a noncallable corporate bond maturing in ten years. Bond Y is also a corporate bond maturing in ten years, and Bond Y is callable at any time beginning three years from now. Both bonds carry a credit rating of AA. Based on this information, identify the *most accurate* statement:
    A. Bond Y will have a higher nominal spread over a 10-year U.S. Treasury security than Bond X.
    B. The option adjusted spread (OAS) of Bond Y will be greater than the nominal spread of Bond Y.
    C. The nominal spread of Bond X will be greater than the option adjusted spread of Bond X.

103. A Treasury bond dealer observes the following Treasury spot rates from the spot rate curve: 1-year 7.40%, 2-year 7.00%, and 3-year 6.3%. The bond dealer also observes that the market price of a 3-year 8% coupon, 100 par value bond is $103.95. Based on this information, the dealer should:
    A. buy the 8% coupon bond in the open market, strip it, and sell the pieces.
    B. sell the 8% coupon bond short, and buy the component cash flow strips with the proceeds.
    C. do nothing since the 8% bond is selling for its arbitrage-free price.

104. David Garcia, CFA, is analyzing two bonds. Bond X is an option free corporate security with a 7% annual coupon and ten years to maturity. Bond Y is a mortgage backed security that also matures in ten years. Garcia is considering two possible interest rate scenarios—one in which rates are flat over the entire 10-year horizon, and one in which the yield curve is sloped steeply upwards. For each bond, Garcia has calculated the nominal spread over the 10-year U.S. Treasury issue as well as the zero-volatility spread. The zero-volatility spread would differ the most from the nominal spread:
    A. for Bond X, when the yield curve is sloped steeply upwards.
    B. for Bond Y, when the yield curve is sloped steeply upwards.
    C. for Bond X, when the yield curve is flat.

105. The bonds of Joslin Corp. are currently callable at par value. The bonds mature in eight years and have a coupon of 8%. The yield on the Joslin bonds is 175 basis points over 8-year U.S. Treasury securities, and the Treasury spot yield curve has a normal, rising shape. As yields on bonds comparable to the Joslin bonds decrease, the Joslin bonds will *most likely* exhibit:
   A. negative convexity.
   B. increasing modified duration.
   C. increasing effective duration.

106. Donald McKay, CFA, is analyzing a client's fixed income portfolio. As of the end of the last quarter, the portfolio had a market value of $7,545,000 and a portfolio duration of 6.24. McKay is predicting that the yield for all of the securities in the portfolio will decline by 25 basis points next quarter. Which of the following statements regarding the portfolio's performance next quarter is *most accurate*?
   A. For the expected change in portfolio yield next quarter, the market value of the portfolio will change by approximately 6.24%.
   B. If the yield curve has a 50 basis point downward parallel shift next quarter, the portfolio will increase in value by approximately $235,404.
   C. The portfolio's ending value after the expected decline in yields will be approximately $7,427,298.

107. Kathy Hurst, CFA, is valuing a 4-year zero coupon security. She is provided the following information:

$_1f_0$	6.0%
$_1f_1$	7.3%
$_1f_2$	?
$_1f_3$	8.9%

The 4-year spot rate is 7.5%.

Calculate the one-year forward rate two years from now ($_1f_2$).
   A. 7.3%.
   B. 7.8%.
   C. 8.0%.

108. ABC Corporation has just issued $200 million of 6.5% $1,000 par value bonds at face value. Which of the following requirements in the indenture for these bonds would *most likely* be considered a negative covenant? ABC must:
   A. maintain its manufacturing equipment in good condition.
   B. make timely semiannual payments of interest and principal when due.
   C. have paid all bond coupon payments due before it can pay cash dividends.

109. Ron Travis, CFA, manages a portfolio of long-term and short-term bonds. The portfolio is equally weighted between 1-year, 2-year, 10-year, and 20-year maturities and currently has a portfolio duration equal to 7.0. Travis is concerned that 1- and 2-year interest rates are going to increase by 100 basis points while 10- and 20-year rates decrease by 100 basis points. If his prediction is correct, Travis' measure of duration will be ineffective at predicting interest rate risk since portfolio duration is only accurate when the:
   A. yield curve does not shift.
   B. shift in the yield curve is parallel.
   C. yield curve steepens.

110. Which of the following *best* describes an option that gives the owner the right to sell 100 shares of stock only on the expiration date three months from now at a strike price of $35, when the current stock price is $25? This option is an:
   A. out-of-the-money American put option.
   B. in-the-money European put option.
   C. out-of-the-money European put option.

111. Roland Carl owns a portfolio of large capitalization stocks. He has a positive long term outlook for the stock market, but Carl is worried about the possible effects of recent changes in monetary policy. Carl would like to protect his portfolio from any sudden declines in the stock market, without selling his holdings. The *most likely* way for Carl to achieve his objective of limiting the downside risk of his portfolio is to:
   A. sell put options on the S&P 500.
   B. sell an S&P 500 futures contract.
   C. buy an S&P 500 forward contract.

112. Julia Chen, a portfolio manager for U.S.-based Dane Investments, has just established a short position in Swiss franc currency futures as part of a currency overlay strategy. The position consists of 100,000 contracts with an initial margin of $4,000, a maintenance margin of $2,500, and a contract price of 0.9120 USD/CHF. If the futures price on the subsequent two days is 0.9300, and 0.8928, respectively, what will be her margin account balance at the end of the second day?
    A. $4,000.
    B. $6,200.
    C. $7,720.

113. Sue Wie, CFA, is the chief financial officer for Garth Company. The company will need to borrow $75 million in the near future to fund a plant expansion. Wie expects interest rates will rise and decides to hedge against this risk using a 3×6 LIBOR based forward rate agreement (FRA). The underlying rate for this FRA is:
    A. 60-day LIBOR.
    B. 90-day LIBOR.
    C. 180-day LIBOR.

114. Call options on the stock of Verdant, Inc., with a strike price of $45 are priced at $3.75. Put options with a strike price of $45 are priced at $3.00. Which of the following *most accurately* describes the potential payoffs for owners of these options (assuming no underlying positions in Verdant)?
    A. The call writer has the maximum loss exposure.
    B. The put buyer has the maximum loss exposure.
    C. The put writer has the maximum potential gain.

115. An analyst is considering buying a call option on ZXC stock, which is currently trading at $33.75 per share. Three month call options with a strike price of $30 are trading at a premium of $4.50. Identify which of the following statements is *most likely* true regarding the ZXC call options.
    A. The ZXC call options are currently out of the money.
    B. The breakeven underlying price for ZXC stock is $38.25 per share.
    C. The potential upside of the ZXC call options is unlimited.

116. IRK Investments is actively engaged in various risk management strategies involving swaps. The company currently has a position as the fixed rate payer in a quarterly fixed for equity swap with an interest rate of 6.8%, a tenor of five years and notional principal of $10 million. Payments on the swap are netted. The underlying equity return is based on the S&P 500 Index. IRK currently owes a payment of $400,000. Which of the following is *most likely* correct?
   A. The underlying equity index experienced a loss greater than 1.7% over the quarter.
   B. The underlying equity index experienced a loss less than 1.7% over the quarter.
   C. The underlying equity index experienced a loss equal to 1.7% over the quarter.

117. An analyst is interested in determining the value of a real estate investment and has estimated the following data for the property:

Net operating income	$50,480	Cost of debt	8.2%
Depreciation	$3,550	Cost of equity	12.5%
Interest expense	$2,720	WACC	9.6%
Tax rate	35%	Cap rate	11.0%

Which of the following is *closest* to the value of the property using the income approach?
   A. $403,900.
   B. $458,900.
   C. $466,500.

118. Bob Kramer, CFA, manages money for high net worth clients. Kramer creates an investment portfolio tailored to his clients' specific needs using mutual funds. Kramer is considering the following Emerging Market Fund and uses a five year time frame. Exhibit 1 details the Emerging Market Fund's fees and expenses.

Exhibit 1 – Fees and expenses for Emerging Market Fund

	Class A	Class B	Class C
Sales charge	2%		
Deferred sales charge		5% first year declining 1% per year	2% for the initial three years
Distribution fee	0.40%	0.50%	0.50%
Management fee	0.40%	0.50%	0.50%
Other expenses	0.20%	0.50%	0.60%

Kramer expects the Emerging Market Fund to earn 12% per year.

Select the class of Emerging Market Fund shares that are *most* appropriate for Kramer's clients.
A. Class A.
B. Class B.
C. Class C.

119. Which of the following statements is *least likely* to be a unique risk associated with a hedge fund?
A. Cash needs arising from marking positions to market.
B. Unexpected absence of normal liquidity under extreme market conditions.
C. Higher volatility of returns as compared to traditional equity funds.

120. A commodity market is in contango if:
A. the spot price is higher than the futures price.
B. the spot price is equal to the futures price.
C. the spot price is lower than the futures price.

End of Morning Session

Exam 1
Afternoon Session

Topic	Questions	Points
Ethical and Professional Standards	121–138	27
Quantitative Analysis	139–152	22.5
Economics	153–165	18
Financial Reporting and Analysis	166–198	49.5
Portfolio Management	199–204	9
Asset Valuation	205–240	54
Total		**180**

Test Answers

121. (A) (B) (C)	161. (A) (B) (C)	201. (A) (B) (C)
122. (A) (B) (C)	162. (A) (B) (C)	202. (A) (B) (C)
123. (A) (B) (C)	163. (A) (B) (C)	203. (A) (B) (C)
124. (A) (B) (C)	164. (A) (B) (C)	204. (A) (B) (C)
125. (A) (B) (C)	165. (A) (B) (C)	205. (A) (B) (C)
126. (A) (B) (C)	166. (A) (B) (C)	206. (A) (B) (C)
127. (A) (B) (C)	167. (A) (B) (C)	207. (A) (B) (C)
128. (A) (B) (C)	168. (A) (B) (C)	208. (A) (B) (C)
129. (A) (B) (C)	169. (A) (B) (C)	209. (A) (B) (C)
130. (A) (B) (C)	170. (A) (B) (C)	210. (A) (B) (C)
131. (A) (B) (C)	171. (A) (B) (C)	211. (A) (B) (C)
132. (A) (B) (C)	172. (A) (B) (C)	212. (A) (B) (C)
133. (A) (B) (C)	173. (A) (B) (C)	213. (A) (B) (C)
134. (A) (B) (C)	174. (A) (B) (C)	214. (A) (B) (C)
135. (A) (B) (C)	175. (A) (B) (C)	215. (A) (B) (C)
136. (A) (B) (C)	176. (A) (B) (C)	216. (A) (B) (C)
137. (A) (B) (C)	177. (A) (B) (C)	217. (A) (B) (C)
138. (A) (B) (C)	178. (A) (B) (C)	218. (A) (B) (C)
139. (A) (B) (C)	179. (A) (B) (C)	219. (A) (B) (C)
140. (A) (B) (C)	180. (A) (B) (C)	220. (A) (B) (C)
141. (A) (B) (C)	181. (A) (B) (C)	221. (A) (B) (C)
142. (A) (B) (C)	182. (A) (B) (C)	222. (A) (B) (C)
143. (A) (B) (C)	183. (A) (B) (C)	223. (A) (B) (C)
144. (A) (B) (C)	184. (A) (B) (C)	224. (A) (B) (C)
145. (A) (B) (C)	185. (A) (B) (C)	225. (A) (B) (C)
146. (A) (B) (C)	186. (A) (B) (C)	226. (A) (B) (C)
147. (A) (B) (C)	187. (A) (B) (C)	227. (A) (B) (C)
148. (A) (B) (C)	188. (A) (B) (C)	228. (A) (B) (C)
149. (A) (B) (C)	189. (A) (B) (C)	229. (A) (B) (C)
150. (A) (B) (C)	190. (A) (B) (C)	230. (A) (B) (C)
151. (A) (B) (C)	191. (A) (B) (C)	231. (A) (B) (C)
152. (A) (B) (C)	192. (A) (B) (C)	232. (A) (B) (C)
153. (A) (B) (C)	193. (A) (B) (C)	233. (A) (B) (C)
154. (A) (B) (C)	194. (A) (B) (C)	234. (A) (B) (C)
155. (A) (B) (C)	195. (A) (B) (C)	235. (A) (B) (C)
156. (A) (B) (C)	196. (A) (B) (C)	236. (A) (B) (C)
157. (A) (B) (C)	197. (A) (B) (C)	237. (A) (B) (C)
158. (A) (B) (C)	198. (A) (B) (C)	238. (A) (B) (C)
159. (A) (B) (C)	199. (A) (B) (C)	239. (A) (B) (C)
160. (A) (B) (C)	200. (A) (B) (C)	240. (A) (B) (C)

Exam 1
Afternoon Session

Ethical and Professional Standards

121. Ryan Brown, CFA, is a portfolio manager for Brinton Investments. Brown has just issued a press release for Brinton regarding the CFA® exam results for several of the company's analysts. The press release states the following: "Two of our analysts passed the Level 3 CFA exam this year after passing the prior two levels on the first attempt. These analysts have demonstrated Brinton's continued commitment to the highest standard of knowledge and ethics in the investment profession and will hopefully allow Brinton to continue its record of outstanding investment performance. Additionally, three other analysts passed the Level 2 CFA exam. These analysts will be able to identify themselves as CFA charterholders next year, a significant addition to the ten CFA charterholders already on staff." Did Brown violate the CFA Institute Standards of Professional Conduct with respect to his comments regarding Brinton's Level 3 or Level 2 CFA candidates?
    A. No violation in either case
    B. No violation in the case of the comments regarding the Level 3 Candidates, but a violation on the comments regarding the Level 2 Candidates.
    C. Both statements are violations of the CFA Institute Standards.

122. Julian Bates, CFA, is a research analyst for a large brokerage house who closely follows the airline industry. He has been asked to accompany two of the firm's top salespeople to visit several important clients who have large holdings in the airline industry. Bates reviews his most recent research report, along with some industry reports written by analysts from rival brokerage firms. He discovers that an analyst at another firm has identified an issue that may hurt the airline industry over the next six months. Bates decides that he concurs with the other analyst's opinion. At the first client meeting, Bates delivers his prepared presentation, and at the end, informs the client of "his important new discovery." According to the CFA Institute Standards of Professional Conduct, Bates:
    A. has not violated any Standard because his own research supports his conclusion.
    B. has violated the Standards by misrepresenting the other analyst's idea as his own.
    C. has violated the Standards by relying on research prepared by a competing firm.

123. Wendy Johnson, CFA, has recently been hired as a junior portfolio manager for Smith Brothers, an investment firm that caters to institutional clients. For the past five years, Johnson has provided investment advice to a local university. Johnson spends approximately five hours per week on the project and is compensated for her time. Johnson does not disclose this arrangement to her supervisor at Smith Brothers because the time involved consulting for the university will in no way interfere with her duties in her new position. Which of the following statements regarding Johnson's actions under the CFA Institute Standards of Professional Conduct is *most* accurate?
    A. Johnson has violated the Standards by failing to disclose a conflict of interest to her employer.
    B. Johnson has violated the Standards by not obtaining written permission from her employer.
    C. Johnson has not violated any Standards.

124. Mark Hanning, CFA, is developing a research report for public distribution on a small avionics firm. Hanning's supervisor, Rob Jannsen, who is not a CFA charterholder, sees an early draft which includes quite favorable earnings projections. A few days later, Hanning obtains additional data that causes him to revise the favorable projections downward. Right before public distribution of this report, Hanning learns that Jannsen has substituted the earlier, more favorable earnings projections into the report without Hanning's knowledge. Hanning should *most* appropriately:
    A. insist that this matter be reported to the regulators immediately, after consulting with internal counsel.
    B. insist that either the report be corrected, or his name be removed from the report.
    C. permit publication of this report, but issue a follow-up report correcting the error.

125. Andrew Pollard, CFA, is employed by a prominent investment bank. While on the elevator one evening, he overhears the CFO from a major multinational oil company discussing an unexpected large earnings increase with the oil company's CEO. When he gets home, he immediately places an order to buy shares in this oil company, based on the information he overheard. The executives from that firm were not aware that he overheard the conversation. Which of the following best describes this situation?
    A. This is a violation of CFA Institute Standards.
    B. There is no violation of CFA Institute Standards, since this was simply an overheard conversation.
    C. Pollard violated CFA Institute Standards by not contacting internal counsel for advice before placing the trade.

126. Jim Whitaker is a managing director of Tiger Partners, an investment banking firm. Tiger is one of three firms preparing to jointly issue a secondary offering on behalf of a computer software company that has experienced tremendous growth over the past three years. There has been strong interest among Tiger's clients in the offering, and consequently, the issue is oversubscribed. According to Tiger's written trade allocation procedures, which are distributed to all clients, an oversubscribed issue must be distributed on a prorated basis among all interested clients, one of which is Whitaker himself. According to CFA Institute Standards of Professional Conduct, this procedure for allocating an oversubscribed issue:
    A. is in violation of the Standards because most clients will be receiving fewer shares than requested.
    B. is in violation of the Standards because Whitaker should forgo an allocation to himself to free up shares for clients.
    C. is not in violation of the Standards because all clients have received copies of Tiger's trade allocation procedures.

127. Martin Crane, CFA, is a portfolio manager. Crane has just been informed by his compliance officer that a new law will require additional disclosures of personal client information, pertaining to investment history, for two of Crane's former clients and one of his current clients. Crane decides to comply with the new law and provide the required client information to the relevant governmental organizations. Has Crane violated CFA Institute Standards of Professional Conduct?
   A. No.
   B. Yes, because he disclosed confidential information about a former client.
   C. Yes, because he disclosed confidential information about a current client.

128. Ron Shipley, CFA, is a portfolio manager for a small investment advisory firm. The firm is preparing to undergo an aggressive marketing campaign and Shipley is creating a presentation that will be delivered at a free investment seminar sponsored by the firm and offered to the public. Since the audience will be made up primarily of retirees, Shipley is going to focus on the performance of the firm's short-term U.S. Treasury fund. He plans to assure the audience that the fund is liquid and contains "guaranteed" securities. According to CFA Institute Standards of Professional Conduct, Shipley's presentation:
   A. does not violate any Standard.
   B. is in violation of the Standards for misleading his audience by using the word "guaranteed."
   C. is in violation of the Standards by misrepresenting the investment performance that can be reasonably expected to be achieved.

129. Katherine White has recently left her position as a portfolio manager at Topham Brothers, a brokerage firm, to start her own investment advisory firm. White, another portfolio manager, and a trading assistant will be the sole employees of the new firm at its start-up. White has arranged for Topham to provide monthly economic and market reviews produced by its research staff to her new firm in return for her executing all of her clients' trades through Topham. In addition, White has negotiated a favorable commission schedule with Topham for the clients of her new firm. Once White's new firm is established, she intends to hire her own research analyst and terminate the arrangement with Topham. According to the CFA Institute's Standards of Professional Conduct, White:
    A. must advise clients at the time when the arrangement is terminated because the commission schedule may change.
    B. does not need to advise prospective clients of the arrangement because she negotiated commission terms that are favorable to the clients.
    C. must advise prospective clients of the arrangement so that they may evaluate any partiality shown in investment recommendations.

130. Joe Howard, CFA, has recently taken on a compliance officer position with a major investment firm. In his new position, he is responsible for reviewing all the firm's marketing and promotional materials. The firm has several CFA charterholders on staff as well as some CFA candidates. Howard has come across three statements in the course of his review:

    Statement 1: "As a CFA charterholder, Mr. Buckmaster is a highly qualified individual who can achieve the highest investment results."

    Statement 2: "Orlin Gravelle, CFA, has recently completed the CFA program thus enhancing his portfolio management skills."

    Statement 3: "Tom Watters, C.F.A., has recently been promoted into his new position of Senior Portfolio Analyst."

    Which of the following best describes these Statements compliance with the CFA Institute Standards?
    A. Statement 2 conforms to CFA Institute Standards. Statements 1 and 3 do not.
    B. Statements 1 and 3 conform to CFA Institute Standards. Statement 2 does not.
    C. None of the Statements conform to CFA Institute Standards.

131. Which of the following actions taken by an investment firm is **NOT** required to be in compliance with Global Investment Performance Standards (GIPS)®?
    A. A firm provides a composite list and composite descriptions to any prospective client that requests them.
    B. A firm hires an independent third-party verifier to prepare a verification report for its largest composite.
    C. A firm makes every reasonable effort to provide a compliant presentation to all prospective clients.

132. Max Steinberg, CFA, manages assets for a mid-sized portfolio management firm in the Cayman Islands. Steinberg receives a call from an American investor who wishes to open an account with his firm. Steinberg agrees to set up an account with an initial deposit of $2 million. After the funds are wired to the account, Steinberg obtains significant evidence to suspect the American investor, the CEO of Slyco Inc., has obtained the $2 million by defrauding Slyco's common stockholders. Steinberg decides not to take any action. One month later, the American investor makes another deposit in the amount of $650,000. Once again, Steinberg obtains evidence of securities fraud. This time he reports both cases of fraud to his company's legal counsel and halts all trading in the account even though the Cayman Island securities laws do not require him to do so. Has Steinberg violated the Code and Standards?
    A. No, since he reported the illegal activities to his firm's legal counsel and halted trading activity.
    B. Yes, since he failed to act the first time he suspected the funds had been obtained illegally.
    C. Yes, since he disclosed confidential information to his firm's counsel in breach of his fiduciary duty.

133. Ken Howell, CFA, a sell-side equity analyst, just issued a strong buy recommendation for an oil company based on an analysis of the company's financial reports along with financial forecasts that Howell developed internally. In addition, Howell suspects that the company will soon announce merger plans with a Japanese oil company. To investigate, Howell attempts to call the CEO, CFO, and COO at the company. Different secretaries inform Howell that the CEO is "attending a conference overseas" and that the CFO and COO are "traveling in Japan." Upon further conversation, Howell is able to confirm that all three men were in the same city in Japan where the potential merger partner is headquartered. Howell feels confident that the merger will go forward. According to CFA Institute Standards of Professional Conduct, Howell may issue a buy recommendation on the oil company:
   A. without taking any further actions to disclose his findings.
   B. only after allowing the companies a reasonable period of time to disclose their merger plans.
   C. only after urging the companies' managements to publicly disclose their merger plans.

134. Guy Sweeney, CFA, is an analyst for Harper, Muench Investment Advisors. Sweeney reports to David Stevage, director of sales and marketing. Sweeney is preparing a research report on a high technology firm, LinkRacer. Sweeney has written a comprehensive report, rating the stock a "strong buy," and has checked his sources carefully. Right before the report is to be printed, Stevage rushes into Sweeney's office and requests that he omit a few items from the report that may temper investor enthusiasm for LinkRacer. To comply with the Code and Standards, what is Sweeney's *best* course of action?
   A. Modify the research report, as requested, but change "strong buy" to "buy."
   B. Modify the report, and show Stevage how the information can be presented in such a way to identify the risks, without putting such strong emphasis on these risks.
   C. Refuse the request, and report this action to the firm's compliance officer, since Stevage's request is a violation.

135. For the past five years, Rafael Garcia has served as a junior portfolio manager for Peak Investments. Garcia has accepted the position of senior portfolio manager at a competing firm. Garcia is not required to sign a non-compete agreement, but knows he may not solicit existing or potential clients of Peak prior to leaving the firm. Shortly after beginning his new job, Garcia discovers several files on his home computer that contain information about Peak's clients and their portfolio allocations. Garcia shares this information with his new employer with the hope of bringing some of these clients over to his new firm. Garcia has:
    A. violated the Standards because he has misused confidential information.
    B. not violated any Standards because he is permitted to have information on former clients to utilize after he begins the new position.
    C. not violated any Standard because he was not required to sign a non-compete agreement.

136. Kelly Kelley, CFA, and Verne Gordon, CFA, are both technology analysts for a major brokerage firm. Kelley and Gordon recently attended a meeting with ADM Microchip's CFO. The CFO invited all the analysts covering the firm, and also invited major shareholders to attend the meeting. During the meeting, the CFO discusses some startling information concerning possible closure of one of ADM's microchip manufacturing plants. Which of the following statements is the *most* accurate?
    A. Kelley and Gordon should urge full public disclosure of the plant closure information.
    B. The meeting is normal and customary, and Kelley and Gordon are free to disclose all information covered in the meeting to their major clients.
    C. The effect on ADM's stock price is indeterminate, thus this information is free to be shared, and is not considered material nonpublic information.

137. Randy Green is a principal in an investment advisory firm that caters to large foundations and pension funds. His firm has recently been retained by the United Teachers Retirement Fund (UTRF), largely due to the fact that the CEO of the UTRF, Bob Harris, is a friend of Green's from graduate school. In appreciation for the business, Green writes Harris a letter that states he will personally oversee the account and will always act in Harris' best interest. According to the Code and Standards, Green:
    A. is not in violation of the Standards by pledging loyalty, prudence, and care of the client's assets.
    B. is in violation of the Standards because his pledge implies that he will give preferential treatment to the UTRF.
    C. is in violation of the Standards because his duty of loyalty is owed to the beneficiaries of the pension fund, not Harris.

138. CFA Institute Bylaws and Rules of Procedure for Proceedings Related to Professional Conduct are CFA Institute's means of enforcing the Code and Standards. These "Rules of Procedure" are based on which primary principles?
    A. Confidentiality of the proceedings and a fair process to the member and candidate.
    B. Good ethics, a fundamental requirement in the investment profession, which forms the basis for the Code and Standards.
    C. The six components of the Code of Ethics and the seven Standards of Professional Conduct.

Quantitative Methods

139. A brokerage company selected 1,200 people at random in New York City to determine a relationship between age and participation in the stock market. Selected New Yorkers were simply asked their age and if they had made at least one stock trade in the last year. The data obtained are listed in the table below. Compute the empirical probability that, in the future, a randomly chosen investor under the age of 30 will have made no stock trades in the last year.

Stock Trades Last Year		
Age	No	Yes
Under 30	325	235
Over 30	550	90

    A. 27%.
    B. 31%.
    C. 58%.

140. Lee Phillips, CFA, calculates that Biolab Inc. should earn $2.00 per share in 2008, with a standard deviation of $1.00. Based on a normal distribution, calculate the approximate probability that Biolab Inc. earns $3.00 or more.
    A. 16%.
    B. 32%.
    C. 34%.

141. Paper Products Incorporated's research department developed a new infant disposable diaper. The marketing department surveyed a random sample of 100 people. The survey is designed to gauge customer interest level in the new product. The sample indicates an average purchase of 2,500 diapers per year with a variance of 160,000 diapers. Calculate the standard error of the sample mean.
    A. 4.
    B. 8.
    C. 40.

142. Five items are being shipped. The weights of the items are: 6, 5, 3, 15, and 11 pounds. What is the standard deviation of the weights of the items sent?
    A. 4.00.
    B. 4.47.
    C. 4.38.

143. Colleagues Lisa McGrow and Nelson Modello recently discussed alternative interpretations of interest rates. During the conversation, McGrow stated that the opportunity cost of holding onto cash rises when interest rates rise. Modello stated that the discounted value of a set of future cash flows rises when interest rates fall. Determine whether the statements made by McGrow and Modello are correct.
    A. Only McGrow is correct.
    B. Only Modello is correct.
    C. Both McGrow and Modello are correct.

144. Which of the following assumptions is *inconsistent* with technical analysis?
    A. Interaction of supply and demand causes trends in stock prices.
    B. Information flow causes the market to reach a new equilibrium abruptly.
    C. Supply and demand is governed by both rational and irrational factors.

145. Determining the end of year bonus structure is always a challenging task for the CEO of Hibbert Asset Management. Seven of the twelve money managers employed by the firm are eligible for a bonus, but only four bonuses are available. The bonuses vary in amounts, rewarding the top performer more than the bottom so the order in which they are awarded is important. The number of ways that the CEO can award the bonuses is *equal* to:

A. 28.
B. 210.
C. 840.

146. Ann Karson, CFA, a drug analyst for KMB Brokerage firm, is evaluating a new drug product of Lancer Pharmaceutical Company. She knows that the new drug must be more effective than the current standard of treatment drugs to receive approval. The appropriate null hypothesis for the hypothesis test is:

A. $H_0: \mu_{New} - \mu_{Std} \geq 0$.
B. $H_0: \mu_{New} - \mu_{Std} \leq 0$.
C. $H_a: \mu_{New} - \mu_{Std} = 0$.

147. An analyst recently conducted a two-tailed test of hypotheses on mean stock returns, using a 5% level of significance. Which of the analyst's following statements is correct?

A. The null hypothesis should be rejected if the critical value for the test statistic exceeds the calculated value of the test statistic.
B. The null hypothesis should not be rejected if the hypothesized mean stock return lies within the 95% confidence interval.
C. The power of the test is the probability that the null hypothesis will not be rejected when it is true.

148. Jack Gallant lends €10,000 to his business partner Alex Wood. In exchange, Wood gives Gallant shares of preferred stock in MM Inc. paying €500 per year in dividends forever. Wood also pays Gallant €6,000 at the end of year 1. The appropriate discount rate on the MM preferred shares is 10%. Gallant sells the MM preferred stock at the end of year 1 after receiving the first dividend. He sells the shares at a price equal to their fair value. Gallant's 1-year holding period return is:

A. 5%.
B. 10%.
C. 15%.

149.   The probability that quarterly earnings for Phone Buddies Inc. will increase in any quarter is 75% and the probability that its quarterly earnings will fall is 25%. The probability that Phone Buddies earnings will increase in any five of the next eight quarters is:
   A. greater than or equal to 0, but less than 5%.
   B. greater than or equal to 5%, but less than 15%.
   C. greater than or equal to 15%, but less than 25%.

150.   In an analyst conference call, the CEO of J&L Materials indicated that there was a 30% chance that the firm would increase its dividend in the coming year as part of its effort to return wealth to shareholders. Other actions under consideration at J&L included the possibility that the company would repurchase its stock. The CEO estimated that the likelihood of the repurchase at the time of the call was 40%. The CEO also indicated that there was a 25% chance that the company would simultaneously increase the dividend and repurchase a portion of the outstanding common stock shares. What is the probability that J&L Materials either increases its dividend or repurchases its stock assuming that the two events are mutually exclusive?
   A. 25%.
   B. 45%.
   C. 70%.

151.   Which of the following statements regarding the Central Limit Theorem is correct?
   A. The distribution of sample means will be approximately normally distributed only if the population is normally distributed and continuous.
   B. Specific inferences about the population mean can be made as long as the sample size is sufficiently large.
   C. The sample mean will have a standard deviation equal to the population standard deviation divided by the sample size.

152.   Danielle Doctor derived a sample of the sales prices for 20 homes recently sold in her city. The data satisfy the requirements of the Central Limit Theorem. Doctor derives the degrees of freedom for the t-statistic for the sample mean and compares the properties of the Student's t-distribution against those of the Normal distribution. Doctor should derive which of the following conclusions about the distribution of her sample mean?
   A. The degrees of freedom for her t-statistic equals 20.
   B. The tails of her Student's t-distribution will be fatter than that of the Normal distribution.
   C. The peak of her Student's t-distribution will exceed that of the Normal distribution.

Economics

153. Pamsark is a nation whose economy has experienced severe cyclical swings over the past 30 years. The country's business cycle has had boom and bust cycles of varying lengths, and policymakers have had little success predicting these swings in economic activity, although the government has taken an active role in managing fiscal policy. The fiscal policy alternative *best* suited to address Pamsark's economic volatility in the future would be:
    A. limiting the growth in the domestic money supply.
    B. reducing marginal tax rates for individuals.
    C. establishing a corporate profits tax.

154. The natural rate of unemployment in Japan is believed to be 3.7%. The current unemployment rate is 4.2%. Identify the type of unemployment that explains the difference between the natural rate and the actual rate, and state whether Japan's potential GDP is greater than or less than its real GDP based on these unemployment figures.
    A. Frictional unemployment explains the difference, and potential GDP is less than real GDP.
    B. Frictional unemployment explains the difference, and potential GDP is greater than real GDP.
    C. Cyclical unemployment explains the difference, and potential GDP is greater than real GDP.

155. In the copper mining industry, environmental reclamation costs to restore the natural habitat after the mine has closed are frequently incurred by citizens who do not receive any direct benefit from the mine's copper production. As a result of the reclamation costs, which of the following is *most likely* to occur?
    A. The market price of copper will equal the equilibrium price.
    B. The marginal cost of copper will exceed the marginal benefit.
    C. The quantity of copper produced will be less than the equilibrium quantity.

156. Wanda Fisher owns and operates a pet store. She likes her work, even though she left a job paying her an annual salary of $70,000 to start the store two years ago. At that time, she borrowed and invested $25,000 in cages, aquariums, shelving and other store fixtures. For the most recent year, her revenue was $120,000, with cash operating expenses of $50,000 and depreciation of $5,000. Interest expense on the loan was $2,000. Wanda does not pay herself any salary. The accounting profit is $63,000 and economic profit of her pet store is:
    A. ($7,000).
    B. $63,000.
    C. $68,000.

157. Assume a cartel is organized and begins practicing collusion. State whether price and output will either increase or decrease under such an arrangement, versus a market with no collusion.
    A. Both will increase.
    B. Price will increase and output will decrease.
    C. Price will decrease and output will increase.

158. The mayor of a large city has proposed that an effective dollar price ceiling be placed on apartment rental rates. Three potential rental rates have been proposed, along with their associated quantity demanded (Q_d) and quantity supplied (Q_s) in millions of square feet.

$ Price per square foot	Q_d	Q_s
$50.00	1.9	5.2
$35.00	3.2	3.2
$15.00	6.0	2.1

    Which of the following *best* describes a price ceiling; its short run effects on the apartment rental market and the potential for a black market in rental properties to exist?
    A. $50.00 ceiling; shortage of apartment space in market, and potential for black market exists.
    B. $15.00 ceiling; surplus of apartment space in market, and no potential for black market exists.
    C. $15.00 ceiling; shortage of apartment space in market, and potential for black market exists.

159. The velocity of transactions has been increasing steadily for the past seven years. Over the same time period, the nation has experienced minimal growth in real output. According to the equation of exchange, inflation over the last seven years:
    A. increased more than the growth in the money supply.
    B. increased minimally, consistent with the growth in real output.
    C. increased at a rate similar to the growth rate in the money supply.

160. Average total costs for Dunhill Corporation's turbine plant are minimized when production is 100,000 units per year. Justin Collins states that (1) average variable cost is minimized at this same level of production, and that (2) profit is maximized at this level of production. Are Collins' statements accurate?
    A. Both statements are accurate.
    B. Neither statement is accurate.
    C. Only one of the statements is accurate.

161. Growth of real GDP in Lower Moesia is at a historically low level. An economic summit invites leading economists to pose a solution to the declining economic situation. Many of the economists in attendance subscribe to supply side economic theory. Their solution is to reduce the marginal tax rate of 68% to 35%. According to the supply-side view, the primary benefit of such a policy is:
    A. higher levels of disposable income and ability to consume goods and services leading to higher GDP.
    B. greater incentive for individuals to spend their income on tax-deductible luxury items.
    C. increased incentive for workers to provide more labor hours, leading to increased potential GDP.

162. BLD Inc. produces pure bottled water. The industry has experienced rapid growth as fitness conscious consumers demand these types of products. The growth has attracted many competitors to the industry. However, marketing campaigns to differentiate their products have proven unsuccessful. The main cost to producers is the filtering system that is required to purify the water. The demand for the filtering systems, as a result of industry growth, has led to a reduction in the cost of the systems. Indicate whether the pure bottled water market is *best* described as a price searcher or price taker and state whether the long-run supply curve is downward- or upward-sloping.
    A. Producers are price searchers and the long-run supply curve is downward-sloping.
    B. Producers are price searchers and the long-run supply curve is upward-sloping.
    C. Producers are price takers and the long-run supply curve is downward-sloping.

163. Which of the following arguments about the efficiency of monopolistic competition in allocating resources is *most* accurate?
    A. Since economic profits in the long run are positive for firms in monopolistic competition, there are efficiency losses.
    B. Product differentiation under monopolistic competition offers benefits that tend to offset inefficiency from the reduction in output compared to perfect competition.
    C. Advertising expenditures under monopolistic competition represent a deadweight loss to society.

164. The *most likely* reason that the Fed does not utilize a money targeting rule in conducting monetary policy is:
    A. unexpected fluctuations in the demand for money.
    B. unexpected fluctuations in the growth of the money supply.
    C. indications that there is a strong link between aggregate demand and demand for money.

Financial Reporting and Analysis

165. A company fails to record accrued wages. What effect will this failure have on the company's owners' equity?
A. No effect.
B. Owner's equity will be overstated.
C. Owner's equity will be understated.

166. There are several differences between the FASB and the IASB frameworks for financial reporting. Which one of the following is *least likely* a difference between the FASB framework and the IASB framework?
A. Constraints.
B. Objectives of financial statements.
C. Purpose of the framework.

167. A company understates year-end depreciation. As compared to the properly stated year-end results, what effect will this understatement have on the company's asset turnover ratio?
A. No impact.
B. Decrease.
C. Increase.

168. A manufacturing company reports research costs and losses on sales of a business segment on its income statement. Which of these expenses would be included in operating expenses?
A. Neither of these expenses.
B. Only one of these expenses.
C. Both of these expenses.

169. Thunderbird Company reported net income of $500 million and the company had 100 million common shares outstanding. In addition, Thunderbird had 5 million shares of convertible preferred and 10 million outstanding warrants during the year. Each preferred share pays a dividend of $4 per share and is convertible into three common shares. Each warrant is convertible into one common share at $25 per share. The company's stock traded at an average $50 per share and the company did not declare any dividends for the year. Thunderbird's diluted earnings per share for the year is *closest* to:
A. $4.00 per share.
B. $4.20 per share.
C. $4.80 per share.

170. At year end, Cleburne Incorporated had 800,000 shares of $1 par value common stock and $5 million of 7% convertible bonds outstanding for the entire year. The convertible debt is convertible into 50,000 shares. Net income for the year was $3,360,000 and the tax rate was 40%. Cleburne's diluted earnings per share for the year is *closest* to:
   A. $3.70 per share.
   B. $4.10 per share.
   C. $4.20 per share.

171. Under U.S. GAAP, how will purchased goodwill related to an acquisition be measured and affect the acquirer's balance sheet following the acquisition?
   A. Measured at excess of purchase cost over the fair value of the assets at acquisition date and recorded as an intangible asset.
   B. Measured at present value of future estimated excess cash flows from the acquisition and recorded as an intangible asset.
   C. No effect. It is an off-balance sheet item.

172. A company's investments include actively traded equity securities, long term bonds available for sale, and an equity investment in a private company. How would the following items affect the income statement?

	Actively traded stock	Bonds for Sale	Private Equity Investment
Change in market value	$200,000 increase	$100,000 decrease	No change
Dividend and interest income	$30,000	$50,000	$10,000

   A. Increase in income of $90,000.
   B. Increase in income of $190,000.
   C. Increase in income of $290,000.

173. During 2008, Salina Manufacturing Company reported the following transactions:
     - Borrowed $4 million from a commercial bank and used the proceeds to purchase land.
     - Purchased a patent for $3 million cash.
     - Decreased accounts receivable by $800,000.
     - Issued 5,000 shares of preferred stock for $3.6 million.
     - Increased deferred tax liabilities $600,000.
     - Paid interest expense of $400,000.
     - Sold held-to-maturity securities with a book value of $1.8 million for $2.1 million.
     - Paid operating lease payment of $900,000.
     - Increased prepaid expenses $100,000.

     Calculate Salina's net cash flow from investing activities under U.S. GAAP for the year-ended December 31, 2008.
     A. –$900,000.
     B. –$4.9 million.
     C. –$7.0 million.

174. During 2008, Salina Manufacturing Company reported the following transactions:
     - Borrowed $4 million from a commercial bank and used the proceeds to purchase land.
     - Purchased a patent for $3 million cash.
     - Decreased accounts receivable by $800,000.
     - Issued 5,000 shares of preferred stock for $3.6 million.
     - Increased deferred tax liabilities $600,000.
     - Paid interest expense of $400,000.
     - Sold held-to-maturity securities with a book value of $1.8 million for $2.1 million.
     - Paid operating lease payment of $900,000.
     - Increased prepaid expenses $100,000.

     Calculate Salina's net cash flow from financing activities under U.S. GAAP for the year-ended December 31, 2008.
     A. $4.6 million.
     B. $4.8 million.
     C. $7.6 million.

175. David Chance, CFA, is analyzing Grow Corp. Chance gathers the following information:

Net cash provided by operating activities	$3,500
Net cash used for fixed capital investments	$727
Cash paid for interest	$195
Income before tax	$4,400
Income tax expense	$1,540
Net income	$2,860

Grow Corp's free cash flow to the firm (FCFF) is *closest* to:
A. $2,260.
B. $2,646.
C. $2,900.

176. For the last few years, firms in the children's toy industry have found it more difficult to keep up with consumer demand despite steadily increasing inventory levels. The Consumer Price Index (CPI) has been at a level of 1050, 1060, and 1087 at the years ended 2006, 2007, and 2008, respectively. Given this situation, a firm in the children's toy industry that seeks to report higher net income would prefer which of the following inventory accounting methods?
A. LIFO.
B. FIFO.
C. Average cost.

177. Spiral Corporation uses the LIFO inventory cost flow assumption and provided the following information for the year just ended.

	Units	Unit cost	Total cost
Beginning Inventory	1,300	$50	$65,000
First Purchase	500	$48	$24,000
Second Purchase	900	$46	$41,400
Total Available	2,700		$130,400
Sold	2,100		

Calculate the *decrease* in ending inventory had Spiral Corporation used the FIFO inventory cost flow assumption.
A. $1,600.
B. $2,400.
C. $3,000.

178. O'Malley Enterprises recently purchased a new forklift for $20,000. O'Malley expects to use the forklift for 5 years and then sell it for $5,000. O'Malley's CFO, Sean Flannigan, is concerned about the financial statement impact of their accounting choice for depreciating the new forklift. He is currently weighing the effects of both the straight-line method and the double-declining-balance method.

Calculate the *difference* in O'Malley's depreciation expense between using straight-line and double-declining-balance in the first year.
A. $5,000.
B. $4,000.
C. $3,000.

179. Mustang Corporation acquired Cobra Company 5 years ago. As a part of the acquisition, Mustang reported goodwill of $750,000. For the year just ended, Mustang gathered the following data:
- Fair value of Cobra $5,000,000
- Carrying value of Cobra (including goodwill) $5,200,000
- Identifiable net assets of Cobra at fair value $4,500,000

Using U.S. GAAP, determine if the goodwill is impaired, and if so, calculate the impairment loss.
A. The goodwill is impaired and a loss of $200,000 is recognized.
B. The goodwill is impaired and a loss of $250,000 is recognized.
C. The goodwill is not impaired and no loss is recognized.

180. POI Corp. has an effective tax rate of 29.6% and a statutory tax rate of 35%. The cause of this difference is *most likely*:
A. warranty expense.
B. accelerated depreciation.
C. permanently reinvested earnings of POI's foreign subsidiary.

181. Lyon Company had pretax earnings of $150 million in its first year of operation. Pretax income included:
- $25 million of interest income from tax-free municipal bonds.
- $35 million of accrued warranty expense that is not yet deductible.
- $15 million of deductible depreciation expense that is not yet accrued.

Lyon's tax rate is 40%. Based on the information provided, calculate the year end amount of income taxes payable Lyon should record.
A. $58 million.
B. $60 million.
C. $70 million.

182. Reek Chemical Company is obligated to decontaminate a processing plant when production is completed in 10 years. Reek has not yet recognized the obligation in its financial statements but plans to do so at the end of this year. Which of the following statements *best describes* the impact of recognizing the asset retirement obligation?
    A. Return on assets will increase and interest coverage will decrease.
    B. Asset turnover will increase and interest coverage decrease.
    C. Debt-to-equity will increase and net profit margin will decrease.

183. Shelby Enterprises recently entered into a new $500 million revolving credit facility. The provisions of the facility require Shelby to repay the loan before any other debt can be retired. In addition, if the company's debt-to-capital ratio is higher than 1.0 and their net worth falls below $2 billion, Shelby will be prohibited from paying any dividends. Shelby would *most likely* agree to these covenants because they reduce:
    A. risk to existing bondholders.
    B. the company's interest cost.
    C. risk to existing shareholders.

184. RGH Aircraft Services recently leased an airplane to Express Delivery Company. The lease agreement provided the following information:

    - The airplane is to be returned to RGH at the end of the lease.
    - Express Delivery can purchase the airplane at any time before the lease expires at the fair value on the purchase date.
    - The term of the lease is 15 years and the airplane has a useful life of 20 years.
    - At the inception of the lease, the present value of the lease payments exceeds the carrying value of the airplane.

    Collectibility of the lease payments is reasonably certain and RGH has no other obligations under the lease. How should RGH treat the lease for financial reporting purposes?
    A. Operating lease.
    B. Direct financing lease.
    C. Sales-type lease.

185. On December 31 of this year, Pinto Company called its $1,000,000, 8% bonds at 101 and reported an extraordinary loss of $12,000. Assuming Pinto's tax rate was 40%, what was the carrying value of the bonds on the call date?
    A. $990,000.
    B. $998,000.
    C. $1,030,000.

186. Pallimen Manufacturing has started a project to improve the firm's profitability ratios. As an alternative to improving its profit margin, Pallimen could improve its return on equity by:
   A. reducing asset turnover.
   B. decreasing the ratio of EBT to EBIT.
   C. increasing financial leverage.

187. At the end of last year, Manhattan Corporation reported a quick ratio of 1.2. During the first quarter of this year, Manhattan reduced its accounts payable with a cash payment of $2 million. Holding all else constant, determine how the cash payment would affect the quick ratio as reported at the end of the first quarter.
   A. No effect.
   B. Increase.
   C. Decrease.

188. An analyst gathers the following selected financial information on Quip Corp.

Partial financials for 2008	Quip Corp
Sales	$350,000
Cost of goods sold	270,000
Net income	35,000
Current assets	165,000
Current liabilities	130,000
2008 LIFO reserve	3,000
2007 LIFO reserve	2,000

To compare Quip and its competitors, an analyst makes the necessary adjustments to restate Quip's financial statements to reflect the FIFO inventory accounting method. Quip's adjusted gross profit margin is *closest* to:
   A. 20%.
   B. 23%.
   C. 26%.

189. Galvin Corporation is currently depreciating its machinery over 18 years. Management has recently determined the actual life of the machinery is 12 years. Management immediately revises its annual depreciation expense to reflect the new information. Which of the following statements *most accurately* reflects the impact of changing the depreciable life of the machinery?
      A. Galvin's taxes increase.
      B. Galvin's interest expense increases.
      C. Galvin's earnings per share decreases.

190. Which of the following cash flows of a company using U.S. GAAP is *least likely* to be classified in the operating activities section of the cash flow statement?
      A. Dividends paid.
      B. Interest paid.
      C. Dividends received.

191. An analyst at HMF Investments is explaining issues that complicate capital budgeting decisions to his firm's new employees. The analyst is focusing on problems caused by project interactions. Which of the analyst's points is *most likely* correct?
      A. The outcome of today's projects can influence future opportunities for investment, which makes today's investment decision more difficult.
      B. Firms are generally able to raise any desired amount of capital, but may have difficulty identifying all available projects.
      C. The identification of many independent projects will require a firm with an unlimited capital budget to select the projects that add the greatest value to the firm.

192. Inverness Corporation is considering investing in one of two mutually exclusive capital projects. The firm's cost of capital is 15%. Project A's NPV profile crosses the Y-axis at $1.8 million and crosses the X-axis at 25%. Project B's NPV profile crosses the Y-axis at $1.2 million and crosses the X-axis at 33%. For the two projects the crossover rate is 18%. Which of the following is *most likely* correct?
      A. Project A and Project B have equal NPVs at a discount rate of 15%.
      B. Inverness should choose Project B since it has a higher IRR.
      C. Inverness should choose Project A since it has a higher NPV.

193. Jay Industrial's capital structure consists of 40% debt and 60% equity. The company's before-tax cost of issuing new debt is 7%, while its cost of issuing new equity is 13%. Jay's marginal tax rate is 35%. Calculate Jay's weighted average cost of capital (WACC).
      A. 7.9%.
      B. 9.6%.
      C. 10.6%.

194. An analyst has collected the following information regarding plastics manufacturer Sturdy Inc.

    Sturdy Inc. Balance Sheet Data for the year just ended (Market Values)

Long-term Debt	$5,625,000
Preferred Stock	$0
Common Equity	$6,875,000
Sturdy Inc. target debt-to-equity ratio	0.65

    Competitor Data

Capital structure	Company A	Company B
Debt	33%	53%
Common Stock	67%	47%

    The analyst wants to calculate Sturdy Inc.'s weighted average cost of capital. Which of the following is *closest* to the common equity weight, using the best available data from the information provided?
    A. 57%.
    B. 61%.
    C. 65%.

195. Jane Redding, an analyst for SDB Investments, is estimating the cost of equity capital associated with a project to give Modanto Corp., a national retailing firm, internet retailing capabilities for its clothing lines. Redding has observed that the common stock of Modanto has 10% more systematic risk than the market. In addition, Redding has observed that the market risk premium is 7%, and the risk-free rate is 3.5%. Based on the historical returns of an internet-only clothing retailer, Redding believes that the project has a beta of 1.3. What is the project cost of equity using the pure play method?
    A. 8.05%.
    B. 11.20%.
    C. 12.60%.

196. While analyzing HMS Inc., Fred Browne noted that the company's liquidity as measured by its quick ratio has decreased over time while its current liabilities have remained constant. Which of the following is the *most likely* reason for weakening liquidity at HMS?
    A. A decrease in the level of inventory.
    B. An increase in the level of marketable securities.
    C. A decrease in the level of accounts receivable.

197. An analyst at a firm is preparing a short-term cash flow forecast. Which of the following adjustments to the cash flow forecast made by the analyst is correct?
    A. Increase cash inflows for an expected $20 million increase in accounts receivable.
    B. Increase cash outflows for an expected $35 million issuance of long-term bonds.
    C. Increase cash inflows for an expected $2 million transfer of funds from a foreign subsidiary.

198. A portfolio manager is evaluating Benson Inc.'s policies related to shareholder rights. The manager is considering investing in Benson if the policies are in the interests of shareholders. Which of Benson's policies has a negative effect on shareholders?
    A. Benson has two classes of publicly traded shares. The class B shares have one tenth the value of and one tenth the voting power of the class A shares.
    B. Benson's board of directors tabulates the results of all proxy votes, which are recorded, and maintained by a third-party entity.
    C. Benson requires a 2/3 majority shareholder approval for any takeover defense proposed by the firm's managers, unless a proposed takeover would damage shareholder value, in which case a simple majority shareholder approval is required.

Portfolio Management

199. Danielle Paftee, age 55, has an investment account designed to fund her granddaughter's college education. Paftee's granddaughter is two years old. Paftee also will use the account for intermittent health care expenses for her elderly parents, whose health plans and retirement plans do not adequately cover their expenses. Which of the following statements regarding Paftee's investment objectives and constraints is *least likely* correct?
    A. Paftee has a long-term time horizon.
    B. Paftee has an significant liquidity requirement.
    C. Paftee should focus on total return with very low current income requirements.

200. Steve McCool is estimating the expected return and standard deviation of his equity portfolio. Steve has estimated a 20% chance that the portfolio will provide an 8% rate of return, a 40% chance that the portfolio will provide a 10% return, and a 40% chance that the portfolio will provide a 12% rate of return. Calculate the standard deviation of McCool's portfolio.
    A. 0.00022.
    B. 0.01497.
    C. 0.02240.

201. Chuck Hill, CFA, is explaining an efficient frontier analysis to one of his clients. Which of Hill's following statements regarding the efficient frontier is correct?
   A. The left endpoint of the efficient frontier is represented by the portfolio with the lowest level of risk.
   B. Portfolios that are further to the right on the efficient frontier dominate portfolios that are to the left.
   C. Only efficient assets are on the efficient frontier.

202. Adding the risk-free asset to a portfolio of risky assets will:
   A. decrease portfolio standard deviation because it is uncorrelated with risky assets.
   B. not affect portfolio standard deviation because it is uncorrelated with risky assets.
   C. decrease portfolio standard deviation due to its negative correlation with risky assets.

203. Bruce Johansen, CFA, is currently fully invested in the market portfolio that lies on the capital market line (CML). Johansen desires to increase the expected return from his portfolio. Johansen is risk averse but willing to accept higher risk if he can increase the expected return from his portfolio. According to capital market theory, Johansen can meet his risk and return objectives *best* by:
   A. allocating a higher proportion of the portfolio to higher risk assets.
   B. borrowing at the risk-free rate to invest in the risky market portfolio.
   C. owning the risky market portfolio and lending at the risk-free rate.

204. Penny Linn, CFA, predicts that both Stock X and Y will return 20% next year. The Treasury bill rate is 5% and the market risk premium is 8%. The beta for Stock X is 1.5 and for Stock Y is 2. The standard deviation for Stock X is 20% and for Stock Y is 30%. Determine if Linn's predictions lie above or below the security market line.
   A. Only Stock X lies below the SML.
   B. Only Stock Y lies below the SML.
   C. Both Stock X and Stock Y lie below the SML.

Asset Valuation

205. Jacques Fontenot wants to place an order to purchase 10,000 shares of BQ Inc. at a price of €75.00 or below. The shares are currently trading for €82.1 bid and €.82.2 ask. What type of order should Fontenot place?
   A. Market order.
   B. Stop loss order.
   C. Limit order.

206. Ned Jones, CFA, manages an endowment fund. The fund's asset allocation includes domestic stocks and bonds, international stocks and bonds, as well as real estate investments. Jones wants to establish an accurate benchmark to compare the fund's performance against. Which of Jones' following statements concerning indexes to be used for benchmarking is *least likely* correct?
    A. The creation of an investment bond index is difficult because of bond pricing issues, and because the universe of bonds is constantly changing.
    B. Correlations between bond index returns for different countries have tended to be lower than correlations between different bond indexes within a single country.
    C. Sovereign bond indexes outside the United States represent after-tax returns.

207. Two stocks have identical risk, but one of them offers a higher expected return than the other. This apparent inefficiency in the market:
    A. indicates that arbitrageurs must be unaware of the mispricing.
    B. may persist and even grow larger before any correction occurs.
    C. can only arise when arbitrageurs lack the capital to exploit the situation.

208. Three equity analysts at Schiler & Company are debating their supervisor's claim that significant excess return can be generated by exploiting inefficiencies in the capital markets. Analyst A states, "… the large number of profit maximizing investors researching investment opportunities creates an efficient market." Analyst B rebuts by stating, "Over the past three years, my technical analysis strategy has outperformed all the major benchmarks, which proves the markets are not efficient." Analyst C states, "High transactions costs improve the information efficiency of capital markets." The statement that is *most likely* to be correct was made by:
    A. Analyst A.
    B. Analyst B.
    C. Analyst C.

209. Rose Half, CFA, is analyzing El Toro Electric Company. She has collected the following data:
    - Stock price is $35.00 per share.
    - Return on equity is 15%.
    - Payout ratio is 30%.
    - Book value is $20.00 per share.
    - Cash flow is $5.00 per share.

    What is El Toro Electric Company's expected long-run rate of return?
    A. 10.5%.
    B. 13.3%.
    C. 15.0%.

210. Peterson Manufacturing has earnings per share of $4.00 and paid a dividend of $1.00 per share. Peterson's return on equity is 16.0%. Peterson is considering a debt issue that would increase its financial leverage. Peterson is also considering increasing its dividend payout ratio. Assuming all other factors are constant, Peterson's potential growth rate:
    A. will increase due to the increased leverage, and increase further due to the higher payout ratio.
    B. will increase due to the higher payout ratio, but this increase will be offset to some extent by the increased leverage.
    C. will increase due to the increased leverage, but this increase will be offset to some extent by the higher payout ratio.

211. Curzon Corp reported the following in its Shareholder's Equity account:
• Preferred stock	($50 par value, 10,000 shares)	$500,000
• Common Stock	($2 par value, 1,000,000 shares issued)	$2,000,000
• Retained Earnings		$8,400,000
• Treasury Stock	(200,000 shares repurchased in 2004)	$(400,000)
• Total Equity		$10,500,000

    In calculating a Price to Book value for Curzon, the appropriate book value per common share is *closest* to:
    A. $10.50.
    B. $12.50.
    C. $13.13.

212. Given the academic research supporting the efficiency of the stock market, which of the following is the *least accurate* description of a portfolio manager's role in an efficient market?
    A. Identifying and specifying a client's objectives and constraints.
    B. Specifying an explicit investment strategy to meet the client's needs.
    C. Diversifying the client's portfolio across all asset classes to eliminate systematic risk.

213. Which of the following is the *least accurate* statement about the price-to-sales multiple?
   A. Price-to-sales is a poor valuation technique for growth companies.
   B. Sales growth drives all subsequent earnings and cash flows.
   C. Revenue has minimal accounting manipulation concerns relative to other numbers.

214. A U.S. investor is considering investing in a security of a company in a developing country. The country's market is characterized by infrequent trading, high inflation, large market volatility, low operating leverage, political unrest, low debt usage, and a depreciating exchange rate. In determining the appropriate country risk premium for the developing country, the investor should consider:
   A. liquidity risk, exchange rate risk, financial risk, business risk, balance sheet risk.
   B. financial risk, liquidity risk, exchange rate risk, country risk, business risk.
   C. business risk, variability risk, country risk, exchange rate risk, financial risk.

215. An advantage of the duration/convexity approach over the full valuation approach is:
   A. its superior accuracy for nonparallel shifts in the yield curve.
   B. it is not based on yield to maturity, which is a summary measure.
   C. it saves considerable time when working with portfolios of bonds.

216. Six-month LIBOR is an interest rate which:
   A. represents the interest rate paid on a CD that matures in 6 months.
   B. is the return available on the shortest term euro-denominated securities.
   C. is determined by adding a small spread to the yield available on a UK government bond maturing in 6 months.

217. An analyst is evaluating an annual-pay bond with a yield to maturity of 7.0%. The bond-equivalent yield of this bond is:
   A. equal to 7.0%.
   B. less than 7.0%.
   C. greater than 7.0%.

218. An economist has forecast that the term structure of interest rates will remain perfectly flat. According to the liquidity preference theory, the economist's forecast implies that future short-term interest rates will:
   A. decrease over time.
   B. increase over time.
   C. equal current short-term interest rates.

219. Identify the *most accurate* statement regarding collateralized borrowing transactions.
    A. Repurchase agreements usually offer the lowest interest cost.
    B. Margin buying usually allows for borrowing a higher percentage of the collateral value.
    C. Margin buying is usually the preferred transaction structure for institutional bond investors.

220. Eric Webb, an individual investor in a high tax bracket, would like to purchase a 5-year zero-coupon security with no credit risk. His investment adviser has recommended U.S. Treasury STRIP securities, and has told Webb that either coupon strips or principal strips would meet his needs. Which of the following statements is **TRUE** regarding the investment adviser's recommendation?
    A. While principal strips have no credit risk, there is credit risk in coupon strips.
    B. The adviser should have informed Webb that the principal strips have higher reinvestment risk than the coupon strips.
    C. The adviser should have informed Webb that STRIP securities may have negative tax consequences related to accrued interest.

221. Jeff Stone, CFA, is evaluating a newly issued mortgage backed security for his bond portfolio. Stone expects interest rates to rise gradually over the next few years. If Stone's interest rate forecast is correct, prepayment risk of the mortgage backed security:
    A. will fall to zero, as borrowers will have no incentive to prepay their loans.
    B. will increase, as curtailments become more likely.
    C. will decrease, although prepayments will still occur.

222. An analyst stated that the purpose of a collateralized mortgage obligation is to redistribute prepayment risk among investors with different risk tolerances while at the same time reducing total prepayment risk for all tranches in the structure. The analyst's statement is correct:
    A. only with respect to redistribution of risk.
    B. only with respect to reducing total prepayment risk.
    C. with respect to both redistribution of risk and reducing total prepayment risk.

223. Jorge Fullen is evaluating a 7% 10-year bond that is callable at par in 5 years. Coupon payments can be reinvested at an annual rate of 7%, and the current price of the bond is $106.50. The bond pays interest semiannually. Should Fullen consider the yield to first call (YTC) or the yield to maturity (YTM) in making his purchase decision?
    A. YTM, since YTM is greater than YTC.
    B. YTC, since YTC is less than YTM.
    C. YTC, since YTC is greater than YTM.

224. PRC International just completed a $234 million floating rate convertible bond offering. As stated in the indenture, the interest rate on the bond is the lesser of 90-day LIBOR or 10%. The indenture also requires PRC to retire $5.6 million per year with the option to retire as much as $10 million. Which of the following embedded options is *most likely* to benefit the investor? The:
    A. 10% cap on the floating interest rate.
    B. accelerated sinking fund provision for principal repayment.
    C. conversion option on the convertible bonds.

225. Richard Wallace manages a portfolio of fixed-income securities for a large multinational investment firm. Wallace's portfolio is exposed to reinvestment risk, which he is attempting to reduce by adding securities with low levels of reinvestment risk. Of the following bonds, Wallace should *most* appropriately choose:
    A. a mortgage-backed security with scheduled principal and interest payments.
    B. an 8%, 10-year Treasury bond with semiannual payments.
    C. a 15-year Treasury strip.

226. Siegel, Inc. has issued bonds maturing in 15 years but callable at any time after the first 8 years. The bonds have a coupon rate of 6%, and are currently trading at $992 per $1,000 par value. If interest rates decline over the next few years:
    A. the call option embedded in the bonds will increase in value, but the price of the bond will decrease.
    B. the price of the bond will increase, but probably by less than a comparable bond with no embedded option.
    C. the price of the bond will increase, primarily as a result of the increasing value of the call option.

227. Bond X carries a rating of BBB-/Baa3. Bond Y has a rating of B/B2. Both bonds are callable after five years, and both bonds mature in ten years. Identify the *most accurate* statement regarding the credit risk of these bonds. Which bond's value would be *most affected* by a ratings downgrade, and which bond has the higher default risk?
    A. Bond X would be more affected by a ratings downgrade, but Bond Y has higher default risk.
    B. Bond Y would be more affected by a ratings downgrade, but Bond X has higher default risk.
    C. Bond X has higher default risk, but both bonds would feel equivalent effects of a ratings downgrade.

228. Karen Callaway is an investor in the 35% tax bracket. She is evaluating a tax-exempt municipal security with a tax-exempt yield of 4.5%. What is the taxable equivalent yield (TEY) of the municipal security?
    A. 2.9%.
    B. 6.9%.
    C. 12.9%.

229. Ron Logan, CFA, is a bond manager. He purchased $50 million in 6.0% coupon Southwest Manufacturing bonds at par three years ago. Today, the bonds are priced to yield 6.85%. The bonds mature in nine years. Identify the *most accurate* statement regarding the pricing and yield of these bonds.
    A. The bonds are trading at a discount, and the yield to maturity (YTM) has increased since purchase.
    B. The bonds are trading at a premium, and the yield to maturity (YTM) has decreased since purchase.
    C. The bonds are trading at a discount and the yield to maturity (YTM) has decreased.

230. Steve Brown is questioned by his superior about the commonly cited criticisms and benefits of the derivatives market. Which of Brown's statements regarding the criticisms and benefits of derivative markets is *most likely* correct?
    A. Derivatives markets are often criticized for being too risky and illiquid for all but the most knowledgeable investors.
    B. Derivatives benefit financial markets due to the price discovery and risk management functions they provide.
    C. Derivatives benefit financial markets by generating high fees for dealers willing to make a market in these securities.

231. Two portfolio managers at an investment management firm are discussing option strategies for their clients' portfolios. The first manager is considering a covered call strategy on Consolidated Steel Inc. (CSI). The manager states that the strategy is attractive since it will increase the expected returns from the anticipated appreciation in CSI, while reducing the downside risk. The second manager is considering a protective put strategy on Millwood Lumber Company (MLC). The manager states that the protective put strategy will allow his investors to retain an infinite profit potential while limiting potential losses to an amount equal to the initial stock price minus the put premium. Determine whether the comments made by the first and second manager are correct.
    A. Only the first manager is incorrect.
    B. Only the second manager is incorrect.
    C. Both the first manager and the second manager are incorrect.

232. An investor takes a long position in a corn futures contract. Initial margin on the contract is 10% of the contract value and maintenance margin is half of the initial margin. If, at the beginning of the second trading day for the contract, the investor receives a margin call, it is *least likely* that:
    A. variation margin is greater than maintenance margin.
    B. the final trade from the previous day is greater than the contract price.
    C. the average of the last few trades from the previous day is less than the contract price.

233. Anne Quincy took the short side of a forward contract on the S&P 500 Index three months ago in an attempt to hedge short-term changes in her index portfolio. The contract had a term of six months at the purchase date, a contract price of $1,221 and Mason Inc. as the counterparty. Quincy is now considering unwinding her short position using either a three-month Mason Inc. contract with a price of $1,220, a three-month JonesCo contract with a price of $1,219, or a three-month Redding Company contract with a price of $1,218. If Quincy wants to minimize credit risk, which of the following should she do? Take the long position in the contract with:
    A. JonesCo.
    B. Mason Inc.
    C. Redding Company.

234. An analyst is evaluating a European call option with a strike price of 25 and 219 days to expiration. The underlying stock is currently trading for $29, and the analyst thinks that by the option expiration date the stock will be valued at $35. If the risk-free rate is 4.0%, what is the lower bound on the value of this option?
    A. $0.
    B. $4.00.
    C. $4.58.

235. Chris Kramer holds three options that expire on the same day. Option 1 is a call option on the stock of Blintz Company with a strike price of $58. Option 2 is an interest rate put option on 90-day LIBOR with a strike price of 5.4% and notional principal of $1,000. Option 3 is a put option on InstaCare stock with a strike price of $23. On the expiration date of the options, if the price of Blintz stock is $64, 90-day LIBOR is 3.0%, and the price of InstaCare stock is $29, which option will have a payoff with the largest present value?
    A. Option 1.
    B. Option 2.
    C. Option 3.

236. Party A enters into a plain vanilla 1-year interest rate swap agreement with Bank B in which he will make fixed-rate payments in exchange for receiving floating-rate payments based on LIBOR plus 100 basis points. Assume that payments are made quarterly in arrears based on a 360-day year. The fixed rate on the swap is 6.5%. The current interest rates on 90, 180, 270, and 360-day LIBOR are 5.2%, 5.5%, 5.8%, and 6.0%, respectively. If the notional principal is $100 million, what will Party A's net cash flow at the end of the first quarter equal?
   A. −$675,000.
   B. −$75,000.
   C. +$75,000.

237. Krissy Steele, CFA, manages money for high net worth individuals. Steele develops unique investment policies for all of her clients and uses various investment funds to construct portfolios. However, Steele has been reluctant to use hedge funds. Which of the following statements made by Steele is *least likely* to be correct?
   A. The volatility of historical returns associated with hedge fund indexes understates their true risk level.
   B. Hedge fund returns are normally distributed.
   C. Published information on hedge fund returns is based on incomplete historical data.

238. When compared to a traditional mutual fund, an ETF will *most likely* offer:
   A. better risk management.
   B. less portfolio transparency.
   C. higher exposure to capital gains distribution taxes.

239. An investor purchases oil commodity futures contracts worth $25 million and an equal amount of 10-year Treasury notes with an interest rate of 3.5%. Assuming that oil prices rise by 10% and the price of the notes remains unchanged, the total return of the position after three months is *closest* to:
   A. $2,500,000.
   B. $2,600,000.
   C. $2,700,000.

240. Archie Boone, CFA, is the managing director at Hoffman Advisors, an alternative investment management company. Boone is reviewing the work of a real estate analyst and finds that in calculating net operating income (NOI) for a property, the analyst has understated vacancy by $3,000, overstated depreciation expense by $4,000, overstated insurance expense by $4,000, and understated interest expense by $2,000. If Boone corrects the analyst's estimates of NOI for all these items, the updated estimate will:
    A. increase by $1,000 as the restatement of vacancy will be partially offset by the restatement of insurance expense.
    B. increase by $1,000 as the restatement of depreciation expense will be partially offset by the restatement of vacancy.
    C. decrease by $1,000 as the restatement of insurance expense will be more than offset by the restatement of vacancy and interest expense.

End of Afternoon Session

Exam 2
Morning Session

Topic	Questions	Points
Ethical and Professional Standards	1–18	27
Quantitative Analysis	19–32	21
Economics	33–44	18
Financial Reporting and Analysis	45–78	51
Portfolio Management	79–84	9
Asset Valuation	85–120	54
Total		**180**

Test Answers

#					#					#			
1.	A	B	C		41.	A	B	C		81.	A	B	C
2.	A	B	C		42.	A	B	C		82.	A	B	C
3.	A	B	C		43.	A	B	C		83.	A	B	C
4.	A	B	C		44.	A	B	C		84.	A	B	C
5.	A	B	C		45.	A	B	C		85.	A	B	C
6.	A	B	C		46.	A	B	C		86.	A	B	C
7.	A	B	C		47.	A	B	C		87.	A	B	C
8.	A	B	C		48.	A	B	C		88.	A	B	C
9.	A	B	C		49.	A	B	C		89.	A	B	C
10.	A	B	C		50.	A	B	C		90.	A	B	C
11.	A	B	C		51.	A	B	C		91.	A	B	C
12.	A	B	C		52.	A	B	C		92.	A	B	C
13.	A	B	C		53.	A	B	C		93.	A	B	C
14.	A	B	C		54.	A	B	C		94.	A	B	C
15.	A	B	C		55.	A	B	C		95.	A	B	C
16.	A	B	C		56.	A	B	C		96.	A	B	C
17.	A	B	C		57.	A	B	C		97.	A	B	C
18.	A	B	C		58.	A	B	C		98.	A	B	C
19.	A	B	C		59.	A	B	C		99.	A	B	C
20.	A	B	C		60.	A	B	C		100.	A	B	C
21.	A	B	C		61.	A	B	C		101.	A	B	C
22.	A	B	C		62.	A	B	C		102.	A	B	C
23.	A	B	C		63.	A	B	C		103.	A	B	C
24.	A	B	C		64.	A	B	C		104.	A	B	C
25.	A	B	C		65.	A	B	C		105.	A	B	C
26.	A	B	C		66.	A	B	C		106.	A	B	C
27.	A	B	C		67.	A	B	C		107.	A	B	C
28.	A	B	C		68.	A	B	C		108.	A	B	C
29.	A	B	C		69.	A	B	C		109.	A	B	C
30.	A	B	C		70.	A	B	C		110.	A	B	C
31.	A	B	C		71.	A	B	C		111.	A	B	C
32.	A	B	C		72.	A	B	C		112.	A	B	C
33.	A	B	C		73.	A	B	C		113.	A	B	C
34.	A	B	C		74.	A	B	C		114.	A	B	C
35.	A	B	C		75.	A	B	C		115.	A	B	C
36.	A	B	C		76.	A	B	C		116.	A	B	C
37.	A	B	C		77.	A	B	C		117.	A	B	C
38.	A	B	C		78.	A	B	C		118.	A	B	C
39.	A	B	C		79.	A	B	C		119.	A	B	C
40.	A	B	C		80.	A	B	C		120.	A	B	C

Exam 2
Morning Session

Ethical and Professional Standards

1. Versoxy Pharmaceuticals has recently hired Meelono Investment Partners to work on a secondary public stock offering. Meelono's brokerage division currently has a "hold" on Versoxy's stock. However, Ed Haskell, investment banking head, has asked Ward Leaver, brokerage head, to consider changing the recommendation from "hold" to "buy." Under the CFA Institute® Standards of Professional Conduct, Leaver's most appropriate action is to:
   A. place Versoxy on a restricted list, giving out only factual information about the firm.
   B. have the currently assigned analyst reexamine the security for consideration of a possible upgrade.
   C. assign a new analyst to do a completely new examination of Versoxy.

2. Zach Ronan, CFA, has a client, Jimmy Deininger, with a large position in a security that is thinly traded. Deininger is insistent that the security be sold right away "whatever the price." Ronan is concerned that the immediate sale will put extraordinary downward pressure on the price. According to CFA Institute Standards of Professional Conduct, Ronan should:
   A. counsel Deininger and encourage a more gradual approach in selling the security in order to maximize his price, but there is no violation by selling the security quickly even if it severely affects the price.
   B. accept the order and has no obligation to counsel the client.
   C. not accept the order, in order to avoid a violation of market manipulation, and should advise the client accordingly.

3. Henry Ketchum works in a mid-sized securities firm. He primarily handles research for the telecommunications industry. One of the major providers of residential phone service, M.A. Ring, has publicly disclosed that it is considering getting out of certain unprofitable segments of the residential phone market. If Ketchum changes his recommendation on M.A. Ring, the firm can comply with Standard III(B) Fair Dealing by determining which clients it will communicate this change to first according to:
    A. size of the client.
    B. known interest of the client in M.A. Ring.
    C. number of shares of M.A. Ring owned by the client.

4. Lyndon Westerburg, CFA, is a respected portfolio manager for a U.S. bank. The portfolios he manages are fully discretionary, and he manages primarily individual accounts over $20 million. One of his clients has offered Westerburg use of his yacht for a week if the client's portfolio exceeds prespecified benchmarks. Westerburg disclosed this to his employer. Is Westerburg completely following CFA Institute Standards of Professional Conduct?
    A. This is a violation of CFA Institute Standards, because Westerburg did not disclose the additional compensation to the other clients.
    B. Westerburg has violated the Independence and Objectivity Standard by accepting a substantial gift which could compromise his independence and objectivity.
    C. No violation of Standards has occurred.

5. Rob Carter is an analyst of the consumer goods industry. Carter is preparing a research report on Clean Bright, a company that manufactures cleaning products. After reviewing industry statistics and consulting with several suppliers of Clean Bright, Carter discovers that Clean Bright has become alarmingly slow in meeting its accounts payable obligations. Carter believes that the company may soon face bankruptcy. Under Standard II(A) Material Nonpublic Information, before Carter can issue a sell recommendation in his research report, Carter is required to:
    A. take no additional action, and can freely issue the report.
    B. wait until suppliers contact other analysts about Clean Bright.
    C. make full disclosure of the conversations with the suppliers to a compliance officer at his firm.

6. Martin Remy, CFA, has just received word from one of his largest clients that she will soon receive a large inheritance that will need to be invested. The client has asked Remy to begin preparations for investing the inheritance which is estimated to be $4.5 million. Remy contacts Johan Walker, who handles the fixed-income portion of the client's portfolio, and gives him the details of the inheritance. Walker informs Remy that he suspects the client's inheritance is actually part of an illegal money laundering scheme. After reviewing Walker's evidence, Remy believes it is highly likely that the supposed inheritance is illegal, but he is not completely sure. Instead of taking the evidence directly to law enforcement officials, however, Remy meets with his firm's primary legal counsel. Did Remy violate CFA Institute Standards of Professional Conduct by sharing the inheritance information with Walker or by informing his firm's legal counsel after discovering the illicit nature of the inheritance funds?
    A. Remy should not have shared the information with Walker, but consulting with the firm's primary legal counsel was appropriate.
    B. Remy acted within the Standards by speaking with Walker and in speaking with legal counsel, but also has an obligation to report the illegal activities to the appropriate authorities.
    C. No Standards violations have occurred.

7. Harriet Kedzie, CFA, is a money manager providing services to the Groeber Foundation. In a recent report to the foundation's directors, Kedzie explained her rationale for investing in ZYX stock as follows: "ZYX was chosen since it further diversifies the Foundation's holdings without sacrificing expected returns. In fact, ZYX's low standard deviation and high expected return ensure that the foundation will benefit from positive returns on this investment." Has Kedzie violated CFA Institute Standards of Professional Conduct?
    A. No.
    B. Yes, because ZYX is an inappropriate investment for the Groeber Foundation's portfolio.
    C. Yes, because she inappropriately guaranteed the return on ZYX stock in her investment report.

8. Milken Corporation, a regional asset management firm, has publicly adopted the CFA Institute Code and Standards as their governing code of ethics. Milken Co.'s president, Kenneth Kozlowski, CFA, recently issued a press release which included the following statement:

    "We are proud to announce that two of our seasoned money managers have earned the right to use the CFA designation. In addition, four of our junior analysts have become Level 3 CFA candidates. These individuals have proven their dedication to the investment community and shown commitment to the highest ethical standards."

    Regarding the press release, which of the following statements is correct?
    A. All statements in the press release are in compliance with CFA Institute Standards.
    B. Milken has violated the Code and Standards by improperly referencing the money managers' right to use the CFA designation.
    C. Kozlowski has violated the Code and Standards by implying superior performance results.

9. Which of the following statements regarding the Disclosures section of the Global Investment Presentation Standards (GIPS)® is *least* accurate?
    A. Disclosures allow firms to elaborate on the raw numbers contained in the presentation.
    B. Disclosures will change from period to period, as circumstances of the reporting firm change.
    C. Some disclosures are required of all firms claiming GIPS compliance, while others are specific to certain circumstances.

10. Teddy Larson, CFA, is drafting a policies and procedures manual for his firm, and is working on the section on "misconduct." He wants to align the procedures with CFA Institute Standards. He accordingly includes prohibitions against any professional conduct involving dishonesty, fraud, etc., and acts that reflect poorly on an individual's professional reputation, integrity, or competence. Larson also includes recommended procedures for compliance. Which of the following would be *least likely* to be included as a prescribed procedure, in order to be in conformity with CFA Institute Standards regarding misconduct?
    A. "A proper ethical code of conduct must be followed and no behavior will be tolerated that reflects poorly on the employee, our company, or the investment industry."
    B. "All prior violations and applicable disciplinary sanctions are shown as follows…"
    C. "All references for potential employees must be checked to ensure good character and eligibility to work within the investment industry."

11. Doug Watson is a senior portfolio manager for Pinnacle Capital. Pinnacle currently holds a substantial position in ATI Corporation, a large oil and gas exploration company. ATI's managers visit Pinnacle's offices to give their financial presentation to Watson and a colleague. After the presentation, ATI's president mentions to Watson that he believes ATI is on the verge of a major natural gas discovery in Texas. News of this potential financial windfall had not been mentioned during the presentation. To comply with CFA Institute Standards of Professional Conduct, Watson should take which of the following measures?
    A. Encourage the president of ATI to make the information public.
    B. Communicate the information to Pinnacle's designated compliance officer before trading or causing others to trade on it.
    C. Prohibit all trading of ATI by Pinnacle until the information is publicly disseminated.

12. Wally Manaugh, CFA, has recently been working on a research report covering BriteCo, a mid-sized energy firm. He has nearly completed all his research, and has elected to rate the firm as a "hold." Subsequently, he meets with other analysts in a social context, and overhears a group talking quite favorably about BriteCo. He is not absolutely certain, but he believes one of the group members is a former employee of BriteCo. Upon returning to his office, he second-guesses his initial analysis and tilts his report to be a bit more favorable, although he retains the "hold" recommendation. Manaugh has violated the Standards because he:
    A. cannot trade or cause others to trade on this information.
    B. does not have a reasonable and adequate basis to change his report.
    C. did not distinguish fact from opinion, and did not first seek compliance approval.

13. Laura Smith, CFA, is an analyst with the trust department of Bright Star Bank. Mega Bank is purchasing Bright Star, to add to their nationwide banking presence. Bright Star's trust department portfolio managers use a proprietary model to select stocks. A few weeks before the Bright Star / Mega Bank merger date, Smith downloads the model to her laptop hard drive, including all the past performance and back testing data. Smith performs major modifications to the model. Mega Bank's Chief Investment Officer has told the Bright Star staff that Mega does not plan to use Bright Star's model. Soon after the merger, Smith is terminated along with the balance of the Bright Star research staff. Smith believes that since Bright Star is "gone" and the model is not being used by Mega Bank, it is acceptable to use the model. Did Smith's actions violate the CFA Institute Standards of Professional Conduct?
    A. No violation occurred because the bank has discontinued use of the model.
    B. No violation occurred because of the material modifications made to the model, combined with the fact that the bank had discontinued use of the model.
    C. This is a violation of CFA Institute Standards.

14. Vanessa Richards, CFA, analyzes growth stocks for Mahoney & Company. Through intense research, Richards has concluded that MegaRx, a pharmaceutical manufacturer, is probably going to require a goodwill write-down in the upcoming year. Richards writes an investment recommendation report with the following statement:

    > "A short strategy is recommended for MegaRx based on the lack of new prescription drugs in the pipeline and the fact that the company will write down goodwill sometime in the near future."

    Richards' supervisor, James Swanson, CFA, reviews the investment recommendation report and approves it for public dissemination without making any changes. Did Richards or Swanson violate any CFA Institute Standards of Professional Conduct?
    A. No violations by Richards or Swanson occurred.
    B. Richards has violated CFA Institute Standards, but Swanson has not.
    C. Both Richards and Swanson are in violation of CFA Institute Standards.

15. A GIPS-compliant firm must:
    A. have its compliance verified by an independent third party.
    B. adjust historical composite returns for relevant changes in firm organization.
    C. make every reasonable effort to provide a compliant performance presentation to every prospective client.

16.   With respect to Standard IV(C) – Responsibilities of Supervisors, those
      with supervisory responsibility:
      A. may not delegate supervisory responsibility.
      B. are in violation of the Standard if an employee under their
         supervision commits securities fraud.
      C. must institute procedures to prevent *and* detect violations of rules
         and regulations by those subject to their supervision.

17.   Phillip Kevil is an investment advisor for Sensible Investments Inc.
      One of Kevil's clients, Alan Miller, has requested that Kevil purchase
      shares of LongShot Technology through a broker that charges higher
      than average fees. Miller maintains a nondiscretionary account and
      makes each investment decision himself. Even though the account is
      not discretionary, Miller does allow Kevil to vote all proxies for his
      account. Kevil generally votes the proxies with management since
      most of the stocks in Miller's account are high-tech companies in
      which the managers are the largest shareholders. Has Kevil violated
      any Standards?
      A. Kevil has not violated any Standards.
      B. Using Miller's choice of broker is not a violation, but the proxy
         voting procedure is not appropriate.
      C. Both of Kevil's actions are violations.

18.   Weston Securities provides investment management services for
      fixed-income and equity investments. If a client seeks investment
      opportunities in other asset classes, Weston refers them to DTI
      Company (for derivatives) and Hurley Inc. (for commodities).
      Weston's client literature, which is distributed to all clients, discloses
      the referral policy and notes that DTI and Hurley provide research
      to Weston in exchange for the referrals. At the initial meeting with
      the referrals from Weston, DTI reiterates the details of the referral
      arrangement with Weston, but does not provide information on the
      volume of referrals received. Hurley does not discuss the referral
      arrangement with clients sent to them from Weston. Which of the
      following statements about DTI and Hurley is **TRUE**?
      A. DTI violated the Code and Standards, but Hurley did not violate the
         Code and Standards.
      B. DTI did not violate the Code and Standards, but Hurley violated the
         Code and Standards.
      C. DTI and Hurley violated the Code and Standards.

Quantitative Methods

19. A portfolio manager for Hansen Investments is responsible for determining the probability weighted return for a portfolio of equity and fixed-income securities. The manager has estimated the likelihood of three return scenarios. In Scenarios 1, 2, and 3, the portfolio is expected to earn 9.0%, –4.0%, or 6.0%. There is a 33.3% chance of Scenario 1 occurring. If the probability weighted return is equal to 3.67%, the probability that Scenario:
    A. 2 will occur is greater than the probability that 3 will occur.
    B. 3 will occur is greater than the probability that 2 will occur.
    C. 2 will occur is equal to the probability that 3 will occur.

20. Reinhart Marcs manages a portfolio whose monthly returns follow a distribution with a kurtosis measure of 4.2. Relative to a portfolio with normally distributed returns, Marcs' portfolio has a:
    A. higher chance of extreme upside returns and higher chance of extreme downside returns.
    B. lower chance of extreme upside returns and higher chance of extreme downside returns.
    C. higher chance of extreme upside returns and lower chance of extreme downside returns.

21. For a skewed distribution that has excess kurtosis, indicate the minimum percentage of the distribution within plus or minus three standard deviations of the mean.
    A. 68%.
    B. 89%.
    C. 99%.

22. Bob Smedly is analyzing a Treasury bill with a par value of $100,000, a maturity of 61 days, and a market price equal to $98,039. Smedly can choose to purchase the T-bill or an alternative investment with an effective annual yield of 12.45%. Calculate the Treasury bill's effective annual yield (EAY).
    A. 11.57%.
    B. 12.58%.
    C. 12.62%.

23. Kenny James, CFA, is calculating the covariance of his large-cap mutual fund returns against the returns generated by intermediate government bonds over the past five years. The following information is provided: (A-a) is the annual return minus the mean return for the large-cap mutual fund; (B-b) is the annual return minus the mean return for the intermediate government bonds):

	(A-a)	(B-b)
Year 1	−23.4	4.2
Year 2	−13.2	−1.6
Year 3	−10.4	4.8
Year 4	19.7	−12.2
Year 5	27.2	4.7

Which of the following is *closest* to the covariance between the mutual fund and government bonds?
A. −47.9.
B. −59.9.
C. −239.6.

24. Mark Miller manages the Young Investments money market fund. Miller is currently evaluating two investment options: a two-year Treasury note with a semiannual yield to maturity of 2.29%, and a 6-month certificate of deposit (CD) with a 2.31% holding period yield. Miller should purchase:
A. the CD.
B. the Treasury note.
C. either the CD or the Treasury note.

25. Penny Street is considering how to select four oil company stocks out of an industry group of seven. She considers the selection of the four stocks as part of an unequally-weighted portfolio. The portfolio is weighted 40% to the first stock, 30% to the second stock, 20% to the third stock, and 10% to the fourth stock in Street's list. The total number of unequally-weighted portfolio possibilities is *closest* to:
A. 35.
B. 168.
C. 840.

26. To determine the value added by active management, a researcher examined the returns of the 20 mutual funds in the large-cap value category that have at least 15 years of returns history available. The results of this analysis *most likely* suffer from:
A. look-ahead bias.
B. time-period bias.
C. survivorship bias.

27.   Joy Inc. produces a variety of ball bearing products. Recently, a competitor filed bankruptcy. The competitor's creditor is auctioning a ball bearing producing machine which Joy is interested in acquiring. Joy calculates the following probability distribution for the price of the machine.

x	f(x)
$50 million	10%
$65 million	20%
$75 million	30%
$95 million	40%

Determine the probability that the machine can be purchased for $75 million or less.
A. 40%.
B. 60%.
C. 90%.

28.   Jane Benson, CFA, manages a portfolio of low beta stocks for a risk-averse client. Her client has expressed a strong need to earn a rate of return on the portfolio of at least 4%. The risk-free rate is currently 2%. Which of the following *best* measures the risk Benson's client is most concerned about?
A. Sharpe ratio.
B. Safety-first ratio.
C. Treynor ratio.

29.   Ricky Gould is assigned the task of examining the relevance of the capital asset pricing model by running hypothesis tests on the risk-free rate and the market risk premium. Starr forms the following hypotheses:

Hypothesis 1: For the CAPM to be valid the mean 1-year Treasury bill rate should equal 4%.

Hypothesis 2: For the CAPM to be valid the mean market risk premium should be positive.

Gould collects historical rate of return data for 1-year Treasury bills and for the annual market risk premiums over the past 30 years. To examine his hypotheses, identify whether Gould should perform one-tailed or two-tailed tests of these hypotheses.
A. Only Hypothesis 1 requires a one-tailed test.
B. Only Hypothesis 2 requires a one-tailed test.
C. Both Hypothesis 1 and 2 require a one-tailed test.

30. Tiffany Green asks the Senior Research Associate at the Paris Hedge Fund to derive an estimate of the risk associated with the firm's primary hedge fund. Green requires that the estimate gets closer to the population parameter value as the number of sampled observations increases. Which of the following *best* describes the estimate property described by Green?
   A. Consistency.
   B. Efficiency.
   C. Unbiasedness.

31. Sydney Burns is considering the purchase of a bond issued by SubPrime Providers. The bond is highly liquid, with a maturity equal to that of a long-term Treasury bond. The SubPrime Providers bond carries a default risk premium of 5%. Burns also notices that the difference in interest rates offered on long-term Treasury bonds and short-term Treasury bills currently equals 4%. The real risk-free rate equals 1% and the expected inflation rate equals 2%. Burns should expect the interest rate on the SubPrime Providers bond to:
   A. be greater than or equal to 4%, and less than or equal to 8%.
   B. be greater than or equal to 5%, and less than or equal to 9%.
   C. be greater than or equal to 7%, and less than or equal to 12%.

32. Portfolio Analytics recently held a symposium contrasting test results that are statistically significant, but that might not be economically significant. Which of the following scenarios would *most likely* explain why a sample statistic for the gross mean rate of return is statistically significant yet not economically significant?
   A. The test statistic is large and the sample size is large.
   B. The test statistic is large and the transactions costs are small.
   C. The test statistic is small and the sample size is large.

Economics

33. Yasuo Noguchi is assessing the effects of the imposition of a new minimum wage on labor costs for two companies. The first company has a unionized work force and the minimum wage will be below the current union wage. Noguchi predicts no effect on wages for this firm. The second company is a monopsonist facing an upward sloping labor supply curve, and the minimum wage is slightly above the current wage the company is paying. Noguchi predicts an increase in wages and employment for this firm. Are Noguchi's predictions *most likely* correct?
   A. Yes.
   B. No. Only his first prediction is correct.
   C. No. Only his second prediction is correct.

34. Which of the following factors is *most likely* to decrease the supply of financial capital?
    A. Higher rates of interest.
    B. Increase in current income.
    C. Increase in expected future income.

35. The Osofine Water Company is the sole provider of water to the city of Charlottesville. Osofine Co. has recently filed with the public utility commission (PUC) the following menu of estimated price (P) per thousand gallons of water, Charlottesville's market equilibrium demand (Q) for water in millions of gallons and the average total cost per thousand gallons. Marginal cost is $10 per thousand gallons of water. The Osofine Water Company pricing schedule is provided below.

Price (P)	Quantity demanded (Q)	Average total cost
$20	2	$18
$15	3	$15
$10	4	$14
$5	4	$13

    The PUC believes it has two basic choices in selecting a regulatory price for Osofine; efficient regulation or average cost pricing. Determine the correct market price per thousand gallons of water associated with each regulatory pricing approach.
    A. The efficient regulation price is $10 and the average cost price is $10.
    B. The efficient regulation price is $10 and the average cost price is $15.
    C. The efficient regulation price is $15 and the average cost price is $10.

36. If the number of employed and the working age population remain the same, what are the effects of a decrease in the labor force on the unemployment rate and the labor force participation rate?
    A. Both of these rates will increase.
    B. Both of these rates will decrease.
    C. One of these rates will increase and the other will decrease.

37. Which of the following statements is the *least accurate* regarding the relationship among inflation, nominal interest rates and the supply of and demand for money?
    A. Lower rates of growth of the money supply lead to higher rates of inflation and, consequently, higher nominal interest rates.
    B. An increase in demand for financial capital combined with a decrease in supply of financial capital increases the equilibrium nominal rate of interest.
    C. The nominal rate of interest is the equilibrium rate determined in the market for savings and investments, and is determined by the sum of the real risk-free rate, the expected inflation rate, and the risk premium.

38. According to the Laffer curve, a(n):
    A. increase in tax rates beyond some level will reduce economic growth.
    B. increase in tax rates can result in a reduction in tax revenues.
    C. decrease in tax rates will always increase GDP growth.

39. BMK Corporation requires a steady source of natural gas to produce their products. Natural gas prices have risen from $2.00 per mcf to $5.50 per mcf. In response, the company's demand for natural gas has fallen from 10,000 mcf per day to 9,000 mcf per day. Calculate BMK's price elasticity of demand for natural gas.
    A. −0.11.
    B. −0.66.
    C. −1.32.

40. Oil Tool Inc. and Jones International Co. are manufacturers in the oil drill bit industry, which economists consider an oligopolistic industry. For years, Oil and Jones have called on the same oil service companies and generally have used any means to undercut each other with their joint customers. Tired of this competition, Oil and Jones have decided to enter a covert pricing agreement to not lower their prices to gain market share. An industry consultant from Stealth Oil Consultants provides Oil and Jones with the following estimated outcomes in millions of U.S. dollars.
    1. Oil complies and loses $40; Jones cheats and gains $110.
    2. Oil complies and gains $30; Jones complies and gains $90.
    3. Oil cheats and gains $110; Jones complies and loses $40.
    4. Oil cheats and gains $20; Jones cheats and gains $80.

    Using the prisoners' dilemma decision rules, which outcome is *most likely*?
    A. Both firms will cheat.
    B. Neither firm will cheat.
    C. Only one of the firms will cheat.

41. The Federal Reserve Bank (Fed) has recently been purchasing off-the-run U.S. Treasury securities in the open market. These purchases have been accompanied by press releases reiterating that the chairman of the Fed remains focused on what he considers the primary objective of the Fed: controlling inflation. The *most likely* interpretation of these actions by the Fed is that the Fed wishes to:
    A. increase the money supply but will closely monitor data to avoid expanding too rapidly.
    B. decrease the money supply but will closely monitor data to avoid decreasing too rapidly.
    C. decrease the money supply in an effort to control inflation.

42. The argument that transferring wealth from the rich to the poor will result in greater overall benefit to society is based on:
    A. the concept of utilitarianism.
    B. a concept called the symmetry principle.
    C. the principle of diminishing marginal utility.

43. According to the quantity theory of money, the *most appropriate* means to combat inflation is to:
    A. reduce the velocity of money.
    B. reduce the money supply.
    C. increase the excess reserves of banks.

44. Which of the following statements about the monetary base is *most accurate*?
    A. The monetary base is the sum of M1 and M2.
    B. The monetary base is one of the least liquid forms of money.
    C. Control of the monetary base is an instrument of monetary policy.

Financial Reporting and Analysis

45. Information concerning the effects of inflation on a company's operations would *most likely* be found:
    A. in the proxy statement.
    B. in the auditor's report.
    C. in management's discussion and analysis.

46. Which one of the following is *most likely* a barrier to creating a coherent financial reporting standards framework?
    A. Transparency.
    B. Comprehensiveness.
    C. Measurement.

47. Finch Incorporated is a defense contractor. In 2006, Finch was awarded a jet fighter contract worth $2,200 million. Finch uses the percentage-of-completion revenue recognition method. The following information was provided in Finch's financial statements:

In millions of dollars	2006	2007	2008
Costs incurred during the year	$500	$850	$450
Estimated remaining costs to complete (as of December 31)	$1,260	$450	0

Based on the information provided, calculate the contract's portion of gross profits to be recognized in 2008.
A. $100 million.
B. $125 million.
C. $175 million.

48. Gus Davy, CFA, is reviewing an industry which has been experiencing rising prices as well as unit volume growth. Davy's investment criteria include selecting companies generating the highest profit margins. If Davy does not adjust companies' financial statements for their inventory cost assumptions, he is *most likely* to select companies that use:
A. FIFO.
B. LIFO.
C. Weighted average cost.

49. A company experiences a number of unusual losses during its current fiscal year. Which of these events would *most likely* qualify as extraordinary gains and losses under U.S. GAAP?
A. Write-down of equipment leased to other companies.
B. Costs of unexpected damage caused by a plane crash at the company's major plant.
C. Foreign currency losses from unexpected currency devaluation.

50. At the beginning of the year, BJC had 40,000 shares of $1 par common stock outstanding. On April 1, BJC issued a 2-for-1 stock split and on July 1, BJC reacquired 20,000 shares. In addition, on October 1, BJC issued 8,000 shares of $10 par, 5% cumulative preferred stock. How many shares should BJC use to calculate dilutive earnings per share?
A. 60,000.
B. 62,000.
C. 70,000.

51. Under accrual accounting, the payment of $15,000 at the end of fiscal year 2008 for a special advertising campaign that will run for the first three months of 2009 would affect the balance sheet by generating a:
   A. decrease in cash of $15,000 and an increase of $15,000 in a prepaid liability account.
   B. decrease in cash of $15,000 and increase in advertising expense of $15,000.
   C. decrease in cash of $15,000 and an increase of $15,000 in a prepaid asset account.

52. A company invests $50 million in a bond portfolio yielding 4% with an average maturity of seven years. After one year interest rates have fallen by 50 basis points. Which one of the following classifications for the securities in the portfolio would result in the company reporting the highest retained earnings?
   A. Held-to-Maturity.
   B. Available-for-Sale.
   C. Trading.

53. Free-X is a gold mining company headquartered in Indonesia but with operations throughout the world. Free-X uses International Financial Reporting Standards (IFRS). When the operations located in the United States and Canada pay dividends to the Indonesian parent company, the dividends are accounted for as:
   A. cash flow from investing only.
   B. cash flow from financing only.
   C. cash flow from either investing or operations.

54. During 2008, Shawnee Corp. reported the following transactions:

   - Collected cash from customers totaling $120 million.
   - Paid cash expenses, including taxes, of $96.5 million.
   - Accrued depreciation expense of $6 million.
   - Acquired 30% equity interest in affiliate for $24 million.
   - Collected dividends on stock investments of $3.5 million.
   - Paid a cash dividend of $1.2 million to common shareholders.
   - Sold $4.5 million of treasury stock with a carrying value of $4.5 million.

   What amount should Shawnee report as net cash flow from operating activities in its 2008 cash flow statement according to U.S. GAAP?
   A. $20.0 million.
   B. $23.5 million.
   C. $27.0 million.

55.   An analyst is responsible for evaluating the inventory accounting of
       companies in the finished lumber industry. The analyst is interested in
       two companies, Harrelson Lumber and Wilson Company. Harrelson
       and Wilson are identical in all respects except that Harrelson uses
       FIFO and Wilson uses LIFO. Inventory information for both companies
       is presented below.

	Units	Cost per unit
Beginning inventory	100	$10
First purchase	20	$8
Second purchase	30	$12
Third purchase	10	$6
Ending inventory	50	

       Which of the following statements is most correct?
       A. Harrelson's cost of goods sold is lower than Wilson's.
       B. Wilson's ending inventory is higher than Harrelson's.
       C. Harrelson's and Wilson's cost of goods sold are the same.

56.   In accordance with U.S. GAAP, JLC Corporation reports its inventory
       at replacement cost under the lower-of-cost-or-market method. Which
       of the following statements must be correct? The original cost is:
       A. greater than replacement cost, and the net realizable value is less
          than replacement cost.
       B. greater than replacement cost, and the net realizable value is greater
          than replacement cost.
       C. less than replacement cost, and the net realizable value is greater
          than replacement cost.

57.   Earlier this year, East Corporation incurred software development
       costs of $108,000 to establish technological feasibility of income tax
       software for personal users. Subsequently, East incurred development
       costs of $90,000. At the same time, West Corporation expended
       $60,000 for special equipment used solely for the development of
       Product X. The equipment has no other use and has an estimated useful
       life of four years and no salvage value. West also incurred $138,000
       for labor and material costs in producing a prototype of the product.
       All else equal, which firm reports the higher total assets under U.S.
       GAAP?
       A. East Corporation.
       B. West Corporation.
       C. East's and West's reported total assets are the same.

58. Laura Cabell, CFA, is analyzing Summit Holdings, a manufacturer of construction and mining equipment, to estimate whether Summit will require higher future capital expenditures. She notes that Summit uses straight line depreciation and has annual depreciation expense of $755 million. Summit's gross fixed assets are $9,510 million and net fixed assets are $5,516 million. The remaining useful life of Summit's fixed assets is:
   A. less than 6 years.
   B. between 6 and 8 years.
   C. more than 8 years.

59. Selected financial information for PLM Corporation appears below:

	Current year	Previous year
Net fixed assets	$200	$200
Deferred tax liability	50	60
Debt	200	100
Equity	300	330

   Based only on this information, the *most likely* explanation for these year-over-year changes is:
   A. the purchase of a new asset.
   B. an asset impairment charge.
   C. an increase in PLM's tax rate.

60. In its first four years of operation, Texas Petroleum Company (TPC) increased their expenditures on deep sea oil platforms and exploration equipment by approximately 14% per year. During their fifth year, however, an oversupply of Middle Eastern oil forced TPC to reduce their expansion to 3% per year. The company's growth has remained depressed for the last three and a half years. As a result of TPC's situation, which of the following is *most likely* to occur?
   A. Deferred tax liabilities will decline.
   B. Inventories will decline.
   C. Off-balance sheet liabilities will increase.

61. Winifred Company's financial statements include the following income tax footnote:

	2008	2007
Gross deferred tax assets	$133,000	$131,500
Valuation allowance	8,100	11,700

   Using the information contained in the footnote only, the future earnings of Winifred are expected to:
   A. increase.
   B. decrease.
   C. remain constant.

62. McAdoo Corporation wants to issue bonds with an equity participation feature. Under U.S. GAAP, McAdoo's debt-to-equity ratio will be:
A. lower if it issues convertible bonds than if it issues bonds with warrants for the same proceeds.
B. lower if it issues bonds with warrants than if it issues convertible bonds for the same proceeds.
C. the same whether it issues convertible bonds or bonds with warrants for the same proceeds.

63. Blue Raider Corporation leases an office building for its administrative staff. From Blue Raider's perspective, which of the following statements is *most accurate*?
A. In the early years, a finance lease will enable Blue Raider to report higher income and higher cash flow from operations as compared to an operating lease.
B. A finance lease will result in a higher total asset turnover ratio and a higher debt-to-equity ratio as compared to an operating lease.
C. An operating lease will result in a higher current ratio and a higher interest coverage ratio as compared to a finance lease.

64. A lessor entered into a non-cancelable 10-year lease at the beginning of this year. The useful life of the asset is expected to be 12 years. The lease agreement calls for annual payments of $10,500 beginning at the end of the year. The interest rate implicit in the lease is 10%. At the inception of the lease, the present value of the lease payments is equal to the lessor's carrying value of the leased asset. How much gross profit should the lessor recognize this year?
A. $0.
B. $2,615.
C. $6,452.

65. During 2008, Lenexa Company purchased inventory totaling $4.8 million. On December 31, 2008, ending inventory was $900,000. Assuming 2008 sales were $7 million and cost of goods sold of $4.2 million, calculate inventory turnover for 2008.
A. 7.0.
B. 6.3.
C. 5.0.

66. Selected data from Olathe Manufacturing Company's 2007 and 2008 financial statements follows:

	2007	2008
Equipment purchases	$3 million	$4 million
Fixed assets, at cost	$12 million	$16 million
Accumulated depreciation	$9 million	$10 million
Fixed asset turnover ratio	2.2 times	2.0 times

Calculate Olathe's revenue for 2008.
A. $9.0 million.
B. $12.0 million.
C. $16.0 million.

67. Selected data from Plano Company's 2008 financial statements follows:

Operating profit (EBIT)	$540 million
Operating profit margin	9%
Interest expense	$20 million
Total assets	$4 billion
Leverage	2.0
Tax rate	32%

Using the extended DuPont equation, calculate Plano's return on equity.
A. 11.8%.
B. 17.7%.
C. 18.4%

68. A company has been increasing its days sales in payables (DSP). What is the impact of increasing DSP on operating cash flow?
A. No impact.
B. A lower operating cash flow.
C. A higher operating cash flow.

69. Al Pike, CFA, is forecasting Red Company's financial statements. Pike is projecting that Red will generate an ROE of 15%. In addition, Pike's forecast includes a profit margin of 10%, financial leverage of 2.5, and total assets of $5 billion. The company's forecasted revenues are *closest* to:
A. $2 billion.
B. $3 billion.
C. $4 billion.

70. A company reports its financial statements according to the Internal Financial Reporting Standards (IFRS) framework. The company's cash flow statement will report interest paid:
    A. in the operating section.
    B. in the financing section.
    C. in either the operating or financing section.

71. The CFO of Langler, Inc. is evaluating two capital projects. Langler has a capital budget of $50 million. Project A has an internal rate of return of 24% and a net present value of $5 million. Project B has an internal rate of return of 18% and a net present value of $12 million. Project A will cost $15 million, and Project B will cost $48 million. Based on this information, the CFO should accept:
    A. Project A to earn the higher return on investment.
    B. Project B to maximize shareholder wealth.
    C. Project B because it uses more of the capital budget.

72. A company is evaluating four investments. Net present values and internal rates of return are shown in the following table. Assuming a required rate of return of 10%, what projects would *most likely* be selected if they are independent?

Project	Net Present Value	Internal Rate Of Return
A	$5 million	25%
B	$10 million	22%
C	$25 million	21%
D	$26 million	16%

    A. Project D.
    B. Projects B and C.
    C. Projects A, B, C, and D.

73. Company A's current capital structure is 50% equity at an average cost of 10% and 50% debt at an average after-tax cost of 3%, assuming a 40% effective tax rate. Company B has totally financed its operations with equity at an average cost of 7% and has an effective tax rate of 40%. If both companies issue debt at par with a coupon rate of 7%, what will be the effect on each company's marginal cost of capital?
    A. Only Company A will have a lower marginal cost of capital.
    B. Only Company B will have a lower marginal cost of capital.
    C. Both company A and B will have a lower marginal cost of capital.

74. To choose the weights for a firm's weighted average cost of capital (WACC), an analyst should *most* appropriately use the:
    A. firm's current debt and equity weights based on market value to calculate WACC.
    B. firm's stated target capital structure even though recent fund raising has diverged slightly from the target weights.
    C. average debt and equity weights based on market value of the firm's competitors to calculate WACC.

75. A company reported the following financial data for 2007 and 2008.

	2007	2008
Cash sales	$1,000,000	$900,000
Credit sales	9,000,000	10,000,000
Accounts receivable	3,000,000	3,400,000

    Calculate accounts receivable turnover for 2008.
    A. 3.13.
    B. 3.41.
    C. 2.93.

76. An analyst has developed a number of projections of key operating and non-operating items.

Sales receipts	Increase in receivables
Increase in inventories	Payment for purchases
Maturing investments	Dividend and interest payments
Proceeds from stock sales	Dividend and interest income
Increases in market values of investments	Tax payments

    What items should be included in the analyst's cash flow forecast?
    A. Sales receipts, increases in receivables and inventories, payment for purchases, dividend and interest payments, proceeds from stock sales, and tax payments.
    B. Sales receipts, payment for purchases, maturing investments, dividend and interest payments and income, proceeds from stock sales, and tax payments.
    C. Sales receipts, increases in receivables and inventories, payment for purchases, maturing investments, dividend and interest income and payments, and tax payments.

77. In early 2008, a company changed its customer credit terms from 2/10, net 30 to 2/10, net 40. Comparisons of accounts receivable aging schedules at the end of 2007 and 2008 are below.

Number of Days	2007 $ millions	2008 $ millions
0–30	380	350
31–60	65	140
61–90	41	35
Over 90	54	55
Total accounts receivable	540	580

At the end of 2008, the number of days of payables totaled 34 days compared to 25 days at the end of 2007. Which of the following *best* interprets the trends in the company's receivables and payables? The trends indicate:

A. an improvement in collections since the percent of outstanding receivables beyond 60 days declined from 2007 to 2008. Slower payments by the company on its trade credit suggest improved liquidity due to better management of cash.

B. an increase in the percent of outstanding receivables in the 31-60 day category indicates a trend of slower customer payments, possibly the result of relaxed credit terms. Along with the increase in the number of days payables, cash may be restrained, costs of trade credit may be rising, and liquidity may be declining.

C. an increase in the percent of outstanding receivables in the 31-60 day category in 2008 indicates the possible impact of more relaxed credit terms. The increase in the number of days payables indicates greater attention to cash conservation, thus improving liquidity.

78. Lawrence Clark, CFA, is analyzing GRE Financial. As part of Clark's investment process, he evaluates GRE Financial's corporate governance. Clark notes the following characteristics regarding GRE Financial's corporate governance:

- A majority of GRE Financial's Board is composed of management, which Clark thinks will allow the Board a better understanding of the complicated issues faced by the company.
- There has been considerable speculation about a potential takeover of GRE Financial. GRE's management initiated a poison pill response, defending the action by stating that the speculation was causing key management personnel to leave the company.

Based on the principles of good corporate governance:
A. only the poison pill is in the best interest of shareholders.
B. only the board composition is in the best interest of shareholders.
C. neither the board composition nor the poison pill is in the best interest of shareholders.

Portfolio Management

79. GBM stock currently trades at $54 per share and is expected to trade at $62 per share in one year. The required return on the market over the same period is 12%. Which of the following statements about GBM stock is *most likely* correct?
   A. GBM stock has greater than average systematic risk and is undervalued.
   B. GBM stock has less than average systematic risk and is overvalued.
   C. GBM stock has average systematic risk and is properly valued.

80. Which of the following statements about security market line (SML) is *least likely* to be true?
   A. The SML must be graphed using the standard deviation of the market portfolio.
   B. The SML measures risk using the standardized covariance of the stock with the market.
   C. Securities plotting above the SML are undervalued.

81. The probability distribution of stock returns for Kokomo Beach Tours, Inc., is provided below.

Future outcome	Probability	Return
Market expansion	0.25	20%
Market status quo	0.50	10
Market contraction	0.25	0%

   From the data provided, the expected standard deviation of returns for Kokomo is *closest* to:
   A. 1.3%.
   B. 2.5%.
   C. 7.1%.

82. Derek Bonney, CFA, is writing an investment policy statement for one of his high net worth clients, Joey Rook. Rook is a retiree who receives Social Security benefits but because he was self-employed, has no pension income. Rook's social security benefits cover all but $1,000 of his monthly living expenses. He has a portfolio of $1.2 million, an effective tax rate of 30%, and recently purchased a vacation cabin with mortgage and maintenance expenses of $6,000 per month. After meeting with his client, Bonney writes the following policy statement: "The total return objective is to earn 7% after-tax. At no time should the principal amount decline in value by more than 15%." The *most valid* criticism of this return objective statement is that:
   A. it considers only the after-tax return.
   B. the return objective is too conservative.
   C. it fails to consider Rook's current income needs.

83. WSX Capital management is considering changing the allocation of its clients' portfolios to include commodities. The portfolios are currently invested in stocks, bonds, real estate, and hedge funds. Which of the following is the *most important* investment attribute to evaluate when adding commodities as an asset class?
   A. The return volatility of commodities.
   B. The relationship between commodity returns and other asset class returns.
   C. The beta of the portfolio after adding commodities.

84. Bill Turner is a security analyst for Secure-Invest Inc. The firm has concerns about the equal borrowing and lending rate assumption made by the traditional capital asset pricing model (CAPM), and, instead, tells Turner to use the zero-beta CAPM when selecting assets. Turner finds that the return on the zero-beta portfolio exceeds the risk-free rate. Which of the following *most accurately* describes the effect of relaxing the equal borrowing and lending assumption?
   A. The slope of the security market line will increase.
   B. The slope of the security market line will decrease.
   C. The slope of the security market line will stay the same.

Asset Valuation

85. An investor purchased a stock for $60 a share using margin from his broker. If the initial margin requirement is 40%, and the maintenance margin requirement is 20%, which of the following *best* describes the price at which a margin call will initially be triggered?
   A. Below $30.
   B. Below $45.
   C. Below $48.

86. In a rebuttal to comments made by Dilbertico's fundamental analyst, Keith Howard states that future changes in stock prices cannot be predicted based on a company's institutional ownership. State which form of the efficient market hypothesis (EMH) Howard's statement supports and also state a type of empirical study which tests that form of the EMH.
   A. Weak form of the EMH and trading rules test.
   B. Semistrong form of the EMH and trading rules test.
   C. Semistrong form of the EMH and event study.

87. Bart Wiggum believes the current level of the S&P 500 index reflects all public information. To convince his supervisor of his hypothesis, Wiggum has downloaded a daily price series for the S&P 500 index for the period 1950 to 2007. Which of the following tests can be used to test Wiggum's belief about public information?
   A. Runs test.
   B. Autocorrelation test.
   C. Earnings surprise test.

88. The constant-growth dividend discount valuation model states that the fair price of a share of common equity is determined by dividing next period's forecasted dividend by the difference between the cost of equity capital and the firm's long-term sustainable growth rate. Using this relationship, the cost of equity capital can alternatively be stated as:
   A. D/V + g.
   B. $RFR - \beta(R_m + RFR)$.
   C. expected growth rate of dividends minus required rate of return.

89. An analyst with Guffman Investments has developed a stock selection model based on earnings announcements made by high P/E stocks. The model predicts that investing in companies with P/E ratios twice that of their industry average that make positive earnings announcements will generate significant excess return. If the analyst has consistently made superior risk-adjusted returns using this strategy, which form of the efficient market hypothesis has been violated?
   A. Weak form of market efficiency.
   B. Semistrong and weak forms of market efficiency.
   C. Strong, semistrong, and weak forms of market efficiency.

90. Mark King, CFA, is valuing Nacho Inc., a food distributor. Nacho is currently selling for $28 per share and has a 3.0% dividend yield. The risk-free rate is 4%, and the expected return on the market is 8%. King has calculated Nacho's beta to be 1.25. Based on King's analysis, Nacho stock's intrinsic value is $30 per share. King should:
   A. invest in Nacho shares.
   B. not invest in Nacho shares because the required rate of return is less than the expected rate of return.
   C. not invest in Nacho shares because the required rate of return is greater than the expected rate of return.

91. An analyst uses a temporary supernormal growth model to value a common stock. The company paid a $2 dividend last year. The analyst expects dividends to grow at 15% each year for the next three years and then to resume a normal rate of 7% per year indefinitely. The analyst estimates that investors require a 12% return on the stock. The value of this common stock is *closest* to:
    A. $48.
    B. $53.
    C. $71.

92. Douglas Morin is discussing market efficiency with some college students who are visiting his firm. Morin states that market efficiency would increase if the cost of trading decreases, if the cost of information decreases, and if arbitrageurs had less capital. Morin is least likely to be correct in his opinion about:
    A. the cost of trading.
    B. the cost of information.
    C. arbitrageurs.

93. James Fry, CFA, is evaluating the potential investment merit of Cushing Corporation. Cushing's most recent year's earnings were $5.00 per share, and Cushing paid a dividend of $1.50 per share. Fry forecasts that Cushing will earn $4.70 per share next year. Fry estimates Cushing's future growth rate will be 10%, with a required rate of return of 12%. Based on the information provided, calculate Cushing's leading price to earnings (P/E) ratio. If the required rate of return is increased, indicate whether Cushing's P/E ratio will be higher or lower.
    A. The P/E ratio is 15.0 and an increase in the required rate of return would results in a higher P/E ratio.
    B. The P/E ratio is 15.0 and an increase in the required rate of return would result in a lower P/E ratio.
    C. The P/E ratio is 17.6 and an increase in the required rate of return would result in a lower P/E ratio.

94. Berger Corporation has a profit margin of 10.0%, total asset turnover of 0.75, financial leverage of 1.6, and debt/equity ratio of 62.5%. Profit margin is defined as Net income/Sales, total asset turnover is Sales/Total assets, financial leverage is Total assets/Equity, and debt/equity ratio is Total debt/Equity. Berger's payout ratio is 60.0%. If these ratios are sustainable for the long term, the best estimate of Berger's growth rate of earnings and dividends is:
    A. 4.8%.
    B. 7.2%.
    C. 7.5%.

95. Increasing which factor in the dividend discount model, without changing the other two, would be *least likely* to increase a stock's price-to-earnings (P/E) ratio?
    A. The expected dividend payout ratio.
    B. The required rate of return on the stock.
    C. The expected constant growth rate of dividends.

96. A drawback of using the price-to-book value ratio as a valuation tool is that book value:
    A. does not reflect human capital.
    B. is not appropriate for valuing firms with large, highly liquid assets.
    C. is only effective in valuing companies that are not expected to continue as a going concern.

97. Antun Blasevic manages a fixed-income mutual fund which holds a variety of high-yield corporate bonds. His largest position is in Garjun Technologies, which currently trades to yield 8.75%, while the equivalent maturity U.S. Treasury yields only 5.25%. Which of the following is the *most accurate* description of the yield spread between Garjun Technologies and U.S. Treasuries?
    A. The yield ratio is 1.67.
    B. The absolute yield spread is 67%.
    C. The relative yield spread is 350 basis points.

98. Kelly Clark, CFA, is a fixed income analyst for Convex Capital. She is evaluating a 15-year bond with a 6.0% coupon. At the current interest rate of 5.5%, the bond is priced at $1,050.62. Clark calculates that a 25 basis point drop in interest rates increases the bond's price to $1,077.20, while a 25 basis point increase in interest rates reduces the bond's price to $1,024.90. Based on the information provided, calculate the bond's effective duration.
    A. 4.98.
    B. 5.06.
    C. 9.96.

99. Assume that there is a widely accepted belief in the U.S. that 1-year interest rates will remain stable at their current level of 3.25%. A yield curve derived from spot rates on U.S. Treasury securities shows the following data:

Maturity	Spot Rate
1 year	3.25%
2 years	4.00%
5 years	6.80%
10 years	7.20%

The yield curve based on this data is least consistent with which theory of the term structure of interest rates?
A. Pure expectations.
B. Liquidity preference.
C. Market segmentation.

100. A 6% U.S. Treasury security maturing 9/30/10 is quoted at a price of 97.625 on July 1. The bond pays interest semiannually on March 31 and September 30. On July 1, the clean price of this bond would be *closest to*:
A. $976.25.
B. $991.17.
C. $946.41.

101. An analyst is considering a bond for purchase. The bond has a coupon that resets semiannually and is determined by the following formula:

coupon = 12% − (3.0 × 6-month Treasury bill rate)

Identify what type of bond this is, and calculate the coupon rate this bond would reset to if the 6-month Treasury bill rate is 4.5%.
A. This bond is an inverse floater, and the coupon would reset to 1.50%.
B. This bond is an inverse floater, and the coupon would reset to 0.00%.
C. This bond is a step up note, and the coupon would reset to 4.50%.

102. Which of the following statements *best* describes the relationship between a valuation factor and its effect on the present value of a bond, holding all else constant?
A. Using a lower discount rate will generate a lower present value.
B. A bond with a lower coupon rate will have a higher present value.
C. Using a higher discount rate will generate a lower present value.

103. Two newly hired fixed income analysts are debating the merits of federal agency backed mortgage securities, specifically mortgage passthroughs and collateralized mortgage obligations (CMOs). Analyst A and Analyst B make the following statements:

Analyst A: Investors in mortgage pass-through securities backed by one mortgage pool have equal exposure to prepayment risk, whereas investors in the CMOs of one pool have different exposures to prepayment risk.

Analyst B: Investors in CMOs have greater protection against default risk than investors in mortgage pass-through securities due to additional credit enhancement.

Identify whether the statements of each analyst are correct or incorrect.
A. Only Analyst A is correct.
B. Only Analyst B is correct.
C. Neither analyst is correct.

104. Sharon Foster owns a portfolio of two bonds. The first bond is a mortgage backed security (MBS) with a coupon rate well above current market rates for securities with similar characteristics. Foster also owns a callable corporate bond with five years to maturity and a coupon rate of 9%. The bond is nonrefundable. Comparable corporate issues brought to market recently were priced to yield 6.5%. The risks that Sharon faces by holding each of these securities could *best* be described as:
A. interest rate risk for the MBS, and call risk for the corporate bond.
B. price compression for the MBS, and reinvestment risk for the corporate bond.
C. prepayment risk for the MBS, and call risk for the corporate bond.

105. Michelle Garcia, CFA, is analyzing two newly issued corporate debt securities for possible purchase by a client. Bond X is a noncallable 10-year coupon bond currently trading at 102.50. Bond Y is a noncallable 10-year coupon bond currently trading at 98.25. Garcia wants to ensure that her client is fully aware of any probable changes in the bonds' values as they approach maturity. Holding interest rates constant, which of the following *best* describes how each bond's price will change as it approaches maturity?
A. The price of both bonds will decrease.
B. The price of Bond X will decrease, and the price of Bond Y will increase.
C. The price of Bond X will increase, and the price of Bond Y will decrease.

106. The bonds of Grinder Corp. trade at a nominal spread of 150 basis points (bp) above comparable maturity U.S. Treasury securities. The option adjusted spread (OAS) on the Grinder Corp. bonds is 75 bp. Using this information, and assuming that the Treasury yield curve is flat, which of the following statements is *most likely* to be true?
    A. The zero-volatility spread should be 75 bp.
    B. The zero-volatility spread for these bonds is 225 bp.
    C. The option cost component of these bonds should be 75 bp.

107. Tony Horn, CFA, is evaluating two bonds. The first bond, issued by Kanon Corp., pays a 7.5% annual coupon and is priced to yield 7.0%. The second bond, issued by Samuel Corp., pays a 7.0% annual coupon and is priced to yield 8.0%. Both bonds mature in ten years. If Horn can reinvest the annual coupon payments from either bond at 7.5%, what would his return be on each bond, assuming the bond was held to maturity?
    A. Greater than 7.0% on the Kanon bonds and less than 8.0% on the Samuel bonds.
    B. Less than 7.0% on the Kanon bonds and less than 8.0% on the Samuel bonds.
    C. Greater than 7.0% on the Kanon bonds and greater than 8.0% on the Samuel bonds.

108. Maria Reyes, CFA, recently purchased a 10 year floating rate bond which is reset semiannually. The bond's coupon is based on the six-month Treasury rate plus 200 basis points with a cap of 8.50%. Identify the **TRUE** statement regarding these floating rate bonds.
    A. The maximum coupon rate on these bonds would occur when the six-month Treasury bill was at 8.50%.
    B. These floating rate bonds have more interest rate risk than comparable floating rate bonds that reset annually.
    C. If the six-month Treasury rate has been greater than 7.00% for the past 12 months, these bonds will be priced similar to comparable fixed rate securities.

109. Chris Renburg owns the following portfolio of option-free bonds:

Bond	Par value	Market value	Duration
A	$3,000,000	$2,400,000	4.625
B	$3,500,000	$3,600,000	7.322
C	$1,500,000	$1,200,000	9.300
	$8,000,000	$7,200,000	

Calculate the duration of Renburg's bond portfolio.
    A. 6.682.
    B. 6.753.
    C. 7.082.

110. A large silver mining corporation in Australia is expecting to have three large inflows of raw silver resulting from a discovery of three silver seams that were previously undetectable. The firm expects the first silver inflow to be ready for sale in nine months, followed by the second inflow three months later and the final inflow six months later. The mining company is expecting the price of silver to begin a downward trend for the next 18 months and wants to hedge the expected inflows without exposing themselves to credit risks. The most appropriate instrument the company should use is a:
    A. series of futures contracts expiring in 9, 12, and 15 months.
    B. series of forward contracts expiring in 9, 12, and 15 months.
    C. swap contract with payments in 9, 12, and 15 months.

111. Consider two options, X and Y. Option X has a strike price of $40 and is selling in the marketplace for $4. Option Y has a strike price of $32 and is selling in the market place for $3. The underlying assets for the options, Stock X and Stock Y, have a current market price of $43 and $29, respectively. Which of the following are *most likely* **TRUE** about Option X and Option Y?
    A. Option X is an expiring call, and option Y is an in-the-money put.
    B. Option X is an in-the-money put, and option Y is an expiring call.
    C. Option X is an in-the-money call, and option Y is an expiring put.

112. Gus McCray, CFA, went long one oil futures contract at a price of $110 on Monday. Oil closed at $115 on Wednesday, and the contract expired on Thursday with oil at $117. To maximize his gain, McCray should:
    A. have closed out his position by selling one oil futures contract close to expiration.
    B. have accepted cash settlement on his long position.
    C. be indifferent between closing out his position by selling the contract and accepting cash settlement.

113. Pete Morris has written a deep out-of-the-money call option on the stock of Omacon, a small capitalization technology company with a very promising medical software product. Omacon stock had risen 365% for the 12 months ended just three weeks ago, but delays with release of the new software have disappointed investors, and the stock has lost 50% of its market value in the past three weeks. When he wrote the options yesterday, Morris received a premium of $3.00 each. Morris would have risk only:
    A. if the stock price rose above the option strike price.
    B. if the stock price fell below the option strike price.
    C. in the amount of the premium he received.

114. KCE stock is currently selling for $51.13 per share in the market. Six-month American put options on KCE with a strike price of $55 are available, and the risk-free rate of interest is 3.66%. Calculate the lower bound for the KCE American put options.
    A. $2.89.
    B. $3.75.
    C. $3.87.

115. Mary Hames has bought a long FRA with a notional principal of $10 million. The agreement expires in 30 days, and is based on 90-day LIBOR. The FRA is based upon an initial rate of 4.75%. Assume that at expiration, 90-day LIBOR is 5.5%, and 60-day LIBOR is 5.25%. Calculate the payoff at expiration.
    A. $12,338 paid to Hames.
    B. $18,496 paid to Hames.
    C. $19,008 paid to Hames.

116. The Pairagain mutual fund has entered into an equity swap with SingleSol, LLC, with a notional principal of $50 million. Pairagain has agreed to pay the quarterly return on the NASDAQ 100 in exchange for a fixed rate of 7.0%. The initial price of the NASDAQ 100 was 1825, and the value at the end of the first quarter, 91 days later, was 1755. The swap uses a 365-day year convention. What is the net payment to be made at the end of the first quarter?
    A. SingleSol pays $2,790,411.
    B. SingleSol pays $1,917,808.
    C. SingleSol pays $872,603.

117. The value of an existing single-family home used for residential purposes will *most likely* be calculated using the:
    A. cost approach.
    B. income approach.
    C. sales comparison approach.

118.	John Gavin, CFA, manages money for high net worth individuals. Gavin utilizes a combination of open-end and closed-end mutual funds to meet each individual's investment objectives. Gavin is evaluating a mutual fund that has assets of $233 million and liabilities of $2 million. In addition, the Fund has a sales charge of 4% and a redemption fee of 1%. The Fund has 16.8 million shares. Gavin makes the following two statements.

Statement 1:	The net asset value (NAV) of the fund is $13.75.

Statement 2:	The primary difference between a closed-end and open-end fund is their method of computing net asset value (NAV).

Indicate whether Statement 1 and Statement 2 are correct.
A. Only Statement 1 is correct.
B. Only Statement 2 is correct.
C. Statements 1 and 2 are both correct.

119.	An analyst valuing the non-controlling shares of a closely held company is using a similar firm quoted on the NASDAQ with relatively high trading volume as his base for a comparable company analysis. He is *most likely* to use the shares of the publicly traded comparable company and apply:
A. only a marketablility discount.
B. only a minority interest discount.
C. both a marketability and minority interest discount.

120.	Wireless Company received venture capital financing that allowed the company to begin commercial manufacturing. This stage of financing is known as:
A. first-stage.
B. second-stage.
C. third-stage.

End of Morning Session

Exam 2
Afternoon Session

Topic	Questions	Points
Ethical and Professional Standards	121–138	27
Quantitative Analysis	139–152	22.5
Economics	153–164	18
Financial Reporting and Analysis	165–198	49.5
Portfolio Management	199–204	9
Asset Valuation	205–240	54
Total		180

Test Answers

121. Ⓐ Ⓑ Ⓒ			161. Ⓐ Ⓑ Ⓒ			201. Ⓐ Ⓑ Ⓒ				
122. Ⓐ Ⓑ Ⓒ			162. Ⓐ Ⓑ Ⓒ			202. Ⓐ Ⓑ Ⓒ				
123. Ⓐ Ⓑ Ⓒ			163. Ⓐ Ⓑ Ⓒ			203. Ⓐ Ⓑ Ⓒ				
124. Ⓐ Ⓑ Ⓒ			164. Ⓐ Ⓑ Ⓒ			204. Ⓐ Ⓑ Ⓒ				
125. Ⓐ Ⓑ Ⓒ			165. Ⓐ Ⓑ Ⓒ			205. Ⓐ Ⓑ Ⓒ				
126. Ⓐ Ⓑ Ⓒ			166. Ⓐ Ⓑ Ⓒ			206. Ⓐ Ⓑ Ⓒ				
127. Ⓐ Ⓑ Ⓒ			167. Ⓐ Ⓑ Ⓒ			207. Ⓐ Ⓑ Ⓒ				
128. Ⓐ Ⓑ Ⓒ			168. Ⓐ Ⓑ Ⓒ			208. Ⓐ Ⓑ Ⓒ				
129. Ⓐ Ⓑ Ⓒ			169. Ⓐ Ⓑ Ⓒ			209. Ⓐ Ⓑ Ⓒ				
130. Ⓐ Ⓑ Ⓒ			170. Ⓐ Ⓑ Ⓒ			210. Ⓐ Ⓑ Ⓒ				
131. Ⓐ Ⓑ Ⓒ			171. Ⓐ Ⓑ Ⓒ			211. Ⓐ Ⓑ Ⓒ				
132. Ⓐ Ⓑ Ⓒ			172. Ⓐ Ⓑ Ⓒ			212. Ⓐ Ⓑ Ⓒ				
133. Ⓐ Ⓑ Ⓒ			173. Ⓐ Ⓑ Ⓒ			213. Ⓐ Ⓑ Ⓒ				
134. Ⓐ Ⓑ Ⓒ			174. Ⓐ Ⓑ Ⓒ			214. Ⓐ Ⓑ Ⓒ				
135. Ⓐ Ⓑ Ⓒ			175. Ⓐ Ⓑ Ⓒ			215. Ⓐ Ⓑ Ⓒ				
136. Ⓐ Ⓑ Ⓒ			176. Ⓐ Ⓑ Ⓒ			216. Ⓐ Ⓑ Ⓒ				
137. Ⓐ Ⓑ Ⓒ			177. Ⓐ Ⓑ Ⓒ			217. Ⓐ Ⓑ Ⓒ				
138. Ⓐ Ⓑ Ⓒ			178. Ⓐ Ⓑ Ⓒ			218. Ⓐ Ⓑ Ⓒ				
139. Ⓐ Ⓑ Ⓒ			179. Ⓐ Ⓑ Ⓒ			219. Ⓐ Ⓑ Ⓒ				
140. Ⓐ Ⓑ Ⓒ			180. Ⓐ Ⓑ Ⓒ			220. Ⓐ Ⓑ Ⓒ				
141. Ⓐ Ⓑ Ⓒ			181. Ⓐ Ⓑ Ⓒ			221. Ⓐ Ⓑ Ⓒ				
142. Ⓐ Ⓑ Ⓒ			182. Ⓐ Ⓑ Ⓒ			222. Ⓐ Ⓑ Ⓒ				
143. Ⓐ Ⓑ Ⓒ			183. Ⓐ Ⓑ Ⓒ			223. Ⓐ Ⓑ Ⓒ				
144. Ⓐ Ⓑ Ⓒ			184. Ⓐ Ⓑ Ⓒ			224. Ⓐ Ⓑ Ⓒ				
145. Ⓐ Ⓑ Ⓒ			185. Ⓐ Ⓑ Ⓒ			225. Ⓐ Ⓑ Ⓒ				
146. Ⓐ Ⓑ Ⓒ			186. Ⓐ Ⓑ Ⓒ			226. Ⓐ Ⓑ Ⓒ				
147. Ⓐ Ⓑ Ⓒ			187. Ⓐ Ⓑ Ⓒ			227. Ⓐ Ⓑ Ⓒ				
148. Ⓐ Ⓑ Ⓒ			188. Ⓐ Ⓑ Ⓒ			228. Ⓐ Ⓑ Ⓒ				
149. Ⓐ Ⓑ Ⓒ			189. Ⓐ Ⓑ Ⓒ			229. Ⓐ Ⓑ Ⓒ				
150. Ⓐ Ⓑ Ⓒ			190. Ⓐ Ⓑ Ⓒ			230. Ⓐ Ⓑ Ⓒ				
151. Ⓐ Ⓑ Ⓒ			191. Ⓐ Ⓑ Ⓒ			231. Ⓐ Ⓑ Ⓒ				
152. Ⓐ Ⓑ Ⓒ			192. Ⓐ Ⓑ Ⓒ			232. Ⓐ Ⓑ Ⓒ				
153. Ⓐ Ⓑ Ⓒ			193. Ⓐ Ⓑ Ⓒ			233. Ⓐ Ⓑ Ⓒ				
154. Ⓐ Ⓑ Ⓒ			194. Ⓐ Ⓑ Ⓒ			234. Ⓐ Ⓑ Ⓒ				
155. Ⓐ Ⓑ Ⓒ			195. Ⓐ Ⓑ Ⓒ			235. Ⓐ Ⓑ Ⓒ				
156. Ⓐ Ⓑ Ⓒ			196. Ⓐ Ⓑ Ⓒ			236. Ⓐ Ⓑ Ⓒ				
157. Ⓐ Ⓑ Ⓒ			197. Ⓐ Ⓑ Ⓒ			237. Ⓐ Ⓑ Ⓒ				
158. Ⓐ Ⓑ Ⓒ			198. Ⓐ Ⓑ Ⓒ			238. Ⓐ Ⓑ Ⓒ				
159. Ⓐ Ⓑ Ⓒ			199. Ⓐ Ⓑ Ⓒ			239. Ⓐ Ⓑ Ⓒ				
160. Ⓐ Ⓑ Ⓒ			200. Ⓐ Ⓑ Ⓒ			240. Ⓐ Ⓑ Ⓒ				

Exam 2
Afternoon Session

Ethical and Professional Standards

121. Ed Socho states in a presentation to his local CFA society that in a GIPS-compliant presentation, (1) total firm value must be based on the market values of all accounts including non-fee-paying accounts and accounts where the client makes the investment decisions, and that (2) the firm must include the performance results of third-party advisors selected by the firm in composite performance. Are Socho's statements accurate?
   A. Both of these statements are accurate.
   B. Neither of these statements is accurate.
   C. Only one of these statements is accurate.

122. Upon completing investment reports on equity securities, sell-side analyst Shannon Mason, CFA, routinely shreds all documents used in preparing the reports. The practice was adopted by Mason's firm four years ago in an effort to reduce information leakage within the firm. In her latest report, Mason has highlighted the investment characteristics of UltraTech Software Inc. Mason's report provides detailed explanations of the upside and downside risks associated with UltraTech, but provides no information on the lack of insider buying over the last 12 months. Which of the following statements regarding Mason's actions is **TRUE**? Mason has violated:
   A. CFA Institute Standards by failing to maintain adequate records.
   B. CFA Institute Standards by neglecting to include the insider buying information in the investment report.
   C. none of the Standards.

123. Denise Chavez, CFA, is speaking with her supervisor, Mary Ellen Savage, CFA, and Savage makes the following statements regarding proper compliance with CFA Institute's Fair Dealing Standard:

Statement 1: "We must make best efforts to get recommendations out to all clients as equally as possible."

Statement 2: "We may differentiate our service to clients, depending on what they pay us."

A. Only Statement 1 is correct.
B. Only Statement 2 is correct.
C. Both statements are correct.

124. Wayne Sergeant, CFA, is an independent investment advisor who works with individuals in his town. A longtime client asks Sergeant if he could recommend an attorney to assist with some estate-planning issues. Sergeant refers his client to Jim Chapman, a local attorney who is also a friend of Sergeant's. Previously, Chapman had offered to perform some free legal work for Sergeant in exchange for the referral of new clients. Does Sergeant's arrangement with Chapman violate CFA Institute Standards of Professional Conduct?
A. No, because the client is under no obligation and is still free to select another attorney.
B. Yes, because Sergeant is prohibited from a making recommendations that could be considered biased due to his friendship with Chapman.
C. Yes, because Sergeant did not disclose the nature of his arrangement with Chapman to his client.

125. Linda Schultz, CFA, is an investment advisor at Wheaton Investments, a small local firm. Schultz has been employed there for five years, and has never signed a "non-compete" clause in her employment contracts with Wheaton. While at Wheaton, Schultz makes preparations to set up her own money management firm. She does not contact any existing clients before leaving Wheaton to solicit their business or take any firm records or files with her. She erases work files stored on her home computer after her employment ends. After her resignation becomes effective, Schultz replicates a list of former clients from memory and uses public sources to get their contact information. She then contacts these former clients and solicits their business for her new firm. Has Schultz violated any CFA Institute Standards?
A. Yes. Schultz may not contact clients of her old firm.
B. No. Schultz is in full compliance with CFA Institute Standards.
C. Schultz would have been in full compliance if she had not solicited new business from her former clients. Schultz is permitted to *notify* clients that she has left her old firm, but she cannot *encourage* them to come with her to the new firm.

126. Thomas Callahan, CFA, is a citizen of Country A where he resides, but is a registered investment advisor in both Country B and Country A. Country B does not allow short selling in its citizens' tax deferred retirement accounts. Country A does permit such short selling. When he deems short sales appropriate for his clients' tax deferred retirement accounts, Callahan will borrow and short sell equity securities in his Country A clients' accounts, sometimes leaving a position open for several days. Callahan also sells equities short in his Country B clients' accounts, but closes the position before the end of the day so that short positions are never posted to the accounts. Has Callahan violated CFA Institute Standards of Professional Conduct with respect to his trades in Country A or Country B?
    A. Callahan's trading in Country A is acceptable, while his trading practices in Country B violate CFA Institute Standards.
    B. Callahan would be in full compliance with CFA Institute Standards if he avoided short selling in both Country A and Country B.
    C. Short selling in tax-exempt retirement accounts is a violation of CFA Institute Standards. So, regardless of the laws in Country A or Country B, Callahan must uphold the "most strict" law or regulation. Thus, he is in violation of CFA Institute Standards in both Country A and Country B.

127. Apex Investments manages three distinct types of portfolios for its clients: a large cap growth fund, a small cap growth fund, and an intermediate term fixed income composite. The firm previously had managed a high yield fixed income fund, but it was liquidated one year ago. Apex has recently decided to adopt the Global Investment Performance Standards (GIPS)® for the next reporting period. Management determines that Apex's current discretionary accounts should be divided into three separate composites based upon their investment objectives. In addition, GIPS:
    A. requires that Apex include the discontinued fund on the firm's list of composites.
    B. does not require that Apex include the discontinued fund on the firm's list of composites or any specific disclosure about it.
    C. requires that Apex include information regarding the discontinued fund in the "Disclosures" section of the presentation, but does not require its inclusion as a composite.

128. Anne Nickel is putting pressure on Marie Hiltop, an analyst and Level 1 CFA candidate, to finish her report on Simple Living Corporation in a short amount of time. Nickel hands Hiltop a competing brokerage firm's report and tells her to use it as a guide while still doing independent research. The report includes several tables with historical market data (from S&P) and earnings projections, along with a management organizational chart and an excellent description of all of Simple Living's lines of business. Hiltop is uncomfortable with simply paraphrasing sections of the competing report, but remembers that certain items can be used without attribution. Which of the following statements is *most accurate* regarding Hiltop's research report preparation?
    A. It is acceptable to include the S&P data without acknowledgement, but the other analyst's report cannot be summarized or paraphrased under any circumstances.
    B. In order to support her own independent analysis, Hiltop may summarize the other firm's report, but Hiltop must acknowledge in her own report her reliance on the other competing report. Hiltop may include the S&P information without acknowledgment.
    C. Hiltop's report can include the S&P tables, but nothing else from the competing report.

129. The Code and Standards prohibit a Member of Candidate who has left one employer and joined another from:
    A. soliciting the old employer's clients.
    B. misappropriating client lists.
    C. transferring files from the old employer to the new employer.

130. Juan Perez is an airline industry analyst for a large Wall Street brokerage firm. Perez does not currently provide analyst coverage on New Jet, a relatively new airline. New Jet believes its new service is unique and has offered two first class tickets to research analysts at the major Wall Street firms in the hopes of receiving increased analyst coverage. Perez believes he can more fully understand the airline's new concept if he is a passenger, so he accepts the tickets and takes his girlfriend on a weekend trip. Perez does not see any differentiation between New Jet and other airlines, and decides the company is too small to warrant analytical coverage. According to the Code and Standards, Perez:
    A. must reject the offer of the airline tickets from New Jet.
    B. should have obtained written permission from his employer before accepting the airline tickets.
    C. does not need written permission from his employer before accepting the tickets because it does not conflict with his employer's interests.

131. Recommended procedures regarding a firm's use of an internal information firewall are *least likely* to specify that:
    A. an information barrier, or firewall, is the strongest procedure a firm should have in place to protect itself from improper communications of material nonpublic information within a firm.
    B. a good firewall procedure contains a reporting system in which authorized personnel review and approve interdepartmental communications.
    C. if an employee behind the firewall believes it necessary to share information, a designated compliance officer should be consulted.

132. Disclosing conflicts of interest is an important component of CFA Institute Standards. Regarding proper disclosure of conflicts, which of the following statements is the *most accurate*?
    A. Disclosures may be included as a footnote in a report, but must be made in plain language.
    B. Within the investment industry, conflicts or perceived conflicts cannot be avoided.
    C. Members and candidates should be most concerned with actual, rather than perceived conflicts.

133. Peter Kent, CFA, is a portfolio manager for Luther Investments. Kent just accepted a new client, Lois Parker, who recently moved to the area. Parker is of the same approximate age, income bracket, and net worth as Kent's other clients. Kent therefore decides to invest Parker's funds according to a standardized model that he uses for his clients that efficiently diversifies funds across all industries. During their one-hour initial meeting, Parker agrees to Kent's investment plan since she has no prior investment experience and prefers to let an expert manage her money. With respect to Standard III(C) Suitability, which statement is the *most accurate*?
    A. Kent has complied with the Standard since the client agreed to the strategy.
    B. Kent violated the Standard by failing to determine Parker's investment objectives and constraints.
    C. Kent violated the Standard by failing to provide a thorough description of the standardized model used to invest the funds.

134. Bob Reynolds, CFA, is "bearish" on JBH Manufacturing Company. Two weeks ago, Reynolds was so convinced that JBH is overpriced that, he shorted 100,000 shares. Today, Reynolds is "surfing" several popular investment bulletin boards on the internet and posting negative claims about company management which are untrue. According to CFA Institute Standards of Professional Conduct, Reynolds has:
    A. engaged in transaction-based market manipulation.
    B. not violated any Standards.
    C. engaged in information-based market manipulation.

135. Judy Nicely, CFA, works for a large brokerage firm based in Cleveland, Ohio, managing portfolios for individuals. In a meeting with a client, Patty Owen, Nicely suggests moving a portion of Owen's portfolio to U.S. bank certificates of deposit. Nicely mentions that the principal is "guaranteed" up to Federal Deposit Insurance Corporation (FDIC) limits. Nicely has:
    A. complied with CFA Institute Standards.
    B. violated the Standards by making an inappropriate assurance or guarantee.
    C. violated the Standards by misrepresenting the terms and character of the investment.

136. Standard III(D) Performance Presentation *least likely* recommends that Members and Candidates:
    A. disclose whether performance is gross or net of fees.
    B. present the performance of an unweighted composite of similar portfolios.
    C. include terminated accounts in performance history.

137. In order to properly comply with the Material Nonpublic Information Standard, is it permissible for a research analyst (for a large multiservice firm) who has responsibility for issuing investment recommendations on a company, to assist the investment banking side during a transaction with that company?
    A. This is never permitted under CFA Institute Standards.
    B. The Member or Candidate may provide limited assistance under tight controls.
    C. This would be allowed only in a circumstance in which the Member or Candidate is making a permanent move to the investment banking side of the firm.

138. William Marsh, CFA, has learned that a friend of his, Hugh Dreyer, CFA, is about to downgrade Custom Bikes Inc., a company for which Marsh would like to provide investment banking services. Marsh knows that a negative report will sour the company's plans to issue new equity. Marsh asks Dreyer to meet him at his condo in Montana for a free ski vacation. Dreyer, aware of Marsh's investment banking aspirations with Custom Bikes, accepts the offer after obtaining written permission from his employer. During the trip, Marsh downplays serious problems with Custom Bikes' inventory management system and continuously highlights the company's projections for its sales growth. Dreyer weighs Marsh's arguments but decides to downgrade his investment rating on Custom Bikes as planned. Did Marsh or Dreyer violate CFA Institute Standards of Professional Conduct related to independence and objectivity?
    A. Only Marsh violated the Standards.
    B. Only Dreyer violated the Standards.
    C. Both Marsh and Dreyer violated the Standards.

Quantitative Methods

139. Jane Wilcott is assigned the task of comparing value and growth stocks in emerging markets. She finds that the data are not normally distributed and is unsure of the exact distribution of the data. Wilcott decides to compute the percentage of months in which value stocks outperform growth stocks. She records a positive sign in any month in which the return on the value stock portfolio exceeds that of the growth stock portfolio. She records a negative sign in any month in which the return on the value stock portfolio is less than that of the growth stock portfolio. She then tests the null hypothesis that the percentage of outperformance of value stocks versus growth stocks equals 50%. Wilcott's research design is an example of a:
    A. conditional test.
    B. binomial test.
    C. nonparametric test.

140. A recent study indicates that the probability that a company's earnings will exceed consensus expectations equals 50%. From this analysis, the odds that the company's earnings exceed expectations are:
    A. 1 to 2.
    B. 2 to 1.
    C. 1 to 1.

141. Mervin Erikson, CFA, is the portfolio manager of a large capitalization mutual fund. Erikson uses the S&P 500 index fund as his benchmark. Erikson provides the following 10-year data:
    - The annual excess return of the large capitalization mutual fund is 8.3%.
    - The annual standard deviation of the large capitalization mutual fund is 43%.
    - The S&P 500 index fund generated a return of 7.9%.
    - The S&P 500 index fund has an annual standard deviation of 26%.
    - The annual risk-free rate is 3.0%.

    Determine whether the large capitalization mutual fund or the S&P 500 index fund had superior risk-adjusted performance.
    A. The S&P 500 index fund had superior risk-adjusted performance.
    B. The Large capitalization mutual fund had superior risk-adjusted performance.
    C. The S&P 500 index fund and the large capitalization mutual fund had the same risk-adjusted performance.

142. George Reily, CFA, manages the Ivy Foundation portfolio. The Ivy Foundation has a minimum acceptable return of 7%. The current risk-free rate is 6%. Reily assumes that returns are normally distributed and wants to choose the optimal portfolio for the foundation. Which of the following strategies *best* describes the approach Reily should take?
    A. Choose the portfolio that maximizes the Sharpe ratio.
    B. Choose the portfolio that maximizes the safety-first ratio.
    C. Choose the portfolio that minimizes the value-at-risk measure.

143. Sharon Reese, CFA, states that security pricing is based solely on the interaction of supply and demand. Reese is evaluating MedTech Inc, a manufacturer of medical devices. Reese is considering purchasing MedTech stock. Which of the following would *most likely* be considered a bullish signal?
    A. The chart of MedTech has broken through its support level.
    B. The chart of MedTech is moving out of a declining trend channel to the upside.
    C. The chart of MedTech has been trading just below the resistance level for several weeks.

144. Kevin Prince is studying the past prices of BHD Corporation's common stock. BHD is a large capitalization stock and a member of the Dow Jones Industrial Average (DJIA). Prince has noticed that the ratio of the price of BHD Corporation to the value of the DJIA has been increasing over time. Prince suggests to his supervisor that BHD stock be added to their clients' portfolios. Which of the following technical analysis tools is Prince using?
    A. Dow theory.
    B. Block up-tick.
    C. Relative strength.

145. Van Drake, CFA, follows Tcom Corporation, a provider of communication products to commercial customers. Tcom is considering a major capital spending program. However, a capital spending increase means a lower stock price in the short run. Drake believes the probability that Tcom will increase capital spending is 60%, with a likely stock price drop of 10% over the short run. If Tcom does not increase capital spending, Drake estimates that Tcom's stock will increase 15%. Tcom's stock currently trades at $25 per share. Calculate a one standard deviation range of Tcom's stock price in the short run.
   A. Between $23 per share and $27 per share.
   B. Between $24 per share and $29 per share.
   C. Between $22 per share and $28 per share.

146. Analyst Shelly King is using a returns and earnings database to examine the past performance of stocks. She uses the historical database to create portfolios at the beginning of each year. She sorts stocks from high to low P/E ratio by dividing the beginning of the year stock price by the reported year-end earnings per share recorded in the database for the prior year. She then examines the performance of the high P/E stocks versus the low P/E stocks. Which of the following biases *most likely* characterizes King's research design?
   A. Time period bias.
   B. Data mining bias.
   C. Look-ahead bias.

147. Don Faust, CFA, is reviewing Metro Utility Corporation. He is focusing on the company's dividend policy. In particular, Faust is interested in the likelihood that Metro will increase its dividend. Based on historical data, Metro will raise its dividend 80% of the time given a rising GDP and 30% of the time given a falling GDP. Faust believes that there is a 30% probability that the GDP level will contract. Calculate the probability that Metro will increase its dividend and GDP will be rising.
   A. 14%.
   B. 24%.
   C. 56%.

148. Joe Bay, CFA, is a portfolio manager of Hark Hedge Fund. He identifies the airline industry as undervalued, but is concerned about the impact of a recent increase in the price of oil on the industry's profitability. What type of test should Bay conduct to examine the change in airline industry profitability after the increase in oil prices? Conduct a:
   A. test of differences between means.
   B. two-tailed Chi-square test.
   C. paired comparisons test.

149. An economist at Forecaster Inc. develops three different forecasts of future GDP growth based on differing U.S. Federal Reserve (Fed) stances on monetary policy. Each forecast is divided into three sets of possible outcomes. Which forecast satisfies the conditions for a probability function?

Fed Stance	Scenario 1 GDP Growth	Probability	Scenario 2 GDP Growth	Probability	Scenario 3 GDP Growth	Probability
Neutral	5.0%	35%	2.5%	35%	−1.0%	35%
50 bp cut	10.0%	50%	4.5%	60%	0%	−10%
75 bp increase	−8.0%	20%	−3.0%	40%	−1.0%	40%

   A. Neutral monetary stance by the Fed.
   B. 50 basis point rate cut by the Fed.
   C. 75 basis point rate increase by the Fed.

150. Wellington Textiles Inc. borrowed $100 million over a ten year period. The company makes annual payments of $15 million. Based on this information, which of the following statements regarding the stated annual interest rate and effective annual interest rate is *most likely* correct?
   A. The stated rate is equal to the effective rate.
   B. The effective rate is higher than the stated rate.
   C. The stated rate is higher than the effective rate.

151. A sample of 250 observations has the following properties:

   Mean   8.6
   Standard deviation 4.9
   Sample kurtosis   3.0
   Median   8.3
   Mode   8.1

   Which of these statements is *most likely* correct regarding this sample?
   A. At least one of the observations is 8.3.
   B. Sample skewness is greater than zero.
   C. The sample has positive excess kurtosis.

152. Jessica Turner, CFA, is a financial analyst with Jet Inc. She is evaluating an investment project with the cash flows shown in the table below. Jet's cost of capital is 8%.

Year	0	1	2
Cash flow	($15,000)	$15,000	$15,000

Which of the following is *closest* to the internal rate of return (IRR) for the project?
A. 41%.
B. 62%.
C. 100%.

Economics

153. Which of the following describes the *most likely* shape of a perfectly competitive firm's supply curve and demand curve in the short-run?
A. The supply curve is upward sloping and the demand curve is horizontal.
B. The supply curve is upward sloping and the demand curve is downward sloping.
C. The supply curve is vertical and the demand curve is horizontal.

154. Demand for a productive resource:
A. will increase if the prices of other inputs increase.
B. will decrease if technological change improves the productivity of the input.
C. is equivalent to the marginal revenue product of the resource when the quantities of other inputs are also allowed to vary.

155. For Tasty Pro Doughnuts, workers who are experienced are able to produce 60 dozen doughnuts per hour. Workers with no experience can produce 40 dozen doughnuts in an hour. Turnover in the industry is fairly high, and inexperienced workers are easy to find, even at a wage of only $6.00 per hour. Experienced workers are scarce, and command a higher wage of $9.50 per hour. Based on this information, if Tasty Pro wants to minimize its labor costs, the appropriate decision would be to employ:
A. both experienced and inexperienced workers such that the marginal revenue product of each group is equalized.
B. only experienced workers to take advantage of their higher marginal productivity.
C. only inexperienced workers to take advantage of their higher marginal revenue product.

156. The minimum wage can be set either above or below the equilibrium wage. Which of the following *most accurately* depicts the influence of a minimum wage on employment in the labor market when the minimum wage is set above or below the labor market equilibrium wage? Setting the minimum wage above the equilibrium wage:
    A. results in increased unemployment, and setting the minimum wage below the equilibrium wage has no effect on unemployment.
    B. has no effect on unemployment, and setting the minimum wage below the equilibrium wage results in increased unemployment.
    C. results in increased unemployment, and setting the minimum wage below the equilibrium minimum wage results in decreased unemployment.

157. Economic officials for the country of Kiwiland have collected extensive amounts of labor market data for the past four years. Kiwiland's statistics on labor force participation, unemployment, and employment-to-population rates are summarized in the table below.

Indicators	2008	2007	2006	2005
Labor Force Participation	69.1%	68.6%	67.9%	67.1%
Unemployment	4.3%	5.1%	5.7%	6.0%
Employment-to-Population	61.9%	61.4%	61.0%	60.3%

Using the data in the table, determine, respectively, whether Kiwiland is creating jobs at a faster or slower rate than its working-age population growth rate and whether Kiwiland has been in the expansion or recession phase of the business cycle over the last four years.
    A. Job creation is at a faster rate; expansion phase.
    B. Job creation is at a slower rate; recession phase.
    C. Job creation is at a faster rate; recession phase.

158. With respect to fiscal policy, a generational imbalance refers to the fact that:
    A. the older portion of the population consumes more government resources than they pay for in taxes.
    B. government benefits promised to the current generation are not fully funded by current taxes.
    C. birth rates have slowed significantly in developed countries so that retired workers will outnumber active workers at some point.

159. Which of the following statements about the U.S. money supply is *most accurate*?
    A. M1 includes all physical money as well as demand deposits. M2 includes M1 in addition to all time-related deposits, savings deposits, and non-institutional money-market funds.
    B. M2 is more liquid than M1.
    C. M2 includes all physical money as well as demand deposits. M1 includes savings deposits and non-institutional money-market funds.

160. Cascade Coal Company is considering the following three alternative methods for extracting 50 tons of coal per day from a mine.

	Quantities of Input	
Extraction Method	*Labor*	*Capital*
Earth moving equipment	4	8
Explosives/dump truck	6	4
Power hand tools	8	3

The daily rate for skilled mining labor is $175 and capital costs $300 per unit. Determine which of the three extraction methods is the *most* economically efficient.
    A. Earth moving equipment.
    B. Explosives/dump truck.
    C. Power hand tools.

161. The policies *most likely* to correct a fiscal budget deficit are to:
    A. increase taxes or decrease government spending.
    B. increase interest rates or decrease government spending.
    C. decrease taxes or decrease government spending.

162. The Bright Star Motor Company of China is currently considering building an automobile manufacturing plant in the United States to insulate itself against future tariffs and build goodwill with potential customers. Bright Star's corporate goal is to be the low cost provider of automobiles. Shinhua Kun is estimating the proposed plant's long-run average cost (LRAC) curve to see if the new manufacturing plant incurs diseconomies of scale, or if the plant approaches its minimum efficient scale. The plant incurs diseconomies of scale if the LRAC is:
    A. falling as output increases, and the plant is at its minimum efficient scale if LRAC is at its lowest level.
    B. falling as output increases, and the plant is at its minimum efficient scale if LRAC is at its highest level.
    C. rising as output increases, and the plant is at its minimum efficient scale if LRAC is at its lowest level.

163. The U.S. economy is currently operating at its potential GDP and the U.S. Congress is considering decreasing the marginal income tax rate by 10%. What is the expected economic effect of a 10% income tax cut on equilibrium employment and potential GDP?
    A. Employment will increase, and potential GDP will increase.
    B. Employment will increase and potential GDP will decrease.
    C. Employment will decrease and potential GDP will increase.

164. In comparing Keynesians, Monetarists, and Classical economists, which of the following statements is the *least accurate*?
    A. Keynesian economists believe equilibrium can only be achieved by directly increasing demand through monetary and fiscal policy.
    B. The classical economists believe that shifts in both aggregate demand and aggregate supply are primarily driven by changes in technology over time.
    C. Unlike the classical economists, the Monetarists believe that the best tax policy is to keep taxes low to minimize the disruption and distortion that they introduce into the economy.

Financial Reporting and Analysis

165. Which of the following statements is *least likely* to be true about a company's interim report?
    A. The report is provided semiannually or quarterly.
    B. The report provides audited results.
    C. The report provides footnotes.

166. A company that records accrued revenue establishes which of the following balance sheet accounts?
    A. Asset.
    B. Liability.
    C. Owners' equity.

167. Sam Jones, CFA, is analyzing a company whose financial information provides reconciliation between net income reported under U.S. GAAP and net income reported under IFRS. Jones makes the following claims:

    Claim 1:   IFRS require three years of comparative financial information, while U.S. GAAP has no specific requirement.

    Claim 2:   Both IFRS and U.S. GAAP permit the use of extraordinary items.

    Is Jones correct with respect to observation 1 and/or observation 2?
    A. Only one claim is correct.
    B. Both claims are correct.
    C. Both claims are incorrect.

168. Kimble Corporation does not record an estimate for the amount of revenues that may be uncollectible. What effect will this omission have on the company's financial statements?
   A. Overstate assets.
   B. Overstate liabilities.
   C. Understate net income.

169. A consumer products retailer reports the following income and expense items.

Net sales	$2,000,000
Cost of sales	1,200,000
Selling expenses	200,000
Interest income	100,000
Interest expense	50,000
Gain on sale of investments	500,000

The company's net non-operating income is *closest* to:
   A. $50,000.
   B. $550,000.
   C. $600,000.

170. Roome Corp. has 5,000,000 common shares outstanding. There are 500,000 warrants outstanding to purchase the stock at $20, and there are 200,000 options outstanding to buy the stock at $60. The average market price for the stock over the year was $40, and the current stock price is $50. The number of shares used to calculate diluted EPS is:
   A. 5,250,000 shares.
   B. 5,300,000 shares.
   C. 5,700,000 shares.

171. Selected common size data for Company A and its industry follow.

% of Total Assets	Company A Year 1	Company A Year 2	Industry Year 1	Industry Year 2
Current assets	0.54	0.60	0.60	0.66
Property & equipment	0.11	0.13	0.08	0.09
Accounts payable	0.45	0.55	0.42	0.48
Long term debt	0.03	0.03	0.03	0.03

Which of these accounts showed the largest increase for Company A from year 1 to year 2 relative to its increase for the industry?
   A. Current assets.
   B. Property & equipment.
   C. Accounts payable.

172. At 12/31/08, a company's liabilities include $100,000 due to trade creditors on 1/31/09, a $200,000 bank note due on 1/28/10, $150,000 bonds due on 9/30/09, and $300,000 bonds due 10/31/12. The company's current liabilities are *closest* to:
   A. $100,000.
   B. $250,000.
   C. $400,000.

173. In 2007, a company acquires two franchises—Franchise A at a cost of $1 million with a five year useful life and Franchise B for $500,000 and no defined useful life. At the end of fiscal year 2008, the company determines that the value of Franchise B has been impaired by $50,000. How will these franchises affect the franchise assets account on the balance sheet in 2008?
   A. $150,000 decrease.
   B. $200,000 decrease.
   C. $250,000 decrease.

174. Which of the following *most* accurately describes cash flow classification under U.S. GAAP and IFRS?
   A. Dividends paid are a financing activity under U.S. GAAP and dividends received may be shown as an operating or investing activity under IFRS.
   B. Dividends received may be shown as an operating or investing activity under U.S. GAAP and dividends paid is a financing activity under IFRS.
   C. Interest expense is a financing activity under U.S. GAAP and interest received may be shown as an operating or investing activity under IFRS.

175. An accountant with Gumble Donut Company is preparing the statement of cash flows. Cash flow from operations is $210 and the change in the cash account on the balance sheet is $340. Using the information below, Gumble's cash flow from financing (CFF) under U.S. GAAP is *closest* to:

Capital expenditures	$100
Investment in joint venture	40
Acquisitions	80
Dividends from affiliates	25

   A. –$220.
   B. +$195.
   C. +$350.

176. During 2008, Tulsa Company sold machinery with an original cost of $100,000 and recognized a $15,000 gain from the sale. At the time of sale, the accumulated depreciation of the machinery was $80,000. Assuming no taxes, determine the effect of the machinery sale on Tulsa's year-end investing cash flows.
    A. $15,000.
    B. $20,000.
    C. $35,000.

177. Skinner Inc. manufactures and sells kitchen utensils. Over time, the cost of Skinner's inventory has been rising. A recent jump in demand for Skinner's products has resulted in a LIFO liquidation. What effect, if any, will the LIFO liquidation have on Skinner's gross profit margin percentage?
    A. Increase.
    B. Decrease.
    C. No effect.

178. Which of the following would be included in inventory cost?
    A. Storage costs for finished goods until they are actually sold.
    B. Shipping cost for delivery to the customer.
    C. An allocation of fixed production overhead.

179. For a firm that reports its long-term debt at market value, a decrease in the rating on its long-term debt will:
    A. decrease its debt ratio.
    B. decrease its equity.
    C. have no effect on its reported solvency ratios.

180. Thomas Light & Power generates electricity for its North Dakota customers using nuclear power plants located in a remote portion of the state. When the company incorporated ten years ago, the state had no regulations regarding the cleanup of toxic waste generated from the production of electricity. However, the state is now requiring full restoration, upon disposal, of land used in utilities' service. Which of the following effects is *most likely* when Thomas Light & Power recognizes this future obligation on its financial statements?
    A. Depreciation expense will be higher and accretion expense will be lower.
    B. Operating profit will be lower and the firm's effective tax rate will be lower.
    C. Net income will be lower and total assets will be higher.

181.   Royt Corp. has experienced a 2-year period of depressed earnings. This has led Royt's management to believe that it will be especially important to meet analysts' earnings estimates for the next several quarters. Assuming Royt follows International Financial Reporting Standards (IFRS), an accounting strategy that is *most likely* to help meet this goal is to:
    A. lower the estimated lives of depreciable assets.
    B. increase asset salvage values.
    C. change to the average cost inventory method.

182.   New government officials were elected in November 2008. In early 2009, the officials enact a tax proposal that includes an increase in the corporate tax rate from 35% to 50%. Use the information below to compute income tax expense for 2009.

    •   2009 taxable income = $5,000.
    •   Deferred tax asset year end 2008 = $2,000.
    •   Deferred tax liability year end 2008 = $1,000.
    •   2009 temporary differences creating deferred tax liabilities = $600.
    •   2009 temporary differences creating deferred tax assets = $200.

    A. $2,272.
    B. $2,500.
    C. $2,700.

183.   Veris Corp. reports under U.S. GAAP and has just acquired a patent to produce the anti-depressant drug Energize for $30 million. The patent expires in 15 years and is not renewable. Based on their experience, Veris management expects that sales of Energize will continue for 10 years, but by that time improved anti-depressant drugs will likely have replaced Energize for the treatment of depression. The *most* appropriate treatment of the cost of the patent is to capitalize:
    A. $20 million of the cost, amortize it over 10 years, and expense $10 million because 5 years of the patent have no expected value.
    B. the $30 million and amortize it over 15 years.
    C. the $30 million and amortize it over 10 years.

184.   Charter Corporation issued $95 million of 8% coupon bonds in 2005. The bonds mature in 2015. In 2005, the market interest rate was 6%. The current market interest rate is 9%. Charter has generated unexpectedly strong profits over the last several years. Given a high cash balance, the company is considering repurchasing the entire bond issue. Assuming Charter repurchases the bonds, what is the immediate effect in Charter's income statement?
    A. A loss is recognized.
    B. A gain is recognized.
    C. No gain or loss is recognized.

185. Jamie Glaze, CFA, is a petrochemical analyst at J&P Investments. He is currently analyzing the financing liabilities of two companies: SatchCo and MaxMill. SatchCo and MaxMill are identical except that SatchCo issues zero coupon debt and MaxMill issues coupon-paying debt at par. Both firms received the same amount when their respective debt instruments were issued. When comparing the two firms, which of the following statements is *least accurate*?
    A. SatchCo's operating cash flow is higher.
    B. SatchCo's interest expense will decrease over time.
    C. MaxMill's financing cash flow is higher.

186. YTR Capital Management uses cash flow from operations rather than net income to value its equity holdings. No adjustments are made for different accounting methods and assumptions. Which of the following accounting conventions would cause YTR to continually overvalue a stock in its portfolio?
    A. Using LIFO rather than FIFO for inventory valuation.
    B. Using accelerated depreciation for book purposes and straight-line depreciation for tax purposes.
    C. Repeatedly selling accounts receivable for cash.

187. Using common size statements based on the selected financial information given below, determine the trend in CutCo's common equity.

CutCo	Prior Year	Current Year
Accounts receivable	550	770
Inventory	645	900
Net Fixed Assets	1,470	1,800
Total Liabilities	1,300	1,770

    A. Common equity is increasing as a percentage of total capital.
    B. Common equity is decreasing as a percentage of total capital.
    C. Common equity has been constant as a percentage of total capital.

188. Carlton Corp, a large manufacturing company, is currently negotiating a new contract with its unionized employees. Which of the following accounting red flags would indicate accounting manipulation to improve the company's bargaining position?
    A. Deferral of expenses.
    B. LIFO liquidation at year-end.
    C. Not capitalizing certain expenses.

189. An analyst states that a company's management is required to report inventory using the lower of cost or net realizable value. Is the analyst's statement **TRUE** under International Financial Reporting Standards (IFRS) standards and/or U.S. GAAP standards?
    A. Only under IFRS standards.
    B. Only under U.S. GAAP standards.
    C. Under both IFRS and U.S. GAAP standards.

190. Which of the following items is *most likely* treated similarly under IFRS and U.S. GAAP standards?
    A. Extraordinary items.
    B. Revenue recognition for long-term contracts.
    C. Discontinued operations.

191. JB Black Incorporated is considering a project with a net present value of $125 million. The project is expected to last ten years, generating $85 million each year in after tax cash flow. JB Black's cost of capital is 8%. Calculate the project's payback period.
    A. 4.11 years.
    B. 4.70 years.
    C. 5.24 years.

192. QuaryCo is determining whether to expand its current production capacity. The firm is reviewing a feasibility study completed one year ago which indicated that the rock in the new quarry site was of sufficient quality. The project would require an increase in working capital to support the project and the use of an empty factory owned by the company. Several existing customers would be expected to purchase materials from the new quarry due to its closer proximity. In its decision to expand production, QuaryCo should *least* appropriately consider:
    A. cash expended to perform the feasibility study.
    B. the increase in working capital required to support the project.
    C. the effects of customers who will switch purchases to the new quarry.

193. Marcy Lomax is analyzing TurboGas, a manufacturer of industrial gas turbines. As a result of strong revenue growth, TurboGas decided to add additional capacity by expanding its existing manufacturing plant. The company plans to issue a bond to finance the expansion. TurboGas issued a 20-year, 8% semiannual coupon bond ten years ago to finance the original construction. The bond currently trades for $1,020. TurboGas has an "A" debt rating and a 40% tax rate. Which of Lomax's following observations about TurboGas's cost of debt is *least likely* correct?
    A. TurboGas's pre-tax cost of debt is estimated to be comparable to other bonds with a debt-rating of "A."
    B. Issues such as the seniority of the debt and the security of the debt must be considered in addition to the rating.
    C. The proceeds of the new debt issue, which will be used to expand TurboGas's operations, will cost the company 8.5% on a pre-tax basis.

194. Janet Adams, CFA, is reviewing Rival Company's financial statements. Rival's long-term debt totals $35 million, while total shareholder equity equals $140 million. Rival's long-term debt has a YTM of 9%. Rival's tax rate is 40% and its beta is 0.9. Adams gathers the following additional facts:

    - Treasury bills earn 4.0%.
    - The equity risk premium is 4.5%.

    Based on the information provided, Rival's weighted average cost of capital is *closest* to:
    A. 4.6%.
    B. 7.5%.
    C. 8.2%.

195. William Mason, CFA, is evaluating the semiconductor division of Mammoth Industries, a conglomerate. The division's projected cash flows are riskier than Mammoth's overall cash flow. Indicate whether Mason should adjust Mammoth's weighted average cost of capital (WACC) when evaluating the semiconductor division.
    A. Mason should increase the WACC.
    B. Mason should decrease the WACC.
    C. Mason should not adjust the WACC.

196. In reviewing the effectiveness of a company's working capital management, an analyst has calculated operating cycle and cash conversion cycle measures for the past three years. The results follow.

	2006	2007	2008
Operating cycle – number of days	55	60	62
Cash conversion cycle – number of days	27	30	32

Which of the following *best* describes how the analyst should interpret the operating cycle and cash conversion cycle trends?
A. The operating cycle is improving as can be seen in the increases in the number of days in 2007 and 2008. The cash conversion cycle is worsening since the company is delaying payment to suppliers.
B. The operating cycle is getting longer, indicating less liquidity as receivables and/or inventory are taking longer to collect and sell, respectively. The cash conversion cycle is also taking longer, which could lead to liquidity problems if the company has already fully delayed its credit payments.
C. The operating cycle is getting longer, indicating less liquidity as receivables and/or inventory are taking longer to collect and sell, respectively. The cash conversion cycle is improving because the company is delaying payment of suppliers so that cash can be used more effectively in other areas.

197. A corporation's governance policies are *most likely* to serve the interests of shareholders when:
A. shareholder-sponsored proposals may only be voted on at the company's annual meeting.
B. management is responsible for taking measures to prevent a hostile takeover of the firm.
C. laws in the company's home jurisdiction permit legal actions against officers and directors of the corporation.

198. Which of the following financing options would be the *least likely* choice to finance $1 million for one month?
A. A bank note at 6.25% interest.
B. Line of credit at 6% with a 0.5% commitment fee on the total amount.
C. A banker's acceptance at 6.25%, an all-inclusive rate.

Portfolio Management

199. Two stocks, Rich Shaw Inc., and Melon Inc., have identical total risk. The Rich Shaw stock risk is comprised of 60% systematic risk and 40% unsystematic risk, while the Melon stock risk is comprised of 40% systematic risk and 60% unsystematic risk. Relative to the Melon stock, the Rich Shaw stock has:
    A. a higher required return.
    B. a lower required return.
    C. the same required return.

200. Bill Smythe and Katherine Banning want to invest 100% of their available funds in the optimal risky portfolio. Smythe invests his money in a portfolio with an expected return of 14% and a standard deviation of 10%. Banning invests her funds in a portfolio with an expected return of 19% and a standard deviation of 12%. Which of the two investors has invested his/her funds in the optimal portfolio?
    A. Smythe, since his portfolio has minimized total risk.
    B. Banning, since the expected return per unit of risk is higher for her investment.
    C. Both, since the optimal portfolio depends on an investor's individual utility function.

201. Greg Burns, CFA, manages a portfolio, P, with expected return equal to 10% and standard deviation equal to 20%. The risk-free rate is 5%. Burns advises Victoria Hull to invest 40% in portfolio P and the remainder in the risk-free asset. The standard deviation for Hull's overall investment will be:
    A. 7%.
    B. 8%.
    C. 12%.

202. Thomas Reid is planning his $1 million retirement fund and decides to invest $300,000 in stocks, $500,000 in bonds, and $200,000 in Treasury bills. Donna Craig decides to invest all of her $500,000 retirement fund in bonds. The expected return on stocks equals 12% and the expected return on Treasury bills equals 4%. Both investors compare their performance against a benchmark portfolio that equally weights stocks, bonds, and Treasury bills. The following data are provided for bonds:

Economic scenario	Probability	Return on bond
Declining interest rates	30%	15%
Stable interest rates	50%	8%
Rising interest rates	20%	–10%

Which portfolio has the highest expected return?
A. Craig's portfolio.
B. Reid's portfolio.
C. The equally weighted benchmark.

203. Omar Henry is a firm believer in capital market theory and the capital asset pricing model. Henry has developed a model to select overpriced stocks as indicated by the security market line. The model identifies the overpriced securities and then executes a short position in the overpriced stocks. Which of the following practical conditions would prevent Henry from using his model to explain capital market behavior?
A. All investors use exactly the same two-stage dividend discount model to evaluate stocks.
B. All investors pay the same commission rate of $0.03/share on all equity trades.
C. All changes in Federal Reserve policy are perfectly anticipated by investors.

204. William Moore is explaining the attributes and importance of asset allocation for investment portfolios to a group of wealthy individual investors. Which of Moore's following statements is *least likely* correct?
A. Asset allocation involves assigning policy weights to relevant asset classes.
B. Asset allocation is the process of selecting specific securities to include in the portfolio.
C. 85–95% of a typical portfolio's return can be explained by the target asset allocation.

Asset Valuation

205. One of the functions of secondary markets is that they:
    A. provide liquidity, and a financial futures contract is an example of a security trading on such a market.
    B. provide liquidity, and a private placement is an example of a security trading on such a market.
    C. provide fees, and a financial futures contract is an example of a security trading on such a market.

206. Mike Bowers has observed that during 2004 the S&P 500 index officially reported a return of 20%. After recalculating the returns on an equally weighted basis, Bowers estimates that the index returned 15%. The difference in the two calculations of return is *best* explained by:
    A. large capitalization stocks outperforming small capitalization stocks.
    B. small capitalization stocks outperforming large capitalization stocks.
    C. the interest expenses on margin accounts.

207. Which of the following is the *least accurate* description of behavioral finance and related investor bias?
    A. Avoiding or ignoring new information that would call a decision into question is an example of overconfidence bias.
    B. Behavioral finance may explain some of the anomalies that tend to refute the efficient markets hypothesis.
    C. Committing more funds to a position that has lost value is an example of escalation bias.

208. Ian Clark, CFA, is a technical analyst. Clark believes that information is incorporated gradually into securities markets and that, as a technician, he can take advantage of this process. However, tests of the efficient market hypothesis indicate security returns are random over time and new information is processed rapidly. Clark makes the following statements:

    Statement 1: Studies have reported that small capitalization stock returns are positive on a risk-adjusted basis.

    Statement 2: Although the academic research indicates that markets are weak form efficient, they are not because many technical analysts beat the market.

    Determine whether Clark's statements regarding tests of market efficiency are correct or incorrect.
    A. Both statements are correct.
    B. Only Statement 1 is correct.
    C. Only Statement 2 is correct.

209. Augusta Sevilla has made the statements about company analysis and stock valuation:

    Statement 1: A growth company is a growth stock. A growth company has opportunities to make investments that yield returns above the firm's required rate of return. A growth company also offers higher rates of return on investments in its shares—they are undervalued and generate high returns when complete information about the company arrives in the marketplace.

    Statement 2: A defensive stock has a low, but not negative, beta. A stock with a negative beta is actually pro-cyclical.

    Are Sevilla's statements *most likely* correct?
    A. Both statements are incorrect.
    B. Only Statement 1 is correct.
    C. Only Statement 2 is correct.

210. Howard Keane is a strategist for Dove Investments. His models indicate that the expected inflation rate will be 3.0%. The real rate of return on the S&P 500 index is expected to be 8.7%, while the real rate of return on U.S. Treasury notes is expected to be 1.0%. Howard is interested in the current equity risk premium. Based on the information above, the equity risk premium is *closest* to:
    A. 4%.
    B. 6%.
    C. 8%.

211. Tim Jan, CFA, relies on the earnings multiplier model in performing his fundamental analysis. His model is based on the constant-growth DDM. Jan is evaluating two stocks, A and B, that have the same 10% required rate of return and the same expected growth rate in dividends. Stock A has a higher retention rate than stock B. Which stock should have the higher P/E ratio?
    A. Stock A.
    B. Stock B.
    C. Both stocks should have the same P/E ratio.

212. Which of the following statements is the *best* description of the ability of arbitrageurs to correct market anomalies?
    A. Only the more significant mispricings may be exploited while others are allowed to persist.
    B. There is a high degree of reliability that apparent mispricings will be corrected.
    C. Investors supply largely unlimited amounts of capital to arbitrageurs because of the reliability of the returns.

213. As an analyst for Donavan Financial Advisors, Lou Marvin must estimate the appropriate inputs for the firm's equity valuation models. Donavan's preferred valuation model is the single-stage dividend discount model (DDM). Members of Marvin's valuation team have supplied him with several pieces of data related to TMQ Utilities, including the company's earnings and dividends from the most recent year, the expected real risk-free rate, and the expected nominal growth in net income. To estimate the value of TMQ Utilities, additional inputs to the DDM that will be necessary include the:
    A. price-to-cash flow ratio and the expected cash flow per share.
    B. expected rate of inflation and the expected earnings retention rate.
    C. historical growth rates in dividends and the required return on the Utility bond index.

214. Fred Fleming is considering working as a security analyst for Sector Investments. In the past, the firm has preferred to employ a top-down investment approach to analyzing potential investments. However, Fred prefers to use a bottom-up approach. Which of the following statements regarding the two analytical approaches is *most* accurate?
    A. Fundamental analysts only employ the bottom-up approach to security selection.
    B. Analysts using the top-down approach begin with forecasts of economic growth, interest rates, and inflation.
    C. The bottom-up approach emphasizes industry analysis for investment selection.

215. Denver Savin, CFA, is an analyst for an investment boutique. Savin is considering investing in one of the following two companies. Savin's evaluation is based on his estimation of price to cash flow.

    Bell United is a producer of aluminum. The company earned record profits in the latest year. Delmar is a major supplier to the worldwide auto industry. U.S. auto industry problems have reduced Delmar's earnings in the latest year.

In $millions, except for per share items	Delmar	Bell United
Revenues	$3,000	$17,000
Taxes	$45	$600
Net Income	$100	$1,500
Depreciation	$250	$800
Outstanding shares	100	500
Stock Price per share	$25	$35

Based on the price to cash flow multiple, state whether Delmar or Bell United is more attractive for purchase.
A. Delmar is more attractive.
B. Bell United is more attractive.
C. Delmar and Bell United are equally attractive.

216. James Martindale, CFA, manages a small mutual fund specializing in defensive equity investments. Martindale has purchased 10,000 shares of BLM stock for the portfolio after deciding that the stock would contribute to meeting the fund's objectives. Which of the following characteristics would make BLM stock suitable for Martindale's mutual fund?
A. A high beta.
B. Low systematic risk.
C. Higher rate of return than other stocks with similar risk characteristics.

217. Martina Profis runs a fixed-income portfolio for the pension fund of Whetherby Whittaker, Ltd. The portfolio contains a $12 million position in the corporate bonds of Dewey Treadmills. Profis is concerned that interest rates are likely to rise and has calculated that a 50-basis point increase in rates would cause a 4% decline in the Dewey bonds. The dollar duration of the position in Dewey Treadmills is *closest* to:
A. $96,000.
B. $480,000.
C. $960,000.

218. A 10-year 5% Treasury bond is issued at a price to yield 5.2%. Three months after issuance, market rates for 10-year Treasuries decline by 100 basis points. The *most likely* price of this bond at issuance and three months later is:
A. above par at issuance, but below par three months later.
B. below par at issuance, but above par three months later.
C. below par at issuance, and below par three months later.

219. The method used by the U.S. Treasury to issue debt is *best* described as a(n):
A. regular cycle auction—multiple price.
B. regular cycle auction—single price.
C. ad hoc auction system.

220.   Peterson Investments has three bond portfolio managers. Manager X invests only in U.S. Treasury STRIPS. Manager Y invests only in putable corporate bonds. Manager Z invests only in mortgage-backed securities guaranteed by GNMA. Which of the following statements is *most likely* to be **TRUE** regarding the risks of each manager's portfolio?
   A. Manager X has more reinvestment risk than Manager Z.
   B. Manager Z has more volatility risk than Manager X.
   C. Manager Y has more interest rate risk than Manager X.

221.   Wendy Jones, CFA, is reviewing a current bond holding. The bond's duration is 10 and its convexity is 200. Jones believes that interest rates will fall by 100 basis points. Calculate the bond's percentage price change based on a 100 basis point decline.
   A. −8.0%.
   B. +8.0%.
   C. +12.0%.

222.   Two analysts have been asked to submit brief summaries to their supervisor on various risks related to bond investing. Included in these summaries were the following statements from each analyst:

   Analyst A: In a decreasing interest rate environment, both callable and amortizing securities will experience the negative effects of price compression.

   Analyst B: The reinvestment risk of a portfolio can be reduced by replacing zero coupon securities with shorter maturity, amortizing securities such as early tranches of a CMO.

   Identify whether the statements of each analyst are correct or incorrect.
   A. Only Analyst A is correct.
   B. Only Analyst B is correct.
   C. Both analysts are correct.

223.   Bartel Corp. has decided to build a new manufacturing facility in a foreign country where production costs will be considerably less than costs at Bartel's aging domestic plant. Bartel expects the increased profits from this off-shore facility will completely pay off the cost of construction within seven years. Bartel hopes to finance the new facility with a single debt issue with the lowest possible coupon rate. The form of borrowing *best* suited to this project would *most likely* be:
   A. medium-term notes (MTN).
   B. debentures with a negative pledge clause.
   C. secured mortgage bonds.

224. Jane Higgins, CFA, is analyzing a corporate bond that she believes is a suitable addition for a client's portfolio. The 10-year security has a 7.50% annual coupon and is non-callable by the issuer. The bond is currently priced at 104.5 to yield 7.177%. According to Higgins' analysis, for a 25 basis point decrease in yield, the bond's price will increase to 107.4166 and for a 25 basis point increase in yield, the bond's price will decrease to 101.3834. Higgins' estimation of the bond's effective duration is *closest* to:
A. 5.77.
B. 10.03.
C. 11.55.

225. Samson Corp. needs to raise $100 million. Delilah Jones, CFA, the Treasurer of Samson, is considering two alternative sources of financing:

   Alternative 1:   Selling a large portion of the company's accounts receivable to a separate entity established solely for this purpose. This entity would then seek to obtain a higher credit rating than Samson's own BB rating, to reduce the required coupon rate on the bond issue.

   Alternative 2:   Issuing bonds, but simultaneously entering into an equity swap so that coupon payments can be covered by appreciation in the underlying equity index. Jones believes the equity index returns will be high for several years.

   Identify the common names for these alternatives.
   A. Both alternatives are structured notes.
   B. Alternative 1 is a structured note, and alternative 2 is a special purpose vehicle.
   C. Alternative 1 is a special purpose vehicle, and alternative 2 is a structured note.

226. Two firms, Groening Inc. and Shearer Co., have just completed simultaneous bond issuances. Both issues have a stated coupon rate of 5%, pay interest semiannually, and have a face value of $1,000 per bond. The Groening and Shearer issues both have a maturity of 15 years and their duration is approximately the same. If the Groening bonds have a higher convexity measure than the Shearer bonds, which issuance will sell for the *higher* price?
   A. Groening, since the bonds will depreciate less in a period of rising interest rates.
   B. Groening, since the bonds will depreciate less in a period of falling interest rates.
   C. Shearer, since the bonds will depreciate less in a period of rising interest rates.

227. Four years ago, the relative yield spread between ten-year A-rated corporate securities with no embedded options, and ten-year on-the-run U.S. Treasuries, was 27.5%. Currently, the nominal yield on ten-year A-rated corporate securities is 5.45%, and the yield on ten-year on-the-run U.S. Treasuries is 4.10%. Calculate the current relative yield spread, and, assuming that any change in the yield spread is due to changes in the credit spread, identify whether the economy has *most likely* weakened or strengthened over the past four years.
    A. The current yield spread is 32.9%, indicating that the economy has weakened.
    B. The current yield spread is 32.9%, indicating that the economy has strengthened.
    C. The current yield spread is 24.8%, indicating that the economy has strengthened.

228. The following three bonds are available for purchase:

    Bond X: Noncallable, accelerated sinking fund
    Bond Y: Nonrefundable, callable, accelerated sinking fund
    Bond Z: Noncallable, no sinking fund

    Based only on the characteristics listed above and the *most likely* effect of those characteristics on yield, identify the correct order for these three bonds, from highest yield to lowest yield.
    A. Bond X; Bond Z; Bond Y.
    B. Bond Y; Bond Z; Bond X.
    C. Bond Y; Bond X; Bond Z.

229. A 1-year U.S. Treasury bill is priced to yield 4.10%. A 2-year U.S. Treasury security is priced to yield 4.65%. The 1-year forward rate one year from now is *closest* to:
    A. 3.55%.
    B. 4.38%.
    C. 5.20%.

230. The 8% McClintock bonds maturing in 10 years are currently trading at 97.55. These bonds are option-free and pay coupons semiannually. Which of the following statements is *most likely* to be **TRUE**?
    A. The yield to maturity is greater than 8.0%.
    B. The current yield is less than 8.0%.
    C. The nominal yield is greater than 8.2%.

231. JonesCorp just entered into a plain vanilla interest rate swap as the fixed-rate receiver. The swap has a tenor of four years and makes payments quarterly on a netted basis. At the time the swap was initiated the LIBOR term structure was flat causing LIBOR to be equal to the swap fixed rate. Under which of the following circumstances would JonesCorp be required to make a future net payment to the swap counterparty?
  A. The LIBOR term structure becomes upward sloping.
  B. The LIBOR term structure remains flat but shifts down.
  C. The LIBOR term structure becomes downward sloping.

232. Gretchen Miller has been analyzing options on the common stock of Spirit Electronics Group (SEG), which last traded on the NASDAQ for $25.96. Miller has collected the following data on put options for SEG stock that expire in three months:

Strike	Put
22.50	0.25
25.00	0.65
27.50	2.00

Miller has been asked by her supervisor to determine the profit on a protective put strategy using a strike price of $25.00 if the stock price is $27.13 on the option expiration date. What figure should Miller report to her supervisor?
  A. $0.00.
  B. $0.52.
  C. $0.65.

233. Black Oil is an oil and gas exploration and production company. Black's management hedges its crude oil production using futures contracts. Which of the following would be the *least likely* method Black would use to close out the futures position?
  A. Holding the cash settled future until expiration.
  B. Physically settling according to exchange rules.
  C. Offsetting the transaction by shorting the oil futures contract on the same exchange.

234. Coleman Industries' stock is currently trading in the market for a price of $21. Three months ago, Myong Packard wrote a 6-month put option on 100 shares of Coleman stock for a premium of $3. The exercise price on the put option is equal to $25. The put option is now trading in the market for $5.25. Determine the moneyness of the put option.
  A. Out-of-the money.
  B. In-the-money.
  C. At-the-money.

235. Janice Grass, CFA, created a gourmet baby food line. To get the production lines up and running, she must borrow $12 million. Grass is concerned that the US Federal Reserve (Fed) will raise interest rates dramatically, so she enters into a 2 × 8 FRA agreement. The FRA is quoted at 6%. LIBOR interest rates on the expiration day of the FRA are presented in the table below.

	Settlement
30-day LIBOR	5.7%
60-day LIBOR	5.8%
120-day LIBOR	5.9%
180-day LIBOR	6.0%
240-day LIBOR	6.1%

Based on the table, calculate the payoff on Grass' transaction.
A. 0.
B. −$2,630.81.
C. −$2,956.39.

236. Two junior portfolio managers at ContraFunds, a hedge fund manager, have been asked to summarize the mechanics of utilizing futures contracts for the firm's training manual. The first manager, Tina Kent, submits a paragraph explaining that administering a futures position will require bringing the margin account balance back to the initial margin level by posting maintenance margin any time the balance falls below the variation margin level. The second manger, Martin Ramsey, submits a paragraph explaining margin requirements are determined according to the daily settlement price which is the average of the last few trades of the day. Are Kent and Ramsey correct or incorrect with regard to their explanation of the mechanics of futures positions?
A. Only Kent is correct.
B. Only Ramsey is correct.
C. Neither is correct.

237. Wilma Green has been following the stock price movements of Bakery Supply International (BSI) and Hull Petrochemical Company (HPC). Green is convinced that the price of BSI stock is going to dramatically increase from its current price of $53.60 and that the price of HPC stock is going to dramatically decrease from its current price of $9.80. She has decided to use options to take advantage of the situation and has thus gathered the following data on three-month put and call options for the two stocks:

	BSI			HPC	
Call	Strike	Put	Call	Strike	Put
8.50	45.00	0.20	2.50	7.50	0.15
4.40	50.00	0.50	0.55	10.00	0.75
1.10	55.00	2.75	0.10	12.50	2.75

If after three months, the price of BSI stock is $54.60 and the price of HPC stock is $8.13, which of the following strategies would have yielded Green the greatest profits?
A. Short BSI put with a $45.00 strike; Short HPC call with a $7.50 strike.
B. Long BSI put with a $45.00 strike; Long HPC call with a $7.50 strike.
C. Short BSI call with a $55.00 strike; Long HPC put with a $10.00 strike.

238. Sandy Hart, CFA, is evaluating the possible purchase of an apartment building. As part of her research, Hart found the following data on three comparable properties:

	Comparable Property Data	
	Net operating income	Transaction price
Property 1	$750,000	$6,000,000
Property 2	$500,000	$3,000,000
Property 3	$1,000,000	$7,000,000

The market cap rate that Hart would be willing to pay for the apartment building is *closest* to:
A. 0.125.
B. 0.143.
C. 0.145.

239.   Which of the following would be the *most likely* reason to use ETFs instead of similar index funds?
       A. Lower market risk.
       B. Intraday valuation and trading.
       C. ETFs do not experience tracking error.

240.   Harold Stone, CFA, is an analyst for Spartacus Venture Capital. Stone is considering investing $3 million in a project with a potential $150 million return over a ten year life. The current risk-free rate is 5%, the equity risk premium is 5%, and the project's beta is 2.0. Stone believes that the project has a 22% probability of failure in the first four years and 13% thereafter. The expected net present value of the project is *closest* to:
       A. $1 million.
       B. $2 million.
       C. $3 million.

End of Afternoon Session

EXAM 3
MORNING SESSION

Topic	Questions	Points
Ethical and Professional Standards	1–18	27
Quantitative Analysis	19–32	21
Economics	33–44	18
Financial Reporting and Analysis	45–78	51
Portfolio Management	79–84	9
Asset Valuation	85–120	54
Total		180

Test Answers

1.	(A)	(B)	(C)	41.	(A)	(B)	(C)	81.	(A)	(B)	(C)

1. (A) (B) (C)
2. (A) (B) (C)
3. (A) (B) (C)
4. (A) (B) (C)
5. (A) (B) (C)
6. (A) (B) (C)
7. (A) (B) (C)
8. (A) (B) (C)
9. (A) (B) (C)
10. (A) (B) (C)

11. (A) (B) (C)
12. (A) (B) (C)
13. (A) (B) (C)
14. (A) (B) (C)
15. (A) (B) (C)
16. (A) (B) (C)
17. (A) (B) (C)
18. (A) (B) (C)
19. (A) (B) (C)
20. (A) (B) (C)

21. (A) (B) (C)
22. (A) (B) (C)
23. (A) (B) (C)
24. (A) (B) (C)
25. (A) (B) (C)
26. (A) (B) (C)
27. (A) (B) (C)
28. (A) (B) (C)
29. (A) (B) (C)
30. (A) (B) (C)

31. (A) (B) (C)
32. (A) (B) (C)
33. (A) (B) (C)
34. (A) (B) (C)
35. (A) (B) (C)
36. (A) (B) (C)
37. (A) (B) (C)
38. (A) (B) (C)
39. (A) (B) (C)
40. (A) (B) (C)

41. (A) (B) (C)
42. (A) (B) (C)
43. (A) (B) (C)
44. (A) (B) (C)
45. (A) (B) (C)
46. (A) (B) (C)
47. (A) (B) (C)
48. (A) (B) (C)
49. (A) (B) (C)
50. (A) (B) (C)

51. (A) (B) (C)
52. (A) (B) (C)
53. (A) (B) (C)
54. (A) (B) (C)
55. (A) (B) (C)
56. (A) (B) (C)
57. (A) (B) (C)
58. (A) (B) (C)
59. (A) (B) (C)
60. (A) (B) (C)

61. (A) (B) (C)
62. (A) (B) (C)
63. (A) (B) (C)
64. (A) (B) (C)
65. (A) (B) (C)
66. (A) (B) (C)
67. (A) (B) (C)
68. (A) (B) (C)
69. (A) (B) (C)
70. (A) (B) (C)

71. (A) (B) (C)
72. (A) (B) (C)
73. (A) (B) (C)
74. (A) (B) (C)
75. (A) (B) (C)
76. (A) (B) (C)
77. (A) (B) (C)
78. (A) (B) (C)
79. (A) (B) (C)
80. (A) (B) (C)

81. (A) (B) (C)
82. (A) (B) (C)
83. (A) (B) (C)
84. (A) (B) (C)
85. (A) (B) (C)
86. (A) (B) (C)
87. (A) (B) (C)
88. (A) (B) (C)
89. (A) (B) (C)
90. (A) (B) (C)

91. (A) (B) (C)
92. (A) (B) (C)
93. (A) (B) (C)
94. (A) (B) (C)
95. (A) (B) (C)
96. (A) (B) (C)
97. (A) (B) (C)
98. (A) (B) (C)
99. (A) (B) (C)
100. (A) (B) (C)

101. (A) (B) (C)
102. (A) (B) (C)
103. (A) (B) (C)
104. (A) (B) (C)
105. (A) (B) (C)
106. (A) (B) (C)
107. (A) (B) (C)
108. (A) (B) (C)
109. (A) (B) (C)
110. (A) (B) (C)

111. (A) (B) (C)
112. (A) (B) (C)
113. (A) (B) (C)
114. (A) (B) (C)
115. (A) (B) (C)
116. (A) (B) (C)
117. (A) (B) (C)
118. (A) (B) (C)
119. (A) (B) (C)
120. (A) (B) (C)

Exam 3
Morning Session

Ethical and Professional Standards

1. Tom Laird, a portfolio manager with over 20 years of investment experience, has decided to leave his position at a major brokerage firm and start his own investment advisory firm. Laird will need to run a streamlined operation until he can greatly increase his assets under management. For his clients, Laird is planning on providing a minimum level of research material, mainly on the economy and the market in general. Laird's intended approach is to subscribe to several different analytical and research reporting services, sift through the research, and present the analysis he likes and supporting data to his clients. Laird's method of providing analysis to his clients:
   A. is not in violation of any Standards.
   B. is not in violation of any Standards, providing that Laird attributes the sources of the third-party material.
   C. requires Laird to obtain permission in order to use any third party ideas, even if properly acknowledged.

2. Mike Chong, CFA, is a newly appointed compliance officer. Chong has just received an inquiry from the SEC regarding the proper use of a "fire wall" within the firm to prevent the improper flow of insider information. Chong is reviewing his firm's compliance manual, and believes the section on firewalls should be updated. Which of the following would **NOT** be suitable as a "minimum element" of a proper fire wall?
   A. There should be regular review of employee trading through maintenance of "watch" and "restricted" lists.
   B. There should be heightened control over relevant interdepartmental communications, preferably through compliance or legal.
   C. Regular meetings between employees of the research and investment banking departments to discuss specific potential conflicts.

3. In order to properly comply with GIPS, the various provisions of GIPS standards must be adhered to. Under "Fundamentals of Compliance," which of the following is NOT a requirement?
    A. GIPS standards must be applied on a firm-wide basis.
    B. Firms should adopt the most broad, meaningful definition of the firm.
    C. Changes in a firm's organization cannot result in changes to historical composite returns.

4. Mark Roman, CFA, has been asked to update his firm's compliance manual regarding proper business practices to deal fairly with all clients relating to dissemination of initial investment recommendations. To comply with CFA Institute's Standard on Fair Dealing, initial recommendations should be made available to:
    A. clients who have indicated a prior interest in that type of security.
    B. all clients.
    C. only selected clients, in accordance with differentiated levels of service.

5. Grace Owen, CFA, has had a successful career with KeysBank, a large regional bank in the Midwest. She has been responsible for managing individual investment portfolios. Owen is preparing to leave this firm, and is moving to a boutique firm in the suburbs. To be in proper compliance with CFA Institute Standards, which of the following can she NOT take with her?
    A. All the names of former clients.
    B. Research that she prepared at KeysBank, but that had been rejected by the firm and never used.
    C. Selected records and files from KeysBank, with written permission.

6. According to the CFA Institute Standards, which of the following statements is incorrect regarding proper IPO allocation?
    A. Regular review procedures should be established to make sure that any conflicts regarding proper IPO allocations are identified and properly dealt with by supervisors.
    B. In situations where there are no conflicts of interest between the employee's participation in an IPO and the client's interests, there is no need to preclear employee participation.
    C. Employees should be aware that participation in an IPO may have the appearance of taking away an attractive investment opportunity from a client, which would be a breach of trust with the client.

7.   Mark Allen, CFA, and Claire Hayes, CFA, are junior sales associates in the corporate bond department of a large financial institution. They have been informed by their supervisor that a bonus will be paid to the sales associates who can sell a large, illiquid debt position in XYZ Corp. that upper management wants off the books by the end of the quarter. Allen contacts several of his best clients, and informs them that they should "buy XYZ Corp. now, because it is a hot issue and he won't be able to offer it for much longer." Hayes places a call to a client seeking to invest a large cash position, and tells them that "an investment in XYZ Corp. is a stable investment because her firm has held a core position in it for as long as she can remember." Which of the following is correct?

A. Allen violated the Standards, but Hayes did not.

B. Allen and Hayes both violated the Standards.

C. Allen would not have violated the Standards if he had contacted all of his clients about the XYZ debt.

8.   Roger Henry, CFA, works as an equity analyst for Jones Brothers, a large brokerage firm in New York City. In his current position, Henry provides analytical coverage of the domestic consumer goods industry. Henry's college roommate, John Brimley, is CEO of a large, publicly traded oil corporation in Texas. Although they have not had contact for nearly 20 years, Brimley calls Henry to invite him and his family to fly on Brimley's private jet for a weekend hunting expedition at his ranch. While there, Brimley would like to discuss with Henry how his company could obtain more favorable investment analysis by Jones Brothers. Henry accepts the offer, but decides not to report it to his supervisor because Brimley is an old friend. Is Henry's acceptance of Brimley's invitation a violation of CFA Institute Standards of Professional Conduct?

A. Yes, because Henry could potentially participate in a future investment banking transaction between Jones Brothers and Brimley's company.

B. Yes, because Henry should not accept any gift that could compromise his independence or objectivity with regard to any analysis of Brimley's company.

C. No, because Henry does not directly participate in the analysis of the energy industry for his firm, and will not issue any analysis of Brimley's company.

9. Hugh Nelson, CFA, a portfolio manager for GMS Investments, has recently been offered a supervisory role at his firm. Nelson will be responsible for managing a large staff of portfolio managers and securities analysts, none of whom is a CFA charterholder, candidate in the CFA program, or member of CFA Institute. Before accepting the position, Nelson reviews the firm's compliance policies and procedures. Nelson feels the procedures and policies are adequate, with one major exception, a trade allocation procedure. Before accepting the new role, Nelson discovers that several of his portfolio managers have been allocating oversubscribed IPO shares based on the amount of fees paid to the firm by the client rather than based on the relative size of the order. The end result has been a filled trade order for high fee clients and only partially filled orders for other clients. What should Nelson do, in order to properly comply with CFA Institute Standards?
   A. Nelson should accept the position with the understanding that the trade allocation procedures will be fixed immediately.
   B. Nelson should decline in writing to accept the promotion until adequate compliance procedures are in place.
   C. Nelson should accept the position, fix the trade allocation procedures, and encourage the firm to adopt policies consistent with CFA Institute Standards.

10. Samantha Cole, CFA, a portfolio manager, recently accepted Greg Brown as a new client. Brown is a relatively young and wealthy professional whose employment compensation has high exposure to the performance of securities markets. Brown has therefore asked Cole to use a market neutral strategy to manage his portfolio. Cole manages other client accounts using similar hedging strategies, which involve combinations of long and short positions with frequent trading. The strategy will create a diversified portfolio with no systematic risk exposure. Through a detailed interview, Cole determines that Brown's suggested portfolio strategy is consistent with his investment objectives and constraints. Cole formalizes an investment policy statement and begins constructing the portfolio, although she receives criticism from her colleagues regarding the high level of risk of some of the individual portfolio positions. Cole also receives criticism for her choice of a brokerage firm that charges higher commissions than those firms used by her colleagues. Cole selected the brokerage firm because it is able to provide the faster trade execution essential to Brown's portfolio strategy. Did Cole violate CFA Institute Standards of Professional Conduct by instituting Brown's portfolio strategy or by her choice of broker?

   A. The choice of brokerage firms is a violation of Standards, and the portfolio strategy is also a violation, because high risk portfolio positions are inconsistent with a market neutral hedging strategy.

   B. The brokerage firm choice is not a violation, as long as it is disclosed to the client, and selecting the portfolio strategy for Brown is also fully compliant with CFA Institute Standards.

   C. The brokerage firm choice is not a violation, but the portfolio strategy is a violation of CFA Institute Standards: systematic risk cannot be eliminated.

11. Andrew Kellogg is a principal with Riley and Smith, a small regional broker/dealer. He has been working on bringing to market a secondary offering for All Pro, a company that manufactures youth sports equipment. One of the reasons All Pro had selected Kellogg's firm to lead the offering is because Riley and Smith has been a market maker for All Pro's stock for the past five years. Kellogg believes that Riley and Smith should refrain from being market makers in All Pro stock beginning immediately and for the duration of the offering period because the firm is in possession of material, nonpublic information. Which of the following actions should Riley and Smith take in order to be in compliance with the Code and Standards? Riley and Smith:

   A. can continue to serve as market maker for All Pro because it is public knowledge that they are underwriters for the offering.

   B. should instruct their market makers to take only the contra side of unsolicited customer trades.

   C. should abstain from making a market in All Pro stock effective immediately, and continuing for five trading days after the offering.

12. Darby Kurtin, CFA, is making a presentation to a prospective client. Kurtin was recently hired as a portfolio manager at Advance Asset Management. Kurtin tells a prospect, "I made an average annual rate of return of 50% over the past two years at my previous firm, and I promise I can duplicate the return for you." Jim Kutcher is also a portfolio manager at Advance Asset Management. Kutcher is a CFA Level 2 candidate and reports his performance data for one year by taking the best year in the past five. Kutcher discloses the basis of his calculation in a footnote at the bottom of his presentation brochure. According to CFA Institute Standards of Professional Conduct, which of the following statements is correct?
   A. Kurtin violated the Standards because he used short-term performance to forecast the future. Kutcher did not violate the Standards since he disclosed the basis of his calculation.
   B. Kurtin violated the Standards because he implied a guarantee of future performance. Kutcher violated the Standards because his presentation is misleading.
   C. Kurtin did not violate the Standards because his past performance is a fact. Kutcher violated the Standards because his method of reporting performance is neither reasonable nor fair.

13. Which of the following statements is *least likely* to be consistent with CFA Institute Standards relating to Preservation of Confidentiality?
   A. The confidentiality of client information is protected only for current clients of the member or candidate.
   B. When permissible under applicable law, a member or candidate may forward confidential information to the CFA Institute's Professional Conduct Program.
   C. If applicable law requires a member or candidate to maintain confidentiality, even if the information concerns illegal activities on the part of the client, the member or candidate should not disclose such information.

14. Which of the following is *least* accurate with regard to CFA Institute Standards regarding supervisory responsibility?
   A. If a supervisor has adopted adequate procedures, and made reasonable efforts to educate and supervise her staff and to detect violations, she has fulfilled the CFA Institute Standard on Responsibilities of Supervisors.
   B. Members and candidates with supervisory roles must personally evaluate each employee's conduct on a regular basis.
   C. Supervisors, whether supervising CFA Institute members, candidates, or non-members, must have comprehensive knowledge of the Code and Standards.

15. According to CFA Institute Standards, which of the following would be *most likely* to be considered material nonpublic information?
    A. Information concerning upcoming management changes.
    B. Information considered material 12 months ago.
    C. Information that, if known, would change the price of a security by at least ten percent, although the direction of the change cannot be predicted.

16. Janet Todd passed Level 2 of the CFA program in June of last year and wants to note on her resume her involvement in the CFA program. She passed both Level 1 and Level 2 of the CFA examination on her first attempts. She plans to register for the Level 3 examination next year. According to CFA Institute's *Standards of Professional Conduct*, which of the following is a proper, dignified, and judicious reference to her participation in the CFA Program? Janet Todd:
    A. is a Level 3 Candidate in the CFA program.
    B. is a Level 2 CFA.
    C. passed the Level 1 and Level 2 CFA examinations on her first attempts.

17. Joe Anderson, after working for U.S. Securities for 20 years as an economist, has decided to retire and move to an island in the South Pacific. U.S. Securities is disappointed at the loss of Anderson's market knowledge and forecasting expertise and wishes to retain his services as an independent contractor. Anderson has negotiated an arrangement where periodically he will provide U.S. Securities with research and analytical data and will be compensated for each report. Anderson will work from his ocean-side home, using his own personal computer. Anderson and his former supervisor orally agree to the terms of this arrangement. Six months after the start of the arrangement, a representative of one of U.S. Securities' largest competitors contacts Anderson about providing similar analytical work for them. According to CFA Institute Standards of Professional Conduct, Anderson must:
    A. abide by the terms of his oral agreement with U.S. Securities.
    B. disclose this potential conflict to U.S. Securities.
    C. disclose the additional compensation to U.S. Securities.

18. Jerry Brock, CFA, is a partner in a small investment advisory firm that caters to high net worth individuals. He has experienced a number of personal and financial setbacks over the past two years. His wife has suffered from a life-threatening illness, and his personal investment portfolio has declined significantly in value. Brock has had increasing difficulty in meeting his personal debt obligations and has filed for bankruptcy protection. Has Brock violated CFA Institute Standards of Professional Conduct and if so, what action should he take?
    A. No, because the circumstances of his personal financial difficulties do not reflect adversely on his professional competence. No action is necessary.
    B. No, but he must disclose the bankruptcy filing to all existing clients of the firm.
    C. Yes, because a member must conduct both their personal and professional business in a manner that protects their reputation and integrity.

Quantitative Methods

19. Zach Mann is examining stock performance after classifying stocks according their market capitalization (firm size) and P/E ratio. First, Mann ranks stocks based on market capitalization by creating decile breakpoints and grouping stocks into the deciles. Then, for each firm size decile, he classifies stocks into P/E ratio quintiles. The total number of classifications created by Mann equals:
    A. 5.
    B. 10.
    C. 50.

20. Calculate the covariance of the returns on Bearl Corporation (R_B) with the returns on ReaCorp (R_R). The following table is provided (entries are joint probabilities).

	$R_R = 25\%$	$R_R = 10\%$	$R_R = 0\%$
$R_B = 16\%$	0.20	0	0
$R_B = 6\%$	0	0.60	0
$R_B = -4\%$	0	0	0.20

    A. 20.
    B. 25.
    C. 50.

21. Martha Lynne, is evaluating the stated performance and standard deviation of STT Mutual Fund over the past ten years to determine how the risk and return of the fund have compared to its overall peer group. To test her hypothesis, Lynne is using the chi-square test. Which of Lynne's statements regarding the chi-square test is *least likely* correct?
    A. The chi-square distribution cannot be lower than zero.
    B. The chi-square test is used to test whether or not a variance equals a certain value.
    C. The chi-square test can be used to make inferences even if the population is not normally distributed.

22. Jeffrey Hogan is an analyst for Maine Investments. Hogan is convinced that technicians provide superior investment advice to their clients. Patrick believes:

    1. Technical analysis is not based on analysis of financial statements, and thus is not bound by accounting conventions that can distort valuation results.

    2. Technicians focus on investment sentiment factors. This focus allows the analyst to consider even irrational investor behavior.

    A technical analyst would *most likely* agree:
    A. only with belief 1.
    B. only with belief 2.
    C. with both belief 1 and belief 2.

23. Colleagues Benjamin Ecko and Bernard Charles recently discussed the application of the normal distribution for random variables. Ecko claimed that the z-statistic measures the distance, in standard deviation units, that a given observation is from the population mean. Charles claimed that there is a 95% chance that the z-statistic lies between positive and negative 1. Are the statements of Ecko and Charles correct or incorrect?
    A. Only Ecko is correct.
    B. Only Charles is correct.
    C. Both Ecko and Charles are correct.

24. David McWyllie derives a scatter plot of the stock price-to-equity ratios and the debt-to-equity ratios for each of 1,000 U.K. companies, for a total of 1,000 paired observations for the same time period. Which of the following *best* characterizes the data examined by McWyllie?
    A. Time-series.
    B. Cross-sectional.
    C. Stratified.

25. Dillon Marshall has determined that the weighted average cost of capital (WACC) for WestStar Inc. is 12%. WestStar is evaluating three capital investment projects with conventional cash flows. Projects 1, 2, and 3 have positive, zero, and negative NPVs, respectively. Which of the following statements regarding WestStar's available investment projects is *least likely* correct?
    A. Project 1 has an internal rate of return greater than the WACC.
    B. Project 2 will increase the size of WestStar, but not its value.
    C. Project 3 assumes reinvestment at a rate higher than the WACC.

26. Bill Foley is reviewing the performance of the EAFE index compared to a small capitalization international stock index for the last 20 years.

	Mean return	Standard deviation
EAFE index	10.6%	21.9%
Int'l Small Cap index	9.4%	31.4%
Difference	1.2%	19.1%

Bill is evaluating the following null hypothesis:

$$H_0: m_{\text{difference}} = 0$$

Based on monthly returns, determine whether or not to reject the null hypothesis at the 0.05% significance level for the 20-year period. Assume that the appropriate test statistic for this decision is 1.98.
    A. Reject the null hypothesis, $t > 1.98$.
    B. Reject the null hypothesis, $t < 1.98$.
    C. Do not reject the null hypothesis, $t < 1.98$.

27. An investment analyst is reviewing the performance of various asset classes. The table below details the performance of the asset classes for the past year.

Asset Class	Risk-free Asset	Real Estate	Fixed Income	Equities
Mean return	4%	25%	8%	20%
Standard deviation	0%	18%	4%	15%

Which of the following statements regarding the asset classes above is *least likely* correct?
    A. The coefficient of variation for real estate is greater than that for equities.
    B. The Sharpe ratio for equities is less than that for real estate.
    C. The Sharpe ratio for fixed income is the lowest of all asset classes.

28. Chester Murphy, CFA, is a stock analyst who screens stocks based on market capitalization and earnings momentum. Specifically, Murphy selects stocks that have market capitalization less than $1 billion ("small cap"), and that have 5-year annualized earnings growth of at least 25% ("high earnings momentum"). The probability that a randomly selected stock is a small cap stock is 20%. The probability that a company has high earnings momentum, given that it is a small cap stock, is 40%. Calculate the probability that a randomly selected stock fits Murphy's dual investment criteria.
    A. 8%.
    B. 12%.
    C. 20%.

29. Larry Brown is evaluating a Treasury bill with a par value of $1,000,000 due 150 days from now. The bill has a holding period yield of 1.52%, and a bank discount yield of 3.60%. Calculate the Treasury bill's money market yield (MMY).
    A. 3.60%.
    B. 3.65%.
    C. 3.74%.

30. Lou Diamond, CFA, is screening all public stocks in the world and grouping them by the industry in which they operate. Each company is further analyzed to determine the best potential investment in the particular industry. The screening process is an example of:
    A. simple random sampling.
    B. systematic random sampling.
    C. stratified sampling.

31. An analyst for BYG Investments Inc. is attempting to estimate the dispersion of quarterly GDP growth in the Korean economy for the last 60 years. He has collected the 240 observations of GDP growth but is unsure of the best method to visually demonstrate the dispersion of his sample data. Which of the following *best* shows the dispersion of a sample distribution?
    A. Covariance.
    B. Histograms.
    C. Time series plots.

32.   Victor Claus, CFA, is the energy analyst for Mercury Brokerage firm. Claus is evaluating a potential major new natural gas discovery of HRF Energy. A consultant hired by Mercury predicts the well will flow at 4 million cubic feet (mmcf) of natural gas per day. The consultant's prediction carries a standard deviation of 0.8 mmcf per day. What is the probability that the well will flow at greater than 5 mmcf per day?

Standard Normal Distribution (z-values)

z	0	0.01	0.02	0.03	0.04	0.05	0.06	0.07	0.08	0.09
0.50	0.6915	0.6950	0.6985	0.7019	0.7054	0.7088	0.7123	0.7157	0.7190	0.7224
0.60	0.7257	0.7291	0.7324	0.7357	0.7389	0.7422	0.7454	0.7486	0.7517	0.7549
0.70	0.7580	0.7611	0.7642	0.7673	0.7704	0.7734	0.7764	0.7794	0.7823	0.7852
0.80	0.7881	0.7910	0.7939	0.7967	0.7995	0.8023	0.8051	0.8078	0.8106	0.8133
0.90	0.8159	0.8186	0.8212	0.8238	0.8264	0.8289	0.8315	0.8340	0.8365	0.8389
1.00	0.8413	0.8438	0.8461	0.8485	0.8508	0.8531	0.8554	0.8577	0.8599	0.8621
1.10	0.8643	0.8665	0.8686	0.8708	0.8729	0.8749	0.8770	0.8790	0.8810	0.8830
1.20	0.8849	0.8869	0.8888	0.8907	0.8925	0.8944	0.8962	0.8980	0.8997	0.9015
1.30	0.9032	0.9049	0.9066	0.9082	0.9099	0.9115	0.9131	0.9147	0.9162	0.9177
1.40	0.9192	0.9207	0.9222	0.9236	0.9251	0.9265	0.9279	0.9292	0.9306	0.9319
1.50	0.9332	0.9345	0.9357	0.9370	0.9382	0.9394	0.9406	0.9418	0.9429	0.9441

A. 2.5%.
B. 10.6%.
C. 14.7%.

Economics

33.   Assume that the long-term equilibrium money market interest rate is 4% and the current short-term money market interest rate is 3%. At this current rate of 3%, there will be an excess:
A. demand for money in the money market, and investors will tend to be net buyers of bonds.
B. demand for money in the money market, and investors will tend to be net sellers of bonds.
C. supply of money in the money market, and investors will tend to be net buyers of bonds.

34.   The U.S. government has just passed a significant tax cut, to take effect immediately. At the same time, the Federal Reserve has reduced the reserve requirement from 18% to 15%. Assuming that long-run aggregate supply does not change, these two policy changes will *most likely* cause aggregate demand to:
A. increase, accompanied by high inflation.
B. increase, leading to real GDP growth with no inflation.
C. decrease, accompanied by high inflation.

35. Harry Miller, CFA, is a commodities analyst for Montrose Commodities, a Swiss-based brokerage firm. Miller is currently engaged in a study of the Egyptian cotton market and an estimation of their cotton production next year. Due to a heavy lobbying effort by an Egyptian farmer trade group, the Egyptian government is paying a 10% price subsidy for each kilo of cotton produced next year. Miller believes that the Egyptian cotton market has gone from being a highly competitive market to a market that is less efficient or suffering a deadweight loss. Identify the effect of the subsidy on the supply of Egyptian cotton, and determine whether the marginal social benefit (MSB) of subsidizing cotton production exceeds the marginal social cost (MSC) of the subsidy.
    A. There will be an oversupply of cotton production and MSB will exceed MSC.
    B. There will be a shortage of cotton production and MSB will be less than MSC.
    C. There will be an oversupply of cotton production and MSB will be less than MSC.

36. Which of the following statements is *least likely* to be associated with monopolistic competition?
    A. A firm in monopolistic competition can earn positive economic profits in the short run.
    B. Firms in monopolistic competition maximize economic profits by colluding and operating as a single seller.
    C. Due to low barriers to entry, firms in monopolistic competition will not earn positive economic profits in the long run.

37. Linda Lopez, CFA, is a pharmaceutical industry analyst. Due to recent large deficit spending, the government is increasing the tax on many products including personal grooming items, such as mouthwash and toothpaste, as well as on drugs used in the treatment of disease. One of the companies under Lopez's coverage is Wigwam Pharmaceuticals, which has the Osobright mouthwash and toothpaste line and the newly approved lung cancer treatment Mabtex. Lopez considers the Osobright market to have low elasticity of supply and high elasticity of demand. The Mabtex drug is believed to have low elasticity of demand and highly elastic supply. Lopez wants to determine whether the higher taxes on each product line will be borne by Wigwam Pharmaceuticals or if they can passed be along to the consumer. Indicate for each product line whether Wigwam or the consumer will *most likely* bear the burden of the higher taxes.
    A. Wigwam bears the burden for Osobright and the consumer bears the burden for Mabtex.
    B. the consumer bears the burden for Osobright and Wigwam bears the burden for Mabtex.
    C. the consumer bears the burden for Osobright, and the consumer also bears the burden for Mabtex.

38. Hanover Industrial operates in a highly competitive market. The CFO conducted a detailed review of Hanover's two main production facilities, located in Paris and Munich. Her final report stated that Hanover's Paris plant produces goods at a marginal cost above market price, while their Munich plant, with identical goods, produces at a marginal cost less than market price. To increase profits, the company's CFO should:
    A. decrease output at both plants.
    B. decrease output at the Paris plant and increase output at the Munich plant.
    C. increase output at the Paris plant and decrease output at the Munich plant.

39. Which of the following *best* describes the cross elasticity of demand for two goods when the two goods complements or substitutes? When two goods are complements, the cross elasticity of demand is:
    A. positive, and for substitutes the cross elasticity of demand is negative.
    B. zero, and for substitutes the cross elasticity of demand is negative.
    C. negative, and for substitutes the cross elasticity of demand is positive.

40. Compared to a competitive market result, a single-price monopolist will:
    A. adopt a marginal cost pricing strategy, which will decrease consumer surplus.
    B. increase price, decrease consumer surplus, and increase producer surplus.
    C. reduce output, create a deadweight loss, and decrease both producer and consumer surplus.

41. Country A and Country B have been experiencing persistent inflation over the last few years. In Country A, large and unexpected increases in the price of coal used in power plants have caused increased price levels, which have caused increased unemployment. The country's central bank has responded by increasing the money supply, further increasing price levels. In Country B, increased government spending on civil defense and social programs has caused increased price levels, which have resulted in increased money wage rates, which in turn have decreased short-run aggregate supply. Determine which type of inflation Country A and Country B are experiencing.
    A. Both countries are experiencing cost-push inflation.
    B. Country A is experiencing demand-pull inflation and Country B is experiencing cost-push inflation.
    C. Country A is experiencing cost-push inflation and Country B is experiencing demand-pull inflation.

42. Walter Johnson is giving a speech on the effects of a recent action by his country's central bank, which recently reduced its target for the rate that banks charge each other for overnight loans. Johnson lists several intended effects of this change in the target rate.
    • Other short-term interest rates fall.
    • The exchange rate rises, his country's currency appreciates.
    • Long-term interest rates fall.
    • Consumption, expenditure, investment, and net exports increase.
    • Aggregate demand increases.

    Is Johnson's description of the effects of the target rate decrease correct?
    A. Yes.
    B. No. Except for the first item (other short-term rates fall), all of his points are incorrect.
    C. No. The second item (the exchange rate rises, his country's currency appreciates) is incorrect. The other items are generally correct.

43. Which of the following *most likely* describes a loss that consumers suffer under an unregulated monopoly compared to a competitive market?
    A. Monopolies produce less goods than a competitive market would.
    B. The costs of production are higher with monopolies.
    C. Monopolists charge the maximum price.

44. Wheelie Incorporated is a domestic producer of bicycle inner tubes and tires. Management at Wheelie has indicated to analysts that in six months the company will be producing between 95% and 98% of their total output capacity. In the short run, Wheelie can expect to experience which of the following cost trends? Average fixed costs:
    A. decrease and marginal costs decrease.
    B. decrease and marginal costs increase.
    C. increase and marginal costs increase.

Financial Reporting and Analysis

45. Information about the operating profits of a company's various business segments can be found in the:
    A. proxy statement.
    B. auditor's report.
    C. supplementary schedule.

46. The following financial information reflects the latest 12-month results for High Corp (in millions).

Revenue	$400
Expenses	$300
Liabilities	$350
Dividends	$10
Beginning retained earnings	$125
Ending retained earnings	$215
Contributed capital	$175

    High Corp's assets are *closest* to:
    A. $565 million.
    B. $650 million.
    C. $740 million.

47. Which one of the following agencies is responsible for carrying out the requirements of the Sarbanes-Oxley Act of 2002?
    A. Securities and Exchange Commission (SEC).
    B. Public Company Accounting Oversight Board (PCAOB).
    C. Financial Accounting Standards Board (FASB).

48. Howard Company has $50 million of intangible assets on its balance sheet. The company has $30 million worth of patents, which have a useful life of ten years with a legal life of fifteen years. The remaining $20 million of intangible assets have an indefinite life. Using the straight line method, Howard's amortization expense is *closet* to:
    A. $2.0 million.
    B. $3.0 million.
    C. $3.3 million.

49. Pepper Company purchased machinery for $1,500,000. The company believes the machine will have a useful life of fifteen years and a $200,000 salvage value. The machine is expected to produce fifteen million units per year. Using the double declining method, the first year's depreciation is *closest* to:
    A. $86,666.
    B. $173,332.
    C. $200,000.

50. Which of the following *best* describes the proper treatment for a change in accounting principles as required by the Financial Accounting Standards Board?
    A. Restate the current period's financial statements and disclose the effect of the change in the footnotes.
    B. Restate financial statements for all fiscal years included in the company's financial report and describe the retrospective changes and rationale in the footnotes.
    C. Include the cumulative effect of the changes on the financial statements and describe the effects of the old standard compared to the new one in the footnotes.

51. Which of the following is included in the statement of comprehensive income?
    A. Net income, minimum pension liability, unrealized gains and losses from available-for-sale securities, and the reacquisition of treasury stock.
    B. Revenues, expenses, realized and unrealized gains and losses from available-for-sale securities, cumulative translation adjustment from foreign subsidiaries, and minimum pension liability.
    C. Revenues, expenses, unrealized gains and losses from available-for-sale securities, cumulative translation adjustment, and stock issued to shareholders.

52. A company did not accrue the December wages that will be paid in January. Which of the following statements is *most likely* correct about the company's year-end balance sheet?
    A. Liabilities and assets are understated.
    B. Liabilities are overstated and owners' equity is understated.
    C. Liabilities are understated and owners' equity is overstated.

53. At the end of 2008, Wichita Incorporated purchased equipment totaling $500,000. The seller of the equipment provided 100% debt financing with payments, including interest, beginning in 2009. How does the equipment purchase impact Wichita's 2008 financing activities on the cash flow statement?
    A. No effect.
    B. Cash inflow.
    C. Cash outflow.

54. Below is selected financial information for James Manufacturing:

Income statement (in millions)	**2008**
Operating Income	$217
Net income	$142

Other information	
Capital expenditures	$48
Change in working capital	−$120
Depreciation	$100
Common dividends declared	$39
Shares outstanding	40

James Manufacturing's 2008 free cash flow per share is *closest* to:
    A. $1.85 per share.
    B. $7.85 per share.
    C. $9.05 per share.

55. Leonard Heavy Industries uses LIFO inventory accounting for financial and tax accounting purposes. An analyst at Goreman Investments believes that Leonard's reported inventory balance and cost of goods sold do not reflect economic reality. Which of the following is a reason that LIFO accounting misrepresents economic reality? LIFO:
    A. understates cost of goods sold in a period of rising prices.
    B. allows for income manipulation through changes in purchasing practices.
    C. leads to an overstatement of inventory when prices are rising.

56. Robert Pernell, CFA, is CFO of Bonanza Company, which operates a specialty retail business in the United States. Bonanza has experienced rising inventory costs and expects this trend to continue into the foreseeable future. Pernell is considering switching Bonanza's inventory accounting from FIFO to LIFO. All else equal, this change will:
A. decrease working capital and decrease income taxes.
B. increase the debt-to-equity ratio and decrease inventory turnover.
C. decrease gross profit margin and decrease the quick ratio.

57. Peney Incorporated is building a new office tower for its administrative personnel. The construction costs are funded using a combination of debt and equity. As compared to expensing the construction costs immediately, capitalizing the construction costs will result in a:
A. higher interest coverage ratio and lower operating cash flow.
B. higher total assets and higher financing cash flow.
C. lower fixed asset turnover ratio and lower investing cash flow.

58. SafeNet Inc. and ProTech Corp. are leading producers of industrial safety equipment. Fixed assets in this industry generally become obsolete after seven years. Using the following financial information, determine which company's cash flow is *most likely* to be constrained by higher capital expenditures in the near future to replace aging equipment.

SafeNet Inc.		ProTech Corp.	
Gross fixed assets	300	Gross fixed assets	520
Net fixed assets	80	Net fixed assets	100
Capital expenditures	60	Capital expenditures	80
Depreciation expense	50	Depreciation expense	70

A. SafeNet, because its remaining useful life of fixed assets is shorter than that of ProTech.
B. ProTech, because the average depreciable life of its fixed assets is shorter than that of SafeNet.
C. ProTech, because the average age of its fixed assets is higher than that of SafeNet.

59. Selected cash flow data from Fritz Company follows:

Net income	$16,000
Depreciation	37,000
Loss on sale of equipment	3,000
Change in working capital	(8,000)
Cash flow from operations	$48,000
Equipment proceeds	$22,000
Capital expenditures	(14,000)
Cash flow from investing	$8,000

The book value of the equipment sold was closest to:
A. $19,000.
B. $22,000.
C. $25,000.

60. Mike Cathey, CFA, is comparing two multinational firms and is concerned about accounting differences for deferred taxes under U.S GAAP and IFRS. Cathey researches the specific standards and summarizes his conclusions. Which of the following conclusions is *least accurate*?
A. Deferred taxes are created from the revaluation of fixed assets under U.S. GAAP.
B. Under IFRS, deferred tax assets and liabilities are classified as noncurrent items on the balance sheet.
C. Under IFRS, the tax rate used to measure deferred tax assets is the enacted tax rate.

61. Manitou Plastics Inc. has been recording large deferred tax assets after incurring operating losses in the previous three years. At the end of the most recent year, Manitou reported $14 million in deferred tax assets but only $3 million in deferred tax liabilities. Manitou has also reported a valuation allowance related to deferred taxes in the amount of $7.5 million. What is the *most likely* cause of Manitou's reported valuation allowance?
A. Accounting earnings have been manipulated.
B. Future profitability is in doubt.
C. Interest rates are high.

62. Barnes Company issues bonds to fund a capital spending program. The $200 million offering has a coupon rate of 6.0% and the bonds yield 6.5% at issuance. If the bonds' yield declines to 5.5% at the end of the year, reported interest expense will be:
A. less than $12 million.
B. more than $12 million.
C. exactly $12 million.

63.   Heritage Corp. issues bonds on January 1, 20X1, with the following characteristics:

Number of bonds outstanding	5,000
Par value	$1,000
Coupon	5.5%
Market rate at issuance	7.5%
Coupon schedule	Annual
Coupon Payment Date	January 1
Maturity date	January 1, 20X6

On January 1, 20X2, Heritage decides to retire its debt and is able to repurchase the debt for $950 per bond. Calculate the gain or loss recorded on Heritage's financial statements due to the retirement of debt.
A. Gain of $154,588.49.
B. Loss of $84,932.63.
C. Gain of $84,932.63.

64.   The footnote below appears in the financial statement of Bongo Copper:

"Bongo is obligated to purchase $200 million per year of natural gas used in the copper smelting portion of operating activities. The annual payment is nonnegotiable for six years even if our natural gas needs are less than expected. Last year Bongo used $400 million worth of gas. Gas prices have been steady for the last three years and Bongo's implicit cost of borrowing is 5.47%."

What adjustment (if any) should an analyst make to Bongo's balance sheet for this obligation?
A. Increase Bongo's debt by $1.2 billion.
B. Increase Bongo's debt by $1 billion.
C. No balance sheet adjustment is necessary.

65. Selected data from Frisco Company's financial statements follows:

Sales	$6 billion
Interest expense	$18 million
Net income	$354 million
Total assets	$4 billion
Leverage	2.0

Using the DuPont model, Frisco's return on equity is *closest* to:
A. 16.8%.
B. 17.7%.
C. 18.1%.

66. Common size analysis is *least likely* to be useful for:
A. comparing companies' financial statements in a single reporting period.
B. analyzing changes in a company's costs and profit margins over time.
C. measuring the relationship between earnings and stock price.

67. Planter Incorporated's inventory has been growing twice as fast as its revenue. The company's inventory growth *least likely* suggests that the company may have:
A. inventory management problems.
B. obsolete inventory recorded on the balance sheet.
C. a higher inventory turnover ratio relative to industry peers.

68. Stock buybacks used to offset earnings dilution from the exercise of stock options are *most likely*:
A. a small percentage of the company's overall cash flow.
B. classified as a financing activity on the cash flow statement.
C. to occur when the stock price is decreasing.

69. Charles Knott, CFA, is reviewing the financial statements of Blue Company. Knott collects the following information:
- Total present value of operating leases is $1,078.
- Rent expense equals $341.
- Average interest rate on debt is 8%.
- EBIT equals $3,172.
- Straight-line depreciation over eight years.
- Interest expense equals $374.

Blue Company's current interest coverage ratio equals 8.5. Knott wants to calculate Blue's interest coverage ratio adjusted for the effects of operating leases. The adjusted interest coverage ratio is *closest* to:
A. 6.4x.
B. 7.3x.
C. 7.9x.

70. An analyst makes the following statements regarding the convergence of accounting standards.

Statement 1: Both IFRS and U.S. GAAP require similar treatment and valuation of goodwill.

Statement 2: U.S. GAAP requires joint ventures be accounted for using the equity method, while IFRS standards require joint ventures to be accounted for using the proportionate consolidation method.

Is the analyst correct with regard to Statement 1 and/or Statement 2?
A. Both statements are correct.
B. Neither statement is correct.
C. Only one of the statements is correct.

71. Bear Company produces gravel hauling equipment. The company recently began producing the Mauler, a new line of equipment. Prior to beginning production of the Mauler, the company spent $10 million in research and development costs. Bear expects the Mauler line to be cash flow positive by the beginning of the fourth year. However, Bear is forecasting a negative cash flow in year 5, due to costs to comply with new government emission standards. The company will use an empty building it already owns to produce the Mauler. Which of the following statements is *least likely* correct?
A. The research and development is a sunk cost.
B. The cash flows for the project are conventional.
C. The use of the empty building is an opportunity cost.

72. A company is evaluating the following capital projects for investment over the next two years—two new machines with costs of $4 million each, a computer software upgrade with a cost of $1 million, and a multi-year replacement of two aging machines involving an investment of $4.5 million for the first machine and another $4.5 million for the second machine if projected savings from the first machine are realized. What will be the *most likely* investment decisions on these projects over the next two years if the available budget is $10 million?
A. Invest $4 million in one of the new machines, $1 million in the software upgrade, and $4.5 million in the replacement of one of the two aging machines in order to improve the overall productivity of the company's equipment.
B. Invest in a mix of these projects based on allocating funds to those projects with the highest expected rates of return over the two-year capital budgeting period.
C. Invest in a mix of these projects based on allocating funds among those projects with the highest present value of expected future cash flows relative to required investment.

73. A graph that shows the relation between the cost of capital and the value that a project adds to the firm is *best* described as a project's:
    A. capital value graph.
    B. net present value profile.
    C. marginal cost of capital curve.

74. Which of the following is *least likely* to lead to an increase in the market risk premium according to either the dividend discount model approach or the capital asset pricing model approach to cost of equity estimation?
    A. An increase in the market beta.
    B. An increase in the market dividend yield.
    C. An increase in the dividend growth rate of the market.

75. A company's schedule of the costs of debt and equity shows that an additional $3 million of debt can be issued at an after tax cost of 3% and additional equity of $9 million at a cost of 6%. The company plans to maintain a capital structure of 30% debt and 70% equity. At what level of new capital financing will the marginal cost of capital change with the issuance of new debt?
    A. $3 million.
    B. $10 million.
    C. $12.86 million.

76. An analyst calculates the following financial ratios for two competitors.

Financial Ratio	Company X Year 1	Company X Year 2	Company Y Year 1	Company Y Year 2
Current ratio	1.95	1.85	1.95	2.00
Quick ratio	0.6	0.85	0.7	0.7

    Which of the following *best* describes the companies' liquidity trends over time?
    A. Liquidity increased for Company X in year 2 compared to Company Y due to the improvement in Company X's quick ratio.
    B. Liquidity was higher for Company Y compared to Company X because Company Y's current ratio in year 2 was higher than Company X's current ratio.
    C. Liquidity declined for Company X due to a decline in its current ratio, while liquidity for Company Y increased due to an increase in the current ratio in year 2.

77. Inventory turnover rates for a company were 8.3x in year 1, 8.1x in year 2, and 7.6x in year 3. The number of days of inventory for the industry averaged 50 in year 1, 49 in year 2, and 48 in year 3. Relative to the industry, the company's inventory management has been:
A. in line with the industry average over the last three years.
B. improving over the last three years.
C. worsening over the last three years.

78. Julie Harris, CFA, is the Chief Financial Officer (CFO) of Logan Associates. Harris was part of the committee that drafted the company's code of ethics. Harris comments that (1) Logan's code of ethics is part of the company's risk management policies, and (2) that ethics committees should meet more frequently than every other year to review Logan's code of ethics and corporate governance policies. Evaluate Harris' statements.
A. Harris is correct only with respect to risk management.
B. Harris is correct only with respect to the frequency of policy reviews.
C. Harris is correct with respect to risk management and the frequency of policy reviews.

Portfolio Management

79. Colin Pollard currently owns a portfolio lying on the Markowitz efficient frontier that has an expected return equal to 15% and a standard deviation equal to 15%. Pollard tells his adviser he would prefer a portfolio lying on the Markowitz efficient frontier with a standard deviation equal to 10%. Which of the following *most likely* describes the expected return on Pollard's new portfolio?
A. The expected return will be equal to 10%.
B. The expected return will be less than 10%.
C. The expected return will be greater than 10%.

80. All portfolios that lie on the capital market line:
A. contain the same mix of risky assets unless only the risk-free asset is held.
B. have some unsystematic risk unless only the risk-free asset is held.
C. contain at least some positive allocation to the risk-free asset.

81. Donald Northerland forecasts the stock return, beta, and standard deviation for three stocks: Cayman, Bonaire, and Lucia. The expected return and standard deviation for the broad market equal 12% and 20%, respectively. The risk-free rate equals 5%.

	Forecast return	Beta	Standard deviation
Cayman	12.0%	1.0	25%
Bonaire	16.3%	1.5	27%
Lucia	18.2%	2.0	26%

Using the capital asset pricing model, determine which of the following statements is *least likely* correct.
A. Cayman is overvalued.
B. Bonaire is undervalued.
C. Lucia is overvalued.

82. Stephanie Dell is evaluating two stocks (X and Y) using the capital asset pricing model. Dell predicts that the betas for the two stocks will be identical, but that the unsystematic risk for Stock X will be much higher than for Stock Y. Using the capital asset pricing model, determine which of the following statements is correct.
A. Stock X will have a higher expected return than Stock Y, but a standard deviation less than or equal to Stock Y.
B. Stock X will have a higher standard deviation than Stock Y, but an expected return less than or equal to Stock Y.
C. Both the expected return and standard deviation for Stock X will be higher than Stock Y.

83. Joe Finn is a highly paid corporate executive who will retire in two years. Over 25 years ago, Finn invested in a portfolio of growth stocks that has performed quite well. Finn has asked his financial adviser to consider switching from stocks to high-yielding bonds. The investment issue of greatest concern in implementing this strategy will be the client's:
A. liquidity needs.
B. time horizon.
C. tax considerations.

84. Daniel Blair recently joined an investment club with several of his coworkers. Members of the club are generally quite conservative and are unwilling to invest in debt securities with credit ratings below AA. New investments are always evaluated in the context of the overall portfolio. Based on the attributes of the investment club members, they will *most likely* pursue an investment strategy that:
A. attempts to reduce a portfolio's standard deviation through diversification.
B. seeks the lowest risk securities.
C. attempts to eliminate standard deviation.

Asset Valuation

85.   Giovanni DiPaglia is VP of strategic planning for Megaquistion
       Holdings, a global conglomerate active in the mergers and acquisition
       market. DiPaglia is looking to invest in a new portfolio company
       for Megaquistion, and has selected Temptytarg, Inc. as a potential
       candidate. He has gathered the following information for Temptytarg,
       Inc.

       - Stock price $18.00
       - Return on equity (ROE)   15%
       - Shares outstanding   6 million
       - Common shareholders' equity $54 million

       Price/Book Value (P/BV) for Temptytarg is *closest* to:
       A. 1.1.
       B. 1.5.
       C. 2.0.

86.   Allen Jackson believes the stock of JMH Corporation is severely
       overvalued. JMH trades for 12.3 times annualized earnings, but
       Jackson thinks the multiple should be 8.1 times. In order to take
       advantage of the expected 35% drop in the price, Jackson decides to
       establish a short position in JMH stock. Which of the following is
       Jackson *least likely* to do in order to establish a short position?
       A. Borrow the stock from another investor.
       B. Reinvest any dividend payments.
       C. Post margin with his brokerage firm.

87.   A buy side analyst is discussing the relative functionality of the
       Australian stock market with her colleagues. She states three specific
       attributes of the Australian stock market that infer that the market is
       a well-functioning securities market. She says, "The Australian stock
       market is characterized by (1) rapid adjustment of prices to reflect new
       information, and (2) price continuity in the absence of significant new
       information." Are these accurate descriptions of attributes of a well
       functioning market?
       A. Both descriptions are accurate.
       B. Neither description is accurate.
       C. Only one of these descriptions is accurate.

88.   The creation of bond indexes is relatively new. Which of the following
       is the *least likely* reason a bond index would be difficult to create?
       A. Lack of continuous trading data.
       B. Constantly changing duration for bonds.
       C. The universe of bonds is limited.

89. Gregory Johansson has collected the following data on Trilby &
    Tribble, Ltd:
    • Sales $680 million
    • Asset turnover   0.9 times
    • Dividends paid $34 million
    • Financial leverage   1.25
    • Net income $85 million

    The sustainable growth rate of the firm is *closest* to:
    A. 6.0%.
    B. 7.1%.
    C. 8.4%.

90. In explaining the factors in the dividend discount model that affect a
    stock's expected price-to-earnings (P_0/E_1) ratio, which of the following
    statements is *least accurate*? Holding other factors constant:
    A. as the difference between k (required rate of return on the stock)
       and g (expected constant growth rate of dividends) widens, the
       value of P_0/E_1 decreases.
    B. as g increases, the value of P_0/E_1 increases.
    C. as the expected dividend payout ratio decreases, the value of P_0/E_1
       increases.

91. Jack George is evaluating Dunger Inc., a waste management firm.
    The company has been experiencing a strong 15% growth rate, which
    is forecasted to continue over the next three years before growth
    settles down to a sustainable level. Dunger's annual return on equity
    is expected to be 10%. The company recently paid a dividend of
    $0.50 per share from reported earnings of $2.50 per share. George has
    calculated a 10% weighted average cost of capital for Dunger Inc. The
    firm has no debt. The company's last reported trade on the New York
    Stock Exchange was $35 per share. Based on the multi-stage dividend
    discount model, George should:
    A. not buy the stock because its intrinsic value is $32 per share.
    B. buy the stock because its intrinsic value is $38 per share.
    C. buy the stock because its intrinsic value is $41 per share.

92. Willa Dowd collected the following information for a small-cap firm that she is evaluating:
    - Stock price per share $20.50
    - Expected sales $920 million
    - Operating expenses (excluding interest) $405 million
    - Depreciation & amortization $44 million
    - Return on equity (ROE)   12%
    - Shares outstanding   31 million
    - Common shareholders' equity $380 million

    The Price/Cash Flow (P/CF) for the small-cap firm is *closest* to:
    A. 7.1.
    B. 8.5.
    C. 9.1.

93. Acquire Corp. has a business model based on making accretive acquisitions each year. The company has historically been successful in implementing its strategy. Earnings per share have grown each of the last five years at a 15% compounded rate. During the past year, Acquire Corp. acquired a services company with large net operating losses, representing a third leg to its business model. The other two business segments are engineering construction and mining. The purchase price was one-half the company's current market value. The *most appropriate* technique to value Acquire Corp. is based on its:
    A. price-to-book value ratio.
    B. forward price-to-earnings ratio.
    C. trailing price-to-sales ratio.

94. Lynn Smith, CFA, and a marketing associate have a disagreement over whether the stock market is truly efficient. The marketing associate believes that the stock market is totally efficient based on academic research that shows actively managed mutual funds do no better than a buy-and-hold strategy. Thus, he invests solely in index funds. Smith counters that academic research indicates that low P/E ratio stocks provide superior risk-adjusted returns. Based on this discussion, indicate which of the following statements regarding the efficient markets hypothesis (EMH) is correct.
    A. The strong form of the EMH is supported by academic research on low P/E stocks.
    B. The semistrong form of the EMH is not supported by academic research on low P/E stocks.
    C. The strong form of the EMH is not supported by academic research on mutual funds.

95. James Larson, CFA, manages a large capitalization growth mutual fund. Larson's benchmark is the Russell 1000 Growth index. Larson's colleague, Kevin Moore, CFA, manages an index fund which mimics the Russell 1000 index. Moore believes that the capital markets are fully efficient, while Larson disagrees. Larson defends his position with the following supporting statements.

    Statement 1: Market participants must be adequately compensated for processing new information to ensure the markets remain efficient. Yet a perfectly efficient market provides no incentive to sufficiently reward investors for processing new information. Hence, markets cannot be fully efficient.

    Statement 2: Low trading costs have led to greater trading activity, which has had the unintended consequence of greater securities mispricing.

    Are Larson's statements correct?
    A. Yes.
    B. Only Statement 1 is correct.
    C. Only Statement 2 is correct.

96. Larry Rile is evaluating the investment merits of Bing Corp., a successful motorcycle manufacturer. Rile is forecasting a dividend in year 1 of $1.50 per share, a dividend in year 2 of $3.00 per share, and a dividend in year 3 of 4.50 per share. After year 3, Rile expects dividends to grow at the rate of 6% per year. Rile calculated a beta of 1.3 for Bing Corp. Rile expects the S&P 500 index to return 8%. The U.S. Treasury bill is yielding 2%. Using the multistage dividend discount model, what is Bing Corp.'s intrinsic value to the nearest dollar?
    A. $92 per share.
    B. $102 per share.
    C. $112 per share.

97. A bond does not pay initial coupon payments but instead accrues them over a pre-determined period and then pays a lump sum at the end of that period. The bond subsequently pays regular coupon payments until maturity. Such a bond is *best* described as:
    A. a step-up note.
    B. a zero-coupon bond.
    C. a deferred-coupon bond.

98. Sara Jones, CFA, recently purchased a U.S. government security that was issued on 6/1/2007 and will mature on 6/1/2014. Jones purchased the security in the secondary market. This security is *most likely* an:
    A. on-the-run Treasury note.
    B. off-the-run Treasury bond.
    C. off-the-run Treasury note.

99. Phillip Green expects the 2-year downward trend in interest rates to reverse next month. Green believes that, in 30 days, interest rates will begin to rise steadily and significantly for at least 12 months.

Bond	Duration	Convexity	Maturity	Coupon
A	8.00	0.153	12 yrs	7.0%
B	4.50	0.235	5 yrs	6.0%
C	7.20	0.212	9 yrs	5.5%

Based on his expectations, Green should only invest in:
    A. Bond A.
    B. Bond B.
    C. Bond C.

100. An entity desiring to issue a fixed-income security has placed $10 million worth of loan receivables in a special purpose vehicle (SPV) that is completely independent of the company. Additionally, the credit rating agencies have suggested the entity secure a third-party guarantee in order to have the security rated AAA. After completing the transfer of assets to the SPV and obtaining a letter of credit from a national bank, the entity issued the AAA-rated security. Which of the following securities did the entity *most likely* issue?
    A. Commercial paper.
    B. International bonds.
    C. Asset-backed securities.

101. A fixed-income portfolio manager at Franken Investments is considering adding a security to his existing portfolio. The bond, issued by KDJ Company, has an option adjusted spread (OAS) equal to 0.23% and a Z-spread equal to 0.15%. The manager is concerned that his portfolio is dominated by callable bonds and will only accept new securities if they contain no call options. Should the portfolio manager add the KDJ bond to his portfolio?
    A. Yes, the negative option cost implies the bond is putable.
    B. No, the positive option cost implies the bond is callable.
    C. No, the negative option cost implies the bond is callable.

102. Leading economists have predicted that the Federal Reserve will continue to pursue a stable monetary policy that has characterized the last five years, keeping the price level constant into the future. Given the Fed's monetary policy, the pure expectations theory and the liquidity preference theory would predict, respectively, the following yield curve shapes:
A. flat and flat.
B. upward sloping and flat.
C. flat and upward sloping.

103. On November 15, 2006, the yield curve was upward sloping with yields of 3%, 4%, and 5.5% on 1-year, 5-year, and 10-year Treasuries, respectively. The following day, the Treasury yield curve experienced an upward parallel shift equal to 112 basis points. Which of the following noncallable bonds would have experienced the *least* percentage change in price as a result of the yield curve shift?
A. A 6% coupon corporate bond maturing in ten years.
B. A 6% coupon corporate bond maturing in five years.
C. A 6% coupon U.S. government bond maturing in ten years.

104. A bond dealer determines that the present value of a particular Treasury note based on Treasury spot rates is greater than its market price. The dealer can generate an arbitrage profit (assuming no transactions costs) by:
A. buying the Treasury note and selling its cash flows as Treasury STRIPS.
B. buying the equivalent Treasury STRIPS and selling them as a Treasury note.
C. buying the undervalued note and selling short the Treasury security with the nearest maturity.

105. Bill Foley, CFA, manages an intermediate tax-exempt bond fund. Foley makes the following two comments about securities in his portfolio.

Statement 1: Revenue bonds usually pay a higher coupon rate than general obligation bonds.

Statement 2: Double barreled bonds are municipal securities that are exempt from both federal and state taxes.

Which of the following *best* evaluates Statement 1 and Statement 2?
A. Only Statement 1 is correct.
B. Only Statement 2 is correct.
C. Both Statements are incorrect.

106. A Japanese auto company announces a new plant to be constructed in San Antonio, Texas. The company will partly finance the project with a dual currency bond offering. The $200 million offering will have a 6.0% coupon payable in yen and mature in 2021 with the final principal payment in U.S. dollars. Indicate whether a U.S.-based investor and/or the company will assume any potential currency exchange risk related to these bonds.
    A. Investor only.
    B. Issuer only.
    C. Both the issuer and the investor.

107. Gerald Snow is a bond manager for Long Vision Investments. Snow is evaluating potential arbitrage opportunities. He has the following list of bonds:
    - Bond X is a 1-year zero coupon bond selling at 950.
    - Bond Y is a 2-year zero coupon bond selling at 850.
    - Bond Z is a 2-year bond with an annual coupon of 8%.

    All three bonds have a par value of $1,000. If no arbitrage opportunity exists, the price of bond Z is *closest* to:
    A. $975.
    B. $995.
    C. $1,015.

108. Rob Ealey, CFA, has just purchased an option-free bond with a 6.50% coupon that is currently selling at 94.73 to yield 7.25%. If yields increase by 50 bps, the new price of the bonds would be 91.41, and if yields decrease by 50 bps the new price of the bond would be 98.20. Determine the approximate new price of the bond if yields decrease by 75 basis points.
    A. 89.64.
    B. 99.82.
    C. 104.92.

109. A bond matures in ten years, pays a 7% semiannual coupon, and is currently priced to yield 6.25%. The bond is callable at par beginning five years from now. Debbie Scott is planning to purchase this bond. Scott can currently reinvest coupon income from the bond at 5.50%. Which of the following statements is *least accurate*?
    A. If the bond is called in six years, Scott's return will be less than 6.25%.
    B. If Scott's reinvestment rate was 6.25%, the bond's yield to worst would be less than 6.25%.
    C. If the bond was priced to yield 5.50%, the current yield would be 7%.

110. Sally Ferguson, CFA, is a hedge fund manager. Ferguson utilizes both futures and forward contracts in the fund she manages. In speaking with a client, Ferguson makes the following statements to answer their questions about futures and forward contracts:

    Statement 1: A futures contract is an exchange traded instrument with standardized features.

    Statement 2: Forward contracts are marked-to-market on a daily basis to reduce credit risk to both counterparties.

    Indicate whether Statement 1 and Statement 2 are *most likely* correct or incorrect.
    A. Only Statement 1 is correct.
    B. Only Statement 2 is correct.
    C. Both statements are correct.

111. Peter Ulrich runs a hedge fund which specializes in using option strategies to enhance the fund's returns. In a training session for newly hired analysts, Ulrich explains option characteristics as follows: "The maximum profit on a short call position is always less than the maximum profit on a long call position and a long at-the-money put option position will break even as soon as the price of the underlying stock decreases." Determine whether Ulrich is correct with regard to his statements about call options and put options.
    A. Ulrich is correct regarding call options only.
    B. Ulrich is correct regarding put options only.
    C. Ulrich is correct regarding both call and put options.

112. Jack Cheney purchases an IBM October 80 put contract for a premium of $5. Cheney holds the option until the expiration date when IBM stock sells for $78 per share. At expiration, what is the loss on the contract?
    A. –$2.
    B. –$3.
    C. –$5.

113. Ken Willis is the portfolio manager of an aggressive growth fund. Ken is concerned about the future performance of his high-beta portfolio in light of his belief that the stock market is currently overvalued. Willis' firm requires that he maintain at least 80% of the portfolio's value in equities at all times. Willis decided his best course of action is to buy put options to protect the portfolio from the potential loss resulting from a market decline. The profits and losses from an equity portfolio combined with long puts would have risk characteristics similar to a:
    A. long call option.
    B. short put and long call position.
    C. covered call position.

114. Bill Turner, CFA, is short a futures contract on wheat. Turner entered into the futures position three months ago at a contract price of $50. The contract expiration is tomorrow. The settlement prices for the past four days (from oldest to most recent) were $56, $53, $49, and $52. If the settlement price on the expiration day is $57, which of the following *best* describes a method Turner is *most likely* to use to terminate his futures contract?
    A. Sell a futures contract for $57 and receive a mark-to-market profit of $5.
    B. Buy a futures contract for $57 and incur a mark-to-market loss of $5.
    C. Leave the contract open, deliver the wheat to the long, and receive a price of $57.

115. A call option on Hartco stock with an exercise price of $50 and an expiration date one year from now is worth $4.00 today. A put option on Hartco stock with an exercise price of $50 and an expiration date one year from now is worth $2.25 today. U.S. Treasury notes maturing in one year are yielding 2.0%. Hartco does not pay a dividend. The value of Hartco's stock is *closest* to:
    A. $43 per share.
    B. $47 per share.
    C. $51 per share.

116. Pamela Burke is a cotton farmer in Texas. Her crop will be ready for harvest in three months, but Burke does not believe prices will remain at their current level. Burke contacts Brooke Anderson, a derivatives dealer, to negotiate a forward contract. Anderson agrees to be the counterparty to a forward contract that will eliminate Burke's exposure to the price of cotton. The contract is structured as a nondeliverable forward with a contract price of $47. If the price of cotton is $49 in three months, which counterparty will be exposed to the greater amount of credit risk and which counterparty will make a payment?
    A. Burke will be exposed to greater credit risk, and Anderson will make a payment.
    B. Anderson will be exposed to greater credit risk, and Burke will make a payment.
    C. Burke will be exposed to greater credit risk, and Burke will make a payment.

117. The annual income and expense figures for a proposed property under consideration for purchase, along with some recent sales data, are given below.

	Proposed Office Building (under construction)	Apartment Complex (recently sold)	Office Building (recently sold)
Potential gross rental income	$324,000		
Vacancy and collection loss	7.50%		
Taxes and Insurance	$27,000		
Depreciation	$37,800		
Other Expenses	$32,000		
NOI		$300,000	$272,000
Price at which property sold		$2,400,000	$1,700,000

The appraised value for the proposed property using the income approach is *closest* to:
A. $1,268,125.
B. $1,504,375.
C. $1,623,200.

118. Jerry Paris, CFA, manages a high yield bond fund. 20% of Paris' portfolio is invested in distressed securities. A colleague commented that investing in distressed securities is analogous to venture capital investing. Which of the following statements concerning distressed securities and venture capital is *least likely* to be true? An investment in distressed securities is similar to an investment in venture capital because both:
A. are illiquid.
B. are normally priced efficiently.
C. require a long time horizon.

119. Kerry Garrett, CFA, manages a hedge fund. The hedge fund industry has enjoyed strong growth over the past ten years. Garrett states that the hedge fund industry has a goal of absolute returns. In addition, Garrett states that the industry's high Sharpe ratio indicates that hedge funds are superior investment vehicles. Is Garrett correct with regard to his statement on hedge fund returns and/or his statement on hedge funds as superior investment vehicles?
A. Only the statement on return is correct.
B. Only the statement on superiority is correct.
C. Both the statements are correct.

120. Wiotech, LLC, a private company, is in the process of developing a revolutionary drug to fight Alzheimer's disease. The drug is in stage 2 development. The management team consists of several experienced clinical doctors. A reputable Wall Street firm has provided venture capital financing. The company would like to go public in the next few years. Which of the following is *least likely* to be a unique risk of this investment compared to other types of investment?
    A. Inexperienced entrepreneurs.
    B. Uncertain time to success.
    C. Limited information.

End of Morning Session

Exam 3
Afternoon Session

Topic	Questions	Points
Ethical and Professional Standards	121–138	27
Quantitative Analysis	139–152	22.5
Economics	153–165	18
Financial Reporting and Analysis	166–198	49.5
Portfolio Management	199–204	9
Asset Valuation	205–240	54
Total		180

Test Answers

121.	Ⓐ	Ⓑ	Ⓒ	161.	Ⓐ	Ⓑ	Ⓒ	201.	Ⓐ	Ⓑ	Ⓒ
122.	Ⓐ	Ⓑ	Ⓒ	162.	Ⓐ	Ⓑ	Ⓒ	202.	Ⓐ	Ⓑ	Ⓒ
123.	Ⓐ	Ⓑ	Ⓒ	163.	Ⓐ	Ⓑ	Ⓒ	203.	Ⓐ	Ⓑ	Ⓒ
124.	Ⓐ	Ⓑ	Ⓒ	164.	Ⓐ	Ⓑ	Ⓒ	204.	Ⓐ	Ⓑ	Ⓒ
125.	Ⓐ	Ⓑ	Ⓒ	165.	Ⓐ	Ⓑ	Ⓒ	205.	Ⓐ	Ⓑ	Ⓒ
126.	Ⓐ	Ⓑ	Ⓒ	166.	Ⓐ	Ⓑ	Ⓒ	206.	Ⓐ	Ⓑ	Ⓒ
127.	Ⓐ	Ⓑ	Ⓒ	167.	Ⓐ	Ⓑ	Ⓒ	207.	Ⓐ	Ⓑ	Ⓒ
128.	Ⓐ	Ⓑ	Ⓒ	168.	Ⓐ	Ⓑ	Ⓒ	208.	Ⓐ	Ⓑ	Ⓒ
129.	Ⓐ	Ⓑ	Ⓒ	169.	Ⓐ	Ⓑ	Ⓒ	209.	Ⓐ	Ⓑ	Ⓒ
130.	Ⓐ	Ⓑ	Ⓒ	170.	Ⓐ	Ⓑ	Ⓒ	210.	Ⓐ	Ⓑ	Ⓒ
131.	Ⓐ	Ⓑ	Ⓒ	171.	Ⓐ	Ⓑ	Ⓒ	211.	Ⓐ	Ⓑ	Ⓒ
132.	Ⓐ	Ⓑ	Ⓒ	172.	Ⓐ	Ⓑ	Ⓒ	212.	Ⓐ	Ⓑ	Ⓒ
133.	Ⓐ	Ⓑ	Ⓒ	173.	Ⓐ	Ⓑ	Ⓒ	213.	Ⓐ	Ⓑ	Ⓒ
134.	Ⓐ	Ⓑ	Ⓒ	174.	Ⓐ	Ⓑ	Ⓒ	214.	Ⓐ	Ⓑ	Ⓒ
135.	Ⓐ	Ⓑ	Ⓒ	175.	Ⓐ	Ⓑ	Ⓒ	215.	Ⓐ	Ⓑ	Ⓒ
136.	Ⓐ	Ⓑ	Ⓒ	176.	Ⓐ	Ⓑ	Ⓒ	216.	Ⓐ	Ⓑ	Ⓒ
137.	Ⓐ	Ⓑ	Ⓒ	177.	Ⓐ	Ⓑ	Ⓒ	217.	Ⓐ	Ⓑ	Ⓒ
138.	Ⓐ	Ⓑ	Ⓒ	178.	Ⓐ	Ⓑ	Ⓒ	218.	Ⓐ	Ⓑ	Ⓒ
139.	Ⓐ	Ⓑ	Ⓒ	179.	Ⓐ	Ⓑ	Ⓒ	219.	Ⓐ	Ⓑ	Ⓒ
140.	Ⓐ	Ⓑ	Ⓒ	180.	Ⓐ	Ⓑ	Ⓒ	220.	Ⓐ	Ⓑ	Ⓒ
141.	Ⓐ	Ⓑ	Ⓒ	181.	Ⓐ	Ⓑ	Ⓒ	221.	Ⓐ	Ⓑ	Ⓒ
142.	Ⓐ	Ⓑ	Ⓒ	182.	Ⓐ	Ⓑ	Ⓒ	222.	Ⓐ	Ⓑ	Ⓒ
143.	Ⓐ	Ⓑ	Ⓒ	183.	Ⓐ	Ⓑ	Ⓒ	223.	Ⓐ	Ⓑ	Ⓒ
144.	Ⓐ	Ⓑ	Ⓒ	184.	Ⓐ	Ⓑ	Ⓒ	224.	Ⓐ	Ⓑ	Ⓒ
145.	Ⓐ	Ⓑ	Ⓒ	185.	Ⓐ	Ⓑ	Ⓒ	225.	Ⓐ	Ⓑ	Ⓒ
146.	Ⓐ	Ⓑ	Ⓒ	186.	Ⓐ	Ⓑ	Ⓒ	226.	Ⓐ	Ⓑ	Ⓒ
147.	Ⓐ	Ⓑ	Ⓒ	187.	Ⓐ	Ⓑ	Ⓒ	227.	Ⓐ	Ⓑ	Ⓒ
148.	Ⓐ	Ⓑ	Ⓒ	188.	Ⓐ	Ⓑ	Ⓒ	228.	Ⓐ	Ⓑ	Ⓒ
149.	Ⓐ	Ⓑ	Ⓒ	189.	Ⓐ	Ⓑ	Ⓒ	229.	Ⓐ	Ⓑ	Ⓒ
150.	Ⓐ	Ⓑ	Ⓒ	190.	Ⓐ	Ⓑ	Ⓒ	230.	Ⓐ	Ⓑ	Ⓒ
151.	Ⓐ	Ⓑ	Ⓒ	191.	Ⓐ	Ⓑ	Ⓒ	231.	Ⓐ	Ⓑ	Ⓒ
152.	Ⓐ	Ⓑ	Ⓒ	192.	Ⓐ	Ⓑ	Ⓒ	232.	Ⓐ	Ⓑ	Ⓒ
153.	Ⓐ	Ⓑ	Ⓒ	193.	Ⓐ	Ⓑ	Ⓒ	233.	Ⓐ	Ⓑ	Ⓒ
154.	Ⓐ	Ⓑ	Ⓒ	194.	Ⓐ	Ⓑ	Ⓒ	234.	Ⓐ	Ⓑ	Ⓒ
155.	Ⓐ	Ⓑ	Ⓒ	195.	Ⓐ	Ⓑ	Ⓒ	235.	Ⓐ	Ⓑ	Ⓒ
156.	Ⓐ	Ⓑ	Ⓒ	196.	Ⓐ	Ⓑ	Ⓒ	236.	Ⓐ	Ⓑ	Ⓒ
157.	Ⓐ	Ⓑ	Ⓒ	197.	Ⓐ	Ⓑ	Ⓒ	237.	Ⓐ	Ⓑ	Ⓒ
158.	Ⓐ	Ⓑ	Ⓒ	198.	Ⓐ	Ⓑ	Ⓒ	238.	Ⓐ	Ⓑ	Ⓒ
159.	Ⓐ	Ⓑ	Ⓒ	199.	Ⓐ	Ⓑ	Ⓒ	239.	Ⓐ	Ⓑ	Ⓒ
160.	Ⓐ	Ⓑ	Ⓒ	200.	Ⓐ	Ⓑ	Ⓒ	240.	Ⓐ	Ⓑ	Ⓒ

Exam 3
Afternoon Session

Ethical and Professional Standards

121. Moe Girard, CFA, covers sports marketing firms for a major New York-based financial services firm. He works in a large group that decides on recommendations by consensus. Girard does not always agree with the group consensus, but he is reasonably confident with his group's decision-making process. Regarding compliance with CFA Institute Standards, which of the following statements is *correct*?
      A. Girard is fully complying with CFA Institute Standards.
      B. On reports he does not agree with, Girard should request that his name be removed.
      C. The other group members should not change Girard's individual recommendations.

122. David Martin, CFA, recently joined Arc Financial as a portfolio manager of an emerging markets mutual fund. For the past three years, he managed an emerging markets mutual fund for Landmark Investments. Upon Martin's arrival, Arc Financial releases a public announcement to existing and prospective clients quoting Martin as follows: "While at Landmark Investments, I was the senior portfolio manager of Alpha Emerging Markets Fund, from 2005-2007. During that time, the returns of this emerging markets stock fund outperformed its benchmarks each year as documented in recent reports by Landmark." Does Martin's statement violate the CFA Institute Standard of Professional Conduct related to performance presentation?
      A. Yes – Standards prohibit showing past performance at a prior firm.
      B. Yes – GIPS require including at least five years of performance history.
      C. No.

123. William Callahan, CFA, is an energy analyst for a large brokerage firm based in Galveston, Texas. His supervisor, Nancy Deininger, CFA, has recently decided to let Callahan cover a few of the firms that Deininger had been covering previously. Deininger gives Callahan specific instructions not to change her prior recommendation on one of these firms, Mayfield Energy. Which of the following actions by Callahan would be *least likely* to be consistent with CFA Institute Standards?
    A. Tell Deininger that he cannot cover Mayfield Energy under those restrictions
    B. Pick up coverage of Mayfield, do his own independent analysis and reach an independent conclusion.
    C. Use subtle, ambiguous language in the report, in order to not mislead the investor, while complying with his employer's instructions.

124. Isabella Wilson is an investment consultant for DOG, Inc. DOG's marketing department is preparing a brochure which outlines each investment consultant's individual qualifications. Wilson recently completed Level 3 of the CFA examination program, and was awarded her CFA charter last month. Which of the following statements, proposed for inclusion in the firm's marketing brochure, would *best* comply with CFA Institute Standards?
    A. Isabella Wilson, CFA, is among a special group of individuals, having passed the three levels of the CFA exam in consecutive attempts.
    B. Wilson recently passed Level 3 and received her CFA, having passed all three levels in consecutive attempts.
    C. Wilson passed all three levels of the CFA examination program in consecutive attempts.

125. Ann Stevens, CFA, is a portfolio manager for Helping Hands, a large non-profit organization. Her husband is the managing partner of a large public accounting firm. Over dinner, he mentions to Stevens that his company has completed its annual audit of Rock Inc., a large manufacturing company, and is going to issue a qualified opinion due to some accounting irregularities that were discovered. The Helping Hands portfolio currently holds a small equity position in Rock Inc., and Stevens feels that the qualified opinion will reduce the value of the stock. What action is recommended by the CFA Institute Standards of Professional Conduct?
    A. Stevens should do nothing.
    B. Stevens should inform her firm's compliance officer.
    C. Stevens should contact upper management of Rock Inc. and encourage them to publicly disseminate the news of the qualified opinion.

126. Terry Welch, CFA, is a portfolio manager for Barr Investments. Welch began using ORH Brokers as his sole broker five years ago. ORH's competitive fees and superior trade execution have drawn the attention of Welch's colleagues, many of whom now only use ORH to place trades. In appreciation for the long-standing relationship, ORH offers Welch tickets to a performance of the local symphony, which he accepts. The tickets have a total value of $90. Welch elects not to report the gift to his employer since it does not meet Barr's reportable threshold value of $100. Do Welch's actions with regard to the symphony tickets violate any CFA Institute Standards of Professional Conduct?
    A. No violation.
    B. Welch is permitted to accept the tickets, however in this instance, written permission is required from his employer.
    C. Welch is in violation of the Standards.

127. Janelle Russ, CFA, is an analyst covering the chemical industry. One of the companies she follows, ETX, is involved in litigation over a hazardous waste disposal site. Russ believes punitive damages resulting from this litigation could virtually bankrupt ETX. In a recent newspaper interview, the ETX chief financial officer (CFO) said that "we are very near a settlement on that lawsuit that we believe is equitable for all parties." In preparing her next pro forma financial report on ETX, Russ should:
    A. be careful not to mention the lawsuit, as her information comes from a material insider.
    B. be careful not to adjust her numbers for the lawsuit until the settlement is established as fact.
    C. use numbers reflecting a settlement, stating that this result is based on her opinion, and cite the CFO's comment.

128. Amy Liu, CFA, and Tom Yang, a CFA candidate, are securities analysts at Roberts Investment Co. In preparing a research report for Tello Industries, Liu includes specific quotations about the company's future earnings prospects, which she attributes to "investment experts." In preparing a research report on another company, Yang includes a table containing earnings and balance sheet ratios he got from a Standard & Poor's report without citing their source. According to CFA Institute's *Standards of Practice*, have Liu or Yang violated the prohibition against plagiarism?
    A. Both analysts have violated the Standards.
    B. Neither analyst has violated the Standards.
    C. Only one of the analysts has violated the Standards.

129. Danielle Roberts, CFA, a sell-side equity analyst for JPS Inc., is finishing a research report on auto manufacturer, Swift & Company. Roberts has owned shares of Swift for over 15 years. Ever since she began covering Swift as an analyst, her shares have been held in a blind trust account. Roberts does not have the ability to direct trades in the trust and is only informed of the holdings through a general list of securities without individual position values or numbers of shares held. According to CFA Institute Standards of Professional Conduct, is Roberts required to make any disclosures of her ownership of shares in Swift?
    A. Roberts does not have to make any disclosures as long as the shares are held in the blind trust.
    B. Roberts should disclose her holdings in Swift in her research report, but no employer disclosure is required.
    C. Roberts should disclose her holdings in Swift in her research report, as well as to her employer.

130. Which of the following is *least likely* a recommended procedure for compliance with CFA Institute Standards related to employees' duties of loyalty, prudence, and care to clients?
    A. Disclose to clients all forms of manager compensation.
    B. Vote proxies in the best interest of the clients and ultimate beneficiaries.
    C. Formulate written performance measurement benchmarks for each client.

131. Roger Anthony, CFA, is an investment adviser to high net worth individuals. Last year, he advised three of his clients to invest in ABCO, an equity issue that Anthony believes possesses above-average growth potential in the near term. All three did in fact purchase the stock, and continue to maintain their positions. Last week, Anthony received a letter from an attorney that his recently deceased uncle has bequeathed $1,000,000 of ABCO stock to him, effectively immediately. Anthony discloses the receipt of the stock to his supervisor, but takes no further action on the matter. Has Anthony violated CFA Institute Standards of Professional Conduct?
    A. No, Anthony has fulfilled all requirements of the Standard regarding the disclosure of a potential conflict of interest.
    B. Yes, Anthony should have immediately and clearly disclosed his position in ABCO to all of his clients.
    C. Yes, Anthony should have immediately transferred management of those affected clients' portfolios to his supervisor, who could then give each client the option to remain with Anthony or change investment advisors.

132. Which of the following statements is **TRUE** regarding the CFA Institute Standard related to Duties to Clients – Suitability?
    A. The income needs of all clients should take precedence over growth needs.
    B. Return objectives should take precedence over risk tolerance.
    C. An investment policy statement should be developed for each client.

133. Brian Lewis, CFA, is an institutional bond sales associate for Kite Brothers, a major financial institution in New York. Kite Brothers has had an incentive program in place for many years in which sales associates are compensated for the successful referral of clients to other operating units of the company. Lewis recommends to a client that the client transfer his personal accounts to the retail area of Kite Brothers. He gives the client supporting documentation that Kite Brothers is the leader in the retail brokerage industry with a very competitive fee structure. The client reviews the material and decides to move his personal accounts to Kite Brothers. Has Lewis violated the CFA Institute Standards of Professional Conduct?
    A. No, because Lewis was participating in a legitimate incentive program established by his employer.
    B. No, because Kite Brothers has a favorable track record and can provide excellent service to the client.
    C. Yes, because Lewis did not disclose the compensation he earned for the referral to another department within Kite Brothers.

134. Which of the following statements is CORRECT regarding situations in which local law may be at odds with CFA Institute Standards?
    A. If the applicable local law or regulation imposes a higher degree of responsibility than the Code and Standards, members and candidates still must follow the Code and Standards.
    B. Legally permitted practices are acceptable, even if inconsistent with CFA Institute Standards, as long as the inconsistency is clearly disclosed.
    C. Members and candidates must comply with all applicable local laws and regulations in their professional activities.

135. Ron Brenner, CFA, manages portfolios of high net worth individuals for Wealth Builders International. One of his clients, John Perlman, offers Brenner several inducements above those provided by his employer to motivate superior performance in managing his portfolio. Perlman offers Brenner and his family the use of his 42-foot yacht and crew for a week in June if Brenner succeeds in earning a return that exceeds his portfolio's benchmark by two percentage points any year during the next three years. Immediately after receiving this proposal, Brenner notifies his manager via e-mail about the terms and conditions of this supplemental, contingent compensation agreement, and his employer grants permission. Which of the following statements is CORRECT, relating to Brenner's compliance with CFA Institute Standard on additional compensation arrangements?
    A. Brenner must notify "all parties involved" which includes his other clients.
    B. Brenner has complied with CFA Institute Standards.
    C. This inducement is excessive and should be declined because it could cause partiality in the handling of other client accounts.

136. Nancy Wiley, CFA, suspects that one of her clients is involved in illegal money-laundering activity, and may have large amounts of unreported income. In order to comply with CFA Institute Standards, what is Wiley's best course of action?
    A. Report the suspected activity to the authorities, as required by law.
    B. Report the activity and resign from managing that particular client's account.
    C. Inform her supervisor, check with her firm's compliance department and possibly outside counsel, and allow her employer to determine the proper steps to take.

137. Clint Durham is a managing director for a regional branch office of a large national brokerage company. Durham oversees all sales personnel on the retail and institutional trade desks in his office. He does not directly manage any client accounts, although from time to time he will assist his sales staff in handling some of the larger clients' needs. The research department has recently issued a downgrade on an equity that represents a significant holding in several of the branch's client accounts. The report was distributed to all clients simultaneously via fax and e-mail as well as a hard copy of the report that was sent through the mail. One of Durham's sales staff has asked Durham to accompany him to lunch with a large client to more fully discuss the implications of the downgrade. According to the Code and Standards, this would:
    A. be in violation because Durham would not be treating all clients equally.
    B. not be in violation because all clients were notified of the downgrade at the same time.
    C. be in violation because to directly handle clients falls outside of Durham's duty to his employer.

138. As an investment counselor, Linda Buck, CFA, makes numerous recommendations about buying and selling securities to her clients. Buck is aware she must maintain appropriate records to support the reasonableness of such recommendations. The Standard of Practice recommends that the minimum amount of time the records should be kept in the absence of local regulatory guidance is:
    A. 4 years.
    B. 7 years.
    C. 10 years.

Quantitative Methods

139. Which of the following is *most likely* a correct statement about the lognormal distribution?
    A. The lognormal distribution is bounded below by zero and skewed to the right.
    B. The lognormal distribution confidence intervals are similar to the normal distribution.
    C. Stock prices must have a normal distribution to use the lognormal distribution.

140. Lauren Pollard is convinced that the mean return on SDC stock is not equal to the mean return on FSE stock. Pollard takes a sample of daily returns on both stocks for a 10-year period and estimates that the mean returns for SDC and FSE stock are 10% and 12%, respectively. Based on a hypothesis test at a 99% confidence level, Pollard has erroneously rejected her null hypothesis that the mean returns on SDC and FSE stocks are equal. Which of the following statements is *least likely* correct?
    A. Pollard has committed a type II error.
    B. The probability of a type I error in this case is 1/100.
    C. The probability of a type II error in this case is greater than 1/100.

141. Merle Newman is forecasting unit demand of Tilt Company, a producer of specialty pinball machines. Newman lists his results in the following table:

Unit Forecast	Probability Function
500	0.20
1,000	0.20
1,500	0.20
2,000	0.20
2,500	0.20

Which of the following is *closest* to the probability that Tilt Company unit demand will be between 1,000 and 2,000 units?
    A. 20%.
    B. 60%.
    C. 80%.

142. The joint probability distribution for the return of two retail stocks, A-Marts and Shops R Us, is provided below.

Retail Scenario	Probability	Return for A-Marts	Return for Shops R Us
Good	0.35	0.20	0.10
Average	0.50	0.04	0.02
Poor	0.15	−0.20	−0.10

The covariance between returns for A-Marts and Shops R Us is:
    A. less than 0.
    B. at least 0, but less than 0.01.
    C. at least 0.01, but less than 0.02.

143. Norton Hurro, CFA, is the portfolio manager for the Universe Fund. The market value of the Universe Fund was $10 million at the beginning of year 1. The following events took place in the Universe Fund over the past two years:

    • Dividends totaling $500,000 were paid to shareholders at the end of year 1.
    • Withdrawals totaling $2 million were made by shareholders at the end of year 1.
    • The per share rate of return on the Universe Fund in year 1 was 10.0%.
    • Dividends totaling $400,000 were paid to shareholders at the end of year 2.
    • The year 2 year-end market value of the Universe Fund was $9 million.
    • The per share rate of return on the Universe Fund in year 2 was 11.5%.
    • No dividends were reinvested by the shareholders.

    Calculate the money-weighted return on the Universe Fund over the 2-year period.
    A. Between 9.5% and 10.0%.
    B. Between 10.0% and 10.5%.
    C. Between 10.5% and 11.0%.

144. William Milhouse conducts a study of factors affecting company return on equity, defined as net income divided by shareholder equity. Initially, Milhouse estimates that the probability that the retail sector ROE will rise next year equals 40% and that the probability that consumer sentiment will increase next year equals 54%. Milhouse also estimates that the conditional probability that consumer sentiment rises given an increase in retail sector ROE equals 70%. Which of the following conclusions is *most likely* correct?
    A. The conditional probability of an increase in retail sector ROE given an increase in consumer sentiment exceeds 40%.
    B. The probability of increases in both consumer sentiment and retail sector ROE exceeds 70%.
    C. The conditional probability of a decrease in retail sector ROE given a decrease in consumer sentiment is less than 40%.

145. Jacques Welch, security analyst for Z-Investments, selects stocks based on a proprietary stock screen. Returns on stocks satisfying Welch's stock screen are assumed to be normally distributed with the following characteristics:

    - Mean annual return = 10%
    - Standard deviation = 5%

    Welch's supervisor at Z-Investments asks Welch to determine the probability that a randomly selected stock satisfying the stock screen will lose money next year. The probability of losing money is *closest* to:
    A. 2.5%.
    B. 5.0%.
    C. 10.0%.

146. A sample of 100 venture capital investments has been examined by VCI, a venture capital firm. VCI conducts tests of hypotheses on venture capital mean rates of return, relying on normal probability distribution theory. The results of their tests lead VCI to not reject the null hypothesis that the population mean rate of return for venture capital investments equals 15%. Tests were conducted over a period during which the market return was 10%. The *best* interpretation of this result is:
    A. most sampled venture capital investments earned a return greater than the market return.
    B. the average rate of return for the 100 sampled venture capital investments equaled 15%.
    C. the sampled average rate of return for venture capital investments did not provide sufficient evidence to contradict the null hypothesis.

147. Harry Lloyd wants to construct a 95% confidence interval for a population mean. Lloyd has gathered 100 observations to calculate the confidence interval, but does not know the variance of the population. In order to construct the confidence interval to be as narrow as possible, which of the following distributions should Lloyd use?
    A. t-distribution.
    B. z-distribution.
    C. either the t-distribution or the z-distribution.

148. Assumptions of technical analysis are *least likely* to include that:
    A. security prices exhibit persistent trends.
    B. current security prices reflect all available information.
    C. both rational and irrational behavior drive supply and demand.

149. An analyst has provided a comparative analysis of the chi-square distribution and the *F*-distribution for a new employee training session she is conducting for her firm. Which of the analyst's following conclusions is correct?
    A. Both chi-square and *F*-statistic test the variance of two normally distributed populations.
    B. Both the chi-square test and F-statistic test are robust to violations of underlying assumptions.
    C. Both the chi-square distribution and *F*-distribution are asymmetrical and defined by degrees of freedom.

150. Jack Long, CFA, is evaluating the retirement account of John Smith. Smith currently has $500,000 and will retire in 12 years. Smith plans to contribute $12,700 per year. If Smith needs $2 million at retirement, which of the following is *closest* to the return required?
    A. 10%.
    B. 11%.
    C. 12%.

151. David Hick, CFA, is reviewing the monthly performance of his fund over the past 20 years. The mean performance was 11.7% with a standard deviation of 21.4%. The return distribution is shown graphically below.

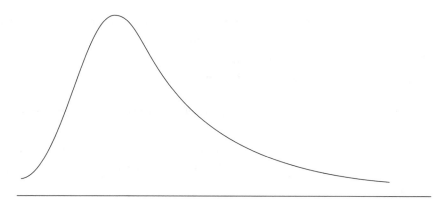

Indicate the relationship of the mean, median, and mode in the above distribution.
    A. Mean < median < mode.
    B. Mean < median > mode.
    C. Mean > median > mode.

152. Assume you bought stock in PQ Inc. at the beginning of year 1 for $20 per share. The price at the end of year 1 was $10, and at the end of year 2 the price was $22. What is the annual geometric rate of return for the 2-year period?
    A. 3.22%.
    B. 4.88%.
    C. 5.00%.

Economics

153. Domino Bank has deposits of $50 million. Domino has loans outstanding in the amount of $41 million. Assume the reserve requirement is 15%. If Domino sells $2 million worth of their short-term U.S. Government securities to the Federal Reserve, then Domino would:
    A. be able to make additional loans of $3.2 million.
    B. be able to make additional loans of $1.7 million.
    C. be able to make additional loans of $1.5 million.

154. When the price of milk in Germany changed from €1.00 per liter to €1.70 per liter, the quantity supplied did not change. The supply of milk in Germany is *closest* to being:
    A. perfectly elastic, meaning elasticity of supply is infinite.
    B. perfectly inelastic, meaning elasticity of supply is zero.
    C. perfectly inelastic, meaning elasticity of supply is infinite.

155. An economist has noted a permanent increase in demand for a certain product in an industry, and a new lower-cost technology adopted in the production of that product. Indicate the *most likely* independent effects of each of these changes on the price of this product in the short run.
    A. The increase in demand and lower cost technology both increase the product price.
    B. The increase in demand increases product price and the lower cost technology decreases product price.
    C. The increase in demand decreases product price and the lower cost technology increases product price.

156. Potential problems in implementing the utilitarian principle *most likely* include:
    A. the costs of income transfer and the shrinking of the economic pie.
    B. the costs of income transfer but not the shrinking of the economic pie.
    C. the shrinking of the economic pie but not the costs of income transfer.

157. An economist finds the following characteristics for the market for two products, S and T:

Product	Firm's Pricing Power	Concentration Ratio
S	Considerable	High
T	Some	Low

Based on the above characteristics, the economist could conclude that the industry for Product S is:
A. an oligopoly and the industry for Product T is also an oligopoly.
B. an oligopoly and the industry for Product T is monopolistic competition.
C. monopolistic competition and the industry for product T is an oligopoly.

158. An economist has noted that at wage rates of both $15 per hour and $35 per hour, the market supply of labor in a particular industry is 50 hours of labor per day. Which of the following *best* explains the economist's observation of the supply of labor at the $35 per hour wage rate?
A. Capital effect.
B. Income effect.
C. Substitution effect.

159. The difference in pricing policy between monopolistic firms and purely competitive firms is *best* explained by which of the following?
A. The profit maximizing output level for monopolists occurs at lower levels of production than for purely competitive firms.
B. Monopolistic firms maximize profits by setting output such that marginal revenue exceeds marginal cost.
C. Monopolistic firms maximize profits by setting output such that marginal revenue is maximized.

160. Which of the following describes the *most likely* relation among the required reserve ratio (RRR), the maximum deposit expansion multiplier (DEM), and the money multiplier (MM)?
A. RRR < DEM < MM.
B. DEM < MM < RRR.
C. RRR < MM < DEM.

161. If there is an increase in the quantity of money at full employment, in the long run there will *most likely* be:
A. an increase in the price level and a decrease in real GDP.
B. an increase in the price level and no effect on real GDP
C. no effect on the price level and no effect on real GDP.

162. An analyst makes the following statements regarding aggregate demand. Which of the analyst's statements is *least likely* to be correct?
    A. The aggregate demand curve is a downward sloping graph of the relationship between the price level and real aggregate demand, which is measured as consumption + investment + government spending + net exports.
    B. An increase in the price level shifts the aggregate demand curve downward (left).
    C. An increase in expected future income shifts the aggregate demand curve outward (right).

163. The Federal Reserve has decided to raise the federal funds rate (the interest rate that banks charge each other for overnight loans). In order to implement this policy, the Federal Reserve will *most likely*:
    A. sell government securities in the open market.
    B. increase currency exchange rates (cause domestic currency to appreciate).
    C. set a lower price on Treasury bills and notes that it is auctioning.

164. Rusty Brown worked at a food processing plant. In a move to reduce costs, the plant automated the production line where Brown worked. Brown was laid off because he was not adequately trained to work the new equipment. Gilda Gold was the bookkeeper for a coal mine that was closed because it could not meet safety standards. Identify which type of unemployment is illustrated by each worker.
    A. Brown and Gold are both examples of frictional unemployment.
    B. Brown is an example of structural unemployment and Gold is an example of regulatory unemployment.
    C. Brown is an example of structural unemployment and Gold is an example of frictional unemployment.

Financial Reporting and Analysis

165. The main objectives of an independent audit are to:
    A. determine whether employees of the entity comply with established policies and to verify inventory amounts and cash balances.
    B. selectively examine evidence supporting the amounts and disclosures in the financial statements and to prepare the necessary financial statements for reporting purposes.
    C. determine whether the financial statements were prepared in accordance with generally accepted accounting principles and to selectively examine evidence supporting the amounts and disclosures in the financial statements.

166. Under U.S. GAAP, dividends paid to shareholders should be classified in the cash flow statement as:
    A. operating activity.
    B. financing activity.
    C. investing activity.

167. Joe's Supermarket has been experiencing rising product prices, while quantities sold have remained stable. The company uses the LIFO method to account for its inventory. If the company had used the FIFO method, what impact would it have had on the company's working capital?
    A. Higher working capital balance.
    B. Lower working capital balance.
    C. No impact on working capital.

168. Gravel Inc. purchased a large crane to improve the production efficiency of its roadway construction division. The cost of the machine was $550,000 and it has a useful life of ten years, at which point the equipment will have a salvage value of $50,000. Depreciation expense for the second year of the asset's life using the double declining balance method is *closest* to:
    A. $50,000.
    B. $88,000.
    C. $110,000.

169. On January 1, National Beverage Vending Corporation (NBV) had 100,000 shares of common stock issued and outstanding. On June 1, the company repurchased 20,000 shares at $12 per share. On August 1, the common stock was split 2 for 1. Weighted average shares outstanding for the year are *closest* to:
    A. 83,333.
    B. 93,333.
    C. 176,667.

170. A food wholesale company has an investment portfolio of frequently traded securities and longer-term investments that are available for sale. U.S. GAAP requires unrealized gains and losses on the longer-term investments to be reported:
    A. in non-operating income and expense.
    B. in a separate section following net income.
    C. as other comprehensive income on the statement of changes in owners' equity.

171. Under U.S. GAAP, costs of a 2-year final testing program for a new drug would be:
    A. measured at actual cost as they occur and recorded as expenses on the income statement.
    B. measured at the present value of expected costs for the 2-year program and capitalized as an intangible asset.
    C. estimated and expensed in equal amounts over the next two years.

172. An analyst makes the following statements relating to the advantages of using off-balance-sheet financing.

    Statement 1: Off-balance-sheet financing reduces the amount of debt reported on the balance sheet and lowers measures of financial leverage.

    Statement 2: Off-balance-sheet financing allows companies to avoid debt restrictions in loan agreements, allowing the use of additional lower cost debt to finance operations.

    Are these statements correct?
    A. Both statements are correct.
    B. Neither statements is correct.
    C. One one of the statements is correct.

173. Registar Corp. reports under U.S. GAAP and has acquired a mining property from the state government that will be used for 10 years, at which time the firm expects to spend $120 million to put the property back in condition to meet the terms of their purchase transaction. What effect will properly accounting for these $120 million in costs have on the firm's equity and return on assets in the third year after the acquisition, compared to not reporting the expected future costs of returning the property to acceptable condition at the end of its useful life?
    A. Both will increase.
    B. Both will decrease.
    C. One will increase and one will decrease.

174. For an analyst, disclosures in the financial statement footnotes and MD&A about financing liabilities would be *most useful* in determining the:
    A. firm's leverage.
    B. market value of the firm's outstanding debt.
    C. timing and amount of future financing cash flows.

©2008 Kaplan Schweser

175. Which of the following is reported as a financing activity on the cash flow statement?
    A. Conversion of debt to equity.
    B. Repayment of long-term debt.
    C. Acquisition of a company through the assumption of its liabilities.

176. The Neptune Company uses the LIFO inventory method and, for the year just ended, its cost of goods sold (COGS) was $70 million. Neptune's beginning inventory was $90 million and ending inventory was $100 million. The market value of Neptune's beginning inventory was $110 million and the market value of its ending inventory was $125 million. Had Neptune used the FIFO inventory method, its COGS for the year just ended would have been *closest to*:
    A. $65 million.
    B. $70 million.
    C. $75 million.

177. Jessica Hightower, CFA, is analyzing the financial statements for a local industrial solvent producer, TYU Corporation. TYU's LIFO reserve fell from $50 million at the end of 2007 to $40 million at the end of 2008. Over the same time period, TYU was able to increase the number of units sold by 7%. In making adjustments to the income statement to reflect economic reality, Hightower should adjust income:
    A. only if the decline was caused by falling prices.
    B. only if the decline was caused by inventory liquidation.
    C. if the decline was caused by either falling prices or inventory liquidation.

178. If Padre Inc. overstates the salvage values of its depreciable assets, which of the following statements is most correct?
    A. Depreciation expense is overstated and fixed asset turnover is overstated.
    B. Net income is overstated and debt-to-equity is overstated.
    C. Depreciation expense is understated and debt-to-assets is understated.

179. Red Company acquired Raider Incorporated at the end of last year. As a part of the acquisition, Red recognized goodwill of $75,000. At the end of this year, the following data was compiled:

Fair value of Red Company	$600,000
Fair value of Raider Company	$400,000
Carrying value of Red Company	$540,000
Carrying value of Raider Company	$385,000*
*including goodwill	

According to U.S GAAP, Red Company should test for impairment and recognize:
A. a $15,000 loss.
B. a $60,000 gain.
C. no gain or loss.

180. Glenn Dock, CFA, is reviewing the financial statements of Dot Corporation, a small oil and gas producer. The company has a large cash position which is invested entirely in tax-free municipal bonds. Also, Dot uses accelerated depreciation for tax purposes and straight-line depreciation for financial reporting. Which of the following statements about Dot's interest income and depreciation method is *most accurate*?
A. Both interest income and the depreciation method will necessitate the use of a valuation allowance account.
B. The interest income will result in a deferred tax asset and the depreciation method will result in a deferred tax liability.
C. The depreciation expense causes a temporary difference between income tax expense and taxes payable, and the interest income creates a permanent difference.

181. JiffyCo's pre-tax income is $1,000 and its tax rate is 40%. JiffyCo purchased a $200 asset with no salvage value which is depreciated on a straight-line basis for four years for tax purposes and five years for financial reporting. At the end of the second year, which of the following statements is *most accurate*?
A. Taxable income for year 1 was $1,010.
B. The asset's carrying value is greater than the tax base.
C. The deferred tax asset has a balance of $8.

182. ABC and DEF are identical firms except the interest rate on ABC's fixed rate debt is lower than DEF's. If interest rates are increasing, which of the following statements is *most accurate*?
    A. ABC has a higher borrowing capacity and is more solvent as compared to DEF.
    B. ABC has a higher borrowing capacity but is less solvent as compared to DEF.
    C. ABC has a lower borrowing capacity but is more solvent as compared to DEF.

183. Jack Capelli, CFA, is reviewing the risk of HYCo. On August 2, 2008, due to the subprime disaster in the United States, the yield spread of HYCo's bonds increased from 250 bps to 450 bps (relative to Treasury securities). Capelli obtained the following information from HYCo's financial statements and footnotes:

Number of bonds outstanding	100,000
Par value	$1,000
Coupon	5.5%
Market rate at issuance	5.5%
Coupon payment schedule	Annual
Coupon payment date	August 1
Maturity date	August 1, 2011
Treasury yield	4.5%

Which of the following adjustments should Capelli make to HYCo's balance sheet in order to reflect the current market conditions of HYCo's debt?
    A. Capelli should reduce the book value of the debt from $100,000,000 to $91,140,469.
    B. Capelli should reduce the book value of shareholders' equity by $8,859,531.
    C. No adjustment is necessary.

184. Which of following would *most likely* be lower if a company used operating leases rather than finance (capital) leases?
    A. Return on assets.
    B. Interest coverage.
    C. Debt-to-equity ratio.

185. Bay Airlines leases a fleet of 100 airplanes used to transport freight. Bay structures the terms of all aircraft leases such that the leases are classified as operating leases. Annual lease payments for Bay's latest airplane acquisition is $1,000. If the company were to capitalize the lease, the reclassification would effectively increase interest expense by $600 and amortization expense by $450. Under U.S. GAAP, the effect of capitalizing the lease on Bay's cash flow is:
   A. a reduction of cash flow from operations.
   B. a reduction of cash flow from financing.
   C. an increase in cash flow from investing.

186. What immediate effect will the issuance of preferred stock have on the reported total debt-to-capital ratio?
   A. No effect on the total debt-to-capital ratio.
   B. A higher total debt-to-capital ratio.
   C. A lower total debt-to-capital ratio.

187. Below are selected data from Denton Corporation's 2007 and 2008 financial statements:

	2007	2008
Preferred stock, 8%, $100 par, nonconvertible	$12.5 million	$12.5 million
Common stock, $10 par	$3 million	$4 million
Additional paid-in-capital, common stock	$30 million	$40 million
Retained earnings	$75 million	$88 million
Treasury stock, at cost	$4 million	$4 million
Net income for the year ended	$9 million	$14 million
Dividends in arrears	$0	$0

Denton's return on common equity for 2008 is *closest* to:
   A. 10.9%.
   B. 11.2%.
   C. 12.1%.

188. BVC Corp. has been experiencing a declining return on equity (ROE) over the past few years. Analysts from Milton Consulting have been hired to determine the reasons for BVC's poor performance. According to the information below, what is the *most likely* reason for the decline in BVC's ROE?

	Prior Year	Current Year
Tax Burden	0.60	0.62
Interest Burden	0.80	0.81
EBIT Margin	0.26	0.26
Asset Turnover	1.06	1.06
ROE	0.15	0.14

   A. Leverage has declined.
   B. The tax rate has increased.
   C. Net profit margin has declined.

189. The table below provides a ratio comparison of Clean Corp and Half Company.

	Clean Corp	*Half Company*
EBITDA/Interest	5.1x	2.3x
Average annual revenues	$25 billion	$9 billion
EBITDA/Average assets	22%	12%
Total debt/EBITDA	12.4x	6.1x

   Based solely on the information provided, state whether Clean Corp *most likely* has a higher, lower, or the same credit rating as Half Company.
   A. The same credit rating.
   B. A lower credit rating.
   C. A higher credit rating.

190. The IFRS Framework for the Preparation of Financial Statements is most useful for decision makers if financial statements exhibit four qualitative characteristics. However, there are potential constraints to realizing this goal. Which one of the following is *least likely* to be a constraint?
   A. Completeness versus reliability.
   B. Cost versus benefits.
   C. Trade-offs between statement characteristics.

191. Darvo Enterprises is considering a machinery replacement project expected to expand production capacity. The project requires the purchase of a machine costing $680,000, plus shipping costs of $13,500 and installation costs of $6,500. A feasibility study costing $25,000 was performed last year to determine the necessity of new machinery. Financial data related to the project is given in the following table:

	Year		
	1	2	3
Net Income	458,000	3,000	−192,000
Cash Flows	675,000	220,000	25,000
Average Book Value = 375,000			
Net Present Value = 71,746			

Which of the following statements regarding Darvo's proposed project is *correct?*
A. The profitability index for the project equals 1.1.
B. The payback period for the project equals 1.3 years.
C. The average accounting rate of return for the project equals 12.8%.

192. Which of the following situations is *least likely* to be problematic when using the internal rate of return (IRR) as an investment decision-making criterion?
A. A five year project requires a net investment today and has positive cash flows in all but the final year.
B. A firm is presented with several independent projects, all of which have an IRR greater than the firm's cost of capital.
C. A firm with a limited capital budget can make a small investment in a project with a large IRR or a large investment in a project with a small IRR.

193. An analyst is studying the tax exposures and capital structures of Alpha Corporation and Beta Corporation. Both companies have equivalent capital structures with both debt and equity components. Pre-tax component costs of capital are the same for both companies. Alpha has total capital of $850 million while Beta has total capital of $370 million. The marginal tax rates for Alpha and Beta are 35% and 40%, respectively. Which of the following statements regarding Alpha and Beta is *least likely* correct?
A. Beta Corporation has a lower current WACC than Alpha Corporation.
B. An increase in Alpha Corporation's tax rate would decrease its WACC.
C. A tax-rate change will affect Alpha Corporation's cost of equity more than Beta Corporation.

194. Allen Company's cost of preferred equity is 6.25%. The preferred pays a $2.50 dividend and has a par value of $50. Which of the following is *closest* to the current price of Allen's preferred equity?
     A. $30 per share.
     B. $40 per share.
     C. $50 per share.

195. In evaluating possible capital projects in the United States, Europe, and a number of developing countries:
     A. a sovereign yield spread should be added to the market risk premium in CAPM calculations to adjust for volatility in the developing country's debt markets.
     B. a reward to risk ratio should be estimated using a large sample of countries with credit ratings and equity markets and should then be applied to the credit rating of the developing country to estimate the cost of equity.
     C. a developing country equity premium should be added to the equity premium in CAPM calculations. This premium includes a sovereign yield spread to adjust for volatility in debt markets and a further adjustment for volatility in the country's equity markets relative to local debt markets.

196. An analyst has calculated the following statistics for Company X and Company Y.

	Company X		Company Y	
	Year 1	Year 2	Year 1	Year 2
Number of days of inventory	18	22	33	24
Number of days of receivables	14	16	14	12
Number of days of payables	19	20	18	20

Which of the following statements provides the *most accurate* calculation and interpretation of the net operating cycle for Company X or Company Y?
     A. Company Y's net operating cycle was 16 days in year 2, an improvement in liquidity compared to year 1.
     B. Company Y's net operating cycle was 36 days in year 2, a decline in liquidity compared to year 1.
     C. Company X's net operating cycle was 18 days in year 2, an improvement in liquidity compared to year 1.

197. A portfolio manager just added to his portfolio $1 million of U.S. Treasury bills maturing in 90 days at a price of $990,390 and discount rate of 3.8%. The existing portfolio consists of the following investments (market values are given).

    - Bank commercial paper maturing in 90 days with a bond equivalent yield of 4.34% and a market value of $100,000.
    - Bank certificates of deposit maturing in six months with a bond equivalent yield of 4.84% and a market value of $200,000.

    The short-term benchmark yield is 4.08%. Which of the following is *closest* to the weighted average yield on the portfolio following the U.S. Treasury bill purchase?
    A. 4.11%.
    B. 3.99%.
    C. 4.06%.

198. For corporations that are publicly traded in the United States, which of the following best describes sources of information related to takeover defenses and proposing shareholder initiatives?
    A. Information on existing takeover provisions can be found in a company's articles of incorporation.
    B. Information on proposed shareholder initiatives can be found in a company's SEC form 10K.
    C. Information on the qualifications of board members can be found in a company's SEC form 10Q.

Portfolio Management

199. An analyst makes the following two statements about the assumptions underlying the use of the efficient frontier to construct an optimal portfolio of assets.

    Statement 1: Investors believe all investments are represented by a probability distribution of expected returns.

    Statement 2: Investors base investment decisions solely on the expected risk of the investment.

    Determine whether each statement correctly describes one of the assumptions.
    A. Only Statement 1 is correct.
    B. Only Statement 2 is correct.
    C. Both Statement 1 and 2 are correct.

200. MNB Capital manages money for high net worth individuals located within the United States. MNB's disciplined investment approach selects a small number of domestic equities selling at significant discounts to book value. If MNB wanted to implement the capital asset pricing theory to evaluate equity investments, which of the following is *least appropriate* as an input to construct the market portfolio?
    A. U.S. Treasury bills.
    B. Noninvestment grade bonds.
    C. Collectible art work sold in Europe.

201. Juliet Kaufman manages a large portfolio of risky assets for a family of investors. The portfolio consists primarily of stocks but also includes a small allocation of fixed-income investments. Currently, the expected return and standard deviation of the portfolio are 14.0% and 12.0%, respectively. Kaufman is considering adding one of three stocks to the portfolio. Data on each stock's expected return, beta, standard deviation, and covariance with the existing portfolio are presented below. Which stock should Kaufman add to the portfolio?

Stock	E(R)	Beta	S.D.	Covariance
A	12.0%	0.85	11.0%	0.00
B	13.0%	1.08	10.0%	−0.01
C	15.0%	0.97	8.0%	0.02

    A. Stock A.
    B. Stock B.
    C. Stock C.

202. Martin Philips evaluates stocks using the security market line while also considering the transaction costs of each buy and sell decision. Philips assumes that both high and low beta stocks incur the same positive percentage transactions costs on all stock trades. Which of the following is *least likely* an effect of Philips' assumptions?
    A. The intercept of the security market line will increase for buy signals.
    B. The intercept of the security market line will decrease for sell signals.
    C. The slope of the security market line will increase for both buy and sell signals.

203. Patrick Manning owns stock in Lumber Providers with a return variance equal to 16%. Manning is considering the addition of Smithson Homebuilders to his portfolio. The variance of returns for Smithson Homebuilders equals 25%, and its correlation of returns with Lumber Providers equals –0.60. The covariance of returns between Lumber Providers and Smithson Homebuilders is *closest* to:
    A. –15.0.
    B. –0.024.
    C. –0.120.

204. A portfolio manager for Klein Capital Management has been slowly increasing the number of stocks in his portfolio randomly over the last five years. Currently, the portfolio contains 20 stocks. Over time, what has *most likely* happened to the risk of the portfolio if macroeconomic variables have remained steady?
    A. Unsystematic risk has been decreasing.
    B. Systematic risk has been decreasing.
    C. Both systematic and unsystematic risk remain at average levels.

Asset Valuation

205. Suppose that stock prices are mean reverting over a three to five year period. Which form of the efficient market hypothesis does this violate?
    A. None.
    B. Weak form only.
    C. Semistrong and weak forms only.

206. Brad Rich uses an investment strategy that assumes stock prices will not reflect quarterly earnings surprises as quickly as suggested by the efficient market hypothesis. Rich believes stocks will earn positive abnormal rates of return over the six months following an earnings surprise. Which form of the efficient market hypothesis would this violate?
    A. None.
    B. Weak form only.
    C. Semistrong and weak forms only.

207. One year ago, Yong Kim bought a preferred stock that had a 6% dividend yield. Now, one year later, Kim sells the stock which is how selling at a 5% dividend yield. The preferred stock pays a fixed annual dividend, which Kim received right before selling. What rate of return did Kim realize on his investment?
    A. 14%.
    B. 20%.
    C. 26%.

208. Roger Templeton, an analyst for Bridgetown Capital Management, is studying past market data to identify risk factors that produce anomalous returns. He tests monthly data on each of 60 financial and economic variables over a 15-year period to find which ones are related to stock index returns. Based on this research, Templeton identifies three variables that show statistically significant relationships with equity returns. He presents his results to Bridgetown's managers and recommends implementing a trading program based on changes in these three variables. What is the *most likely* reason why Bridgetown's management should be skeptical of the anomalies Templeton has identified? The results suffer from:
   A. data mining bias.
   B. survivorship bias.
   C. small sample bias.

209. Horace Lance, CFA, states that the efficient market hypothesis and its rigorous testing have yielded many benefits to investors. Lance makes the following statements concerning an efficient market.

   Statement 1: The Efficient Market Hypothesis (EMH) assumes that changes in security prices occur in a random fashion.

   Statement 2: Portfolio managers should reduce trading turnover of client accounts.

   Statement 3: The EMH establishes that the expected rate of return is the risk-free rate plus a risk premium that is the security beta times the market price of risk.

   Which of Lance's statements is *least likely* to be correct?
   A. Statement 1
   B. Statement 2
   C. Statement 3

210. George Judas, CFA, manages a small capitalization mutual fund. Judas only invests in companies with low price to earnings ratios. Judas states that research suggests that returns on both small capitalization and low P/E companies are anomalous, in that they will provide investors with superior risk-adjusted long-term returns. Judas' supervisor counters with the following two observations.

Observation 1: The research does not adequately account for the level of risk of small capitalization and low price to earnings ratio companies.

Observation 2: The research on small capitalization and low price to earnings ratio companies suffers from a small sample bias.

Are the supervisor's observations *most likely* correct?
A. Yes.
B. Only Observation 1 is correct.
C. Only Observation 2 is correct.

211. At the end of the last 12-month period, Romano's Italian Foods had net income and ending equity for the company of $16.68 million and $115 million, respectively. Romano's declared a $7.5 million dividend for the year. Using internally generated funds, Romano's can grow its equity by approximately:
A. 8.0% per year.
B. 10.0% per year.
C. 14.5% per year.

212. Van Jeffery, CFA, utilizes price multiples to evaluate the attractiveness of potential investment opportunities. However, Jeffery's supervisor does not support using price multiples exclusively in making investment decisions. The supervisor points out the following:

Statement 1: P/S ratios are not able to capture the different cost structures of companies.

Statement 2: The P/CF ratio is more stable than the P/E ratio.

Statement 3: An advantage of the P/B ratio (unlike the P/E ratio) is that the P/B ratio cannot be negative.

Which of the supervisor's three statements is *least likely* to be correct?
A. Statement 1
B. Statement 2
C. Statement 3

213. Rock Inc. maintains a policy of paying 30% of earnings to its investors in the form of dividends. Rock is expected to generate a return on equity of 9.3%. Rock's beta is 1.5. The equity risk premium is 6% and U.S. Treasury notes are yielding 3%. Rock's required rate of return is closest to:
    A. 9.0%.
    B. 9.3%.
    C. 12.0%.

214. Ben Click is analyzing an equity security using price-to-earnings, price-to-sales, price-to-book value, and price-to-cash flow ratios. Which statement correctly identifies a drawback of using one of the listed ratios?
    A. Earning power is a chief driver of investment value.
    B. Accounting effects may compromise the use of book value.
    C. Sales are generally less subject to distortion or manipulation than are other fundamentals.

215. Darlene Villanueva provides analytical support for portfolio managers at a small investment management firm. Villanueva's latest report highlights two companies, Company X and Company Y. Company X has consistently earned a higher rate of return on assets than their cost of capital, but the stock price is substantially greater than the fair value. Company Y's earnings have been pulled down by the recent economic slowdown, but its stock price has remained stable despite the negative returns on the overall market. Which of the following statements correctly categorizes the two companies?
    A. Stock X is a value stock and Company Y is a defensive company.
    B. Stock X is a growth stock and Company Y is a cyclical company.
    C. Company X is a growth company and Stock Y is a defensive stock.

216. Jim Boo, CFA, is analyzing Justin Corp., a maker of home appliances. Boo's research provides the following facts:

    - Justin's stock price is $60 per share.
    - Expected growth rate of dividends is 5%.
    - Expected retention ratio is 60%.
    - Justin's book value is $90 per share.
    - Required rate of return is 10%.

    Calculate Justin's expected price to earnings ratio (P_0/E_1).
    A. 8.0x.
    B. 10.0x.
    C. 12.0x.

217. A 10-year, semiannual-pay $1,000 bond with a 6% coupon is currently priced at $864.10, to yield 8%. If yields increase by 50 basis points (bp), the new price of the bond would be $833.82. If yields decrease by 50 bp, the new price of the bond would be $895.78. The expected percentage change in the price of this bond for a 100 bp change in yield is *closest* to:
    A. 3.6%.
    B. 7.2%.
    C. 14.4%.

218. The current price of a $1,000 par value, 6-year, 4.2% semiannual coupon bond is $958.97. The bond's PVBP is *closest* to:
    A. $0.50.
    B. $4.20.
    C. $5.01.

219. Jack Hare, CFA, is a fixed income analyst. Hare is evaluating a 15-year zero-coupon bond, which is priced at $30.83. Determine the issue's *approximate* yield to maturity.
    A. 6%.
    B. 7%.
    C. 8%.

220. Bond X and Bond Y were issued at a premium to par value three years ago. Bond X matures in five years, and Bond Y matures in ten years. Both bonds carry the same credit rating. Bond X has a coupon of 7.25%, and Bond Y has a coupon of 8.00%. Currently the required yield for both bonds is 7.60%. Determine whether each bond is currently priced at a premium or discount to par value.
    A. Both bonds are priced at a premium.
    B. Bond X is priced at a premium, and Bond Y is priced at a discount.
    C. Bond X is priced at a discount, and Bond Y is priced at a premium

221. Charlotte Villa, CFA, is a portfolio manager analyzing two securities. The 10-year bonds of Zehmer Corp. are callable beginning in two years. The 10-year bonds of Cavalier Inc. are not callable, but have a floating coupon that adjusts annually based on a margin above comparable maturity U.S. Treasury issues with no limits on the rate adjustment. Both bond issues are rated AA. Villa uses a computer model to value individual bonds based on their zero-volatility spread and/or option-adjusted spread (OAS). She decided to increase the interest rate volatility assumption in her model without changing any of the other model inputs. Identify how this change in assumption will affect the OAS for each bond.
    A. The OAS for both bonds will increase.
    B. The OAS for both bonds will decrease.
    C. The OAS for the Zehmer bond will decrease, but the OAS for the Cavalier bond will be unchanged.

222. Rob Pirate is considering investing in a subordinated tranche in a collateralized mortgage obligation (CMO). If Pirate wishes to measure his interest rate risk for this debt security, which measure would be *most appropriate*?
    A. Modified duration
    B. Effective duration
    C. Effective convexity

223. Mark Davidson and James Case are bond traders at a large fixed-income investment firm. Both Davidson and Case have developed bond valuation models for bonds with embedded options. Using their respective valuation models, the traders have calculated the price of BMC Corp.'s callable and putable bonds. Davidson uses a yield volatility assumption of 23%, while Case uses an assumption of 31%. Other than the volatility assumption, the traders use identical inputs for the valuation models. Which of the following *best* summarizes the output of the two valuation models?
    A. Davidson's model will calculate a lower value for the call option and a lower value for the putable bond.
    B. Case's model will calculate a higher value for the call option and a lower value for the putable bond.
    C. Davidson's model will calculate a lower value for the put option and a lower value for the callable bond.

224. James Volley, CFA, is evaluating a number of municipal bonds. One of the revenue bonds on his list is marked as "prerefunded." When Volley asks his assistant about the bonds, the assistant tells him that the collateral behind the bonds is a portfolio of U.S. government securities, and that, therefore, these bonds have "less credit risk than insured municipal bonds." Which of the following statements regarding these bonds is *most accurate*?
    A. The bonds do indeed have less credit risk than insured municipal bonds.
    B. Only general obligation bonds can be prerefunded, not revenue bonds.
    C. Prerefunded bonds are secured by a cash escrow account, not by US government securities.

225. Laura Mack, is considering purchasing two Treasury securities. The first is the 7-year on-the-run Treasury issued last week that has a coupon rate of 4.98%. The second is a 7-year off-the-run Treasury that was issued two months ago and has a coupon rate of 4.74%. Which of the following statements regarding the two issues under consideration is *most accurate*?
    A. The on-the-run issue has higher reinvestment risk because of its higher coupon rate.
    B. The on-the-run issue has higher interest rate risk because of its higher coupon rate.
    C. Both the on-the-run and the off-the-run issues have equivalent interest rate risk.

226. An investor wants to take advantage of the 5-year spot rate, currently at a level of 4.0%. Unfortunately, the investor just invested all of his funds in a 2-year bond with a yield of 3.2%. The investor contacts his broker, who tells him that in two years he can purchase a 3-year bond and end up with the same return currently offered on the 5-year bond. What 3-year forward rate beginning two years from now will allow the investor to earn a return equivalent to the 5-year spot rate?
    A. 3.5%.
    B. 4.5%.
    C. 5.6%.

227. Eileen Hart, CFA, is a fixed income portfolio manager for MTY Investment Management. Hart's portfolio includes US agency mortgage-backed securities. Which of the following statements about U.S. agency mortgage-backed securities is *least accurate*?
    A. Cash flows from mortgage loans include prepayments, which could affect the future performance of Hart's portfolio.
    B. Pass-through securities issued by Ginnie Mae guarantee the timely payment of interest and principal.
    C. Collateralized mortgage obligations (CMO) redirect cash flows from the underlying mortgage pool to eliminate prepayment risk.

228. Which of the following statements about debt retirement features is **TRUE**?
    A. A bond issue must be retired in its entirety when exercising a call feature.
    B. A make-whole premium provision and call price are identical terms.
    C. A bond can be retired early even if it is nonrefundable.

229. Allison Coleman, CFA, owns a bond portfolio that includes Bond X, a callable bond with ten years to maturity that is callable at any time beginning one year from today. Coleman's portfolio also includes Bond Y, a noncallable security with ten years to maturity that carries the same credit rating as Bond X. Coleman expects interest rates to drift steadily lower over the next few years. Based on this assumption, Coleman should expect that:
    A. Bond Y will experience a larger decrease in value than Bond X.
    B. Bond X will benefit from positive convexity as rates decline.
    C. the option embedded in Bond X will increase in value.

230. Jefferson Blake invests only in bonds and other fixed-income securities. Blake believes there is a good opportunity to purchase an undervalued 4% annual pay corporate bond with three years left until maturity and a par value of $1,000. Blake observes that 1-year, 2-year, and 3-year Treasury strip rates are currently 4.0%, 4.5%, and 4.75%, respectively. What is the maximum price Blake should be willing to pay for the bond?
    A. $1,069.58.
    B. $979.93.
    C. $958.36.

231. Mark Walters' risk aversion is relatively high compared to other individual investors. Walters is interested in generating some income on his equity portfolio. Walters decides to establish a covered call position on CGF stock and simultaneously establish a protective put position on HSD stock. After establishing the covered call and protective put positions, which of the following would *least likely* describe Walters' portfolio, relative to the positions before adding the options?
    A. The HSD position will have a higher breakeven price and less downside risk.
    B. The CGF position will have a lower breakeven price and more upside potential.
    C. The HSD position will have lower upside potential and less downside risk.

232. In futures markets, the role of the clearinghouse is to:
    A. prevent arbitrage and enforce federal regulations.
    B. act as guarantor to both sides of a futures trade.
    C. reduce transaction costs by making contract prices public.

233. Morgan Dexter has been asked by his supervisor to present the features of interest rate swaps to a group of newly hired risk managers. In his presentation, Dexter notes that in a plain-vanilla interest rate swap, there is one floating rate-payer and one fixed-rate payer. Dexter points out that the netting arrangements typical to plain vanilla swaps reduce the credit risk for both counterparties. Dexter also states that some interest rate swaps may have two floating rate payers. Are Dexter's statements regarding swaps correct or incorrect?
    A. Only Dexter's statement about reduced credit risk from netting is correct.
    B. Only Dexter's statement about two floating rate payers is correct.
    C. Both statements are correct.

234. Debbie Chon, CFA, is evaluating a put option on Lincoln Industrial. Lincoln's current stock price is $64 per share and the company will pay a $0.56 dividend. The 90-day U.S. Treasury bill is yielding 5.3%. Lincoln's 3-month European call option with a strike price of $70 has a premium of $3.50. Based on the put-call parity, calculate the value of the associated Lincoln put option.
    A. $8.05
    B. $8.60
    C. $9.15

235. Peter Black is an options trader for HighSmith Investments. Black trades options on the U.S. and U.K. stock exchanges. Over the past three weeks, Black has been following the price movements of options on two companies: U.S.-based Pacific Chemicals Inc. (PCI), and U.K.-based Merchant Clothing Co. (MCC). Black has observed that over the past few days, the price of put options on PCI stock have suddenly increased, and the price of call options on MCC stock have suddenly increased. Which of the following provides the *most accurate* explanation of Black's observations? Interest rates in:
    A. the U.S. have risen and the volatility of MCC stock has risen.
    B. the U.K. have fallen and the volatility of PCI stock has risen.
    C. the U.S. have fallen and the volatility of MCC stock has risen.

236. An investor holds a long position in a futures contract on the S&P 500 Index. The futures contract has a term of three months, requires 10% margin, and has a futures price of 1,574. The investor posted $37,500 into the margin account at contract initiation. After the contract initiation, the futures price on the index experienced infrequent but dramatic drops. Two days ago, the investor received a margin call and was required to post an additional $17,500 to the margin account. Which of the following is *most likely* the maintenance margin on the contract?
    A. $17,500.
    B. $18,750.
    C. $22,500.

237. Frank Holmes, CFA, is reviewing Martha Inc, a distributor. Holmes is interested in the company's European-style call option, which has a value of $5.90. Currently, Martha's stock is trading at $33 per share and pays no dividend. The exercise price of both the call and put options is $30, with 80 days to expiration. The current risk-free rate is 5.50%. Martha's put option sells for $2.75. Calculate the synthetic call option value.
    A. $3.35
    B. $5.75
    C. $6.10

238. Kim Lee is valuing a closely held private shoe retailing company. She compares the company to other shoe retailing competitors that are publicly traded and are highly liquid. Relative to the private company, the shares of the publicly traded competitors *most likely* include a:
    A. marketability discount.
    B. minority interest discount.
    C. control premium.

239. Nina Foch, CFA, is considering investing in an exchange traded fund (ETF). However, she is unsure how the ETF compares to open-end and closed-end funds. Which of the following statements comparing ETFs with open-end and closed-end funds is *least likely* to be true?
    A. ETF shares can be sold short, while open-end fund shares cannot be shorted.
    B. The legal structure of an ETF is similar to a closed-end fund.
    C. ETF shares trade like closed-end fund shares.

240. Ann Fowler, CFA, has a client that wants to invest in hedge funds. Fowler recommends the client invest in a Fund of Funds (FOF), which will invest in a variety of hedge funds. Fowler makes the following statements:

    Statement 1:   Investing in several different types of hedge funds will reduce risk compared to investing in a single fund.

    Statement 2:   An important part of the selection process is due diligence to resolve any transparency issues.

    Which statements are correct?
    A. Only statement 1 is correct.
    B. Only statement 2 is correct.
    C. Both statements 1 and 2 are correct.

End of Afternoon Session

Exam 1
Morning Session Answers

To get valuable feedback on how your score compares to those of other Level 1 candidates, use your Username and Password to gain Online Access at schweser.com and choose the left-hand menu item "Practice Exams Vol. 2."

1. C	31. B	61. C	91. A
2. A	32. C	62. B	92. C
3. B	33. C	63. A	93. A
4. A	34. B	64. B	94. B
5. A	35. A	65. C	95. C
6. B	36. C	66. B	96. A
7. B	37. C	67. B	97. A
8. C	38. B	68. A	98. C
9. B	39. A	69. A	99. C
10. A	40. B	70. C	100. B
11. B	41. A	71. B	101. C
12. B	42. B	72. B	102. A
13. C	43. C	73. B	103. A
14. C	44. A	74. B	104. B
15. A	45. A	75. A	105. A
16. A	46. C	76. B	106. B
17. C	47. C	77. C	107. B
18. C	48. C	78. C	108. C
19. A	49. C	79. B	109. B
20. B	50. A	80. C	110. B
21. A	51. A	81. A	111. B
22. B	52. B	82. C	112. B
23. B	53. B	83. B	113. B
24. B	54. C	84. B	114. A
25. B	55. A	85. A	115. C
26. C	56. A	86. B	116. A
27. A	57. B	87. C	117. B
28. C	58. B	88. A	118. A
29. B	59. B	89. A	119. C
30. B	60. C	90. B	120. C

Exam 1
Morning Session Answers

Ethical and Professional Standards

Answers referencing the Standards of Practice are all Study Session 1, LOS 2.a, b.

1. **C** Standard VII(A) Conduct as Members and Candidates in the CFA Program. The Standard does not prohibit expressing opinions about the program or CFA Institute. Thus, Smith is not in violation. Jones and Burkett violated the Standard because they compromised the integrity of the exam process during the call by sharing information about the content of the exam.

2. **A** GIPS. Evaluating the suitability of an investment for a particular client is a concept addressed by the CFA Institute's Standards of Practice, but is not one of the concerns addressed by GIPS.

3. **B** Standard II(B). According to the Standard, members are prohibited from intentionally misleading market participants through the artificial manipulation of prices or trading data. Wilson's actions with regard to BNR stock are not intended to mislead market participants but are related to a legitimate trading strategy and thus do not violate the Standards. Even though taking the short position may have played a part in moving the price of BNR stock, it was not intended to manipulate the price. Wilson did, however, deceive market participants through his message board post related to HTC stock. Thus, Wilson violated Standard II(B) in this situation.

4. **A** Standard I(A). When applicable law and the Code and Standards have differing requirements, candidates and members must follow the stricter of either the local law or the Code and Standards.

5. **A** Standard V(B). According to the standard, clients must be made aware of the investment process used by the member and must be informed of any changes to this process. Additionally, members must include factors relevant to the analysis, determined using their reasonable judgment, in communications with clients. A change in the firm's valuation model is likely important information to clients. Green has informed all clients and prospects of the change in the model and has stated an expectation of improved results from the model without guaranteeing results or stating the improvement as fact. Smith has not violated the Standards.

6. **B** GIPS. Firms are required to present, at a minimum, five years of investment performance, or if in existence less than five years, all years since inception. After five years, the firm must present an additional annual performance history up to ten years at a minimum. Firms may link a present non-compliant history to their compliant history so long as the firm discloses the period of noncompliance and explains how the presentation is not in compliance. "Non-compliant performance periods" cannot include any time periods subsequent to 1 January 2000.

7. **B** Standard VI(B) states that family accounts that are client accounts should be treated equally with other firm accounts and should not be given special treatment nor be disadvantaged due to a family relationship with the member. However, Smith may be subject to the pre-clearance or reporting requirements of his employer.

8. **C** Standard VI(A). According to the Standard, members and candidates must disclose to their clients, prospects, and employer all situations that could reasonably be expected to compromise their independence and objectivity. Stock ownership of a company in which clients are invested would need to be disclosed to clients and the employer since a member may be tempted to purchase more stock for client accounts in order to increase the value of personal holdings. Participation on the board of directors of a company in which clients are invested would also need to be disclosed to both clients and the employer. Board positions may inhibit the member's ability to objectively determine when to sell the stock of the company and may expose the member to material nonpublic information.

9. **B** According to Standard II(A), an analyst may not use material nonpublic information. The information was material to the company's future profitability, and it was nonpublic because the lawsuit had not yet been filed and was not a matter of public record. The mosaic theory does not apply here, because the mosaic theory assumes that the information gathered is nonmaterial. The mosaic or "perceptive analyst" defense allows combining material public with nonmaterial nonpublic information, and forming investment conclusions.

10. **A** According to Standard III(A), members must put client's interest ahead of their employer's or their own interests. Members have a duty of loyalty, prudence, and care. Also, members must comply with any applicable fiduciary duties in the client relationship. Welch has violated his duty of prudence by investing the Craig Family Trust assets in a manner inconsistent with the trust investment mandate which stated the trust should have a risk/return profile that mirrors the S&P 500 Index using a passive strategy [this is also a violation of Standard III(C)]. Welch intentionally deviated from this policy statement. It is irrelevant that the strategy was successful.

11. **B** Rutherford is not treating all clients fairly and is thus violating Standard III(B) Fair Dealing. If he has an opinion regarding a possible surprise earnings announcement, this needs to be shared with all clients for which this security is appropriate.

12. **B** Standard III (C). The investment advisor should consider the following in writing an investment policy statement (IPS) for each client: (1) client identification (type and nature of clients, existence of separate beneficiaries, and approximate portion of total client assets; (2) investment objectives (return objectives and risk tolerance); (3) investor constraints (e.g., liquidity needs, expected cash flows, time horizon, tax considerations, and regulatory and legal circumstances); and (4) performance measurement benchmarks. Standard VI(A) Disclosure of Conflicts requires that members and candidates disclose all potential areas of conflict to clients but this disclosure is not part of a client's IPS.

13. **C** Standard III(B). Issuing a press release is the best way to achieve fair public dissemination. Notifying any specific analysts first is a violation, regardless of any help they may have provided in the past.

14. **C** Standard II(B), Market Manipulation, is not intended to prohibit transactions that are done in order to minimize income taxes or trading strategies that are not intended to distort prices or artificially inflate trading volume. Thus, neither Gordon nor Turpin is in violation.

15. **A** Standard V(A). Group consensus is not required in the course of preparation of analytical reports. If it were a situation in which there is no justification for the changes, Pickler may wish to have her name removed from the report. In this case, she is a junior analyst, and the investment committee has every right to make any necessary adjustments based on their expertise. In this situation, the presumption is that the investment committee, due to its superior experience, had a reasonable and adequate basis for making the changes.

16. **A** Under Standard VI(A) Disclosure of Conflicts, Malone is required to disclose to his employer all matters, including beneficial ownership of securities or other investments that reasonably could be expected to interfere with his duty to his employer or ability to make unbiased and objective recommendations. In addition, under Standard VI(A), Malone must disclose to clients all matters, including beneficial ownership of securities or other investments that reasonably could be expected to impair his ability to make unbiased and objective recommendations. Members beneficially own securities or other investments that they or a member of their immediate family own or that are held in trust for them or their immediate family.

17. **C** Standard I(D). Although she was arrested, the Standard is not intended to cover acts of "civil disobedience."

    Standard IV(A). Chavez has a duty of loyalty to her employer. While she will not be compensated for the Greensleeves' Board position, the duties may be time-consuming and should be discussed with her employer in advance.

18. **C** According to Standard IV(B), members and candidates must not accept benefits that might create a conflict of interest with their employer's interest unless they obtain prior written consent from all parties involved. After accepting this gift, Potts might be tempted to show favoritism to this client.

Quantitative Analysis

19. **A** Expected eps = $(5.2 \times 0.1) + (2.5 \times 0.4) + (1 \times 0.3) + (-1 \times 0.2) = 1.62$

    Std Dev = $\{[0.1(5.2 - 1.62)^2] + [0.4(2.5 - 1.62)^2] + [0.3(1 - 1.62)^2] + [0.2(-1 - 1.62^2)]\}^{0.5}$

    = $\{[1.282] + [0.310] + [0.115] + [1.373]\}^{0.5} = 1.75$ (Study Session 2, LOS 8.k)

20. **B** Since the median is higher than the mean, the distribution is negatively skewed. If the mean were higher than the median the distribution would be positively skewed. (Study Session 2, LOS 7.i, j)

21. **A** The question gave you the conditional probability of recession given higher oil prices as 40%. You must determine the joint probability of recession and higher oil prices using the multiplication rule for probability: $P(AB) = P(A \mid B)P(B)$. In this case, $P(A \mid B) = 0.40$ and $P(B) = 1 - 0.7 = 0.3$ (the probability of higher oil prices). Putting the two together, we get the joint probability of higher oil prices and recession: $(1 - 0.7) \times 0.4 = 0.12$. The probability of oil prices rising is an unconditional probability because it is not based on any other event. (Study Session 2, LOS 8.d, e)

22. **B** A normal probability distribution is completely identified by its *mean* and standard deviation and has a mean equal to its mode and median. (Study Session 3, LOS 9.f)

23. **B**   Since Investment 1 is compounded annually, its effective annual interest rate is equal to the stated annual rate of 6.1%.

Investment 2 has an effective annual interest rate equal to:

$$[1 + (0.06/12)]^{12} - 1 = 6.17\%$$

Investment 3 has an effective annual interest rate equal to:

$$[1 + (0.059/4)]^{4} - 1 = 6.03\%$$

Jones should choose Investment 2 since it has the highest effective annual interest rate. (Study Session 2, LOS 5.c)

24. **B**   Relative class frequency = 25/500 = 0.05; class frequency is number of observations; for lowest class (0 up to 10), there are 25 observations. (Study Session 2, LOS 7.c)

25. **B** $\ln\left(\dfrac{80}{20}\right)^{\frac{1}{5}} = 0.277 \approx 0.28$ or 28%   (Study Session 3, LOS 9.k)

26. **C**   The accumulated interest possibilities are limited because of the existence of the interest floor and cap on the floating rate and because the interest payments are made in increments of $0.01. Therefore, the accumulated interest payments are an example of a discrete random variable. Because the interest payments are paid in increments of $0.01, the graph of the probability distribution will not be a curve or a line, but rather a series of points, indicating that there is zero probability that accumulated interest will equal a value between the $0.01 increments (e.g., $500.01 and $500.02 are possible, $500.015 is not). (Study Session 3, LOS 9.a)

27. **A**   The level of significance is the probability of rejecting the null hypothesis when it is true. (Study Session 3, LOS 11.b)

28. **C**   A random number generator is used to ensure that each member of the population has an equal chance of being selected. A sample in which each member has an equal chance of being selected is known as a simple random sample. In contrast, for stratified random samples, the population is split into mutually exclusive groups or strata, and simple random samples are extracted from each strata. In the example above, however, only one group is being sampled (growth stocks). So, Weaver is not correct. The distribution of a sample statistic, such as the sample mean, is known as a sampling distribution. Alternatively, the sampling distribution is the probability distribution of the sample means obtained from repeated sampling from the same population. The distribution of the sampled stock returns is not the sampling distribution. Thus, Palmer also is incorrect. (Study Session 3, LOS 10.a)

29. **B**   Since John focuses on contrary opinion rules, he is looking for evidence that other investors are bearish. Low mutual fund cash positions suggest that mutual fund managers are fully invested – this favorable outlook would not support John's contrary bullish opinion. An investment advisory reading above 60% bearish is an indication of widespread pessimism in the market. A high put-call ratio indicates that more investors are buying put options in anticipation of lower stock prices; this bearish attitude would be bullish for a contrarian. (Study Session 3, LOS 12.c)

30. **B** $-100,000 = \text{PV}$; $6 = \text{N}$; $-100,000 = \text{PMT}$; $950,000 = \text{FV}$; $\text{CPT} \rightarrow \text{I/Y} = 10\%$. (Study Session 2, LOS 5.d)

31. **B** Time-weighted returns are used when the client exercises discretionary control over timing and amount of additions and withdrawals to the portfolio.

    Time-weighted $=[(1 + 0.15)(1 + (-0.05))]^{0.5} - 1 = 0.0452$ or 4.52%. (Study Session 2, LOS 6.c)

32. **C** Rao uses an ordinal scale. A nominal scale places data in groups but with no meaningful ranking content. An ordinal scale groups data according to a characteristic that can be ordered, such as grouping stocks based on their rates of return. Ratio scales are the strongest scale of measurement. Ratio scale amounts can be meaningfully added, subtracted, multiplied, and divided. Rao's ranking does not rise to this level (e.g., a group 4 firm does not necessarily have twice the interest coverage of a group 2 firm). (Study Session 2, LOS 7.a)

Economics

33. **C** If demand elasticity differs between different groups of consumers, the firm can maximize profits by setting different prices for each group—in this case the idea would be to raise weekend prices to take advantage of the low elasticity, and lower weekday prices to take advantage of the high elasticity. (Study Session 5, LOS 19.c)

34. **B** Consumer surplus is calculated as 1/2[quantity demanded(maximum price – market price)]. Quantity demanded is the quantity at which the market price falls on the demand curve. In this question, if the market price were $2 per gallon, the demand curve would intersect the market price at 30 gallons of gasoline. The maximum price is the highest price a consumer is willing to pay for a good. In this question the consumer is only willing to pay $5 or less per gallon of gasoline. From the consumer surplus equation, it is clear that as the market price of the good falls and/or the quantity demanded increases, the consumer surplus increases. The limit would be a price of zero at which point the consumer would be able to obtain a good with positive value for free. Answer A is incorrect. The marginal benefit of consuming a good is equal to the difference between the maximum price the consumer would pay for a given quantity of a good and the market price of the good. For a given market price, the marginal benefit is greatest for the first unit of consumption. In the question, the consumer would be willing to consume the first gallon of gas at a price of $5. If the market price of gasoline is $2, the marginal benefit of the first gallon of gas is $5 – $2 = $3. The marginal benefit decreases with each successive gallon of gas consumed. Answer C is incorrect because the marginal benefit to the consumer decreases as the market price increases. (Study Session 4, LOS 14.b)

35. **A** The MC curve would cross both curves at their minimum points. Both AVC and ATC would be declining until the marginal cost exceeded the respective AVC or ATC level. Once MC exceeded those levels, the higher MC would increase both average variable costs and average total costs. (Study Session 4, LOS 17. c,d)

36. **C** When the Federal Reserve purchases Treasury securities in the open market, the supply of loanable funds increases and interest rates decrease, with the likely result of increasing economic growth. One of the Fed's intermediate targets is the federal funds rate that banks charge each other for loans. When the Fed conducts open market operations, it is generally to adjust the federal funds rate to its target level. The Fed cannot simply dictate the federal funds rate as it can the discount rate, so it must use open market operations to achieve its target. The purpose of using the federal funds rate is to achieve the Fed's primary goal of price level stability (or predictable inflation rates). In pursuing price level stability, the Fed also attempts to achieve its secondary goal of sustainable real GDP growth, which occurs when real GDP and potential GDP are close to each other. (Study Session 6, LOS 27.a)

37. **C** By liberalizing Country Beta's labor immigration laws and allowing more of Country Delta's labor force into Country Beta, the full-employment quantity of labor has increased. As the full-employment labor force increases, aggregate supply increases; more of this incremental labor is put to work producing goods and services for Country Beta. Thus, the long-run aggregate supply (LAS) and the short-run aggregate supply (SAS) curves are pushed to the right creating a higher real GDP and the same price level. Note that price level and money wage changes merely move up and down the LAS or along the SAS and ultimately back to the same LAS, creating no real long lasting incremental increases in aggregate supply. (Study Session 5, LOS 23.a)

38. **B** When a market is subsidized by a government, the supply curve (marginal cost curve) shifts to the right while the demand curve (marginal benefit curve) stays constant. Producers in the market end up receiving more than the equilibrium price for their product and consumers in the market end up paying less than the equilibrium price for the product. In addition, the quantity produced and consumed is greater than the equilibrium quantity. In this situation, the marginal cost of the product is greater than the marginal benefit resulting in a deadweight loss due to overproduction. (Study Session 4, LOS 15.d)

39. **A** Herfindahl-Hirschman (HHI) index formula: $HHI = M_1^2 + M_2^2 + ... + M_N^2$; where M_N is the market share of the Nth firm.

    $HHI = (20^2 + 20^2 + 10^2 + 10^2 + 10^2 + 6^2 + 6^2 + 6^2 + 6^2 + 6^2) = 1,280$

    (Study Session 4, LOS 16.g)

40. **B** For any sloping demand curve, the elasticity changes as you move along the curve. Elasticity will be higher at low levels of demand (or high price levels) and lower at high levels of demand (when prices are low). (Study Session 4, LOS 13.a)

41. **A** For all firms, profit is maximized at the output where the incremental revenue from selling an additional unit (marginal revenue) is equal to the incremental cost of producing it (marginal cost). Since marginal revenue is still higher than marginal cost, Tetra can expand output. (Study Session 5, LOS 19.b)

42. **B** This is a good example of monopolistic competition which has free entry and exit, and product differentiation. Unfortunately, there is no guarantee of a profit, and monopolistic competition has no excess profit in the long run. (Study Session 5, LOS 20.a)

43. **C** Potential deposit expansion multiplier = (1/required reserve ratio) = 1/0.2 = 5

    Excess reserve = (actual reserves − required reserves) = 30 − (105 × 0.2) = 30 − 21 = 9

    Potential increase in the money supply = (potential deposit expansion multiplier x increase in excess reserve) = 9 × 5 = 45 (Study Session 6, LOS 24.e)

44. **A** This is a classic example of cost-push inflation. (Study Session 6, LOS 25.b)

Financial Reporting and Analysis

45. **A** The proxy statement provides information about management and board member compensation, as well as any conflicts of interest. (Study Session 7, LOS 29.e)

---

46. **C**   Strategic investments in companies are considered long-term in nature and would not be converted into cash over the next year or less. All the other answers are considered cash or convertible into cash over the next year. The asset category represents an element, while cash or receivables represent account sub-classifications. (Study Session 7, LOS 30.b)

47. **C**   Statement 1 is true. However, a more complete answer would include all users of the information including employees, lenders, suppliers, customers, government agencies, and others. The usefulness of the financial information is based on four qualitative characteristics: understandability, relevance, reliability, and comparability. Relevance states that the level of detail presented is driven by materiality (statement 2 is true). (Study Session 7, LOS 31.d)

48. **C**   The development of raw land is one example of a situation in which it is appropriate to use the cost recovery method. The uncertainty of collection requires a delayed revenue method. (Study Session 8, LOS 32.b)

49. **C**   The jet will have constant usage. To best match the usage and the total costs, the declining method is the most appropriate method. The declining method combines the higher depreciation costs and lower maintenance costs in the early years with lower depreciation costs and higher maintenance costs in the later years. The level total costs match the constant usage. (Study Session 8, LOS 32.d)

50. **A**   Restructuring and plant shutdown costs are considered part of a company's normal operations. The gains and losses related to discontinued operations are reported separately in the income statement because these activities are no longer included as part of the company's continuing operations. (Study Session 8, LOS 32.f)

51. **A**   Since Upton's capital structure does not have potentially dilutive securities, the company has a simple capital structure.

$$\text{Basic EPS} = \frac{\text{Net income} - \text{preferred dividends}}{\text{weighted average number of common shares outstanding}}$$

$$\text{Basic EPS} = \frac{830,000 - (6.5 \times 20,000)}{500,000} = 1.40$$

(Study Session 8, LOS 32.h)

52. **B**   Diluted EPS is computed assuming conversion of the options using the treasury stock method. Accordingly, an additional 50,000 shares are added to compute diluted EPS [{($15 average market price – $10 exercise price) / $15 average market} × 150,000 options = 50,000 shares]. 2,000,000 shares + 50,000 shares = 2,050,000 shares. (Study Session 7, LOS 32.h)

53. **B**   Cash in December would increase $1 million by the amount of collections and accounts receivable would be increased by $2 million, the amount not collected from customers until January. (Study Session 8, LOS 33.c)

54. **C** Rather than learn all the things that might be included, remember that generally only longer-term adjustments are made to stockholder's equity. Thus changes in short-term investments are excluded. The total change in stockholder's equity is:

$45,000,000 − [(1,000,000 + 500,000 shares) × $1.3/share] + (500,000 × $20/share) = $53,050,000

(Study Session 8, LOS 33.h)

55. **A** According to U.S. GAAP, issuances of common stock and dividend payments are financing cash flows. Interest payments are included in operating cash flows. Depreciation is a non-cash operating expense, added to net income in calculating operating cash flows. Acquisitions, divestitures, and investments in joint ventures are all considered investing cash flows. −$175M + 86M − 50M = −$139M. (Study Session 8, LOS 34.a)

56. **A** Operating cash flow is equal to $36.1 million [$43.7 million net income + $4.2 million depreciation expense − $8 million gain on sale − $1.5 million increase in receivables − $2.3 million decrease in payables]. Net capital expenditures are equal to $20 million [$35 million equipment purchased − $15 million proceeds from sale]. Free cash flow is equal to $16.1 million [$36.1 million operating cash flow − $20 million net capital expenditures]. (Study Session 8, LOS 34.i)

57. **B** The total cost of goods available for sale is $14,700 [(100 units × $15) + (200 units × $21) + (100 units × $18) + (300 units × $24)]. The average cost per unit is $21 ($14,700 / 700 units available for sale). Stanley sold 550 units (700 units available − 150 remaining). Thus, COGS is $11,550 (550 units sold × $21 per unit). (Study Session 9, LOS 35.c)

58. **B** The difference in working capital is the sum of the change in the inventory balance (in this case the LIFO reserve) and the tax savings effects. Under FIFO, MNB would have paid $240 more in income taxes ($600 LIFO reserve × 40% tax rate). Thus, working capital would be $360 higher under FIFO ($600 increase in inventory − $240 decrease in cash for taxes). (Study Session 9, LOS 35.f)

59. **B** Reversing capitalized interest will increase interest expense. Higher interest expense will reduce the interest coverage ratio (higher denominator). (Study Session 9, LOS 36.a)

60. **C** Box Packaging is using the double-declining balance method (DDB) to calculate the first year depreciation of $10 million [$75 million × (2 / 15 year life)].

As compared to DDB, the straight-line method will result in lower depreciation expense in the early years of the equipment's life which, in turn, results in higher net income, higher assets, and higher equity. Thus, the lower depreciation expense in the early years (straight-line relative to DDB) results in *lower* fixed asset turnover (higher denominator), and *higher* ROA and ROE (higher numerators). (Study Session 9, LOS 36.d)

61. **C** Since the asset's future undiscounted cash flows exceed its carrying value, no impairment is recognized. Thus, both ratios are correctly stated. (Study Session 9, LOS 36.i)

62. **B** Deferred tax assets result from gains that are taxable before they are recognized in the income statement, while deferred tax liabilities result from gains that are recognized in the income statement before they are taxable. Deferred tax assets result from losses that are recognized in the income statement before they are tax deductible, while deferred tax liabilities result from losses that are tax deductible before they are recognized in the income statement. (Study Session 9, LOS 37.b)

63. **A**   It is the coupon payment, not the interest expense, that results in an outflow of cash. The difference in the coupon payment and interest expense is the discount amortization. The amortization does not result in a cash outflow. Under U.S. GAAP, the coupon payment is reported as an operating activity. The discount, when paid at maturity, is reported as a financing activity. (Study Session 9, LOS 38.a)

64. **B**   The $50 current market price significantly exceeds the conversion price of $25 per share ($1,000 bond / 40 shares). Thus, the bonds should be treated as equity for the purposes of calculating leverage ratios. Consequently, the analyst should decrease debt and increase equity by the book value of the bonds ($1,000 × 100,000 bonds = $100,000,000). This will decrease the debt-to-equity ratio. Since the bonds are long-term, the adjustment does not affect the current ratio. (Study Session 9, LOS 38.e)

65. **C**   As compared to an operating lease, a finance lease will result in higher interest expense. Thus, the interest coverage ratio is lower (higher denominator). A finance lease would add debt to the balance sheet, generating a *higher* debt-to-capital ratio. Because interest expense is higher in the early years of a finance lease, net income will be lower in the early years as compared to operating lease. Over time, interest expense decreases as the liability is reduced through principal payments. Thus, ROE will be lower in the early years (lower numerator) and higher in the later years (higher numerator). (Study Session 9, LOS 38.g)

66. **B**   The appropriate adjustment is to reverse the sale of the receivables and treat the transaction as a short-term loan. Thus, accounts receivable and current liabilities should both increase by $40 million. Cash from operations should be reduced by $40 million and cash from *financing* should increase by $40 million. Investing cash flow is unaffected. Although interest expense should be increased, sales are not affected. (Study Session 9, LOS 38.i)

67. **B**   Although Keller's current assets have remained constant as a percentage of total assets, its liquidity position has fallen since both cash and accounts receivable have fallen as a percentage of total assets, while inventory has increased as a percentage of total assets. (Study Session 10, LOS 39.a)

68. **A**   These are all warning signs associated with the Enron accounting scandal. Sunbeam's financials showed negative operating cash flow, primarily due to increases in inventory and receivables. WorldCom warning signs are not covered in the curriculum but did not include all the items listed here. (Study Session 10, LOS 40.h,i)

69. **A**   Given the cash conversion cycle, days in inventory, and days in receivables, solve for days in payables [65 days in inventory + 43 days in receivables – 58 days cash conversion cycle = 50 days in payables]. Use days in payables to compute accounts payable turnover [365 / 50 days in payables = 7.3]. Use cost of goods sold and accounts payable turnover to solve for average accounts payable [$3.65 million / 7.3 = $500,000]. (Study Session 10, LOS 39.c)

70. **C**   IFRS standards require certain borrowing costs to be capitalized, such as interest that accrues during the construction of a capital asset. IFRS standards define expenses to include losses. GAAP standards differentiate expenses from losses. (Study Session 10, LOS 43.b)

71. **B**   Net cash outflow = $25,000

        Increase in annual after-tax cash flows: NCF = $5,000

        Present value of annual cash flows: PV = $5,000 (5.6502) = $28,251

        NPV = 28,251 − 25,000 = $3,251; NPV is thus positive. Buy the new Freeze II machine. (Study Session 11, LOS 44.d)

72. **B**   Observation 1 is incorrect. The payback period is as popular as either the NPV or IRR techniques, particularly among small companies as well as in Europe. Observation 2 is correct. The capital budgeting process can provide insight about management's willingness to accept the goal to maximize shareholder value and how successful they are in accomplishing that goal. (Study Session 11, LOS 44.f)

73. **B**   Recall that the marginal cost of capital (MCC) is the cost of the last dollar of new capital raised by the firm. Marginal cost increases as increasing amounts of capital are raised during a set period. In general, firms in riskier businesses, or with riskier projects, have higher costs of common equity and thus higher MCC and WACC. The increase in the tax rate would reduce the after-tax cost of debt, reducing the MCC. (Study Session 11, LOS 45.a, b)

74. **B**   The cost of common equity capital can be calculated using the CAPM approach, the dividend discount model approach, or the bond yield plus risk premium approach. In this question, the information given is only sufficient to use the CAPM approach. Using the CAPM approach, Net-Zone's cost of common equity is calculated using the following formula:

$$E\left(R_i\right) = R_f + \beta_i \left[E\left(R_m\right) - R_f\right]$$

        where :
        $E\left(R_i\right)$ = Return on stock i
        R_f = Risk-free rate
        $E\left(R_m\right)$ = Return on the market
        β_i = sensitivity of stock i to the market

        Because the analyst is analyzing a long-term project for Net-Zone, it is most appropriate to use a risk-free rate with a similar term. In this case, the 10-year Treasury bond yield is the appropriate risk-free rate. The cost of Net-Zone's common equity is thus: 4.8% + 1.8(10.7% − 4.8%) = 15.4%. (Study Session 11, LOS 45.h)

75. **A** Flotation costs are the fees charged by an investment bank to underwrite the issuance of debt, preferred stock, or common stock. Flotation costs for debt and preferred stock are generally not incorporated in the cost of capital since the costs are small. Instead, flotation costs for debt and preferred stock are treated as a cash outlay reducing the proceeds received from the issuance. For common stock, flotation costs are significantly higher. One study estimated the average flotation cost of common equity in the U.S. at 7.11% of the issue price. Some argue this cost should be incorporated in the cost of equity capital. While this method reflects the higher cost of issuing additional equity capital (as opposed to using internal equity capital from retained earnings), it ignores the fact that flotation costs are a cash outflow that occurs at the beginning of the project. The recommended method is to reduce the NPV of the project by the flotation costs by treating the flotation costs as a cash outflow at project initiation, rather than as a component of the cost of equity. For YHM, the flotation costs of its recent debt and equity issuances are as follows:

Source of capital	$ flotation cost	% flotation cost
Debt	$0.132 million = (12 × 0.011)	1.1%
Equity	$2.05 million = (25 − 22.95)	8.2% = (2.05 / 25)

The appropriate adjustment to account for flotation costs is to reduce the NPV of the associated project by the dollar flotation costs of $2.18 million = $2.05 + $0.132. (Study Session 11, LOS 45.l)

76. **B** In order to answer this question, you must first recall the definition of net operating cycle.

$$\text{net operating cycle} = \frac{\text{number of days}}{\text{of inventory}} + \frac{\text{number of days}}{\text{of receivables}} - \frac{\text{number of days}}{\text{of payables}}$$

The net operating cycle (also called the cash conversion cycle) measures the amount of time between paying the firm's suppliers for raw materials and collecting cash through the sale of finished goods. As a firm reduces the net operating cycle, it essentially increases its ability to generate cash flows from its operating activities. Thus, the firm can hold fewer liquid assets and will rely less on short-term financing to maintain its liquidity. A shorter net operating cycle indicates a more liquid firm. In order to decrease the net operating cycle, a firm must do at least one of three things: decrease the number of days of inventory (i.e., more efficiently manage inventory purchases, processing, and fulfillment); decrease the number of days of receivables (i.e., reduce credit terms to customers and reduce collection times); or increase the number of days of payables (i.e., lengthen the amount of time to pay suppliers). In the question, GTS Company has decreased its net operating cycle over the last three years indicating it has become more liquid by reducing number of days of inventory or number of days of receivables or increasing number of days of payables. The industry, however, has increased its average net operating cycle over the same period, indicating the industry has become less liquid by increasing number of days of inventory or number of days of receivables or decreasing number of days of payables. (Study Session 11, LOS 46.b)

77. **C** An investment policy for short-term portfolios should have the following elements: purpose, authorities, limitations / restrictions, quality, and other items. The purpose section should state the general reason the portfolio exists and the general strategy that will be followed. The authorities section should state the executives who will oversee the portfolio. The limitations section generally states the types of investments that are or are not acceptable and should note only categories of securities rather than specific issuers of securities (making answer choice C incorrect since it is too specific). The quality section should state guidelines for the credit quality of the investments in the portfolio. The other section may be used for portfolio requirements not covered in the first four sections, such as auditing or reporting requirements. (Study Session 11, LOS 46.e)

78. **C** Since Ross's sister is a partner for a company working as an advisor to Grambling, Ross's independence should be called into question. Since Ross's son is only a mid-level manager, his influence at Grow Company is limited. Furthermore, Ross's son does not have any potential influence on internal Grambling decisions and should not compromise Ross's independence. However, care must be taken so that Ross's position does not result in any supply contracts going to his son's employer to the detriment of Grambling. The fact that Ross's wife has a non-controlling equity interest in Grambling through a mutual fund is not reason to question his independence. The interest may more closely align Ross's interests with those of the other shareholders, which is one goal of corporate governance. (Study Session 11, LOS 48.b,c)

Portfolio Management

79. **B** The formula for the expected return for any asset, i, equals:

$$E(R_i) = \sum p_i R_i$$

where p_i is the probability that event (or scenario) i will occur. In the problem above p_1 = 20%, p_2 = 50%, and p_3 = 30%. R_i is the return associated with scenario i. Therefore, the expected return for the S&P 500 market index equals:

$$E(R_{S\&P}) = (20\% \times -10\%) + (50\% \times 10\%) + (30\% \times 20\%) = -2\% + 5\% + 6\% = 9\%$$

The formula for the expected return for a portfolio is the weighted average of the individual asset expected returns:

$$E(R_p) = \sum w_i E(R_i)$$

where w_i is the percentage of the portfolio, p, allocated to asset i. For Choudra's portfolio: $w_{S\&P\ 500}$ = 60% and w_F = 40%. The expected return on the risk-free rate equals 5%. There are no calculations for the expected return on the risk-free rate because the return on the risk-free asset is known with certainty. It will equal 5% regardless of the state of the economy over the stated investment horizon. And, as shown above, the expected return on the S&P 500 equals 9%. Therefore, the expected return on Choudra's portfolio equals:

$$E(R_p) = (40\% \times 5\%) + (60\% \times 9\%) = 7.4\% \text{ (Study Session 12, LOS 50.c)}$$

80. **C** The security market line (SML) is the diagram of the capital asset pricing model:

$$E(R_i) = R_F + \beta_i[E(R_m) - R_F].$$

The SML graphically illustrates the linear relationship one should expect between returns on assets and their risks (as represented by beta). Low beta assets have low expected returns, and high beta assets have high expected returns. The expected returns for the individual assets are plotted along the vertical axis and the betas for the individual assets are plotted along the horizontal axis. The beginning point for the SML (the intercept) is the risk-free rate; e.g., the expected return equals the risk-free rate if beta equals zero. The SML slope (rise over run) equals the market risk premium $E(R_m) - R_F$. (Study Session 12, LOS 51.d)

81. **A** If the covariance is negative, the correlation must be negative. Calculate the correlation as follows: $\dfrac{-0.10}{\left[\left(\sqrt{0.25}\right) \times \left(\sqrt{0.20}\right)\right]} = \dfrac{-0.10}{0.22} = -0.45$.

(Study Session 12, LOS 50.d)

---

82. **C** Diversification reduces the portfolio standard deviation below the weighted average of the standard deviations if they are less than perfectly positively correlated. However, the minimum standard deviation occurs when the correlation is equal to negative one, not zero. (Study Session 12, LOS 50.e)

83. **B** The capital asset pricing model is the equation for the security market line: risk-free rate plus beta times market risk premium, where the market risk premium equals the difference between the expected market return and the risk-free rate. For Royal Company, the required return equals $0.05 + 1.5(0.11 - 0.05) = 14\%$. The analyst predicts the stock will return 15%, implying that she thinks Royal Company stock is undervalued by 1 percentage point (15% minus 14%). (Study Session 12, LOS 51.e)

84. **B** Lywie faces a precarious situation with his lack of sufficient insurance coverage and low income expectations. Consequently, he cannot pursue a high risk strategy. His risk tolerance will be fairly low. Risk and return are positively related, so Lywie's return expectations also will be low. In contrast Stromek has high net worth and long-term earnings potential. He will be able to withstand high levels of risk in his portfolio and will therefore also earn higher returns. (Study Session 12, LOS 49.b)

Asset Valuation

85. **A** An unweighted index (or equal weighting) does not reflect the size bias in Johnson's portfolio. Price-weighted indexes can be affected by a stock split in the long run. A stock with a high stock price and splits should have good growth characteristics. If these characteristics continue, the lower weighting of the stock due to the split will cause the index to have lower long-run returns than if the stock did not split. DJIA is an example of a price-weighted index. (Study Session 13, LOS 53.a)

86. **B** In an efficient market, price adjustments may be imperfect but they are unbiased. Thus, the market will sometimes over-adjust and under-adjust at other times, but market participants cannot predict which will occur at any given time. Answers A and C are assumptions upon which market efficiency is based. (Study Session 13, LOS 54.a)

87. **C** In the fourth market, securities are traded using alternative trading systems, either electronic communication networks or electronic crossing networks, without using a broker. NASDAQ allows stocks to be traded whenever the market is open (continuous market). (Study Session 13, LOS 52.e)

88. **A** Escalation bias occurs when an investor chooses to increase the amount invested in a poorly performing investment rather than admit that the investment was a bad decision. Often the investor ignores bad news that would confirm the value of the investment had truly declined or that the original valuation was incorrect. Overconfidence bias (also called confirmation bias) occurs when investors look for information to support their decision to invest in growth companies. As a result, investors with this bias misvalue the subject company. Momentum bias is not a behavioral bias. (Study Session 13, LOS 54.d)

89. **A** In a short sale transaction, the lender of stock would not receive dividends from the issuing company. Therefore, if the company paid a dividend, the short seller would be required to pay that amount to the lender. The short seller must post some collateral or margin (usually the proceeds of selling the stock). The good faith money protects the brokerage house. (Study Session 13, LOS 52.f)

90. **B**   Next year's dividend is $D_1 = D_0(1 + g) = \$1.90(1 + 0.06) = \$2.014$

   Determine k_e using the CAPM: $RFR + \beta(R_{mkt} - RFR) = 5\% + 1.3(12\% \times 5\%) = 14.1\%$

   Note: The market risk premium is $R_{mkt} - RFR$.

   Calculate the stock's value using the infinite period dividend discount model (DDM):

   $$V_0 = \frac{D_1}{k_e - g} = \frac{2.014}{0.141 - 0.06} = 24.86$$

   Answer A incorrectly uses the current dividend (D_0) of \$1.90 instead of the next-year dividend (D_1) of \$2.014. Answer C uses the correct dividend but the wrong denominator, dividing by g instead of $k_e - g$. (Study Session 14, LOS 56.c)

91. **A**   The dividend payout ratio is $1 -$ expected retention ratio $= 1 - 0.625 = 0.375$ or 37.5%.

   The leading (forward) P/E ratio is:

   $$\frac{P_0}{E_1} = \frac{D_1 / E_1}{r - g} = \frac{0.375}{0.11 - 0.06} = 7.50$$

   Multiplying the leading P/E ratio times forecasted earnings per share gives the stock value:

   $P_0 = (P_0/E_1)\,(E_1) = 7.50\,(\$4.24) = \$31.80$. (Study Session 14, LOS 56.d)

92. **C**   Demographics best exemplifies the strategic initiative of targeting the Hispanic audience. The large growth of this demographic group is the reason Radio Corp. is targeting them. The regulatory rules that allow clustering of ownership of local radio stations allow the company to pursue the acquisition strategy. (Study Session 14, LOS 57)

93. **A** $RFR_{nominal} = (1 + RFR_{real})(1 + IP) - 1 = (1.04)(1.05) - 1 = 1.0920 - 1 = 0.0920 = 9.20\%$

   Using the CAPM, the required rate of return (k_e) $= RFR_{nominal} + \beta(R_{mkt} - RFR_{nominal}) = 9.20\% + 1.4(14.0\% \times 9.2\%) = 9.20\% + 6.72\% = 15.92\%$

   The retention ratio (RR) $= 1 -$ dividend payout ratio $= 1 - 0.30 = 0.70$

   The growth rate (g_c) $= (RR)(ROE) = (0.70)(10\%) = 7.00\%$

   $D_0 = E_0$(dividend payout) $= \$4.00(0.30) = \$1.20$

   Next year's dividend (D_1) $= D_0(1 + g_c) = \$1.20(1 + 0.07) = 1.284$

   $P_0 = D_1 / (k_e - g) = 1.284 / (0.1592 - 0.07) = 14.39$.

   (Study Session 14, LOS 56.f)

94. **B**   Since Barco Company's earnings are cyclical, the earnings multiplier is reduced versus a company with a stable earnings profile. (Study Session 14, LOS 58.a)

95. **C**   Willow Corp. does not exhibit growth company characteristics (e.g. growth rate substantially above WACC), but does exhibit growth stock characteristics with the potential of positive earnings surprises. The substantial risks of Vision Inc. as outlined reflect a speculative company, while valuation relative to potential growth does not support a speculative stock characterization. (Study Session 14, LOS 58.a)

96. **A**   Reported loss of $2.50 per share plus $2.00 nonrecurring loss equals –$0.5. However, this results in a meaningless P/E calculation of –100. Using the long run return on equity multiplied by total equity, divided by outstanding shares equates to a long run earnings per share. ($1 billion × 0.25)/50 million = $5 per share. P/E = 50/5 = 10. (Study Session 14, LOS 59.b)

97. **A**   The analyst is correct with respect to bond maturity but incorrect with respect to coupon rate. As the maturity of a bond increases, an investor must wait longer for the eventual repayment of the bond principal. As the length of time until principal payment increases, the probability that interest rates will change increases. If interest rates increase, the present value of the final payment (which is the largest cash flow of the bond) decreases. At longer maturities, the present value decreases by greater amounts. Thus, interest rate risk increases as the maturity of the bond increases. As the coupon rate decreases the interest rate risk of a bond increases. Lower coupons cause greater relative weight to be placed on the principal repayment. Because this cash flow occurs farther out in time, its present value is much more sensitive to changes in interest rates. As the coupon rate goes to zero (i.e., a zero-coupon bond), all of the bond's return relies on the return of principal which as stated before is highly sensitive to interest rate changes. (Study Session 15, LOS 61.c)

98. **C**   Most CDOs are structured into tranches like CMOs. CDOs are not limited to U.S based entities at all. If the CDO has bonds as the underlying, it is called a collateralized bond obligation (CBO). (Study Session 15, LOS 62.j)

99. **C**   The risk most likely to have increased is call risk, as the bonds have appreciated well above par value, quite possibly due to falling rates, which might motivate the issuer to call the bonds and replace them with lower cost debt. Credit risk has decreased, since the bonds have improved in rating from A to AA. There is no information to suggest that liquidity risk has changed, although a higher rated bond would likely be somewhat more liquid (less liquidity risk). (Study Session 15, LOS 61.a)

100. **B**   The OAS provides a method of valuing the yield differential of certain fixed income securities versus Treasury securities with similar maturities. The OAS represents the higher yield of a non-Treasury security that compensates the investor for some amount of credit and liquidity risk. The OAS, by definition, excludes any compensation for the risk related to the embedded option. This broker's OAS model has calculated that for this issue, the investor should receive 75 bps over a comparable Treasury security for the assumption of the additional credit and liquidity risk. The embedded option will increase the yield further, thus creating a total spread that is more than 75 bps. (Study Session 16, LOS 65.g)

101. **C**   Since the U.S. Treasury does not currently issue securities for every point on the yield curve, simple linear interpolation is the method used to estimate the yields for those maturity points where there is no on-the-run issue. In fact, most yields along the Treasury yield curve are interpolated yields rather than observed yields. (Study Session 16, LOS 65.e)

102. **A** Bond Y will have the higher nominal spread due to the call option embedded in the bond. This option benefits the issuer at the expense of the investor, and investors would demand a higher yield to compensate for this feature. The option-adjusted spread removes the value of the option from the spread calculation, and would always be less than the nominal spread for a callable bond. Since Bond X is noncallable, the nominal spread and the OAS will be the same. (Study Session 15, LOS 63.g)

103. **A** First, determine the arbitrage-free price of the bond:

$$\frac{8}{(1+0.074)^1} + \frac{8}{(1+0.070)^2} + \frac{108}{(1+0.063)^3} = 104.35$$

The pieces can be sold for a profit over and above the cost of the bond ($103.95). Buy the bond and sell the pieces individually (strip the bond). (Study Session 16, LOS 64.f)

104. **B** If the yield curve is flat, the zero volatility spread would be the same as the nominal spread. A steeper curve would give rise to a greater difference between the spreads. An amortizing security (Bond Y) will exhibit greater difference in spreads than a non-amortizing one (Bond X). (Study Session 16, LOS 65.f)

105. **A** As yields decline, callable bonds experience price compression and negative convexity. Declining yields should lead to decreases in duration. (Study Session 16, LOS 66.b,c)

106. **B** A portfolio's duration can be used to estimate the approximate change in value for a given change in yield. A critical assumption is that the yield for all bonds in the portfolio change by the same amount, known as a parallel shift. For this portfolio the expected change in value can be calculated as: $7,545,000 \times 6.24 \times 0.0050 = $235,404. The decrease in yields will cause an increase in the value of the portfolio, not a decrease as suggested by answer C. (Study Session 16, LOS 66.f)

107. **B** $(1+S_4)^4 = (1+ {}_1f_0)(1+ {}_1f_1)(1+ {}_1f_2)(1+ {}_1f_3)$

$(1.075)^4 = (1.06)(1.073)(1+x)(1.089)$

$0.078 = x$

(Study Session 16, LOS 65.h)

108. **C** This is an example of a negative covenant. Affirmative covenants are what the issuer must do (e.g. make timely payments of interest and principal, maintain equipment). A negative covenant refers to something the issuer is restricted from doing, such as paying dividends on stock when bond interest is in arrears. (Study Session 15, LOS 60.a)

109. **B** Duration is an estimate of the percentage price change of a bond for a 1% parallel shift of the yield curve. When the shift in the yield curve is not the same for all maturities, it is a poorer estimator of the bond/portfolio price change. (Study Session 15, LOS 61.g)

110. **B** European options can only be exercised at expiration. A put option gives the owner the right to sell the underlying asset. Put options are in-the-money when the strike price is above the underlying asset price. In this case, the option is in-the-money by $35 – $25 = $10. (Study Session 17, LOS 70.a)

111. **B** Losses on Carl's portfolio of large cap stocks should be offset by gains on the short position in a futures contract. Note, however, that gains on the portfolio will be offset by futures losses. He could also *buy* put options on the S&P 500. A long position in an S&P 500 forward contract would not offer any downside protection. (Study Session 17, LOS 67.b)

112. **B** Because Chen is short the futures contracts which are denominated in dollars per Swiss franc, an increase in the futures price means that Chen receives fewer dollars per franc sold than could a person contracting at the new price. Therefore her position decreases in value and the decrease is subtracted from her margin account. The reverse is true if the futures price decreases in value. Thus on the first day, the futures price increases by 0.0180 = 0.9300 − 0.9120. This is a loss of $1,800 = 100,000(0.0180). At the end of the first day the margin balance is 2,200 = 4,000 − 1,800. Because the account balance is below the maintenance margin level, Chen would receive a margin call on the next morning (the 2nd day) and would need to deposit enough to bring the account balance back to the initial margin level of $4,000. Thus on the third day, Chen must deposit 1,800 = 4,000 − 2,200. The following table summarizes the account balance changes.

Day	Beginning Balance $	Funds Deposited $	Futures Price $	Price Change $	Gain/Loss $	Ending Balance $
0	0	4,000	0.9120			4,000
1	4,000	0	0.9300	0.0180	(1,800)	2,200
2	2,200	1,800	0.8928	(0.0372)	3,720	7,720

On the second day, the futures price falls and allows Chen to realize a margin account gain of $3,720 = 100,000(0.9300 − 0.8928). Thus the account balance at the end of the second day is $7,720 = 2,200 + 1,800 + 3,720. (Study Session 17, LOS 69.c)

113. **B** A 3 x 6 FRA expires in 90 days (3 months from now) and is based on interest that will be paid 90 days after the expiration (6 months from now), which is 90-day LIBOR. (Study Session 17, LOS 68.f)

114. **A** The writer of an option can only profit from the premium received, but has exposure to moves in the underlying asset price. The put writer could lose $42, but the call writer's potential loss is unlimited. The put buyer's loss exposure is limited to the premium paid. The put writer's potential gain is limited to the premium received. (Study Session 17, LOS 72.a)

115. **C** For a long call position, the profit is equal to the value of the call at expiration minus the initial cost of the call. If the call expires in the money, the value is equal to the final stock price minus the exercise price. Since the final stock price has no upper limit (i.e., it can rise infinitely), the expiration value of the call (and thus the profit) is unlimited. Since the current market price of ZXC ($33.75) is greater than the strike price of the call options ($30), the options are in the money, i.e. they would have value if exercised today. Breakeven occurs when the stock price is equal to the exercise price plus the cost of the option. For ZXC stock, the breakeven stock price is $34.50, not $38.25. (Study Session 17, LOS 72.a)

116. **A** The quarterly fixed rate payments on the swap are equal to $170,000 [10,000,000 × (0.068 / 4)]. This is the amount that IRK Investments must pay each quarter. In exchange for this payment IRK will receive the return on the S&P 500 Index. If the return on the index is positive, the payment received from the counterparty will offset the payment that IRK must make. In this situation, the payment IRK must make will be lower than $170,000 or may even be a cash inflow if the return on the index exceeds 1.7%. If, however, the return on the index is negative, IRK will have to make an additional payment on top of the fixed payment. Since IRK owes $400,000, the most likely explanation is that the underlying index experienced a negative return. If the loss on the index had been 1.7%, IRK's payment would have been double the ordinary payment. The actual amount owed is more than double, which indicates the loss was greater than 1.7%. (Study Session 17, LOS 71.b)

117. **B** The income approach to valuing a real estate investment is simply NOI / cap rate. The cap rate is the discount rate being used in the market to discount the NOI of comparable properties. In this question, the value of the property is $458,909 = 50,480 / 0.11, which is approximately equal to $458,900. (Study Session 18, LOS 73.f)

118. **A** Assuming a $1 investment, the terminal value for each class over the five year period is:

$$\text{Class A} = (\$1 \times (1-0.02)) \times (1+0.12)^5 \times [1-(0.004+0.004+0.002)]^5 = \$1.642$$

$$\text{Class B} = (1+0.12)^5 \times [1-(0.005+0.005+0.005)]^5 = \$1.634$$

$$\text{Class C} = (1+0.12)^5 \times [1-(0.005+0.005+0.006)]^5 = \$1.626$$

Select Class A shares because they have the highest terminal value.

(Study Session 18, LOS 73.a)

119. **C** Hedge funds have been shown to exhibit less volatility than traditional equity funds. (Study Session 18, LOS 73.k)

120. **C** A commodity market is contango if the futures price is higher than the spot price. (Study Session 18, LOS 74.a)

Exam 1
Afternoon Session Answers

To get valuable feedback on how your score compares to those of other Level 1 candidates, use your Username and Password to gain Online Access at schweser.com and choose the left-hand menu item "Practice Exams Vol. 2."

121. B	151. B	181. A	211. B
122. B	152. B	182. C	212. C
123. B	153. C	183. B	213. A
124. B	154. C	184. C	214. B
125. A	155. B	185. A	215. C
126. B	156. A	186. C	216. A
127. A	157. B	187. B	217. B
128. A	158. C	188. B	218. A
129. B	159. A	189. C	219. A
130. A	160. B	190. A	220. C
131. B	161. C	191. A	221. C
132. B	162. C	192. C	222. A
133. A	163. B	193. B	223. B
134. B	164. A	194. B	224. C
135. A	165. B	195. C	225. C
136. A	166. A	196. C	226. B
137. C	167. B	197. C	227. A
138. A	168. C	198. B	228. C
139. C	169. A	199. C	229. A
140. A	170. C	200. B	230. B
141. C	171. A	201. A	231. C
142. C	172. C	202. A	232. B
143. C	173. B	203. B	233. B
144. B	174. C	204. B	234. C
145. C	175. C	205. C	235. A
146. B	176. B	206. C	236. B
147. B	177. B	207. B	237. B
148. C	178. A	208. A	238. A
149. C	179. B	209. B	239. C
150. C	180. C	210. C	240. A

Exam 1
Afternoon Session Answers

Ethical and Professional Standards

Answers referencing the Standards of Practice are all Study Session 1, LOS 2.a, b.

121. **B** Standard VII(B). According to the standard, members are not allowed to misrepresent or exaggerate the meaning of the CFA designation, membership in CFA Institute, or candidacy in the CFA program. This applies when the member references their relationship to the CFA Institute or CFA program verbally, or in writing (both print and electronic). Brown's statements regarding the Level 3 candidates at Brinton are acceptable. Stating that the analysts passed all three CFA exams on the first attempt is a statement of fact and is acceptable. Brown has also made acceptable statements regarding the rigor of the CFA program and has not over-promised investment results in connection with employing CFA charterholders and candidates. However, Brown's statement regarding the Level 2 CFA candidates at Brinton does violate Standard VII(A), which prohibits citing an expected completion date for any level of the CFA program. There is also a presumption that these Level 2 candidates will meet the work experience requirement, which may not be the case.

122. **B** Standard I(C). Bates plagiarized in violation of Standard I(C), because even though Bates might have eventually come to the same conclusion, he utilized other analyst's work and represented it as his own.

123. **B** Standard IV(A). It is likely that Johnson's outside work competes with her employer, especially since Smith Brothers caters to institutional clients. Standard IV(A) – Duties to Employer – Loyalty requires that Johnson not engage in conduct that harms her employer. Permission from employer for the outside work is required.

   Standard IV(B). This is also a violation of Standard IV(B) – Duties to Employer – Additional Compensation Arrangements. Even though the independent practice was in place at the time of being hired by the employer, the employee should still seek consent from the employer for any additional compensation or benefits.

124. **B** Standards I(B) and V(A), Independence and Objectivity, require the member to use reasonable care and judgment to achieve and maintain independence and objectivity in making investment recommendations or taking investment action. Hanning must be independent and objective in his analysis—if the report violates the integrity of his opinion, even if it is at the direction of this supervisor, Hanning should not be associated with the report. C is not correct—a follow-up report does not excuse the initial attempt to mislead investors.

125. **A** Standard II(A). Pollard has enough information to determine that the overheard information is indeed material nonpublic information. No matter how this information was obtained, even through an overheard conversation, it may not be traded on, and Pollard cannot cause others to trade on this same information. Even if he had contacted internal counsel before placing the trade, Pollard would have violated Standard II(A).

126. **B** Standard III(B). Members and candidates must deal fairly and objectively with all clients and should forgo any sales to themselves or their immediate families to free up additional shares of oversubscribed stock issues for clients.

127. **A** Standard III(E). According to the Standard, members and candidates must keep information about former, current, and potential future clients confidential unless client information is legally required to be disclosed, the information pertains to potential illegal client activities, or the client gives permission for the information to be disclosed. Crane is complying with current legal reporting requirements which happen to require disclosure of personal client information for both former and current clients. Thus, Crane has not violated the Standard by disclosing the client information.

128. **A** Standard I(C) does not prohibit members and candidates from making truthful statements that some investments are guaranteed in one way or another. Shipley must be careful to explain that there are still elements of risk involved. While U.S. Treasury securities are guaranteed, there is still interest rate risk.

129. **B** Standard III(A). Members and candidates have a duty of loyalty, prudence, and care to their clients. As part of this duty, research obtained using soft dollars (i.e., purchased through directing brokerage to a specific broker) must benefit the client. When the soft dollar arrangement does not benefit the client, the member or candidate must disclose the conflict to clients. In this case, however, White has negotiated favorable brokerage terms for her clients in order to receive research that will benefit client accounts. Thus, she is not in violation of the CFA Institute Standards and is not required to disclose the arrangement to clients.

130. **A** Standard VII(B). Statement 1 is an improper use of the CFA designation. Standard VII(B) – Responsibilities as a CFA Institute Member or CFA Candidate – Reference to CFA Institute, the CFA Designation, and the CFA Program prohibits any claim of superior results. It is acceptable to attest to the credibility and rigor of the CFA program, but Statement 1 improperly implies superior investment results. Statement 2 is acceptable, since it does not improperly exaggerate the value or meaning of the CFA designation. Statement 3 improperly references "C.F.A." with periods after the letters, which is not allowed.

131. **B** Firms are encouraged, though not required, to have an independent third party verify the performance results for the whole firm, not just for a single composite.

132. **B** Standard I(A). Steinberg has clearly violated Standard I(A) Knowledge of the Law. As a CFA charterholder, Steinberg has a duty to uphold the laws of his home country, laws of foreign countries in which he does business, or the Code and Standards, whichever is strictest. Since the American investor has illegally obtained funds and Steinberg knows about it, he is required to report the activity to his firm's counsel and dissociate from the illegal activities. Steinberg waited until the investor provided a second deposit of questionable funds before taking any action. By not taking action the first time, Steinberg has violated Standard I(A).

133. **A** Standard II(A). According to the Standard, members are not allowed to trade or induce others to trade on material nonpublic information. An exception exists under the mosaic theory which states that a combination of material public information and non-material nonpublic information can be used to trade even if the combination amounts to material nonpublic information. Howell is using publicly available financial reports from the oil company as well as non-material nonpublic information regarding the travel plans of the company's executive officers that led him to suspect that the company was planning a merger with a Japanese oil company. Howell's buy recommendation was based on his analysis of the firm's financials and his own forecasts, in combination with the executives' travels. Thus, Howell formed his conclusion using the mosaic theory and did not violate the Standards.

134. **B** Standard V(B). "A" is incorrect, because Sweeney would have omitted the negative information and changed his recommendation. "B" is correct—Stevage is still including the negative information, just not emphasizing it as strongly. The investor is not being misled. "C" is not correct because Stevage's request is not a violation.

135. **A** Standard IV(A). Garcia has violated the standard because work performed on behalf of the firm, whether at the office or at home, is property of the firm. It should be returned to the firm or destroyed unless the firm gives permission to keep the information after employment ends. Standard IV(A) Duties to Employers – Loyalty specifically addresses use of "client lists." Simple knowledge of client information is acceptable to have, but taking and/or misusing specific client information such as portfolio allocations is unacceptable.

136. **A** Standard II(A). Although analysts and shareholders were present in the meeting, it is not considered public disclosure. It is likely that this information *would* have an impact on ADM's stock price, thus it is considered to be material nonpublic information. Kelley and Gordon are not allowed to trade or cause others to trade on the information. ADM should be encouraged to officially release this information to the public.

137. **C** Standard III(A). Members and candidates must identify the "client" to whom the duty of loyalty is owed. In this case, the client is not the person or entity who hired the manager, but the beneficiaries of the pension fund.

138. **A** CFA Institute Professional Conduct Program. The Rules of Procedure are based on two fundamental principles – fair process and confidentiality. CFA Institute's Board of Governors has oversight and responsibility for the Professional Conduct Program (PCP) and enforces this responsibility through the Disciplinary Review Committee (DRC) whose job it is to enforce the Code and Standards.

Quantitative Methods

139. **C** An empirical probability is established by analyzing past data. Note that the question is only asking about investors under the age of 30. In the survey, the number of investors under 30 was 325 + 235 = 560. The number of investors under 30 who did not make a stock trade was 325 / 560 = 0.58 or 58%. (Study Session 2, LOS 8.b)

140. **A** We can determine the probability of interest using the approximations of areas under the normal distribution. Phillips is interested in the probability of observing a result that is one standard deviation above the EPS expected value $(3 - 2)/1 = 1$. Approximately 68% of observations fall within plus or minus one standard deviation of the mean. Therefore, $1 - 0.68 = 0.32$ or 32% remains in the tails. Since we are interested in the upper tail, we can say that there is $0.32/2 = 0.16$ or 16% probability of observing an EPS greater than 3. (Study Session 3, LOS 9.h)

141. **C** The standard error of the sample mean is calculated as the standard deviation of the sample data divided by the square root of the sample size. Standard deviation is equal to the square root of the variance.

$$\text{Standard deviation} = \sqrt{\text{Variance}} = \sqrt{160,000} = 400;$$

$$\text{Standard error} = \frac{400}{\sqrt{100}} = 40. \qquad \text{(Study Session 3, LOS 10.e)}$$

142. **C**

Mean = (6+5+3+15+11)/5=8	Deviations	Std Deviation
	6: 6-8 = −2	$-2^2 = 4$
	5: 5−8 = −3	$-3^2 = 9$
	3: 3−8 = −5	$-5^2 = 25$
	15: 15−8 = 7	$7^2 = 49$
	11: 11−8 = 3	$3^2 = \underline{9}$ 96
		96/5 = variance = 19.2
		Std Dev = 4.38

(Study Session 2, LOS 7.f)

143. **C** An opportunity cost is the amount foregone by pursuing a specific course of action. By holding onto cash, the individual is foregoing interest that could be earned by investing the cash. As interest rates rise, the opportunity cost of holding onto the cash also rises. Therefore, McGrow is correct. Interest rates are used to "discount" future cash flows in order to determine today's (present value) equivalent of the future cash flow amounts. The present value is inversely related to the discount rate. Therefore, Modello is also correct. (Study Session 2, LOS 5.a)

144. **B** Technical analysts believe the flow of information into the market is gradual, causing the market to adjust prices to a new equilibrium over a significant period of time. Fundamental analysts believe that the market receives information quickly and efficiently, causing abrupt price changes as the market moves to a new equilibrium. (Study Session 3, LOS 12.a)

145. **C** If the order in which a combination is determined is important, then the permutation formula is used. The permutation formula is used to select r objects from a set of n total objects (i.e., select 4 managers for a bonus out of the 7 managers eligible for a bonus). The permutation formula is as follows:

$n!\ /\ (n − r)!$, where the ! indicates the factorial function. To determine the number of ways to award bonuses, we substitute 7 for n and 4 for r in the permutation formula as follows:

$7!\ /\ (7 − 4)! = 7!\ /\ 3! = 5,040\ /\ 6 = 840.$ (Study Session 2, LOS 8.n)

146. **B** This is a difference of means test where we want to know if the mean of the new drug is greater than the mean of the old drug. The decision rule for the null hypothesis is H_0: $\mu_{New} − \mu_{Std} \leq 0$. (Study Session 3, LOS 11.a)

147. **B** The 95% confidence interval is the range of possible stock returns that has 95% chance of including the hypothesized population mean. For example, a 95% confidence interval of [−50%, +80%] indicates that there is a 95% chance that the population mean stock return lies somewhere between −50% and +80%. The decision rule is to not reject the null hypothesis if the hypothesized mean lies within the 95% confidence interval, and to reject the null hypothesis if the hypothesized mean lies outside the 95% confidence interval. The decision rule is to reject the null hypothesis whenever the (absolute value of the) calculated test statistic exceeds its critical value (i.e., the test statistic lies in the "rejection tail"). The power of a hypothesis test is the probability of rejecting the null hypothesis when it is not true. (Study Session 3, LOS 11.c)

148. **C** Gallant receives a €500 dividend on the MM preferred shares plus a €6,000 payment from Wood at the end of year 1. The preferred shares offer a perpetuity of €500, which Gallant sells at the end of year 1. At the end of year 1, the fair value (price received by Gallant) for the preferred stock equals:

Fair Value of perpetuity = €500/0.10 = €5,000.

So, at the end of year 1, Gallant receives a €500 dividend payment, €5,000 from selling the preferred shares, and a €6,000 payment from Wood. His one-year holding period return equals:

$$\text{Holding period return} = \frac{5{,}000 + 6{,}000 + 500 - 10{,}000}{10{,}000} = 15\%.$$

(Study Session 2, LOS 6.b)

149. **C** The random variable in this question can be viewed in only two ways: success (earnings increase) or failure (earnings decrease). Any event that produces just one of two possible outcomes is called a Bernoulli trial. The number of successes in a Bernoulli trial is called a binomial random variable. The formula for finding the probability for x successes out of n trials is:

Probability for a Binomial Random Variable = $_nC_x p^x (1-p)^{(n-x)}$

where:
$_nC_x$ = the number of combinations of a set of x successes from a total of n trials
p = the probability of a success in one randomly selected trial (0.75)
1−p = the probability of a failure in one randomly selected trial (0.25)

$$_8C_5 = \frac{8!}{5!(8-5)!} = \frac{8!}{5!3!} = 56$$

Probability of five successes out of eight trials = $_8C_5 (0.75)^5 (0.25)^3 = 56(0.2373)(0.0156)$ = 0.2073. (Study Session 3, LOS 9.d)

150. **C** If the events are mutually exclusive, then the probability of J&L Materials either increasing its dividend or repurchasing its stock is 30% + 40% − 0 = 70%. Note that if the events are not mutually exclusive, the probability of either event occurring is 30% + 40% − 25% = 45%. (Study Session 2, LOS 8.e)

151. **B** According to the Central Limit Theorem, if the sample size is large, the sample mean will be distributed normally regardless of the population's distribution, specific inferences can be about the population mean, and the sample mean will have a standard deviation equal to the population standard deviation divided by the square root of the sample size (also known as the standard error). (Study Session 3, LOS 10.d)

152. **B** Degrees of freedom for the *t*-statistic calculated for the sample mean equals the number of sampled observations minus 1. The number of sampled observations equals 20, so the degrees of freedom equal 19. The shape of the Student *t*-distribution changes depending on the degrees of freedom. Specifically, the Student *t*-distribution becomes closer to the Normal distribution as the degrees of freedom become large. As the degrees of freedom get smaller, the tails of the Student *t*-distribution get fatter relative to the Normal distribution, and the distribution becomes less peaked relative to the Normal distribution. (Study Session 3, LOS 10.i)

Economics

153. **C** Corporate profits taxes act as automatic stabilizers because they have a countercyclical effect. Limiting money supply growth is a monetary policy alternative; reducing marginal tax rates will decrease the countercyclical (and stabilization) effects of personal income taxes. (Study Session 6, LOS 26.d, e)

154. **C** The natural rate of unemployment is the unemployment rate that is present in the economy at full employment. The difference between the actual unemployment rate and the natural rate is cyclical unemployment. The natural rate includes both frictional and structural unemployment. When unemployment is above the natural rate, the economy is not operating at full capacity, and potential GDP is greater than real GDP. (Study Session 5, LOS 22.c)

155. **B** External costs are costs associated with a market that are paid for by people other than producers in that market. In this question, the mining industry producers are creating environmental damage that must be cleaned up after mining operations cease. The cost of the cleanup is borne by citizens not involved with the mine's production of copper. Thus, the reclamation costs are external costs. Producers in the mining industry are unlikely to consider the reclamation costs when determining the amount of copper to supply to the market. The result is production in excess of the efficient quantity. When overproduction occurs, marginal cost exceeds marginal benefit at the quantity produced, creating a deadweight loss. (Study Session 4, LOS 14.e)

156. **A** Accounting profit = revenue less cash expenses less depreciation (this is an explicit cost, just not a cash outlay) less interest expense (also an explicit cost, and interest expense is NOT included in operating expenses) = $120,000 − 50,000 − 5,000 − 2,000 = $63,000. To derive the economic profit, Wanda would also deduct the opportunity cost of foregone salary ($70,000), leaving an economic loss of $7,000. The $25,000 investment in fixtures is accounted for by the depreciation. (Study Session 4, LOS 16.a)

157. **B** Collusion is an agreement among firms to avoid various competitive practices. The cartel or oligopolists practicing collusion will be similar to a monopoly, in which prices increase and output decreases. (Study Session 5, LOS 20.a)

158. **C** The effective dollar price ceiling ($15.00) is below the equilibrium price of $35.00 per square foot and therefore generates a shortage of 6.0 − 2.1 = 3.9 million square feet. With such a large shortage, the potential for a black market exists. (Study Session 4, LOS 15.a)

159. **A** The equation of exchange is MV = PY. If velocity (V) is increasing faster than real output (Y), inflation (P) would have to be increasing faster than the money supply (M) to keep the equation in balance. (Study Session 6, LOS 24.i)

160. **B** Both statements are wrong. The minimum average variable cost will occur at a lower production level than the minimum average total cost. Profit is maximized where marginal profit equals marginal cost, not where average total cost is minimized. (Study Session 4, LOS 17.c)

161. **C** Marginal tax rates affect the reward derived from additional work. Reducing the marginal tax rate will provide incentives to increase the amount of labor supplied, which increases long-run aggregate supply (potential GDP). (Study Session 6, LOS 26.a)

162. **C** The pure bottled water market meets the four conditions (large number of competitors, similar product, no company has a dominant market share, no barriers to enter or exit) of the price taker model. Increased volume for filtering systems has reduced their cost. Since the industry cost curve is decreasing, the long run supply curve is downward-sloping. If the industry cost curve were increasing the long run supply curve would be upward-sloping. (Study Session 5, LOS 18.a)

163. **B** Economic profits are zero in the long run under monopolistic competition, but since average cost includes the costs of product differentiation and advertising (branding), there is disagreement over the efficiency of long-run output. Both advertising and product differentiation can create value as consumers prefer more choices and use the advertising and branding information to make purchase decisions. Whether there is an efficient amount of product differentiation or not, the benefits of product differentiation do tend to offset its costs. Whether the benefits of differentiated products totally offset the costs compared to a competitive market with a single (undifferentiated product) is open to debate. (Study Session 5, LOS 20.b,c)

164. **A** The money targeting rule assumes stable demand for money and a stable velocity of money. When demand for money is stable, the money targeting rule works. However, technological advances in the banking system have led to unexpected and unpredictable variability in the demand for money, making the model unreliable. The goal of the money targeting rule was to stabilize the money supply, and so fluctuations in the money supply are not the problem with the rule. The money targeting rule assumes that there is a strong link between demand for money and aggregate demand. If this link is strong, that would be an argument for using the model. (Study Session 6, LOS 27.d)

Financial Reporting and Analysis

165. **B** Failing to record accrued wages will understate wage expense, which leads to net income being overstated. Since net income is overstated, retained earnings and owners' equity are both overstated. (Study Session 7, LOS 30.f)

166. **A** Both the FASB and IASB frameworks have similar constraints. Each of the other answers reflects a difference between the two frameworks. The IASB framework gives underlying going concern and accrual assumptions greater importance than the FASB framework. The IASB framework provides one objective for all entities, while the FASB framework has separate objectives for business entities versus nonbusiness entities. In developing new standards, the IASB framework requires management's input into the process, while the FASB framework does not. (Study Session 7, LOS 31.f)

167. **B** Asset turnover equals sales / average total assets. Understating depreciation expense has no effect on sales. The lower depreciation will result in understatement of the accumulated depreciation account, so assets will be overstated. The higher level of assets will decrease the asset turnover ratio. (Study Session 8, LOS 32.c)

168. **C** These expenses are ongoing costs of operations. Losses or gains from the sale of a business segment are included in operating expenses. (Study Session 8, LOS 32.f)

169. **A** Diluted EPS $= \dfrac{\$500\,\text{million} - \$20\,\text{million}}{100\,\text{million} + 5\,\text{million} + 15\,\text{million}} = \$4.00\,\text{per share}$

Preferred dividend = 5 million × $4 = $20 million

$$\text{Warrant} = \left[\frac{\$50 - \$25}{\$50}\right] \times 10\,\text{million shares} = 5\,\text{million shares}$$

Preferred = 5 million shares × 3 shares = 15 million shares

(Study Session 8, LOS 32.h)

170. **C** Diluted EPS $= \dfrac{\$3,360,000 + \$210,000}{800,000 + 50,000} = \$4.20\,\text{per share}$

After-tax interest on convertible debt = ($5 million × .07) × (1 − 0.4) = $210,000

Add 50,000 shares from potential conversion of the convertible debt for a total of 850,000 diluted shares.

(Study Session 8, LOS 32.h,i)

171. **A** U.S. GAAP requires that goodwill associated with an acquisition be measured at the excess of cost over fair value of the acquired company's assets and recorded as an intangible asset. (Study Session 8, LOS 33.e)

172. **C** Unrealized gains and losses for actively traded securities are reported in the income statement. The dividends and interest income on all the securities would also be included. $200,000 + 30,000 + 50,000 + 10,000 = $290,000 (Study Session 8, LOS 33.g)

173. **B** The land purchase resulted in a $4 million outflow of cash, the patent resulted in a $3 million outflow, and the sale of the held-to-maturity securities resulted in a $2.1 million inflow. Thus, investing activities resulted in a net outflow of $4.9 million [−$4 million − $3 million + $2.1 million]. (Study Session 8, LOS 34.a)

174. **C** The bank loan resulted in a $4 million inflow of cash and the preferred stock issuance resulted in a $3.6 million inflow. Thus, financing activities resulted in a net inflow of $7.6 million ($4 million + $3.6 million). Note that under U.S. GAAP, Interest Expense is an operating cash flow. (Study Session 8, LOS 34.a)

175. **C** FCFF = CFO + Int(1 − tax rate) − capital expenditures

$$\text{FCFF} = 3,500 + \left[195 \times \left(1 - \left(\frac{1,540}{4,400}\right)\right)\right] - 727 = 2,899.75 \approx 2,900$$

(Study Session 8, LOS 34.i)

176. **B** In a period of rising prices and rising inventory levels, FIFO results in the highest net income (lowest COGS). (Study Session 9, LOS 35.c)

177. **B** There are 600 units remaining in ending inventory (2,700 units available – 2,100 units sold). Under LIFO, ending inventory is $30,000 (600 units × $50) and under FIFO, ending inventory is $27,600 (600 units × $46 per unit). Thus, FIFO will result in lower ending inventory of $2,400 ($30,000 LIFO inventory – $27,600 FIFO inventory). (Study Session 9, LOS 35.c)

178. **A** Under straight line (20,000 – 5,000)/5 = $3,000, under DDB 20,000× 2/5 = 8,000 (remember no salvage value). $8,000 – $3,000 = $5,000. (Study Session 9, LOS 36.d)

179. **B** Since the carrying value of Cobra exceeds the fair value of Cobra, the goodwill is impaired. The implied goodwill of Cobra is $500,000 ($5,000,000 fair value – $4,500,000 FV net assets). The impairment loss is equal to $250,000 ($750,000 goodwill carrying value – $500,000 implied goodwill). (Study Session 9, LOS 36.i)

180. **C** The effective rate and the statutory rate can vary because of permanent differences, such as permanently reinvested earnings from an unconsolidated affiliate. Depreciation expense and warranty expense result in temporary differences, which create deferred tax liabilities and assets. (Study Session 9, LOS 37.i)

181. **A** Taxable income is $145 ($150 pretax income – $25 municipal interest + $35 warranty expense – $15 depreciation). Income tax payable = $58 ($145 taxable income × 40%). (Study Session 9, LOS 37.d)

182. **C** Recognizing an asset retirement obligation (ARO) will result in a higher debt-to-equity ratio. Debt is higher by the amount of the ARO and equity is lower by the depreciation and accretion expense. Net profit margin is lower because of the depreciation and accretion expense (lower numerator). Asset turnover and ROA are both *lower* because the ARO is added to assets (denominator). Interest coverage is *lower* because of the accretion expense (higher denominator). (Study Session 9, LOS 36.g)

183. **B** Shelby's management will agree to the lending covenants to lower the interest rate on the credit facility. The existing bondholders and shareholders may have more risk since their respective interests are subordinate to the credit facility. (Study Session 9, LOS 38.b)

184. **C** The lease meets the criteria of a finance lease since the term is 75% of the airplane's life, collectibility is reasonably certain, and the lessor has substantially completed performance. The lease is treated as a sales-type lease since the present value of the lease payments exceeds the carrying value of the airplane. (Study Session 9, LOS 38.h)

185. **A** An extraordinary item is reported net of tax. At a 40% tax rate, the before tax loss was $20,000 [$12,000 extraordinary loss / (1 – 40% rate)]. In an extinguishment, a loss occurs when the reacquisition price exceeds the carrying value. Thus, given the reacquisition price of $1,010,000 ($1,000,000 × 101%), the carrying value must have been $990,000 ($1,010,000 – $20,000). (Study Session 9, LOS 38.a)

186. **C** Within the DuPont framework, the only choice that will increase the ROE is C. (Study Session 10, LOS 39.e)

187. **B** Since the quick ratio is greater than one, the percentage decrease in the denominator (current liabilities) is greater than the percentage decrease in the numerator (cash + accounts receivable + marketable securities). The denominator will decrease relatively more than the numerator. As a result, the quick ratio will increase. (Study Session 10, LOS 39.c)

188. **B** adjusted cost of goods sold Quip = 270,000 − (3,000 − 2,000) = 269,000

adjusted gross profit margin Quip = (350,000 − 269,000)/350,000 = 0.231 ≈ 23%

(Study Session 10, LOS 42.e)

189. **C** Galvin's depreciation expense will increase as a result of reducing the useful life. The higher depreciation expense translates into lower earnings per share. Higher depreciation expense will result in *lower* taxes. Interest expense would not be affected. (Study Session 9, LOS 36.d)

190. **A** GAAP standards require that dividends paid be reported in the financing section of the cash flow statement. GAAP standards require interest paid, dividends received and interest received be reported in the operating section of the cash flow statement. (Study Session 10, LOS 43.c)

191. **A** Three project interactions that complicate the capital budgeting process include: project sequencing, capital rationing, and mutually exclusive projects. Project sequencing complicates the capital budgeting process since certain investment projects may provide opportunities for future investment depending on the outcome of the first investment project or future economic conditions. Since the outcome of the project and future economic conditions are difficult to predict, the decision to invest today is more complicated. Under capital rationing, a firm with a *limited* budget for investment projects must select the mix of investments that increases shareholder value by the largest amount. Generally firms are not able to raise an unlimited amount of capital and must choose investments within their budget. Mutually exclusive projects occur when only one project may be selected from a group of projects. In this situation, a criteria for selecting the best investment out of the group must be determined. Independent projects do not cause problems for firms with unlimited capital budgets. Firms in this situation will select all positive NPV projects. (Study Session 11, LOS 44.c)

192. **C** A project's NPV profile crosses the Y-axis at the NPV associated with a discount rate of zero. This is also equal to the sum of the undiscounted cash flows of a project. As the discount rate increases, the NPV profile falls. At some point the NPV profile crosses the X-axis. At this point, the NPV is zero and the point of intersection is the project's IRR (the discount rate that causes NPV to equal zero). When two projects' NPV profiles are graphed together, one Project's NPV will be higher than the other project's NPV until the profiles reach the crossover rate. At the crossover rate, the NPVs of the two projects are equal. In our example, the NPV of Project A starts out higher than Project B. This trend will continue until the NPV profiles reach the crossover rate of 18%. At rates higher than the crossover rate, the NPV of Project B will be higher than the NPV of Project A (opposite of the initial trend at lower discount rates). Because Project A and Project B are mutually exclusive, we should select the project with the higher NPV if the NPV and IRR rankings conflict. Recall that at rates lower than the crossover rate of 18%, the NPV of Project A is greater than Project B. The relevant rate for calculating NPV for investment decisions is the firm's cost of capital. Inverness has a cost of capital of 15%, implying the NPV of Project A is greater than Project B at that discount rate. The IRR rankings would indicate Project B is the appropriate choice since it has the higher IRR. Since the rankings conflict, use the NPV criteria to select Project A. (Study Session 11, LOS 44.e)

193. **B** WACC = 0.4 × 0.07 × (1 − 0.35) + 0.6 × 0.13 = 0.096. The WACC is also referred to as a company's marginal cost of capital when the weighted average cost of capital reflects the cost of raising additional capital. (Study Session 11, LOS 45.a)

194. **B** In order to calculate the weighted average cost of capital, weights must be chosen for each component cost of capital. Weights can be determined using several methods, including: using the current market values of the firm's capital to determine weights, examining historical trends in the capital structure to determine the optimal structure, and using an average of the capital structure of competitors. The fourth (and preferred) method is to use the company's target capital structure. The target capital structure is the proportion of debt, preferred stock, and common stock that the firm would like to maintain as it obtains additional financing. Individuals outside a company generally are unaware of the target capital structure. However, this information is given for Sturdy Inc in the form of the target debt-to-equity ratio, which is therefore the best available data provided. We can transform the debt-to-equity ratio into capital weights as follows.

$$w_d = \frac{(D/E)}{(1+D/E)} = \frac{(0.65)}{(1.65)} = 0.39 = 39\%$$

Since the company has no preferred stock, the weight of equity can be calculated as follows.

$$w_e = (1 - 0.39) = 0.61 = 61\%$$

(Study Session 11, LOS 45.c)

195. **C** Note that the market risk premium is not the same as R_M, or return of the market. The pure play cost of equity uses the SML equation but replaces the overall company beta of 1.1 with the project beta of 1.3 obtained by observing the systematic risk of an internet only clothing retailer. The pure play cost of equity is thus: 12.6 = 0.035 + 1.3(0.07). (Study Session 11, LOS 45.h)

196. **C** The quick ratio is defined as: (cash + marketable investments + accounts receivable)/ current liabilities. The question states that for HMS Inc., the quick ratio has been decreasing over time while the current liability balance has remained constant. Given this information, we know that the numerator of the ratio must be decreasing over time. The only possible explanation is that cash, marketable investments, or accounts receivable has decreased. Note that inventory is not included in the quick ratio calculation. (Study Session 11, LOS 46.a)

197. **C** A cash flow forecast should include those items that reflect real cash inflows and outflows. Examples of real cash inflows include cash receipts from operations, transfers of funds from a subsidiary or other related entity, long-term investments that are coming due, debt issuance, interest income, tax refunds, and other items. Examples of real cash outflows include payroll, payment of accounts payable balances, fund transfers to a subsidiary or other related entity, cash used to enter long-term investments, debt repayment, interest payments, dividend payments, and tax payments. Items that would not affect the cash flow forecast include non-cash expenses such as depreciation or accruals for future expenses. Also, sales made on credit would not affect the cash flow forecast since these sales would be collected at a later date. (Study Session 11, LOS 46.c)

198. **B** Form 8A describes the rights of a company's shareholders. From the investor viewpoint, the company should hire a third-party agent to conduct voting tabulation to ensure confidentiality and accuracy. The third party should also maintain the voting records. Having two classes of shares is not a problem for shareholders as long as the shares have proportional economic and voting rights. For example, anyone could acquire ten shares of Benson class B stock and have the exact same economic and voting rights as one class A share. Obviously there is an economic difference between one share of class A and one share of class B. However, both classes of shares are publicly traded so there is nothing stopping a class B shareholder from acquiring the same rights as a class A shareholder. Benson's takeover defense approval system is also not a problem for shareholders. Requiring shareholder approval protects shareholders from management's refusal of a beneficial takeover. For example, if an acquirer offered twice the market value of Benson's common stock, shareholders can prevent Benson managers (who want to protect their jobs) from initiating a takeover defense since a 2/3 majority shareholder approval would be needed. (Study Session 11, LOS 48.g)

Portfolio Management

199. **C** Paftee's granddaughter is at least 15 years away from entering college. Therefore, the time horizon constraint is long-term. Paftee also faces a significant liquidity constraint because she must withdraw funds occasionally from her investment account to pay for health care expenses for her parents. (Study Session 12, LOS 49.d)

200. **B** Compute the expected return first:

$$(0.2 \times 0.08) + (0.4 \times 0.10) + (0.4 \times 0.12) = 0.104$$

Then compute the squared differences multiplied by their probabilities:

$$[0.2(0.08 - 0.104)^2] + [0.4(0.10 - 0.104)^2] + [0.4(0.12 - 0.104)^2] = 0.000224$$

Next, take the square root of the variance to find the standard deviation:

$$\sqrt{0.000224} = 0.01497$$

(Study Session 12, LOS 50.c)

201. **A** The efficient frontier is the set of portfolios that are the most efficient in terms of risk and return. Each portfolio on the efficient frontier provides the maximum expected return for its level of risk. The leftmost endpoint of the efficient frontier is the efficient portfolio with the lowest risk (the minimum risk portfolio). Points on the efficient frontier represent portfolios, not individual assets (with the exception of the rightmost point when short sales are not allowed). (Study Session 12, LOS 50.f)

202. **A** The return of the risk-free asset is certain, so its standard deviation will be zero; therefore, covariance and correlation with other assets will also be zero. Therefore, adding the risk-free asset to a risky portfolio will decrease the portfolio standard deviation. (Study Session 12, LOS 51.a)

203. **B** Investing on margin in the market portfolio will raise both risk and expected returns. This strategy would be mean-variance efficient. Other strategies such as shifting a portion of total funds to higher risk assets would achieve the higher return goal but would leave the portfolio below the CML and thus would not be an optimal strategy. (Study Session 12, LOS 51.b)

204. **B** The capital asset pricing model is the equation for the security market line (SML): risk-free rate plus beta times market risk premium, where the market risk premium equals the difference between the expected market return and the risk-free rate. The starting point (intercept) for the SML is the risk-free rate (5%), and the slope for the SML is the market risk premium (8%). For Stock X, the required return equals 0.05 + 1.5(0.08) = 17%, and for Stock Y equals 0.05 + 2(0.08) = 21%. Linn predicts 20% for each stock. Therefore, Linn's predicted return for Stock X (20%) lies above the SML and for Stock Y (20%) lies below the SML. (Study Session 12, LOS 51.e)

Asset Valuation

205. **C** This is a limit order. If the shares trade for €75 or below, Fontenot's broker will purchase the shares for him. If Fontenot had wanted to sell shares he already owned when the price dropped to €75.00, that would be a stop loss order. (Study Session 13, LOS 52.e)

206. **C** The statements in answer choices A and B are correct. Answer choice C is incorrect because sovereign bond index returns are not adjusted for taxes. (Study Session 13, LOS 53.b)

207. **B** Inefficiencies such as this often arise and often grow larger before there is any correction. The internet stock bubble of the late 1990s is an example of just such a situation. Arbitrageurs may be unaware of the situation, but that is not necessarily true. Similarly, arbitrageurs may lack capital to exploit the mispricing, but this is not the only way such inefficiencies can arise. (Study Session 13, LOS 55.b)

208. **A** Analyst A is correct. The large number of investors motivated by profits provides a very efficient market, making it difficult to outperform the market benchmarks. Analyst B is incorrect. Although his strategy has outperformed over three years, a significantly greater period of time is needed before the strategy can be considered an anomaly to the efficient market. Analyst C is incorrect because market frictions (such as transactions costs) reduce efficiency. (Study Session 13, LOS 54.b)

209. **B** We will use the relation $k_i = \dfrac{D_1}{P_0} + g$

g = ROE(1 − payout ratio) = 0.15(1 − 0.3) = 0.105;

EPS = ROE × BV = 0.15 × 20 = 3

D_0 = EPS × payout = 3 × 0.3 = 0.9

D_1 = 0.9 × (1.105) = 0.9945

$k_i = \dfrac{0.9945}{35} + 0.105 = 0.1334 = 13.34\%$

(Study Session 14, LOS 56.f)

210. **C** A company's potential growth is estimated by ROE × retention rate. The increase in leverage will increase Peterson's ROE, and increase the potential growth rate. However, the increased payout ratio will decrease the retention rate, and have a negative effect on growth potential offsetting the higher ROE to some extent. (Study Session 14, LOS 56.f)

211. **B** The book value for common stock should exclude preferred stock, but should include common stock and retained earnings, adjusted for any Treasury stock:

$$\frac{2,000,000 + 8,400,000 - 400,000}{1,000,000 - 200,000} = 12.50 \quad \text{(Study Session 14, LOS 59.b)}$$

212. **C** Diversification eliminates unsystematic risk, not systematic risk. The portfolio manager's duties require a thorough understanding of the client's current objectives and constraints. In addition, the portfolio manager must monitor them for any possible future changes. (Study Session 13, LOS 54.c)

213. **A** Price-to-sales is acceptable for evaluating growth companies, and can be superior to other measures when earnings are negative or nonexistent. (Study Session 14, LOS 59.a)

214. **B** Balance sheet risk and variability risk are not considered part of the five components of country risk premiums. (Study Session 14, LOS 56.e)

215. **C** For large portfolios, the full valuation approach requires that each bond be valued under each interest rate scenario. The duration/convexity approach would calculate the effect based on the overall portfolio characteristics, and would be much quicker. (Study Session 16, LOS 66.a)

216. **A** LIBOR is the rate paid by banks borrowing from each other in the London Interbank market. The loan is made by way of a certificate of deposit (CD). The lending bank deposits funds into a CD account at the borrower bank. In this case the CD would mature in 6 months. LIBOR can be denominated in several currencies, including the dollar, the pound, and the euro, but 6 month LIBOR is not the return on the shortest maturity euro-denominated instrument. LIBOR is not based on UK government security yields. (Study Session 15, LOS 63.j)

217. **B** The bond equivalent yield (BEY) is calculated by doubling the semiannual yield that, when compounded for two periods, would equal the annual yield. The BEY will always be less than the yield to maturity of an annual pay bond.

$$\text{Annual Yield} = \left(1 + \frac{\text{BEY}}{2}\right)^2 - 1 \Rightarrow \text{BEY} = 2 \times \left[(1 + \text{Annual Yield})^{0.5} - 1\right]$$

BEY = 2 × [(1.07)^{0.5} − 1] = 0.0688 = 6.88%

(Study Session 15, LOS 65.d)

218. **A** The liquidity preference theory states that investors require a liquidity premium for investing in longer-term bonds. This liquidity premium is compensation for interest rate risk and increases as maturities get longer. The liquidity preference theory can explain a flat or downward sloping term structure of interest rates as an expectation of decreasing future short-term interest rates. For the term structure to remain flat, according to this theory, the increasing liquidity premium must be accompanied by decreasing short-term interest rates so that the total interest rate (short-term rate + liquidity premium) is constant throughout time. A similar argument is made to justify a downward sloping term structure of interest rates. (Study Session 15, LOS 63.c)

219. **A** The implied rate on a repurchase agreement is generally less than the rate charged by banks for margin buying, especially when a service fee is added on to the margin interest rate by the broker. Margin buying restricts the loan amount to a set percentage of the collateral value. While in a repurchase agreement, the loan value is the value of the collateral reduced only by the implied interest (repo) rate. Repurchase agreements are much more common for institutional bond investors than margin buying. (Study Session 15, 60.f)

220. **C** Neither coupon nor principal strips have credit risk or reinvestment risk. They are direct obligations of the U.S. government that have no interim cash flows to be reinvested. There can be negative tax consequences, however, since the interest accrued each year is taxed even though nothing is received until the strip matures. (Study Session 15, LOS 62.c)

221. **C** Prepayment risk refers to the EARLY repayment of principal. In a rising rate environment, borrowers will be less likely to refinance their mortgages, but there will still be prepayments as homes are sold. Note that the increasing amount of principal payments through a standard amortization schedule does not give rise to prepayment risk – that amount of prepayment is assumed. (Study Session 15, LOS 62.e)

222. **A** The analyst is correct with respect to the redistribution of risk, but is incorrect with respect to total risk. Collateralized mortgage obligations (CMOs) were devised as a way of redistributing the prepayment risk of a mortgage backed security. In a CMO, the cash flows from the underlying assets are collected and distributed to different tranches according to a predetermined schedule. This reduces the uncertainty associated with prepayments for some tranches while increasing the uncertainty for other tranches. The total prepayment risk, however, is unchanged. (Study Session 15, LOS 62.f)

223. **B** The bond is trading at a premium, and if the bond is called at par that premium would be amortized over a shorter period, resulting in a lower return. The lower return is the more conservative number, so the YTC should be used. You could use your financial calculator to solve for YTC assuming 10 semiannual coupon payments of $35 (FV = 1,000; PMT = 35; PV = -1,065, N = 10; solve for i = 2.75; × 2 to get annual YTC = 5.5%. Calculation of YTM would use the same inputs except N = 20, to get YTM = 6.12% (Study Session 16, LOS 65.b)

224. **C** The conversion privilege is an option granted to the bondholder. The cap benefits the issuer. The accelerated sinking fund might reduce the investor's default risk, but the conversion option is the most likely benefit to the investor. (Study Session 15, LOS 60.e)

225. **C** Zero-coupon bonds (such as a Treasury Strip) have no reinvestment risk over their lives but have a high degree of interest rate risk. The mortgage-backed security would have higher reinvestment risk due to the need to reinvest not only the coupon payments, but amortized principal payments as well. (Study Session 15, LOS 61.i)

226. **B** Remember the formula:

price of callable = price of option free – price of embedded option

The value of the call option would increase, but this increase benefits the issuer, not the investor. The value of the bond would increase due to the lower rates, but the increasing value of the option would offset some portion of this benefit. (Study Session 15, LOS 61.d)

Exam 1
Afternoon Session Answers

227. **A** Bond X carries the lowest investment grade rating – if it is downgraded, it will fall to a speculative rating, and many investors will be restricted from owning it. A downgrade would therefore have a more significant impact on Bond X. Bond Y carries a highly speculative rating that implies more risk of default than the higher rated Bond X. (Study Session 15, LOS 61.j)

228. **C** Taxable equivalent yield = 0.045 / (1 – 0.35) = 0.0692 (Study Session 15, LOS 63.i)

229. **A** The yield on the bonds has increased, indicating that the value of the bonds has fallen below par. The bonds are therefore trading at a discount. If a bond is selling at a discount, the bond's current price is lower than its par value and the bond's YTM is higher than the coupon rate. Since Logan bought the bonds at par (coupon = YTM = 6%), the YTM has increased. (Study Session 16, LOS 61.b)

230. **B** The derivative markets require a high degree of leverage in their payoffs, thus are considered too risky or similar to gambling for investors with limited knowledge of derivatives. However, illiquidity is not a commonly cited criticism of derivatives markets. The benefits most frequently cited are: price discovery, risk management, and the derivative markets' relatively low transaction costs. (Study Session 17, LOS 67.c)

231. **C** A covered call strategy reduces the risk of the position by cushioning losses with the premium received on the short call option. In order to gain this risk reduction, however, the covered call strategy gives up the possibility of experiencing large upside gains. Therefore, the expected return is reduced, not increased, as the first manager incorrectly states. The profit potential on a protective put is indeed infinite. The protective put strategy requires the purchase of a put option, but the long position in the stock may increase in value without limit. Therefore, the overall profit of the protective put may also increase without limit. The maximum loss, however, is equal to the cost of the initial position (stock price at initiation plus the put premium) minus the exercise price of the put option: $S_0 + p_0 - X$. The second manager incorrectly stated the maximum loss on the protective put strategy. (Study Session 17, LOS 72.b)

232. **B** In a futures contract, margin calls occur when the balance in the margin account has fallen below the maintenance margin level. When this occurs, a deposit must be made to bring the margin account balance back to the initial margin level. This deposit is called variation margin. If the maintenance margin is half of the initial margin, then a margin call after the first day of trading (which would be issued at the beginning of the second day) would mean that the balance in the margin account is less than half the initial margin. The variation margin would therefore be more than half the initial margin and more than the maintenance margin. Daily gains and losses are determined by the settlement price relative to the futures price. The settlement price is the average of the last few trades of the day, not the final trade of the day. Since the contract in the question has only traded for one day, the futures price used as a reference for gains/losses is also the original contract price. In order for a long futures contract to experience a loss, and thus require a margin call, the settlement price for the first trading day must have been lower than the contract price. (Study Session 17, LOS 69.b)

233. **B** Quincy should enter into a long S&P 500 Index forward contract with Mason Inc. to minimize credit risk. Since the original short forward contract was with Mason Inc., entering into an offsetting position would allow for cancellation of the contracts between the two parties. Since Quincy is required to sell the underlying for $1,221, and the long contract has a price of $1,220, Quincy and Mason can terminate the original contract by having Mason pay Smith $1. Contracting with JonesCo or Redding Company would increase credit risk since Quincy would be exposed to potential default from another entity in addition to Mason. (Study Session 17, LOS 68.b)

234. **C** $C_0 \geq Max[0, S_0 - X/(1+ r)^{(219/365)}] = Max[0, 29 - 25/1.04^{0.6}] = Max[0, 29 - 24.42] = 4.58$. (Study Session 17, LOS 70.h)

235. **A** A long position in a put option pays off when the underlying interest rate falls below the strike rate on the option. Since on the day of expiration LIBOR is 3.0%, Kramer's interest rate put option, Option 2, is in the money. The payoff on Option 2 would be $6 = [$1,000 × (0.054 – 0.030) × 0.25]. However, the payoff would occur 90-days after the expiration date, making the present value at expiration of the payoff on Option 2 less than $6. At expiration, Kramer's call option on Blintz Company stock, Option 1, is also in the money. Recall that call options on common stock are in the money when the stock price is greater than the strike price. The payoff on Option 1 is equal to $6 = ($64 – $58). The payoff would occur on the expiration day, making the present value at expiration of the payoff on Option 1 equal to $6. Thus, the present value of the payoff on Option 1 is greater than the present value of the payoff on Option 2. Option 3 is out of the money. Therefore it has a payoff of zero. (Study Session 17, LOS 70.e)

236. **B** Party A wants to swap his fixed-rate payment, so he will pay the fixed payments in the swap and receive the floating- rate payments based on LIBOR plus 100bp. First calculate the first fixed-rate payment as: $100,000,000 × [0.065 × (90 / 360)] = $1,625,000.

Next calculate the first floating-rate payment as: $100,000,000 × [(0.052 + .01) × (90 / 360)] = $1,550,000

Since Party A is paying fixed and receiving floating, the net payment from Party A is $1,625,000 – $1,550,000 = $75,000 (a cash outflow). Notice you need only 90-day LIBOR since payments were being calculated quarterly and the question asked for the first net payment. (Study Session 17, LOS 71.b)

237. **B** Hedge fund indexes are biased toward the success stories of the industry. Inclusion of the unsuccessful hedge funds would increase the historical volatility of the hedge fund industry. The investment strategies of hedge funds generate asymmetrical returns (not normally distributed). Hedge fund indexes do suffer from incomplete historical data. (Study Session 18, LOS 73.l)

238. **A** Compared to a traditional mutual fund, an ETF will most likely have options and futures traded on the index. In addition, ETF prices are available on an intra-day basis and an investor can take a short position in the ETF. All these advantages should lead to better risk management when investing in an ETF. ETF portfolios are more transparent, as ETF sponsors publish portfolio holdings on a daily basis. ETF shareholders generally face lower capital gains tax liabilities than holders of traditional mutual funds. (Study Session 18, LOS 73.c)

239. **C**   Total return = capital gains plus interest income

Capital gains = 25,000,000 × 0.1 = 2,500,000

Interest income = $25{,}000{,}000 \times 0.035 \times \dfrac{90}{360} = 218{,}750$

Total return = \$2,500,000 + \$218,750 = \$2,718,750 ≈ \$2,700,000

(Study Session 18, LOS 73.r)

240. **A**   Net operating income (NOI) is calculated as gross operating income less estimated vacancy, collections, and other operating expenses. The calculation does not consider depreciation (properties are assumed to be maintained to offset depreciation) or interest expense (NOI is used to value the real estate investment independent of its financing). Since the analyst at Hoffman advisors underestimated vacancy by \$3,000 and overestimated insurance expense (an operating expense) by \$4,000, updated NOI would \$1,000 higher (NOI decreases by \$3,000 for the vacancy but increases \$4,000 for the insurance expense for a net increase of \$1,000). (Study Session 18, LOS 73.f)

Exam 2
Morning Session Answers

To get valuable feedback on how your score compares to those of other Level 1 candidates, use your Username and Password to gain Online Access at schweser.com and choose the left-hand menu item "Practice Exams Vol. 2."

1. A	31. C	61. A	91. B
2. A	32. A	62. B	92. C
3. B	33. A	63. C	93. C
4. C	34. C	64. A	94. A
5. A	35. B	65. A	95. B
6. C	36. B	66. A	96. A
7. C	37. A	67. B	97. A
8. A	38. B	68. C	98. C
9. B	39. A	69. B	99. A
10. B	40. A	70. C	100. A
11. A	41. A	71. B	101. B
12. B	42. A	72. C	102. C
13. C	43. B	73. B	103. A
14. C	44. C	74. B	104. C
15. C	45. C	75. A	105. B
16. C	46. C	76. B	106. C
17. B	47. A	77. B	107. A
18. B	48. A	78. C	108. C
19. C	49. B	79. A	109. B
20. A	50. C	80. A	110. A
21. B	51. C	81. C	111. C
22. B	52. C	82. C	112. C
23. B	53. C	83. B	113. A
24. A	54. C	84. B	114. C
25. C	55. C	85. B	115. B
26. C	56. B	86. C	116. A
27. B	57. A	87. C	117. C
28. B	58. B	88. A	118. A
29. B	59. B	89. B	119. A
30. A	60. A	90. A	120. A

Exam 2
Morning Session Answers

Ethical and Professional Standards

Answers referencing the Standards of Practice are all Study Session 1, LOS 2.a, b.

1. **A** Standard I(B). An analyst's recommendation should be his or her own objective view—there must be no yielding to pressure from the investment banking department or any other department. To avoid even the appearance of impropriety or a conflict of interest, Meelono must discontinue issuing recommendations about Versoxy, and perhaps put the stock on a restricted list.

2. **A** Standard II(B). There is not a violation of Standard II(B) – Integrity of Capital Markets – Market Manipulation. This is not a manipulative transaction. Also, in accordance with Standard III(C) – Duties to Clients – Suitability, it would be a good idea to counsel the client, and at minimum encourage a more systematic sale of the thinly traded security. Some type of confirmation, in advance, from the client, would be a good idea, acknowledging that the price of the security may be severely affected by an immediate sale.

3. **B** Standard III(B). Although simultaneous distribution of information is preferred, recommendations, or changes of recommendations, only need to go to those clients who have previously expressed a known interest in these types of securities.

4. **C** Standard I(B) and Standard IV(B). Standard IV(B) – Duties to Employers – Additional Compensation Arrangements requires Westerburg to obtain permission from his employer for any additional compensation from clients. He has done so. There is no requirement to notify other clients. It is true that the nature of this arrangement (use of the yacht) may result in partiality to one account to the detriment of others. The intent of the Standard is that the employer must grant permission to receive such a supplemental benefit. If the *employer* believes that such compensation may result in partiality to a certain account, then the employer can deny permission. Standard I(B) – Professionalism – Independence and Objectivity restricts compensation, but only from parties which may influence behavior, such as brokers.

5. **A** Standard II(A). According to Standard II(A), the analyst's conclusions are covered by the mosaic theory, so no additional disclosure is required. Carter has appropriately conducted perceptive analysis, combining material public with nonmaterial nonpublic information.

6. **C** Standard III(E). According to the Standard, members must maintain the confidentiality of all clients, prospects, and former clients unless the member has information concerning illegal activities, a disclosure of information is necessary by law, or the client grants permission to share the information. Members can best comply with the Standard by avoiding disclosure of confidential client information to anyone but authorized employees working for the client. Remy is allowed to inform Walker of the client's expected inheritance since Walker manages a portion of the client's portfolio and will likely need to prepare for the infusion of new funds into the account. Remy has also taken appropriate action with regard to his suspicion that the client's inheritance is actually part of an illegal money laundering scheme. Since he is

not completely sure of the legality of the inheritance, it is appropriate to first speak with his firm's compliance or legal department before contacting law enforcement authorities. Remy has not violated Standard III(E). – Duties to Clients – Preservation of Confidentiality.

7. **C** Standard I(C). According to the Standard, members and candidates are prohibited from knowingly making misrepresentations related to investment analysis, recommendations, actions, or professional activities. Kedzie has violated the Standard by effectively guaranteeing the return on ZYX stock will only be positive. The stock may be suitable for the portfolio, but the investment success of inherently volatile investments cannot be guaranteed. The troublesome phrase is "ensure that the foundation will benefit from positive returns." This implies a guarantee.

8. **A** Standard VII(B), I(C). Milken is allowed to make a statement of fact such as the money manager's right to use the CFA designation. All of the statements are acceptable. Milken Co. may reference the participation of its employees in the CFA program if the employees are currently registered to take one of the exams. They may also state that certain employees have earned the right to use the CFA designation as long as it is a statement of fact. The statement regarding dedication to the investment community and commitment to the highest ethical standards are proper references regarding the CFA program.

9. **B** GIPS. Disclosures are to be considered static information that does not change from period to period. Included in the Disclosure section would be information on such topics as the firm definition, the currency used in the presentation and a complete list and description of all of the firm's composites.

10. **B** Standard I(D). According to Standard I(D) – Professionalism – Misconduct, the other choices are consistent with the recommended procedures for compliance. However, it is instead appropriate to distribute to employees a list of *potential* violations and associated sanctions.

11. **A** Standard II(A). Standard II(A) states that if a member or candidate possesses material nonpublic information, they should make a reasonable attempt to have the information publicly disseminated, usually by encouraging the issuer company to inform the general public of the relevant information through a formal press release. Choice C is not appropriate because it might give a signal to the market.

12. **B** Standard V(A). According to the Standard, members must conduct professional activities in a diligent, independent, and thorough manner. Additionally, members must be able to support a reasonable and adequate basis for their professional activities with proper research. Standard V(A) – Investment Analysis, Recommendations, and Actions – Diligence and Reasonable Basis requires Manaugh to exercise independence in analyzing investments and making investment recommendations. If Manaugh chooses to update his report, it must be based on his own independent research and analysis, not an overheard conversation.

13. **C** Standard I(C). According to the Standard, members are prohibited from making any misrepresentations relating to investment analysis, recommendations, actions, or other professional activities. By downloading Bright Star's proprietary model to her hard disk plus the performance and back testing data, Smith has copied proprietary computerized information without authorization of the creator, Bright Star Bank and now Mega Bank. Even if Bright Star has been absorbed by Mega Bank, the assets of the trust department, including the model, now belong to the new owner Mega Bank, even if they choose not to use them. Smith should have properly sought a licensing agreement with Mega Bank to use the model and data.

14. **C**   Standard V(B). Richards has violated Standard V(B) – Investment Analysis, Recommendations, and Actions – Communication with Clients and Prospective Clients by failing to appropriately distinguish between fact and opinion. It is her *opinion* that MegaRx will require a write-down, not a fact. Swanson violated Standard IV(C) – Duties to Employers – Responsibilities of Supervisors by failing to recognize that the report he was personally reviewing contained a violation of the Code and Standards, which both he and Richards are bound to uphold.

15. **C**   Verification is not required. Compliant firms must meet all GIPS requirements so there is no disclosure related to requirements that are not met. Firms are not permitted to alter historical composite performance because of changes in firm organization.

16. **C**   Standard IV(C) – Duties to Employers: Responsibilities of Supervisors requires members and candidates with supervisory responsibility to make reasonable efforts to detect and prevent violations of rules and regulations (as well as of the Code and Standards) by those under their supervision. The fact that violations occur is not necessarily evidence that reasonable efforts were not made. In large organizations, delegating supervisory responsibility may be necessary, but this does not relieve the person with overall authority of supervisory responsibility.

17. **B**   Standard III(A) Loyalty, Prudence, and Care. Kevil has violated his duty under Standard III(A). He must consider all proxy issues carefully and ensure that the proxies are voted in the best interest of his client. He cannot rely on the assumption that because a company's management happens to be the largest shareholders, they have his client's best interest in mind. He is allowed to use a more expensive broker for any client if the client specifically requests the use of the broker (client directed brokerage).

18. **B**   Standard VI(C). Members and candidates must disclose referral fees to their employer, clients, and prospects. DTI has noted the details of the referral arrangement with Weston and has, thus, complied with the Standard. It is not necessary to provide the exact number of referrals received, just the details of the compensation given or received as a result of the referral relationship. Hurley has not provided any disclosure to clients regarding the referral arrangement with Weston and has thus violated the Standard. They cannot rely on Weston's disclosure, but must make the disclosure themselves.

Quantitative Methods

19. **C**   Begin by setting up the following probability weighted return calculation:

$(0.333 \times 0.09) + (P_2 \times -0.04) + [(1 - 0.333 - P_2) \times 0.06] = 0.0367$

Then solve for P_2 (the probability Scenario 2 will occur):

$0.03 + -0.04 P_2 + 0.06 (0.667 - P_2) = 0.0367$

$P_2 = 0.333$

The probability of Scenario 3 equals: $P_3 = (1 - 0.333 - P_2)$ Solving for P_2 and P_3 reveals that there is an equal probability (33.3%) of each scenario occurring. (Study Session 2, LOS 7.d)

20. **A**   A leptokurtic distribution (a distribution with kurtosis measure greater than 3) is more peaked in the middle (data more clustered around the mean) and has fatter tails at the extremes (greater chance of outliers). (Study Session 2, LOS 7.j)

21. **B** Chebyshev's inequality holds for samples/populations regardless of the shape of the distribution. For +/− k standard deviations, the probability underneath the distribution in general is $\geq 1 - 1/k^2$. Thus, for +/− 3 standard deviations, the percentage underneath the distribution is $\geq 1 - 1/3^2 = 1 - 1/9 = 89\%$ Risk management is not concerned with the mean, but with the distribution of returns in the tails of the distribution. (Study Session 2, LOS 7.g, j)

22. **B**
$$EAY = (1+HPY)^{\frac{365}{t}} - 1$$

$$HPY = \frac{P_1 - P_0 + D_1}{P_0}$$

$$HPY = \frac{100,000 - 98,039 + 0}{98,039} = .02 \text{ or } 2\%$$

$$EAY = (1+.02)^{\frac{365}{61}} - 1 = .1258 \text{ or } 12.58\%$$

(Study Session 2, LOS 6.d)

23. **B**

	(A-a)	(B-b)	(A-a)(B-b)
Year 1	−23.4	4.2	−98.3
Year 2	−13.2	−1.6	21.1
Year 3	−10.4	4.8	−49.9
Year 4	19.7	−12.2	−240.3
Year 5	27.2	4.7	127.8
			−239.6

−239.6/4 = −59.9   (Study Session 2, LOS 8.j)

24. **A** The bond equivalent yield on a semiannual coupon paying bond is calculated by doubling the semiannual yield to maturity. Similarly, the bond equivalent yield on a 6 month money market instrument is calculated by doubling the holding period yield.

Treasury note: 0.0229 × 2 = 0.0458

CD: 0.0231 × 2 = 0.0462

Select the CD. (Study Session 2, LOS 6.d)

25. **C** The number of unequally-weighted portfolios is determined using the permutation formula:

$$_7P_4 = \frac{7!}{(7-4)!} = \frac{7!}{3!} = 840$$

In this answer, the ordering of the 4 selected stocks matters (each stock receives an allocation that differs depending on its place in the ordering of the four stocks). For example, ABCD and ACBD are counted as two portfolios. (Study Session 2, LOS 8.n)

26. **C** Selecting only funds that managed to survive for 15 years should bias the value added upward, as poor-performing funds are more likely to have failed or been rolled into better performing funds (an example of survivorship bias). While the time period can affect results, with 15 years of data, the time period is likely to be less important than survivorship bias. (Study Session 3, LOS 10.k)

27. **B** Using the cumulative distribution function, we can calculate that the probability the machine will be purchased for $75 million or less is: 0.3 + 0.2 + 0.1 = 0.6 or 60%. (Study Session 3, LOS 9.c)

28. **B** Benson's client is most concerned with getting less than a 4% return. Thus, the safety-first ratio is appropriate to measure risk. Notice, however, that using the risk-free rate in the safety-first ratio gives you the Sharpe ratio. If the client was concerned about achieving a return less than the risk-free rate, then the Sharpe ratio would be appropriate. (Study Session 3, LOS 9.i)

29. **B** Gould states that "*the mean 1-year Treasury bill rate should equal four percent.*" Therefore, the null hypothesis is: H_o: mean Treasury bill rate equals 4%; and the alternative hypothesis is H_a: mean Treasury bill rate does not equal 4%, which is a two-tailed test. Gould also states that "*the mean market risk premium should be positive.*" Therefore, the null hypothesis is: H_o: mean market risk premium is less than or equal to zero; and the alternative hypothesis is H_a: mean market risk premium is greater than zero, which is a one-tailed test. (Study Session 3, LOS 11.a)

30. **A** A consistent estimator is one that gets better as the sample size increases. An unbiased estimator is one whose expected value (average) equals the true population parameter. (Study Session 3, LOS 10.g)

31. **C** The interest rate equals the sum of the real rate, the expected inflation rate, the total risk premium (which equals the sum of the maturity risk premium, the liquidity risk premium, and the default risk premium). The real rate equals 1%, the expected inflation rate equals 2%, the maturity risk premium equals 4%. Treasury bonds have no liquidity or default risk, so the interest rate on a long-term Treasury bond would be expected to equal 7%. Since the SubPrime Providers (long-term) bond incurs default risk, its interest rate must exceed that of the long-term Treasury bond (i.e., 7%). The SubPrime Providers bond is highly liquid, so it has no liquidity premium. The default risk premium for SubPrime Providers bond equals 5%. Taken together, this implies that the SubPrime Provider bond interest rate should exceed the Treasury bond interest by 5 percentage points (12%). (Study Session 2, LOS 5.b)

32. **A**   A test statistic (e.g., such as a *t*-statistic) is "statistically significant" if it exceeds its critical value. Therefore, a large test statistic indicates that the sample statistic (e.g., the sample mean) is statistically significant (i.e., significantly different from the hypothesized value under the null hypothesis). A sample statistic can be statistically significant yet not economically meaningful. This happens when the sample statistic differs only slightly from the hypothesized value, while the standard error is extremely small. In that case, the test statistic may still be statistically significant, even though the sample mean differs only slightly from the hypothesized value (was not economically significant). This situation is most likely to occur in large samples because the standard error shrinks as the sample size grows. For example, the test statistic for testing the sample mean equals:

$$t = \frac{\bar{X} - \mu_o}{s.e.}$$

where:
s.e. = the standard error, which equals $S/\sqrt{n}$
S   = the sample standard deviation
n   = the sample size.

Note how the standard error shrinks as *n* grows large. Imagine a sample with 100,000 observations. The numerator of the *t*-statistic could be very small (economically insignificant), yet the *t*-statistic could still exceed the critical value (which equals 1.96 for extremely large samples). (Study Session 3, LOS 11.d)

Economics

33. **A**   A union restricts the supply of labor, increasing the wage rate and decreasing the quantity supplied. (A union may also try to increase the demand for labor by political means, which can further increase the wage rate.) If the minimum wage is below the union wage, it will have no effect on the first firm. A monopsonist maximizes profit where the marginal cost of labor equals the marginal revenue product. Because the monopsonist is the only buyer of labor, the monopsonist pays a wage rate lower than the marginal cost of labor. If the minimum wage is above this wage rate, the monopsonist will be forced to pay the higher rate and have higher employment on the upward-sloping supply curve of labor. In this circumstance, the minimum wage increases both the wage rate and amount of labor supplied. (Study Session 5, LOS 21.d)

34. **C**   An increase in expected future income will decrease individuals' willingness to trade current consumption for future consumption, making them save less now. Lower current saving decreases the supply of capital in the market. Alternatives A and B would most likely increase the supply of capital. (Study Session 5, LOS 21.f)

35. **B**   The **efficient regulation price** occurs when price is equal to marginal cost. This occurs for Osofine when marginal cost is $10 and price is equal to $10. Since marginal cost is only being covered under this scenario, this natural monopoly is then saddled with a loss of $40 because it is selling 4 units at $10 when average total costs are $14, or a "loss" of $4 per unit sold. (ATC – Marginal Cost = Fixed Costs). Since no contribution is being made toward covering fixed costs under this efficient regulatory price, Osofine could never afford to replace its worn out fixed capital. The **average total cost pricing** occurs at P = ATC, or in this case when price equals $15 and ATC equals $15 per thousand of gallons of water. At this point P = ATC and Osofine has all of its costs covered, including a normalized profit and depreciation. **Average total cost pricing** will allow Osofine to continue to operate as a utility and it is thus likely that the Charlottesville PUC will adopt this regulatory pricing. (Study Session 5, LOS 19.e)

36. **B**   Since the labor force is the sum of employed and unemployed, a decrease in the labor force with the number employed held constant will decrease the unemployment rate (the number of unemployed divided by the labor force). The labor force participation rate is the labor force divided by the working-age population. If the labor force decreases while the working-age population remains the same, the participation rate will decrease. (Study Session 5, LOS 22.a)

37. **A**   A is inaccurate because higher (not lower) rates of growth of money supply lead to higher rates of inflation, and consequently, higher nominal interest rates. The other statements are correct. (Study Session 6, LOS 25.e)

38. **B**   Arthur Laffer's theory states that at a sufficiently high tax rate (i.e., at the peak of the Laffer curve), an increase in the tax rate causes a decrease in tax revenues even though the tax revenue per dollar earned is higher. The Laffer curve does not include any measure of economic growth. (Study Session 6, LOS 26.a)

39. **A** $$\text{percentage change in quantity} = \left[(9,000-10,000)\right]/\left[(10,000+9,000)/2\right] = -0.105$$

$$\text{percentage change in price} = \left[(5.50-2.00)\right]/\left[(5.50+2.00)/2\right] = 0.933$$

Price elasticity of demand for natural gas $= -0.105/0.933 = -0.11$

(Study Session 4, LOS 13.a)

40. **A**   Applying prisoners' dilemma to a duopoly pricing decision, Oil will make the best possible decision based on Jones' potential decisions and Jones will make the best possible decision based on Oil's potential decisions. Clearly, if Oil complies, then it must depend on Jones to comply, but complying is not in the interest of Jones. If Jones were to comply, then it must depend on Oil to comply, but complying is also not in the best interest of Oil. Individually, it clearly pays for Oil and Jones to cheat. (Study Session 5, LOS 20.d)

41. **A**   Purchasing securities in the open market is an expansionary move, as the funds used to buy the securities will increase the money supply. The comments about inflation indicate that the Fed would be careful not to overstimulate the economy by increasing the money supply too rapidly. (Study Session 6, LOS 24.d)

42. **A**   Utilitarianism is the idea that decisions should be those that create the greatest benefit overall for society. This idea, along with the idea that a poor person gets more utility from an additional dollar than a rich person does, supports the argument that transferring a dollar of wealth from the rich to the poor will increase the overall benefit to society. Diminishing marginal utility of wealth means that for each individual, additional dollars of wealth each provide less and less additional (marginal) utility or satisfaction. It does not extend to comparisons between individuals. (Study Session 4, LOS 14.f)

43. **B**   The quantity theory focuses on the quantity of money. The quantity theory states that velocity is not affected by monetary policy. Choice C would most likely lead to higher inflation. (Study Session 6, LOS 24.i)

44. **C**   Central banks adjust the monetary base to control inflation. Monetary base is the sum of banknotes, coins and commercial banks' reserves with the central bank. Monetary base is one of the most liquid forms of money. (Study Session 6, LOS 24.f)

Financial Reporting and Analysis

45. **C**   Management's discussion and analysis must include results of operations, trends, significant events, company's liquidity, effects of inflation, changing prices, capital resources, and material events that could impact future operations. (Study Session 7, LOS 29.c)

46. **C**   The characteristics for effective financial reporting system include: transparency, comprehensiveness, and consistency. However, barriers to creating a coherent financial reporting framework arise in trying to achieve all three characteristics simultaneously. Thus, any financial reporting standards framework has three areas of conflict. They are valuation, standard-setting approach, and measurement. These three areas of conflict are barriers to creating a coherent financial reporting framework. (Study Session 7, LOS 31.g)

47. **A**   Gross profits from contract for each year:

$$2006: \frac{500}{(500+1260)} = 0.28409; \ 2,200 \times 0.28409 = 625; \ 625 - 500 = 125$$

$$2007: \frac{(850+500)}{(850+450+500)} = 0.75; \ 2,200 \times 0.75 = 1,650; \ 1,650 - 625 = 1,025; \ 1,025 - 850 = 175$$

$$2008: \frac{(450+850+500)}{(850+450+500)} = 1.00; \ 2,200 \times 1.00 = 2,200; \ 2,200 - 625 - 1,025 = 550; \ 550 - 450 = 100$$

Note: In 2007 the estimated cost of the contract increased by $40 million. (Study Session 8, LOS 32.b)

48. **A**   The FIFO method recognizes the oldest costs in the cost of goods sold. When the FIFO method is combined with rising prices, net income will be higher as compared to the LIFO method. The higher net income means higher profit margins. (Study Session 8, LOS 32.d)

49. **B**   To qualify as an extraordinary loss, the loss must be both unusual and infrequent. The plane crash would most likely meet these criteria as it is unusual and would not be expected to recur. The other items would be unlikely to be considered unusual and infrequent. (Study Session 8, LOS 32.g)

50. **C**   The shares from the stock split are retroactively restated to the beginning of the year. Since the preferred stock is not convertible, there is no impact on the number of dilutive shares outstanding. [Beginning shares (40,000 shares × 12 months) + split shares (40,000 shares × 12 months) − reacquired shares (20,000 shares × 6 months)] / 12 months = 70,000 shares. (Study Session 8, LOS 32.h)

51. **C**   When cash is paid before the expense is recognized in the income statement, a prepaid asset for this expense is increased and cash is decreased by the amount paid. Selection A is incorrect because a prepaid liability account would not be set up unless the expense was recorded before the cash payment is made. (Study Session 8, LOS 33.c)

52. **C**   The trading portfolio classification includes the unrealized gain from the bond portfolio on the income statement, which is then recorded in retained earnings. The available-for-sale portfolio classification directly records the unrealized gain as part of other comprehensive income within owner's equity. The held-to-maturity classification does not record any unrealized gain on the financial statements. (Study Session 8, LOS 33.g)

53. **C** Under IFRS, interest and dividends received may be shown as either cash flow from operations or cash flow from investing. Remember that in most cases international standards are more flexible in reporting cash flow. (Study Session 8, LOS 34.c)

54. **C** Cash flow from operating activities is equal to $27.0 million [$120 million cash collected from customers – $96.5 million cash expenses + $3.5 million dividends received]. (Study Session 8, LOS 34.a)

55. **C** Both firms sold 110 units (100 units in beginning inventory + 60 units purchased – 50 units in ending inventory). Using FIFO, Harrelson's COGS is $1,080 [(100 units × $10) + (10 units × $8)]. Using LIFO Wilson's COGS is $1,080 [(10 units × $6) + (30 units × $12) + (20 units × $8) + (50 units × $10)]. (Study Session 9, LOS 35.c)

56. **B** When the replacement cost is between net realizable value and net realizable value less a normal profit margin, then market is defined as replacement cost. When original cost is greater than replacement cost, under LCM, inventory is reported at replacement cost. (Study Session 9, LOS 35.b)

57. **A** Once technological feasibility is established, software development costs must be capitalized under U.S. GAAP. R&D expenditures that have no other use are expensed as incurred. Thus, East's reported assets are higher since East must capitalize $90,000 of development costs. All of West's R&D costs must be expensed as incurred. (Study Session 9, LOS 36.c)

58. **B** The remaining useful life is 7.3 years ($5,516 ending net investment / $755 depreciation expense). (Study Session 9, LOS 36.e)

59. **B** An impairment charge could lead directly to a decrease in the deferred tax liability. An increase in the tax rate would, other things equal, increase the firm's deferred tax liability. Purchasing a new asset would not cause a decrease in the DTL. (Study Session 9, LOS 36.i)

60. **A** Deferred tax liabilities increase when capital spending is growing as a result of depreciation that is deducted on the tax return before expense is recognized in the income statement. Once the capital spending slows, the temporary difference reverses and deferred tax liabilities decline. (Study Session 9, LOS 37.b)

61. **A** The valuation allowance account decreased from $11,700 to $8,100. The most likely explanation is the future earnings are expected to increase, thereby increasing the portion of the DTA that is likely to be realized. (Study Session 9, LOS 37.g)

62. **B** When convertible bonds are issued, the conversion option is not valued separately under U.S. GAAP. All of the issue proceeds are reported as debt. When bonds are issued with detachable stock purchase warrants, the value assigned to the warrants is reported as equity. The remainder is reported as debt. Thus, the debt-to-equity ratio is *lower* than if a convertible bond is issued. (Study Session 9, LOS 38.e)

63. **C** An operating lease will improve leverage and turnover ratios by transferring debt and assets off-balance sheet. A finance lease will have higher cash flow from operations because part of the lease payment is considered a financing activity. All of the operating lease payment is treated as an operating activity. The lessee will have lower income under a finance lease in the early years, because the interest and depreciation expense are higher as compared to the rent expense of an operating lease. (Study Session 9, LOS 38.g)

64. **A** Since the present value of the lease payments is equal to the carrying value of the leased asset, no gross profit is recognized by the lessor, whether the lessor accounts for the lease as an operating or capital lease.(Study Session 9, LOS 38.h)

65. **A** Inventory turnover is equal to COGS / average inventory. Given COGS, purchases, and ending inventory, solve for beginning inventory [$4.2 million COGS + $900,000 ending inventory − $4.8 million purchases = $300,000 beginning inventory]. Next, calculate average inventory [($300,000 beginning inventory + 900,000 ending inventory) / 2 = $600,000 average inventory]. Finally, calculate inventory turnover [$4.2 million COGS / $600,000 average inventory = 7.0]. (Study Session 10, LOS 39.c)

66. **A** Fixed asset turnover is equal to revenue / average net fixed assets. Calculate average net fixed assets [($12 million 2007 gross fixed assets − $9 million 2007 accumulated depreciation + $16 million 2008 gross fixed assets − $10 million 2008 accumulated depreciation) / 2 = $4.5 million average net fixed assets]. Solve for 2008 revenue given 2008 fixed asset turnover and average net fixed assets [$4.5 million average fixed assets x 2.0 fixed asset turnover = $9 million revenue]. (Study Session 10, LOS 39.c)

67. **B** Using the extended DuPont equation, ROE is equal to tax burden (net income / EBT) × interest burden (EBT / EBIT) × EBIT margin (EBIT / revenue) × asset turnover (revenue / average total assets) × leverage (average total assets / average shareholders' equity). First, calculate tax burden [1 − 0.32= 0.68 or 68%]. Next, calculate interest burden [(540 − 20) / 540 = 0.963]. EBIT margin is given at 9%. Next, solve for revenue given operating profit and operating profit margin [$540 million operating profit / 9% operating profit margin = $6 billion sales]. Next, calculate Asset turnover [$6 billion sales / $4 billion assets = 1.5]. Leverage is given at 2.0. Finally, calculate ROE [0.68 × 0.963 × 0.09 × 1.5 × 2.0 = 17.7%]. (Study Session 10, LOS 39.e)

68. **C** As DSP increases, operating cash flow will also increase. If a company stretches out the payment of its account payables, operating cash flow will increase. (Study Session 10, LOS 41)

69. **B** $ROE = \dfrac{Revenues}{Total\ assets} \times \dfrac{Net\ income}{Revenues} \times \dfrac{Total\ assets}{Equity}$

$0.15 = \dfrac{x}{5} \times 0.10 \times 2.5$

$0.6 = \dfrac{x}{5}$

x = $3 billion   (Study Session 9, LOS 39.e and Study Session 10, LOS 42.b)

70. **C** IFRS standards allow interest paid to be reported in either the operating or financing section of the cash flow statement. U.S. GAAP standards require interest paid to be reported in the operating section of the cash flow statement. (Study Session 8, LOS 34.c and Study Session 10, LOS 43.c)

71. **B** When the IRR and NPV methods conflict, the general rule is to take the higher NPV project, as NPV measures the expected increase in the value of the firm from undertaking the project. IRR is not the best measure for ranking mutually exclusive projects of different sizes, and the capital budget is not large enough to do both projects. (Study Session 11, LOS 44.d,e)

72. **C** If there are no monetary constraints on capital investments and all projects are independent, then all would be selected because net present values are positive and internal rates of return are higher than the required return. If the projects were mutually exclusive, the project with the highest present value, Project D, would be selected. (Study Session 11, LOS 44.e)

73. **B** Company A's current cost of debt capital is 3%. Since the after tax cost of the new debt will be 4.2% ($0.07 \times 1 - 0.40$ tax rate), the marginal cost of capital is higher. For Company B, the issuance of debt will lower the marginal cost of capital because the after tax cost of the new debt of 4.2% is lower than the current cost of equity capital of 7%. (Study Session 11, LOS 45.a,b)

74. **B** The analyst should always use the target capital structure weighting if possible. In this case, the firm has stated its target weights. However, often the targets are unknown, so the analyst must estimate the weights. Three methods can be used: observing the company's current capital structure weights; estimating weights by evaluating trends within the company; or using averages of comparable companies to compute the firm's weights. The analyst can use either an unweighted or weighted arithmetic average to compute comparable companies' capital structures as the target for the capital structure of the firm being analyzed. (Study Session 11, LOS 45.c)

75. **A** The correct calculation for accounts receivable turnover is credit sales / average accounts receivable. Credit sales were $10 million in 2008. Average accounts receivable were $3.2 million for 2008 ($3 million + $3.4 million) / 2. Accounts receivable turnover is 3.13 = $10 million / $3.2 million for 2008. (Study Session 11, LOS 46.a)

76. **B** Only expected cash inflows and outflows should be included. These are all the cash elements in the list. The projected increases in receivables, inventories, and market values of investments do not affect cash. (Study Session 11, LOS 46.c)

77. **B** Slower customer payments after the change in credit terms along with slowing payments by the company to its creditors may indicate liquidity problems. These trends do not usually suggest liquidity improvements as stated in the other selections. (Study Session 11, LOS 46.f)

78. **C** GRE Financial's Board should be made up of a majority of independent board members to maintain its unbiased viewpoint. Any type of executive action that is potentially detrimental to shareholders, such as a poison pill provision, should be viewed as a negative. (Study Session 11, LOS 48.b, c, g)

Portfolio Management

79. **A** GBM stock's expected return for the coming year can be calculated as follows:

$(62 / 54) - 1 = 14.8\%$

The expected return on the market is equal to 12%. According to the CAPM, only systematic risk (i.e., beta risk) is rewarded by the market. Thus, assuming equilibrium (i.e., all assets properly priced), in order to have an expected return greater than the market, an asset must have greater than average systematic risk. If we don't assume equilibrium, then an asset with an expected return greater than the market could have the same level of systematic risk as the market, but be undervalued by the market. A second alternative is that the stock could have less than average systematic risk and be undervalued. Finally, the stock could have greater than average systematic risk and be over, under, or properly valued. Note that without knowing the required return on GBM stock, if we assume it has greater than average systematic risk, we cannot determine the relative valuation. All we know for sure is that the required return on GBM is greater than the required return on the market. (Study Session 12, LOS 51.c,e)

80. **A**   The SML uses either the covariance between assets and the market or beta as the measure of risk. Beta is the covariance of a stock with the market divided by the variance of the market. Securities that plot above the SML are undervalued and securities that plot below the SML are overvalued. So, the statements provided in Answers B and C are correct and the statement in Answer A is incorrect. (Study Session 12, LOS 51.d, e)

81. **C**   The formula for the standard deviation for an individual asset is the square root of $\sum pt[Rt - E(R)]^2$, where pt is the probability for outcome t, R_t is the return associated with outcome t and $E(R)$ is the expected return for the stock. $E(R)$ is calculated as follows:

$$E(R) = \sum p_t R_t = 0.25(20\%) + 0.50(10\%) + 0.25(0\%) = 10\%$$

The variance is calculated as:

$$\text{variance} = \sum p_t [R_t - E(R)]^2 = 0.25(20\% - 10\%)^2 + 0.50(10\% - 10\%)^2 + 0.25(0\% - 10\%)^2 = 0.5$$

The standard deviation is the square root of the variance:

$$\text{standard deviation} = (0.5\%)^{1/2} = 7.07\% \text{ (Study Session 12, LOS 50.c)}$$

82. **C**   For any retiree current income must always be considered, and in this case the current income needs appear quite high relative to the portfolio. Rook needs ($6,000 + $1,000) × 12 = 84,000 just for his monthly living expenses, including his vacation home. A 7% after-tax return on $1.2M would yield $84,000, just enough to cover his expenses. The focus of the policy statement on after-tax return is appropriate. The 7% after-tax return requirement, which translates into 7% / (1 − 0.3) = 10% on a pre-tax basis is not particularly conservative, especially given that inflation has not been factored into the requirement. (Study Session 12, LOS 49.c)

83. **B**   Adding assets classes (such as commodities) with little correlation to the existing portfolio will reduce the overall standard deviation of the portfolio, even if the standard deviation of the asset class to be added is somewhat high. Thus, the relationship between the new asset class and the existing portfolio (i.e., the correlation) is the most important factor to consider. (Study Session 12, LOS 50.e)

84. **B**   Secure-Invest relaxes the equal borrowing and lending assumption by using the zero-beta CAPM rather than the traditional CAPM. The equation for the traditional CAPM is:

$$E(R_i) = R_F + \beta_i[E(R_m) - R_F]$$

where:
R_F is the risk-free rate

The graph of the CAPM is called the security market line (SML). The intercept equals the risk-free rate and the slope equals the market risk premium, $E(R_m) - R_F$. The CAPM assumes the investor can borrow and lend at the same rate (R_F). In practice, borrowing and lending rates differ. To address this violation of the CAPM, Secure-Invest employs the zero-beta version of the CAPM:

$$E(R_i) = E(R_Z) + \beta_i[E(R_m) - E(R_Z)]$$

where:
asset Z is the zero-beta portfolio, which has a beta equal to zero

Turner finds that the expected return on the zero-beta portfolio exceeds the risk-free rate. Therefore, the slope of the zero-beta CAPM is less than the slope of the traditional CAPM (the slope of the SML decreases):

$$E(R_m) - E(R_Z) < E(R_m) - R_F$$

(Study Session 12, LOS 51.d)

Asset Valuation

85. **B** Below $45. Using the following formula for the trigger price of margin purchases, the investor will receive a margin call when the stock goes below $45.

trigger price (margin purchases) =

$$P_0 \left(\frac{1 - \text{initial margin}\%}{1 - \text{maintenance margin}\%} \right) = \$60 \left(\frac{1 - 0.40}{1 - 0.20} \right) = \$60(0.75) = \$45.00$$

Answer A is incorrect because the trigger price (margin purchases) equation incorrectly uses the percentage borrowed (60%), not the initial margin (40%). Answer C is incorrect because it is $60(1 − maintenance margin) = $60(0.80). (Study Session 13, LOS 52.g)

86. **C** Semi-strong form EMH asserts that current security prices fully reflect all public information, including institutional ownership. Studies of past trading rules test the weak form. Event studies test semi-strong form efficiency. (Study Session 13, LOS 54.a,b)

87. **C** The earnings surprise test is used to test the semi-strong form of the efficient market hypothesis, which holds that stock prices reflect all publicly available information. The other tests are only applicable to the weak form of the EMH. (Study Session 13, LOS 54.b)

88. **A** $k = D/V + g$ = required rate of return = cost of equity capital. (Study Session 14, LOS 56.g)

89. **B** Semi-strong form of EMH states that security prices rapidly adjust to reflect all publicly available information. If the analyst can use his model to earn above average returns, which is based on publicly available information, the semi-strong form of the EMH has been violated. (Study Session 13, LOS 54.a)

90. **A** Because the intrinsic value is more than the price, the investor should buy the stock. The required return is calculated using the following formula:

$E(R) = RFR + \beta(R_M - RFR) = 0.04 + 1.25(0.08 - 0.04) = 0.09$

Because the intrinsic value (30) exceeds the price (28), King should purchase the shares. Furthermore, because intrinsic value exceeds price, the expected return is above 0.09. With an expected return greater than the required return, King should buy Nacho Inc. stock. (Study Session 14, LOS 56.c)

91. **B** Calculate the dividends during the supernormal growth period using $g_s = 15\%$.

$D_1 = D_0(1 + g_s) = \$2.00(1.15) = \$2.30$

$D_2 = D_0(1 + g_s)^2 = \$2.00(1.15)^2 = \$2.645$

$D_3 = D_0(1 + g_s)^3 = \$2.00(1.15)^3 = \$3.042$

Calculate the first dividend when the normal constant growth resumes at $g_c = 7\%$.

$D_4 = D_3(1 + g_c) = \$3.042(1.07) = \$3.255$

Calculate the terminal value of the stock at the end of the supernormal growth period using the infinite period DDM.

$$P_3 = \frac{D_4}{(k_e - g)} = \frac{3.255}{0.12 - 0.07} = 65.100$$

Calculate the present value of the cash flows discounted at k_e of 12%.

PV of $D_1 = \$2.30/(1.12) = \$2.054$

PV of $D_2 = \$2.645/(1.12)^2 = \$2.109$

PV of $D_3 = \$3.042/(1.12)^3 = \$2.165$

PV of $P_3 = \$65.100/(1.12)^3 = \underline{\$46.337}$

$V_s = \$52.664$

Answer A incorrectly discounts the \$46.337 value of the stock at the end of the supernormal growth period in year 4 instead of year 3. Answer C fails to discount the \$65 value of the stock at the end of the supernormal growth period. (Study Session 14, LOS 56.c)

92. **C** Morin is incorrect in his assessment of arbitrageurs. One of the limits to arbitrage that can make markets less efficient is when arbitrageurs have inadequate capital. Morin is correct about decreases in the cost of trading or the cost of information, both of which would increase market efficiency. (Study session 13, LOS 55.a)

93. **C** $D_1 = 1.5 \times 1.1 = 1.65$

$$\frac{P_0}{E_1} = \frac{\left(\dfrac{D_1}{E_1}\right)}{(k-g)} = \left(\frac{\dfrac{1.65}{4.70}}{(0.12-0.10)}\right) = \left(\frac{0.351}{0.02}\right) = 17.6$$

Note that the trailing P/E, which is P_0 / E_0, has a different value. Raising the required rate of return, k in the equation above, results in a lower P/E. (Study Session 14, LOS 56.d)

94. **A**   The return on equity = profit margin × asset turnover × financial leverage

ROE = 10% × 0.75 × 1.6 = 12.0%

The retention rate = 1 − payout rate = 100% − 60% = 40%

g = (Retention rate) × (Return on equity) = 40% × 12.0% = 4.8%

(Study Session 14, LOS 56.f)

95. **B**   An increase in the required rate of return would decrease the P/E ratio. An increase in the other two (the dividend payout rate and the growth rate) would increase the P/E ratio. This can be seen by inspecting the equation for the expected (P_0/E_1) ratio, which is:

$$\frac{P_0}{E_1} = \frac{D_1 \big/ E_1}{k-g}$$

where:
D_1/E_1 = the expected dividend payout ratio.
k   = the required rate of return on the stock.
g   = the expected constant growth rate of dividends.

(Study Session 14, LOS 56.d)

96. **A**   An important drawback of book value is that it does not account for human capital, which may represent a substantial asset of financial service companies. (Study Session 14, LOS 59.a)

97. **A**   The effect of rising or falling market rates is best captured by relative yield or the yield ratio. The yield ratio is 8.75%/5.25% = 1.67. The absolute yield spread is 8.75% − 5.25%, which is 3.50% or 350 basis points. The relative yield spread is 3.5%/5.25% = 0.67 = 67%. (Study Session 15, LOS 63.e)

98. **C** $\text{effective duration} = \dfrac{(1077.20-1024.90)}{2 \times 1050.62 \times .0025} = \dfrac{52.3}{5.2531} = 9.956$

(Study Session 16, LOS 66.d)

99. **A**   The observed yield curve is upward sloping despite stable short-term rates. The pure expectations theory would predict a flat yield curve. The market segmentation theory can explain any shape of the yield curve, depending on supply and demand conditions for each time horizon. (Study Session 15, LOS 63.c)

100. **A** Clean price is the price excluding accrued interest, given as 976.25. The dirty price would add the accrued interest to get 976.25 + 14.92 = 991.17. (Study Session 15, LOS 60.c)

101. **B** The bond is an inverse floater because the coupon rate will move opposite to any move in the reference rate. Inverse floaters have a floor such that the rate cannot drop below zero. (Study Session 15, LOS 60.b)

102. **C** An important property of the present value of a bond is the inverse relationship between discount rate and present value: the higher the discount rate, the lower the present value, and vice versa. For a bond that has level cash flows over its life, the present value of each cash flow progressively decreases each period in the future. Another way of expressing this relationship is that as time (t) increases, present value$_t$ decreases. (Study Session 16, LOS 64.c)

103. **A** Analyst A is correct. Passthrough securities distribute monthly cash flows on a proportionate basis, whereas CMOs are structured to reapportion prepayment risk among the different tranches. Analyst B is incorrect. CMOs do not provide credit enhancement. (Study Session 15, LOS 62.e)

104. **C** Both bonds have higher coupons than comparable securities today. For the MBS, this implies a risk that prepayments will be higher than anticipated, as the underlying mortgages are refinanced at today's lower rates. For the callable corporate bond, the drop in rates increases the likelihood that the bond will be called. Reinvestment risk and price compression are two components of call and/or prepayment risk, which are the same thing. Call/prepayment risk also includes the uncertainty of the cash flows from the bond. (Study Session 15, LOS 61.a)

105. **B** One of the many factors affecting a bond's value is time. As a premium bond approaches maturity, its value will decrease over time, while a discount bond will increase in value. A bond selling at par will remain unchanged. A change in discount rate will also affect a bond's value. In general, the higher the discount rate, the lower a security's value, and vice-versa. (Study Session 16, LOS 64.d)

106. **C** The option cost is the difference between the zero volatility spread and the OAS, or 150 − 75 = 75 bp. With a flat yield curve, the nominal spread and zero volatility spread will be the same. (Study Session 16, LOS 65.f, g)

107. **A** The yield to maturity calculation assumes that all interim cash flows are reinvested at the yield to maturity (YTM). Since Horn's reinvestment rate is 7.5%, he would realize a return higher than the 7.0% YTM of the Kanon bonds, or a return less than the 8.0% YTM of the Samuel bonds. (Study Session 16, LOS 65.c)

108. **C** The cap on these bonds is 8.5%, which would be reached when the six-month Treasury yield reached 6.5%. The interest rate risk of floating rate bonds will be lower if the reset period is shorter, so an annual reset would mean higher risk than these bonds. Once a floating rate security hits its maximum (cap) rate, it will be priced similar to fixed rate bonds, since the ability of the coupon reset to keep pace with higher rates will be lost. (Study Session 15, LOS 61.e)

109. **B** Portfolio duration is the weighted average of component securities, using market values:

    (2,400,000 / 7,200,00) × 4.625 + (3,600,000 / 7,200,000) × 7.322 + (1,200,000 / 7,200,000) × 9.3 = 6.753.   (Study Session 16, LOS 66.f)

110. **A** Forward contracts are private transactions in an unregulated market and the terms can be customized. However, forward contracts do have higher default risk as there is no clearinghouse to guarantee the performance of each party. Since the company is unwilling to accept credit risk from the counterparty, swaps and forwards will not be appropriate. (Study Session 17, LOS 67.b)

111. **C** Both options appear to be in-the-money. Since Option X has a strike lower than the stock price, it could be a call option. Assuming it is a call, Option X has the following intrinsic value: 43 − 40 = 3. Option X has a premium greater than the intrinsic value which indicates there is time value left and it is not about to expire. Since Option Y has a strike higher than the stock price, it could be a put. Assuming it is a put, Option Y has an intrinsic value equal to 32 − 29 = 3. The intrinsic value is equal to the premium for Option Y, indicating no time value. Option Y is about to expire. (Study Session 17, LOS 70.a,f)

112. **C** It does not matter whether McCray sells the contract or accepts cash settlement. His payoff should be the same under either method. (Study Session 17, LOS 69.d)

113. **A** The risk in writing a call is if the stock price increases. The premium is his maximum gain, but his potential loss is unlimited since the stock could have an infinite increase in value. (Study Session 17, LOS 72.a)

114. **C** The minimum value of an American put option is $\text{Max}(0, X - S_0)$. Thus the lower bound for the put options on KCE stock is $\text{Max}(0, 55 - 51.13) = \$3.87$. (Study Session 17, LOS 70.h)

115. **B** We are told that the agreement is based on 90-day LIBOR and that Hames is long the FRA. Since rates increase, she receives a payment equal to:

$10M[(0.055 − 0.0475)(90 / 360)] / [1 + 0.055(90 / 360)] = $10M(0.001875 / 1.01375) = $18,496. (Study Session 17, LOS 68.g)

116. **A**
Fixed rate payment is $50M × 0.07 × (91 / 365) = $872,603
Equity payment is $50M × (1755 / 1825 − 1) = <u>−$1,917,808</u>
Total payment $2,790,411

The negative equity payment increases the amount due from SingleSol. (Study Session 17, LOS 71.b)

117. **C** An existing single-family home for residential purposes will most likely be valued using the sales comparison method. (Study Session 18, LOS 73.e)

118. **A** Net asset value $= \dfrac{\left(233\,\text{million} - 2\,\text{million}\right)}{16.8\,\text{million}} = 13.75$

Statement 1 is correct. During the year the appreciation or depreciation of assets less liabilities will yield the NAV. The sales charge is a one time cost to purchase the fund. The redemption fee is a charge to exit the fund. Statement 2 is incorrect. The method of capitalization is the main difference between an open-end and closed-end investment company. (Study Session 18, LOS 73.a)

119. **A** The non-controlling shares of a closely held company will be relatively illiquid when compared to a firm that is quoted on an exchange. Hence, the analyst will apply a marketability discount. Since the valuation is being done for a non-controlling interest and the shares quoted on the exchange also represent a non-controlling interest, no minority interest discount is applicable, (Study Session 18, LOS 73.n)

120. **A** The first-stage represents financing for the initial production of a product. Second-stage represents expansion financing for a company that has a product, but is not yet profitable. The third-stage represents financing for a major expansion of plant, equipment, or a major marketing campaign. (Study Session 18, LOS 73.g)

EXAM 2
AFTERNOON SESSION ANSWERS

To get valuable feedback on how your score compares to those of other Level 1 candidates, use your Username and Password to gain Online Access at schweser.com and choose the left-hand menu item "Practice Exams Vol. 2."

121. A	151. B	181. B	211. B
122. A	152. B	182. A	212. A
123. B	153. A	183. C	213. B
124. C	154. A	184. B	214. B
125. B	155. C	185. B	215. A
126. A	156. A	186. C	216. B
127. A	157. A	187. B	217. C
128. B	158. B	188. C	218. B
129. A	159. A	189. A	219. B
130. C	160. A	190. C	220. B
131. A	161. A	191. C	221. C
132. B	162. C	192. A	222. A
133. B	163. A	193. C	223. C
134. C	164. C	194. B	224. C
135. A	165. B	195. A	225. C
136. B	166. A	196. B	226. A
137. B	167. C	197. C	227. A
138. C	168. A	198. B	228. C
139. C	169. B	199. A	229. C
140. C	170. A	200. C	230. A
141. B	171. C	201. B	231. A
142. B	172. B	202. B	232. B
143. B	173. C	203. B	233. C
144. C	174. A	204. B	234. B
145. C	175. C	205. A	235. A
146. C	176. C	206. A	236. B
147. C	177. A	207. A	237. C
148. C	178. C	208. B	238. C
149. C	179. A	209. A	239. B
150. A	180. C	210. C	240. C

Exam 2
Afternoon Session Answers

Ethical and Professional Standards

Answers referencing the Standards of Practice are all Study Session 1, LOS 2.a, b.

121. **A** Both statements are correct. Total firm assets must include fee-paying and non-fee-paying accounts. If a sub-advisor who manages firm assets is selected by the firm, the performance of assets under the sub-advisor's control must be included in the performance of the firm's composite for those assets.

122. **A** Standard V(C). This Standard requires CFA charterholders and candidates to maintain appropriate records to support investment recommendations. Shredding all of the supporting documents is clearly a violation of the standard. Mason did not violate Standard V(B), however, since she fully described the basic characteristics of the investment. The relatively little insider buying is not a basic characteristic of an equity security.

123. **B** Standard III (B). Statement 1 is incorrect. Fair is not the same as equal. It is virtually impossible to get recommendations out to all interested clients at precisely the same time, but best efforts should be made to do so. Also, all clients do not need to receive all recommendations – only those clients who have expressed a prior interest in that type of security. Statement 2 is correct. Differentiated levels of service are allowed, as long as they do not disadvantage or negatively affect clients.

124. **C** Standard VI(C). Members must disclose to their clients any compensation or benefit received by, or paid to, others for the recommendation of services. Full disclosure would include the nature and value of the benefit and should be made in writing. Sergeant's failure to disclose that he receives free legal services for his referral of clients to Chapman is in violation of the Standards.

125. **B** Standard IV(A). Standard IV(A) – Duties to Employers – Loyalty is not being violated. Schultz continued to act in her employer's best interest while still employed and did not engage in any activities that would conflict with this duty until her resignation became effective. The Standard does not prohibit her from contacting clients from her previous firm if she does not get the contact information from the records of her former employer or violate an applicable non-compete agreement. In this situation, she used public information to contact former clients and she did not have a non-compete agreement.

126. **A** Standard I(A). According to the Standard, members and candidates must comply with applicable laws and regulations or the Code and Standards, whichever is most strict. Callahan does not appear to have violated the Standards by making short sales in Country A client accounts. Local laws permit such sales and Callahan appears to have assured the suitability of such trades for the clients. Callahan has violated Standard I(A) by selling stock short for Country B client accounts. Even though the trades are suitable, Country B's laws prohibit such trades. Since Callahan is a registered investment advisor in Country B, he must abide by the country's laws, even though he is a citizen of, and resides in, Country A. It is irrelevant that the trades occur intraday and do not post to the accounts, Callahan knowingly violated the laws of Country B and has thus violated the Standard.

127. **A** GIPS. According to GIPS section 0.A.12, firms must list discontinued composites on the firm's list of composites for at least five years after discontinuation.

128. **B** Standard I(C). Summarizing another report in some instances is acceptable, as long as acknowledgement is clearly given. Hiltop may use recognized sources of factual information without acknowledgment, such as data from statistical services like S&P.

129. **A** Standard IV(A). Solicitation of an old employer's clients is only prohibited prior to ceasing employment with the old firm. Misappropriation of clients or client lists is never permitted. It is permissible to take records or files from the old employer if written permission is received.

130. **C** Standard IV(B). Standard IV(B) requires that members obtain their employer's written consent before accepting any gift or benefit that may create a conflict of interest with their employer. However, in this situation the gift is coming from a company seeking only to demonstrate their product. Two tickets here are the firm's product, not a lavish gift.

131. **A** Standard II(A). A firewall, or information barrier, is actually the minimum procedure a firm should have in place. Companies should go further, and consider restrictions / prohibitions on personal trading, periodic reports on personal transactions, placing securities on restricted or watch lists when appropriate, etc.

132. **B** Standard VI (A). A is incorrect – disclosure must be prominent and in plain language. C is incorrect – in fact, a mere appearance of a conflict can be problematic for members / candidates and the employer. B is correct. The member / candidate must take reasonable steps to determine if a conflict exists, and disclose it to the employer. It is accurate to say that conflicts or perceived conflicts cannot be avoided – the key issue is disclosure, according to Standard VI(A) – Conflicts of Interest – Disclosure of Conflicts.

133. **B** Standard III(C). According to Standard III(C) – Duties to Clients – Suitability, when a member is in an advisory role, he must determine the investor's objectives (risk and return) and constraints, as well as investment experience, thereby creating an Investment Policy Statement (IPS) for his client. The IPS must be updated at least annually. Afterwards, a customized investment strategy is developed. Since each investor's constraints and objectives are different, Kent has violated the Standards by not working out an appropriate IPS for Ms. Parker. Providing a description of the model would not satisfy this requirement.

134. **C** Standard II(B). According to Standard II(B) – Integrity of Capital Markets - Market Manipulation, Reynolds is guilty of information-based manipulation by spreading false rumors to induce trading by others.

135. **A** Standard I(C). According to Standard I(C) – Professionalism – Misrepresentation, members must not intentionally allow misrepresentations to occur in their research, recommendations, or other professional duties. All indications are that Nicely did nothing inappropriate – The CDs are in fact guaranteed. Nicely correctly points out that only the principal is guaranteed. This Standard does not prohibit members and candidates from providing clients with data on investment products that have guarantees built into their structures.

136. **B** Standard III(D). According to Standard III(D) – Duties to Clients – Performance Presentation, members must ensure the accuracy, fairness, and completeness of performance presentations. Recommendations for Standard III(D) specify that the performance of the *weighted* composite of similar portfolios should be presented.

137. **B** Standard II(A). According to Standard II(A) – Integrity of Capital Markets – Material Nonpublic Information, there are situations in which an employee can be allowed to temporarily move to the investment banking side of the "wall", and act as a temporary insider until all the information is publicly disclosed. Clearly he cannot use any of this information in research, or share it with colleagues. "C" is incorrect because of inclusion of the word "only".

138. **C** Standard I(B). According to the Standard, Members and Candidates must maintain their independence and objectivity and must not offer or accept any gifts or compensation that would affect their own or someone else's independence and objectivity. Marsh is clearly in violation of this Standard. His offer of a free ski vacation at his condo in Montana was intended to influence Dreyer to change his investment rating downgrade, despite evidence that such a move may be appropriate. Marsh's motivation is only to provide investment banking services to Custom Bikes. Dreyer has also violated the Standard. Even though the trip was approved by his employer, Dreyer knew Marsh was trying to secure an investment banking relationship with Custom Bikes. Dreyer should therefore reject the offer since it could reasonably be expected to compromise his independence and objectivity. It does not matter that Dreyer ultimately did not change his decision to downgrade Custom Bikes. Dreyer accepted a gift that put his independence and objectivity at risk and therefore violated the Standard.

Quantitative Methods

139. **C** A nonparametric test is often used when the researcher is unsure of the distribution of the data. Nonparametric tests often transform the original data into ranks, or into signs (greater than or less than). The null hypothesis for a nonparametric test is stated in terms of ranks or signs. Wilcott finds that the data do not follow a normal distribution. She transforms the original data (monthly returns for value and growth stock portfolios) into signs: positive sign for months in which the value stock portfolio return exceeds the growth stock portfolio return, and negative sign for months in which the value stock portfolio return is less than the growth stock portfolio return. Finally, she states the null hypothesis as a statement about the signs of the differences between the two portfolios (null hypothesis: 50% of the signs are positive). (Study Session 3, LOS 11.g)

140. **C** Odds for an event equals the ratio of the probability of success to the probability of failure. If the probability of success is 50 percent, then there are equal probabilities of success and failure, and the odds for success are 1 to 1. (Study Session 2, LOS 8.c)

141. **B** The Sharpe ratio for the large cap fund = 0.083/0.43 = 0.193. Remember the excess return, $(R_p - RFR)$ already reflects the risk-free rate. The Sharpe ratio for the S&P index fund = $(0.079 - 0.03) / 0.26 = 0.1885$. The large capitalization mutual fund has a higher Sharpe ratio, and hence superior risk adjusted returns, compared to the S&P 500 index fund. (Study Session 2, LOS 7.h)

142. **B** Because the Ivy Foundation has a minimum acceptable return that is greater than the risk-free rate, the safety-first ratio is a more suitable criterion than the Sharpe ratio for choosing the optimal portfolio. Given a set of available portfolios, the one that maximizes the safety-first ratio will minimize the probability that the return will be less than the minimum acceptable return if we assume returns are normally distributed. This is the optimal portfolio. Minimizing value-at-risk (VaR) could lead to choosing a portfolio with an expected return below Ivy Foundation's desired expected return, or worse, below the minimum acceptable return. (Study Session 3, LOS 9.i)

143. **B** If MedTech stock breaks a support level, technicians believe this is bearish because the stock is seeking a lower support level. Moving out of a declining channel to the upside is considered bullish because it signifies a reversal of a downward trend. Trading just below a resistance level is not necessarily bullish or bearish. If the price were to rise above the resistance level, this would be a bullish sign. (Study Session 3, LOS 12.c)

144. **C** Analyzing the ratio of stock prices to a stock index is known by technical analysts as relative strength analysis. If upward or downward trends are observed the technical analyst will take an appropriate position in the stock. (Study Session 3, LOS 12.c)

145. **C** First calculate the expected return:

$(0.6 \times -0.1) + (0.4 \times 0.15) = -0.06 + 0.06 = 0$

Next calculate the standard deviation of returns:

$$\sqrt{\left((-0.1-0)^2 \times 0.6\right) + \left((0.15-0)^2 \times 0.4\right)} = 0.122$$

Finally, calculated a one standard deviation range of stock prices:

$(0.122 \times 25) \pm 25 = 22$ to 28 (Study Session 2, LOS 8.k)

146. **C** King has designed a trading strategy based on P/E ratios. All the necessary accounting information must be available at time t in order to implement the strategy. At the beginning of a new year, the earnings from the recently ended fiscal year will not be released for several weeks and perhaps months into the new year. By assuming the fiscal year-end earnings are available at the beginning of the new fiscal year, King is introducing a look-ahead bias into her research design. Instead, she should lag the earnings at least 3 months, ranking stocks based on the ratio of current stock price to lagged earnings, P_t/E_{t-3}, to ensure that the accounting data (earnings) are available at the time the strategy is implemented. Of the remaining biases, time period bias refers to a research design in which results are time-specific and cannot be generalized reliably outside the sample period. Data mining refers to repeated testing of data for various strategies or patterns. Eventually, given a large number of examined strategies, a pattern will emerge even by chance. (Study Session 3, LOS 10.k)

147. **C** $P(AB) = P(A \mid B)P(B) = 0.7 \times 0.8 = 0.56$. The historical data is conditional, where one event impacts another event. (Study Session 2, LOS 8.d, e)

148. **C** The change in airline industry profitability given higher oil prices can be examined through the paired comparisons test. In a paired comparisons test the two samples are not independent. A test of differences between means is used to compare independent random samples. A chi-square test is used to test hypotheses about the variance of a population. (Study Session 3, LOS 11.e)

149. **C** The sum of the scenario probabilities for the neutral monetary stance is 105%, which is greater than 100%; the 50 basis point rate cut contains a negative probability, which violates the rule that probabilities are non-negative. (Study Session 3, LOS 9.c)

150. **A** Since the interest on the loan is compounded annually, the effective rate and nominal rate are the same. If the problem used different compounding periods, the effective rate would be higher than the nominal rate. (Study Session 2, LOS 5.c)

151. **B** Mean > median > mode, which means this sample is right skewed. When a sample is right skewed, sample skewness is positive. Because the sample has an even number of observations, we cannot say with certainty that there is an observation equal to the median. Sample kurtosis of 3.0 is the same as the kurtosis of the normal distribution, so excess kurtosis is zero. (Study Session 2, LOS 7.i,j)

152. **B** On a financial calculator: PV = –15,000; FV = 0; PMT = 15,000; N=2; Solve for i, I = 61.8% (Study Session 2, LOS 6.a)

Economics

153. **A** In the short run, a perfectly competitive firm's supply curve is upward sloping, because if prices increase, the quantity supplied increases. The demand curve for a perfectly competitive firm is horizontal. Each firm in a competitive market is a price taker and has no influence on the price of the product. Firms will not charge a below-market price, because this results in lower total revenue. If the firm attempts to sell above the market price, the firm will sell nothing. Thus, whatever quantity the firm sells will be at the market price, causing the demand curve to be flat. (Study Session 5, LOS 18.c)

154. **A** An increase in the prices of other productive inputs will cause a shift toward the resource in question, increasing the demand for the resource. The other statements are false. (Study Session 5, LOS 21.b)

155. **C** Experienced workers generate a unit cost of $9.50/60 dozen doughnuts, or $0.158 per dozen. Inexperienced workers generate a unit cost of $6.00/40 = $0.150 per dozen. Since all the doughnuts sell for the same price, the marginal revenue product will be higher for inexperienced workers. At some higher level of output, the law of diminishing returns might result in a situation where adding experienced workers increases productivity, but the question does not provide any information to support hiring experienced workers at expected output levels. (Study Session 5, LOS 21.a)

156. **A** If the minimum wage rate is set above the equilibrium wage rate, it is in conflict with market forces and therefore increases unemployment in the labor market. If the minimum wage is set below the equilibrium wage, then the minimum wage has no effect because workers would always take the higher market wage rather than work at a lower minimum wage. (Study Session 4, LOS 15.b)

157. **A** The employment-to-population ratio is defined as the percentage of working age people who are employed. If this ratio is increasing over time (as it is in the table), then job growth is occurring at a faster rate than working-age population growth. Labor market indicators can be used to determine which phase of the business cycle an economy is in. During an expansionary phase, unemployment falls, labor force participation increases, and the employment-to-population ratio increases. The data presented by Kiwiland clearly shows an expansionary period over the last four years. Note that the years are presented from right to left. (Study Session 5, LOS 22.a,c and Study Session 6, LOS 25.f)

158. **B** A generational imbalance occurs when the present value of government benefits to the current generation is not fully paid for by taxes on the current generation so that future generations are obligated to pay for them. (Study Session 6, LOS 26.c)

159. **A** These statements best express the definitions of M1 and M2. Answer choice B is incorrect because M1 is more liquid than M2, as the monetary aggregates are classified according a liquidity scale (from more liquid to less liquid). (Study Session 6, LOS 24.b)

160. **A** Economic efficiency occurs when a given output, such as 50 tons of coal, is produced at the least cost. In this case, the explosives/dump truck is the least expensive because 6 units of labor @ $175 per day equals $1,050 in labor costs and 4 units of capital @ $300 per unit equals $1,200 per day or a total per day operating cost of $2,250. This cost is less than either of the other alternatives and so is the most economically efficient for CCC.

Earth moving equipment: 4 × $175 + 8 × $300 = $3,100;
Power hand tools: 8 × $175 + 3 × $300 = $2,300.

(Study Session 4, LOS 16.c)

161. **A** Restrictive Fiscal Policy – the fiscal deficit can be corrected by increasing taxes or decreasing government spending. (Study Session 6, LOS 26.c)

162. **C** When Bright Star incurs diseconomies of scale in its auto manufacturing process, the LRAC rises as output increases. In auto manufacturing this rise in costs may be due to increasing complexity of plant management and inefficiencies resulting from miscommunication. The minimum efficient scale is the smallest quantity of output at which the LRAC reaches its lowest level. (Study Session 4, LOS 17.d)

163. **A** A decrease in the marginal income tax rate shifts the labor supply curve up and to the right, increasing the supply of labor. An increase in the supply of labor will increase equilibrium employment and increase potential GDP. (Study Session 6, LOS 26.a)

164. **C** Both the classical economists and the Monetarists believe that the best tax policy is to keep taxes low to minimize the disruption and distortion that they introduce into the economy. The other statements are correct. (Study Session 5, LOS 23.d)

Financial Reporting and Analysis

165. **B** The interim report is generally not audited. The report provides financial information semiannually or quarterly, which includes all of the company's financial statements and footnotes. (Study Session 7, LOS 29.e)

166. **A** When the company records unbilled or accrued revenue, an asset such as unbilled revenue or accounts receivable is recorded. (Study Session 7, LOS 30.e,g)

167. **C** IFRS requires only one year of comparative financial information. IFRS does not allow the use of extraordinary items. U.S. GAAP permits extraordinary items. (Study Session 7, LOS 31.f)

168. **A** This account is a contra asset account to accounts receivable, thus assets are overstated. The omission of estimated bad debt expense will result in net income being overstated. In addition, the allowance for doubtful accounts is understated. Liabilities are not affected. (Study Session 8, LOS 32.c)

169. **B** Net non-operating income includes interest income, interest expense and the gain on investment sales. Sales, cost of sales and selling expenses are operating income items. $100,000 – $50,000 + $500,000 = $550,000 (Study Session 8, LOS 32.f)

170. **A** 5,000,000 + [500,000 – (500,000 × $20)/$40] = 5,250,000 shares. The options will be anti-dilutive, because their exercise price is higher than the stock price. (Study Session 8, LOS 32.h)

171. **C** Accounts payable increased from 45% to 55% of total assets in Year 2 compared to an increase for the industry from 42% to 48% of total assets. If accounts payable totaled $450 and $550 for Year 1 and Year 2 and the industry reported $420 and $480 for Year 1 and Year 2, the percent increases would be 22% for Company A and 14% for the industry. (Study Session 8, LOS 33.i)

172. **B** Current liabilities are obligations due within one year from the date of the balance sheet. The $100,000 trade credit due on 1/31/09 and $150,000 bonds due on 9/30/09 are current liabilities. The other bonds are non-current since they do not mature until after 2009. $100,000 + $150,000 = $250,000 (Study Session 8, LOS 33.d)

173. **C** Franchise A's asset value will be reduced by the $200,000 annual amortization of the original cost of $1 million and Franchise B's asset value will be reduced $50,000 for the impairment. A total of $250,000 decrease in the franchise assets account. (Study Session 8, LOS 33.e)

174. **A** Interest received, dividends received and interest paid are operating cash flows under SFAS 95. Dividends paid are financing cash flows under SFAS 95. Interest received and dividends received may be shown as operating or investing cash flows under IAS 7. Interest paid and dividends paid may be shown as operating or financing cash flows under IAS 7. (Study Session 8, LOS 34.c)

175. **C** CFI includes capital expenditures, the investment in a joint venture, and acquisitions: –100 – 40 – 80 = –220. The dividend from affiliates is included in operating cash flow. CFF is equal to total cash flow minus CFO minus CFI: 340 – 210 – (–220) = 350. (Study Session 8, LOS 34.a)

176. **C** With no taxes, the only cash flows are the sale proceeds. The sale proceeds of $35,000 are equal to the $15,000 gain + the $20,000 book value [$100,000 cost – $80,000 accumulated depreciation]. The proceeds are reported as an inflow from investing activities. The $15,000 gain on sale is NOT an operating cash flow. (Study Session 8, LOS 34.f)

177. **A** The LIFO liquidation causes old inventory to be sold that was accumulated at lower costs thereby decreasing COGS as a percentage of sales. Lower COGS as a percentage of sales will result in higher gross profit as a percentage of sales. (Study Session 9, LOS 35.g)

178. **C** An allocation of fixed production overhead based on normal production capacity is included in inventory cost. Neither storage costs that are not required as part of the production process nor shipping costs for delivery to the customer are included in inventory cost. (Study Session 9, LOS 35.a)

179. **A** A decrease in the firm's bond rating will increase the required yield on its debt and decrease the market value of its debt. A decrease in the market (and book) value of its debt will decrease the firm's reported debt-to-assets ratio (a solvency ratio). A decrease in balance sheet liabilities will increase equity as long as assets are unchanged. (Study Session 9, LOS 38.d)

180. **C** The future obligation is known as an asset retirement obligation (ARO). Recognizing an ARO will result in lower net income and higher total assets. Net income is lower because of higher depreciation expense and *higher* accretion expense. Total assets are higher because the present value of the future obligation is added to total assets. The effective tax rate is not changed by an ARO. (Study Session 9, LOS 36.g)

181. **B** Increasing salvage values will lower depreciation expense and increase net income. Lowering the estimated life will *increase* depreciation expense. We need additional information about the direction of prices to determine the impact of switching to the average cost method. (Study Session 9, LOS 36.d)

182. **A** 2009 taxes owed = $0.5 \times 5000 = \$2,500$

    2009 deferred tax asset addition = $0.5 \times 200 = \$100$

    2009 deferred tax liability increase = $0.5 \times 600 = \$300$

    adjustment of deferred tax asset = $(0.5 / 0.35) \times 2000 - 2000 = \$857$ (increase in tax rate makes asset more valuable)

    adjustment of deferred tax liability = $(0.5 / 0.35) \times 1000 - 1000 = \$429$

    Income tax expense = taxes owed + ΔDTA $-$ ΔDTL = $2,500 + (300 + 429) - (100 + 857)$ = $\$2,272$. (Study Session 9, LOS 37.d,e)

183. **C** The cost of intangible assets with finite lives is capitalized and amortized over their useful lives. In this case, the useful life of the asset is expected to be 10 years. (Study Session 9, LOS 36.f)

184. **B** The bonds were issued at a premium in 2005 because the 8% coupon rate exceeded the 6% market interest rate. Since the current market interest rate of 9% is above the coupon rate, Charter can repurchase the bonds at a price below the carrying value. When the carrying value exceeds the reacquisition price, a gain is recognized in the income statement. (Study Session 9, LOS 38.a)

185. **B** Coupon payments are reported in the cash flow statement as operating outflows. For zero coupon debt, there is no outflow of cash until the debt matures. At maturity, the outflow of cash is reported as a financing activity. Therefore, firms with zero coupon debt will report higher CFO and lower CFF when compared to firms with coupon-paying debt. When debt is issued at a discount, interest expense *increases* over time as the carrying value of the debt increases. (Study Session 9, LOS 38.a)

186. **C** The effects of using LIFO versus FIFO would depend on the direction of inventory price changes. The deferred tax effect may eventually reverse. Selling accounts receivable would always overstate cash flow from operations. (Study Session 9, LOS 38.i)

187. **B** Common equity as a percentage of total capital is calculated as:

    $$1 - \left[\frac{1,300}{(550 + 645 + 1,470)}\right] = 1 - 0.488 = 51.2\% \text{ in Prior Year and}$$

    $$1 - \left[\frac{1,770}{(770 + 900 + 1,800)}\right] = 1 - 0.510 = 49.0\% \text{ in Current Year.}$$

    (Study Session 10, LOS 39.a)

188. **C** A company negotiating a new labor contract is likely to understate earnings to get a more favorable contract. By expensing rather than capitalizing costs, the company will reduce its reported net income. LIFO liquidation at year-end will result in a lower COGS and higher net income, offset by higher tax expense. By deferring expenses, the company will report higher net income. (Study Session 10, LOS 40.a)

189. **A** IFRS require inventories to be stated at the lower of cost or net realizable value. U.S. GAAP requires inventory to be reported at the lower of cost or *market*. (Study Session 10, LOS 43.a)

190. **C** IFRS (No. 5) and U.S. GAAP (SFAS No.144) have aligned their standards on the reporting requirements for discontinued operations. IFRS standards do not permit extraordinary items. U.S. GAAP standards require the completed contract method be used when the outcome of a contract cannot be reliably estimated, while IFRS standards require revenue to be recognized to the extent possible. (Study Session 10, LOS 43.b)

191. **C** On a financial calculator: PMT = 85 million; i = 8%; n = 10 years; PV = ?
    PV = 570,356,918

    Calculate the amount invested in the project: 570,356,918 − 125,000,000 = 445,356,918

    Payback period = 445,356,918 / 85,000,000 = 5.24 years. (Study Session 11, LOS 44.d)

192. **A** Cash previously spent to perform a feasibility study is a sunk cost which should be ignored. Working capital requirements and cannibalization are factors that should be considered in capital budgeting. (Study Session 11, LOS 44.b)

193. **C** N = 20(10 × 2); FV = 1000; PMT = 40; PV = −1020;

    CPT → I / Y = 3.85 × 2 = 7.70 = YTM

    The debt-rating approach uses the company's debt rating to estimate before-tax cost of debt. The yield on the existing bonds is currently 7.7%, which is considerably less than 8.5%, so C is incorrect. Based on the information given, there is no reason to assume TurboGas's pretax cost of debt is not comparable to other "A" rated entities. The seniority and security of the debt should be considered in estimating the cost of debt. (Study Session 11, LOS 45.f)

194. **B** $Weight_{debt}$ = 35 / (35 + 140) = 0.2

    $Weight_{equity}$ = 140 / (35 + 140) = 0.8

    WACC = (0.2 × 0.09 × (1 − 0.4)) + (0.8 × (0.04 + (0.9 × 0.045))) = 0.0752

    (Study Session 11, LOS 45.a)

195. **A** Mason must increase Mammoth's weighted average cost of capital (WACC) to adjust for the semiconductor's higher cash flow risk. (Study Session 11, LOS 45.d, e)

196. **B** Longer operating and cash conversion cycles are frequently signs of liquidity problems since timeframes for realizing sales and credit collections are increasing without offsetting increases in the time delay to repay suppliers. (Study Session 11, LOS 46.b)

197. **C** Shareholders' interests are served when they have the right to bring legal actions against management or the board to enforce ownership rights or in case of fraud. The rights to hold a special meeting to vote on shareholder-sponsored initiatives and vote to approve or disapprove any takeover defenses are also supportive of shareholders' interests. (Study Session 11, LOS 48.g)

198. **B** The line of credit is the most costly alternative, therefore the least likely choice.

Calculations for the alternatives are:

Bank note = 6.25%

$$\text{Line of credit} = \frac{\left(0.06 \times 1,000,000 \times \frac{1}{12}\right) + \left(0.005 \times 1,000,000 \times \frac{1}{12}\right)}{1,000,000} \times 12$$

$$= \frac{(5,000) + (416.67)}{1,000,000} \times 12 = 0.065 = 6.5\%$$

$$\text{Banker's acceptance} = \frac{\left(0.0625 \times 1,000,000 \times \frac{1}{12}\right)}{1,000,000 - \left(0.0625 \times 1,000,000 \times \frac{1}{12}\right)} \times 12$$

$$= \frac{5,208.33}{994,791.67} \times 12 = 0.0628 = 6.28\%$$

(Study Session 11, LOS 46.g)

Portfolio Management

199. **A** Both stocks have the same total risk, but Rich Shaw stock has more systematic risk than the Melon stock. Systematic risk is the part of the stock's total risk that is non-diversifiable. In contrast, unsystematic risk is the part of the stock's total risk that is diversifiable. Unsystematic risk is affected by factors unique to the firm, and is also known as unique risk. Rich Shaw stock has more non-diversifiable (systematic) risk than Melon (60% vs. 40% of total risk). According to rational investment behavior assumptions, investors demand a higher return for stocks with greater systematic risk. A stock's unsystematic (diversifiable) risk has no effect on the stock's required return because it is assumed that this risk can be diversified away. (Study Session 12, LOS 51.c)

200. **C** By definition, the optimal portfolio is the point of tangency between the efficient frontier and the utility function of a particular investor. Since every investor has their own set of utility curves (based on their attitudes toward risk and return), every investor could have a different optimal portfolio. (Study Session 12, LOS 50.g)

201. **B** The standard deviation for a combination of a risky asset, A, and a risk-free asset, F, equals $w_A \sigma_A$ because the standard deviation of a risk-free asset, by definition, is zero. So, Hull's standard deviation equals 0.40(0.20) = 8%. (Study Session 12, LOS 51.a)

202. **B** Craig invests all her savings in bonds. The formula for the expected return for any asset, i, equals:

$$E(R_i) = \Sigma p_i R_i$$

where p_i is the probability that event or scenario i will occur.

For Craig's investment, $p_1 = 30\%$, $p_2 = 50\%$, and $p_3 = 20\%$. R_i is the return associated with scenario i: $R_1 = 15\%$, $R_2 = 8\%$, and $R_3 = -10\%$. Therefore, the expected return for bonds equals:

$$E(R_{bonds}) = (30\% \times 15\%) + (50\% \times 8\%) + (20\% \times -10\%) = 4.5\% + 4\% - 2\% = 6.5\%$$

The formula for the expected return for a portfolio is the weighted average of the individual asset expected returns:

$$E(R_p) = \Sigma w_i E(R_i)$$

where w_i is the percentage of the portfolio, p, allocated to asset i.

Reid invests 30% in stocks, 20% in Treasury bills, and 50% in bonds: $w_{stocks} = 30\%$, $w_{tbills} = 20\%$, and $w_{bonds} = 50\%$. The problem provides the expected returns for stocks and Treasury bills (the risk-free asset): $E(R_{stocks}) = 12\%$ and $R_F = 4\%$. And, we have calculated the expected return on bonds: $E(R_{bonds}) = 6.5\%$. Therefore, the expected return on Reid's investment equals:

$$E(R_p) = (30\% \times 12\%) + (20\% \times 4\%) + (50\% \times 6.5\%) = 7.65\%.$$

The equally-weighted benchmark invests 33.33% in each of the 3 asset classes. The expected return for the equally-weighted benchmark is simply the arithmetic average of the 3 asset class expected returns:

$$E(R_{bench}) = \frac{12\% + 4\% + 6.5\%}{3} = 7.5\%$$

Therefore, Reid's expected return exceeds the equally-weighted benchmark, whereas Craig's expected return falls below the equally-weighted benchmark. (Study Session 12, LOS 50.c)

203. **B** Capital market theory assumes no transaction costs, not equal transaction costs. (Study Session 12, LOS 51.a)

204. **B** Asset allocation refers to the process of allocating funds across various asset classes such as stock, bonds and cash. It does not refer to the selection of specific securities within each asset class. Target asset allocation refers to the normal weights assigned to each asset class. Studies have shown that between 85 to 95% of the total portfolio return is attributable to the portfolio's target asset allocation. (Study Session 12, LOS 49.e)

Asset Valuation

205. **A** An important reason for secondary markets is to provide liquidity to investors after securities are issued. Financial futures are traded on secondary markets. Private placements are not traded, but issued directly to an investor. (Study Session 13, LOS 52.b)

206. **A** Because the S&P 500 index is market capitalization weighted, stocks with higher market capitalization have greater influence on the performance of the index. Because the index outperformed its equally weighted version, larger capitalization stocks performed better than smaller capitalization stocks. (Study Session 13, LOS 53.a)

207. **A** Avoiding or ignoring new information that would call a decision into question is an example of confirmation bias. Overconfidence bias refers to evidence that analysts' overconfidence in their earnings forecasts and their (high) estimated growth rates of earnings lead them to overemphasize the impact of good news and to underestimate the negative value implications of bad news. The other choices are accurate statements. (Study Session 13, LOS 54.d)

208. **B** Statement 1 is correct. Research indicates that there is a small capitalization effect. Excess returns can be generated by investing in small capitalization stocks, but some question whether this is a function of an incomplete measure of risk. Statement 2 is incorrect. Research offers strong support for the weak form of the efficient market hypothesis. If markets are weak-form efficient, abnormal returns to technical analysis should be positive about 50% of the time. (Study Session 13, LOS 54.c)

209. **A** Both statements are incorrect. A growth company has good internal investment prospects. A growth stock, on the other hand, is a stock with higher rate of return prospects than other stocks in the market with similar characteristics. A defensive stock can have a low or even negative beta. A stock with a negative beta is not pro-cyclical, but counter-cyclical. (Study Session 14, LOS 58.a)

210. **C** Nominal return on Treasurys = $(1.01 \times 1.03) - 1 = 1.0403 - 1 = 0.0403 = 4\%$

     Nominal return on S&P = $(1.087 \times 1.03) - 1 = 1.1196 - 1 = 0.1196 = 12\%$

     $12\% - 4\% = 8\%$. (Study Session 14, LOS 56.e)

211. **B** The P/E model that Jan is using is: $P/E = \dfrac{D_1/E_1}{k - g}$. Because k – g is the same for both stocks, the stock with the highest payout rate (D_1/E_1) has the highest P/E. The stock with the lowest retention rate (and highest payout rate) is Stock B. (Study Session 14, LOS 56.d)

212. **A** There is no guarantee concerning when, or even if, apparent mispricings will be corrected and it may be difficult or impossible to find securities with exactly the same risk. Arbitrageurs do not have unlimited funds. The providers of capital to arbitrageurs may place limits on the arbitrage trades and position sizes that restrict the ability of arbitrageurs to completely exploit mispricings. Given the limitations on the funds that investors make available for exploiting mispricings, only the more significant mispricings may be exploited while others are allowed to persist. (Study Session 13, LOS 55.b)

213. **B** Since Marvin is given the real risk-free rate and nominal growth in net income, he will need the inflation rate to either state all inputs on a nominal or real basis. Marvin will also need the expected long-term earnings retention rate to estimate the long-term growth rate for the company. (Study Session 14, LOS 56.c)

214. **B** Fundamental analysts use both a top-down and bottom-up approach to investing. The top-down approach requires a three-step process. The bottom-up approach focuses on the individual investment to be considered. The other statements are incorrect. (Study Session 14, LOS 56.a)

215. **A**

	Delmar	*Bell United*
Stock price per share	$25	$35
Cash flow = NI + depreciation	$100 + 250 = 350	$1,500 + 800 = 2,300
Cash flow per share	350 / 100 = 3.5	2,300 / 500 = 4.6
Price to cash flow ratio	25 / 3.5 = 7.14×	35 / 4.6 = 7.61×

The price/CF multiple indicates that Delmar is a less expensive stock. (Study Session 14, LOS 59.b)

216. **B** A high beta stock could be either a cyclical or a growth stock. Defensive stocks (with low betas and low systematic risk) are less sensitive to economic cycles. (Study Session 14, LOS 58.a)

217. **C** The duration of the Dewey bonds = – (percentage change in price) / (change in yield in percentage points) = – (–4.0) / 0.50) = +8.0. Dollar duration = duration/100 × portfolio value = 8/100 × $12 million = $960,000. (Study Session 15, LOS 61.f)

218. **B** A bond issued at a yield higher than its coupon will be priced below par, or at a discount. Apparently, the market believed that the 5% coupon was too low relative to market yields. Three months later, when market yields have declined, the 5% coupon will be more attractive, and the bond will trade at a premium to par, reflecting the fact that the coupon is now higher than the yield available on comparable bonds. (Study Session 15, LOS 61.b)

219. **B** Under the regular cycle auction – single price method the debt is auctioned periodically according to a cycle and the highest price (lowest yield) at which the entire issue to be auctioned can be sold is awarded to all bidders. This is the system used by the U.S. Treasury. (Study Session 15, LOS 62.a)

220. **B** Increased volatility reduces the value of bonds with embedded call options, such as mortgage backed securities. The STRIPS are zero-coupon securities with no reinvestment risk. Putable bonds have less interest rate risk than straight bonds; if rates rise they can be put back to the issuer. (Study Session 15, LOS 61.a, n)

221. **C** percentage change in price = $\{[\pm\ duration \times (\Delta y)^2]\} + [convexity \times (\Delta y)^2]\} \times 100$

decrease in rates = $\{[10 \times 0.01] + [200 \times (0.01)^2]\} \times 100 = 12\%$

(Study Session 16, LOS 66.g)

222. **A** Analyst A is correct. Price compression refers to the situation where callable bonds will not appreciate as much as option free bonds in a falling interest rate environment, because such bonds can be called by the issuer. This risk also applies to amortizing securities. Analyst B is incorrect. Zero coupon securities have no reinvestment risk, while amortizing securities require reinvestment of periodic payments of both principal and interest. (Study Session 15, LOS 61.h, i)

223. **C** Since this is a one-time expenditure, the MTN format with debt issued repeatedly on a best-efforts basis would not be particularly appropriate. The secured bonds would be lower risk for investors than debentures (which are unsecured) and so would probably have the lowest coupon. (Study Session 15, LOS 62.h)

224. **C** The duration of a bond can be estimated using the following equation:

$$\frac{\text{Price if yields decline} - \text{price if yields rise}}{2 \times (\text{initial price}) \times (\text{change in yield in decimal})} = \frac{107.4166 - 101.3834}{2 \times 104.5 \times 0.0025} = 11.547$$

(Study Session 16, LOS 66.d)

225. **C** Creation of a separate entity in search of a higher credit rating is a common type of asset backed security financing, known as a special purpose vehicle. Combining a debt issue with a derivative instrument such a swap is referred to as a structured note. (Study Session 15, LOS 62.h,i)

226. **A** Bond prices fall when interest rates increase; convexity reduces the price decline. (Study Session 16, LOS 66.c)

227. **A** The relative yield spread is calculated as $\frac{5.45 - 4.10}{4.10} = 0.329$ Since the spread has

widened from 4 years ago, it would appear that the economy has weakened. A weaker economy would result in a "flight to quality" as investors sought the safety of low risk issues. Higher risk issues would fall in price, widening the yield spread. (Study Session 15, LOS 63e,f)

228. **C** Bond Z has no provisions for early retirement (which favor the issuer), so it should yield the lowest. Note that a bond that is noncallable will also be nonrefundable. Bond X is noncallable, but allows the issuer to redeem principal through an accelerated sinking fund. Bond Y also has an accelerated sinking fund and is callable, giving the issuer the most options, and therefore, yielding the highest rate. (Study Session 15, LOS 60.d,e)

229. **C** Forward rate: $(1 + 0.0465)^2 = (1 + 0.041)(1 + f)$

$0.052 = f$ (Study Session 16, LOS 65.h)

230. **A** A bond trading at a discount will have a YTM greater than its coupon. The current yield is $8 / 97.55 = 8.2\%$. Know the terminology: nominal yield = coupon rate. (Study Session 16, LOS 65.b)

231. **A** In a plain vanilla interest rate swap the net payments are calculated using the following formula:

$$(\text{net fixed-rate payment})_t = (\text{swap fixed-rate} - \text{LIBOR}_{t-1})\left(\frac{\text{number of days}}{360}\right)(\text{notational principal})$$

In order for JonesCorp as the fixed-rate receiver to make a net payment (i.e., the floating-rate payer), LIBOR must increase above the swap fixed rate. Since LIBOR is currently equal to the fixed-rate on the swap, the LIBOR term structure would need to either remain flat but shift up or become upward sloping. In either of these scenarios, future LIBOR will be higher than the fixed-rate on the swap and JonesCorp will owe more to the counter party than it will receive. (Study Session 17, LOS 71.b)

232. **B** The profit on a protective put strategy is $V_T - S_0 - p_0$. The term V_T in the profit equation is equal to $S_T + \max(0, X - S_T)$. Since the put is out of the money at expiration, the value of V_T is simply the value of the stock at expiration. Combining this value with the rest of the profit equation, we can calculate the protective put profit as $27.13 - 25.96 - 0.65 = \$0.52$. (Study Session 17, LOS 72.b)

233. **C** Since Black is hedging part of its production, the company will be short futures. To close out the position, Black would offset the position with a long position on the same exchange. (Study Session 17, LOS 69.d)

234. **B** Since the market price is below the exercise price, it is 25 − 21 = $4 in-the-money. (Study Session 17, LOS 70.a)

235. **A** A 2 × 8 FRA agreement means that in 60 days (2 months) Grass will need to borrow the $12 million and the agreement is based on the 180-day (6 months) LIBOR.

$$\text{Transaction gain(loss)} = (12,000,000)\left(\frac{(0.06 - 0.06)\left(\frac{180}{360}\right)}{1 + (0.06)\left(\frac{180}{360}\right)}\right) = 0$$

(Study Session 17, LOS 68.f,g)

236. **B** When an investor establishes a futures position, he must deposit an amount called the initial margin which is pre-set dollar amount determined by the exchange. As the value of the underlying asset (and thus the futures contract) changes, the balance in the margin account will also change as the account gets marked to market. If the balance falls below a certain level, known as the maintenance margin, then the investor will need to deposit additional funds in order to bring the margin account balance back to the initial margin level. The amount required to bring the balance back to the initial level is known as the variation margin. Kent incorrectly reversed the definitions of maintenance and variation margin. Ramsey's statement about the daily settlement price is correct. (Study Session 17, LOS 69.b)

237. **C** If the price of BSI stock is $54.60 at the expiration date, then the short BSI call with a strike price of $55.00 will be out of the money and will have a profit equal to the option premium of $1.10. If the stock price of HPC stock is $8.13 at expiration, then the long HPC put option with a strike price of $10.00 will be in the money and will have a profit of 10.00 − 8.13 − 0.75 = $1.12. The total profit of the strategy would be 1.10 + 1.12 = $2.22. A long BSI call with a strike of $55.00 combined with a short HPC put would have a profit of −$2.22, the exact opposite of the previous strategy. Note that this demonstrates the symmetrical nature of option profits. A short BSI put with a $45.00 strike combined with a short HPC call with a $7.50 strike would have a profit of $2.07. A long BSI put with a $45.00 strike combined with a long HPC call with a $7.50 strike would have a profit of − 2.07. (Study Session 17, LOS 72.a)

238. **C**

Property 1	750,000/6,000,000 = 0.125
Property 2	500,000/3,000,000 = 0.167
Property 3	1,000,000/7,000,000 = 0.143
Average	(0.125 + 0.167 + 0.143)/3 = 0.145

(Study Session 18, LOS 73.f)

239. **B** ETFs can be priced and traded throughout the day, rather than only after the market closes. ETFs have similar market risk to index funds. ETFs are just as likely as index funds to experience tracking error. (Study Session 18, LOS 73.c)

240. **C** The probability of survival is the product of the annual probabilities as follows:

$Probability = (1 - 0.22)^4 \times (1 - 0.13)^6 = 0.16$

$Cost\ of\ Capital = 0.05 + (0.05)2.0 = 0.15$

The NPV of the project, assuming it survives, is:

$$\text{Survival NPV} = -3 + \frac{150}{(1+0.15)^{10}} = 34.08$$

The NPV if the project fails is:

Project failure = -3

The overall expected project NPV is then a probability weighted average:

Expected NPV = $(0.16 \times 34.08) + [(1 - 0.16) \times -3] = 2.93$ million

(Study Session 18, LOS 73.h)

EXAM 3
MORNING SESSION ANSWERS

To get valuable feedback on how your score compares to those of other Level 1 candidates, use your Username and Password to gain Online Access at schweser.com and choose the left-hand menu item "Practice Exams Vol. 2."

1. B	31. B	61. B	91. A
2. C	32. B	62. B	92. A
3. B	33. B	63. B	93. B
4. A	34. A	64. B	94. B
5. B	35. C	65. B	95. B
6. B	36. B	66. C	96. B
7. B	37. A	67. C	97. C
8. B	38. B	68. B	98. C
9. B	39. C	69. B	99. B
10. B	40. B	70. C	100. C
11. B	41. C	71. B	101. A
12. B	42. C	72. C	102. C
13. A	43. A	73. B	103. B
14. B	44. B	74. A	104. A
15. A	45. C	75. B	105. A
16. C	46. C	76. A	106. C
17. A	47. A	77. C	107. B
18. A	48. B	78. C	108. B
19. C	49. C	79. B	109. C
20. C	50. B	80. A	110. A
21. C	51. B	81. A	111. A
22. C	52. C	82. B	112. B
23. A	53. A	83. C	113. A
24. B	54. B	84. A	114. B
25. C	55. B	85. C	115. C
26. C	56. A	86. B	116. B
27. A	57. C	87. A	117. B
28. A	58. C	88. C	118. B
29. B	59. C	89. C	119. A
30. C	60. A	90. C	120. C

Exam 3
Morning Session Answers

Ethical and Professional Standards

Answers referencing the Standards of Practice are all Study Session 1, LOS 2.a, b.

1. **B** Standard I(C). Members and candidates can employ ideas from others with proper acknowledgement. Members and candidates must be careful not to misrepresent to clients the extent of their work. In accordance with Standard I(C) – Professionalism – Misrepresentation, Laird must also ensure that the third-party research has a reasonable and adequate basis. Permission is not required when the ideas of others and research results are properly acknowledged.

2. **C** Standard II(A). Any material nonpublic information should only be distributed to those with a need to know. Although the number of parties who know the information should be limited, some employees may need the information in order to do their job (e.g.,the investment banking department). Tight controls are extremely important regarding these specific communications. Regular meetings to discuss potential conflicts would be more likely to create additional breaches of sensitive information. Additional review of employee trading is a suitable element. Either a designated supervisor or a compliance officer can serve as the "clearance" person considering whether or not information is material or sufficiently public.

3. **B** GIPS. "B" is a recommendation, not a requirement. The other two choices are both requirements, under the "Fundamentals of Compliance".

4. **A** Standard III(B). The best business practice is one that dictates that initial recommendations be made available to clients who have previously indicated an interest in the specific security type. The firm does not need to communicate a recommendation to all clients, but choosing which clients receive the recommendation should be based on suitability and known interest rather than the amount of assets invested with the firm or other favored status. According to Standard III(B) – Duties to Clients – Fair Dealing, differentiated levels of service are acceptable, but not if any client group is disadvantaged or negatively affected. Not sharing a recommendation with clients who have expressed an interest would disadvantage them.

5. **B** Standard IV(A) states that in matters related to employment, members must act for the benefit of their employer and not deprive their employer of their skills, divulge confidential information, or otherwise cause harm to their employer. "Simple knowledge" of former clients is acceptable. It is also acceptable to take records if permission is received from the old employer. "Discarded" research cannot be taken, since it is a work product produced during Owen's tenure with the old firm.

6. **B** Standard VI(B). Members must give investment transactions for clients and employers priority over transactions for either direct or indirect benefit of the member. Preclearance is still required for participation in all IPOs, even if there do not appear to be any conflicts.

7. **B** Standard I(C). According to the Standard, Members and Candidates must not knowingly misrepresent any investment recommendation or action. Allen and Hayes were motivated by the offered bonus, rather than the needs of their individual clients. Allen's statement implies that he will not be able to offer the XYZ issue for long because it is such an attractive investment, not because management has ordered its disposal. Hayes' statement may be correct, but the statement is giving a false impression that the firm held the position on purpose, not because it is illiquid.

8. **B** Standard I(B). According to the Standard, members must use reasonable care and judgment to remain independent and objective in their professional activities. This includes both the solicitation and acceptance of gifts or other consideration that could potentially compromise their objectivity. Henry should not accept the invitation, given the fact that Brimley has stated his desire to obtain more favorable analytical coverage, and the fact that they had no contact for nearly twenty years.

9. **B** Standard IV(C). According to the Standard, members are required to make a reasonable effort to prevent their subordinates from violating laws, regulations, rules, and the Code and Standards and must also make a reasonable effort to identify such violations. Standard IV(C) – Duties to Employers – Responsibilities of Supervisors is quite clear on this point – supervisory responsibility should be *declined* until proper procedures are in place.

10. **B** Standard III(A). According to the Standard, members must put client's interest ahead of their employer's or their own interests. Members have a duty of loyalty, prudence, and care. Also, members must comply with any applicable fiduciary duties in the client relationship. Cole has not violated the Standards. She has considered the client's investment objectives and constraints in assessing the appropriateness of the investment strategy. In addition, Cole has selected a broker that will help ensure the success of the investment strategy. Members can pay higher commissions for brokerage as long as there is a corresponding benefit to the client. Cole has maintained loyalty to her client by ensuring that the portfolio strategy is appropriate and by arranging for trade execution that will allow the strategy to be successful.

11. **B** Standard II(A). A complete withdrawal from market-making activities would be a signal to outsiders that a significant transaction is underway. The firm should continue making a market, but in a passive way that would not give them an unfair advantage over those who do not posses material, nonpublic information.

12. **B** Standard III(D). Investment performance information must be fair, accurate, and complete. Although Kurtin's performance may have been fact, he is in violation for implying a guarantee (also a violation of Standard I(C) Misrepresentation), for using short-term performance, and for imputing past performance in the future. Kutcher is in violation because most investors would assume that one-year performance data was for the previous year. His presentation is neither reasonable nor fair. Footnoting the basis for his presentation does not make him in compliance.

13. **A** Standard III (E). The standard protects the confidentiality of client information even if the person or entity is no longer a client of the member or candidate. Regarding "C", the critical point is to always follow applicable law. Conversely, there may be situations in which applicable law *requires* disclosure of client information. When in doubt, check with compliance or counsel.

14. **B** Standard IV(C). According to Standard IV(C) – Duties to Employers – Responsibilities of Supervisors, the supervisor must see that proper procedures are in place, and make best efforts to train employees and detect any possible violations. A supervisor cannot personally evaluate each employee's actions, particularly in instances of large staffs.

15. **A** Standard II(A). According to Standard II(A) – Integrity of Capital Markets – Material Nonpublic Information, there are several examples of likely material nonpublic information, including "changes in management". Information with an ambiguous effect on price of the security may not be material nonpublic information, and once certain information is dated, it also may not be considered material nonpublic information.

16. **C** Only Choice C complies with Standard VII(B) – Reference to the CFA Institute, the CFA Designation, and the CFA Program. Choice A: Todd may not claim that she is a "Level 3 candidate in the CFA program" because she has not registered for the next Level 3 CFA examination. Choice B: Todd may not claim that she is a Level 2 Chartered Financial Analyst because there is no designation for someone who has passed Level 1, Level 2, or Level 3 of the CFA examination.

17. **A** Standards IV(A) & IV(B). Anderson is an independent contractor, rather than an employee of U.S. Securities. Therefore, Standard IV(A) and IV(B) do not apply, and Anderson only needs to abide by the terms of his oral agreement with U.S. Securities.

18. **A** Standard I(D). Members are prohibited from participating in any professional conduct that reflects adversely on their professional reputation or integrity. Declaring personal bankruptcy does not by definition reflect adversely on the individual's integrity or trustworthiness. If the circumstances of the bankruptcy included any fraudulent or deceitful conduct on the part of the Member, then that would be considered a violation.

Quantitative Methods

19. **C** First, Mann created 10 firm size groups (deciles). Then, within each of the 10 deciles, he created 5 P/E groups (quintiles), for a total of 50 classifications. (Study Session 2, LOS 7.e)

20. **C**

Expected Return Bearl Corporation		Expected Return ReaCorp	
16×0.2	= 3.2	25×0.2	= 5
6×0.6	= 3.6	10×0.6	= 6
-4×0.2	= _–0.8_	0×0.2	= _0_
Sum	= 6.0	Sum	= 11

Deviations Bearl Corporation	Deviations ReaCorp	Product of Deviations	Probability of Condition	Probability-Weighted Product
$16 - 6 = 10$	$25 - 11 = 14$	$10 \times 14 = 140$	0.2	$140 \times 0.2 = 28$
$6 - 6 = 0$	$10 - 11 = -1$	$0 \times -1 = 0$	0.6	$0 \times 0.6 = 0$
$-4 - 6 = -10$	$0 - 11 = -11$	$-10 \times -11 = 110$	0.2	$110 \times 0.2 = \underline{22}$
				Sum = 50

(Study Session 2, LOS 8.l)

21. **C**   The chi-square test is sensitive to violations of its assumptions. If the population from which the sample is drawn is not normally distributed, then inferences based on the chi-square test will be flawed. The other statements concerning chi-square are correct. (Study Session 3, LOS 11.f)

22. **C**   Both beliefs are correct, and are considered to be advantages of technical analysis. (Study Session 3, LOS 12.b)

23. **A**   The z-statistic is defined as: $z = \dfrac{X - \mu}{\sigma}$, where X is the value for a randomly selected observation from the population, μ is the mean value for the population, and σ is the standard deviation of the population. Therefore, as indicated by the formula, the z-statistic is the number of standard deviations X is from the mean (Ecko is correct). According to the normal distribution, 95% of the observations lie within 1.96 standard deviations of the mean, which implies that 95% of the z-statistics lie within plus and minus 1.96 (Charles is not correct). (Study Session 3, LOS 9.h)

24. **B**   Time-series data refer to observations spread out over time for one entity (company, fund, etc.). In contrast, cross-sectional data refer to observations spread out over many entities, but measured over one period of time. McWyllie examines the relationship between price-to-equity and debt-to-equity ratios for many companies, over a single period of time. He uses data representing a broad cross-section of the U.K. market, over a specific period of time. (Study Session 3, LOS 10.c)

25. **C**   The IRR method assumes reinvestment at the internal rate of return, while the NPV method assumes reinvestment at the opportunity cost of capital (i.e., the weighted average cost of capital). A positive NPV project will have an IRR greater than the WACC, while a negative NPV project will have an IRR less than the WACC. A project with zero NPV has an IRR equal to the WACC. NPV measures the additional shareholder wealth created by an investment project. A project with zero NPV will increase the size of the firm, but will not add to shareholder wealth. (Study Session 2, LOS 6.a)

26. **C**   This is a test of paired differences, also called a paired comparisons test.

$$t = \frac{\bar{d} - \mu_{d0}}{s_{\bar{d}}}, \text{where } s_{\bar{d}} = \frac{s_d}{\sqrt{n}}$$

$$\bar{d} - \mu_{d0} = 1.2 - 0 = 1.2$$

$$s_{\bar{d}} = \frac{s_d}{\sqrt{n}} = \frac{19.1}{\sqrt{240}} = 1.2329$$

$$t = 1.2 / 1.2329 = 0.9733$$

Do not reject, $0.9733 < 1.98$

Note: this is a two-tail test. (Study Session 3, LOS 11.e)

27. **A** Coefficient of Variation $= \dfrac{\text{Standard Deviation}}{\text{Mean Return}}$

Sharpe Ratio $= \dfrac{\text{Asset Return} - \text{Risk-free Rate}}{\text{Standard Deviation}}$

	Coefficient of Variation	Sharpe Ratio
Real Estate	0.18/0.25 = 0.72	(0.25-0.04)/0.18 = 1.17
Fixed Income	0.04/0.08 = 0.50	(0.08-0.04)/0.04 = 1.00
Equities	0.15/0.20 = 0.75	(0.20-0.04)/0.15 = 1.07

(Study Session 2, LOS 7.h)

28. **A** Murphy selects stocks based on two events: small cap stock and high earnings momentum stock. The probability of two or more events occurring together is called a joint probability, and is calculated as the product of the probabilities of the two events. In Murphy's case, the two investment screen events are dependent. That is, the probability of high momentum (M) is conditional on the stock being among the small cap stocks (S). The conditional probability of finding a high earnings momentum stock given that the stock is small is expressed as:

$$P(M \mid S) = 0.40$$

To satisfy Murphy's criteria, a stock must be a small stock and have high earnings momentum. The joint probability is calculated as the product of the conditional and marginal probabilities:

$$P(M \text{ and } S) = P(M \mid S)\, P(S) = 0.40 \times 0.20 = 8\% \text{ (Study Session 2, LOS 8.e)}$$

29. **B** $r_{MM} = \dfrac{360 \times r_{BD}}{360 - (t \times r_{BD})}$

$r_{MM} = \dfrac{360 \times .036}{360 - (150 \times .036)} = .0365 \text{ or } 3.65\%$ (Study Session 2, LOS 6.d)

30. **C** Stratified sampling is a process that divides the population according to common characteristics and then selects samples from each subgroup in proportion to the subgroup's representation in the overall population. If these samples are selected randomly then the process is called stratified random sampling. If additional criteria are applied in selecting the samples, then the process is simply called stratified sampling since the samples created are not random. (Study Session 3, LOS 10.b)

31. **B** A histogram is a bar chart representing the relative frequencies of observations in the sample (i.e., the frequency distribution). The other choices are not measures or displays of dispersion. (Study Session 2, LOS 7.c)

32. **B** Use the standard normal distribution table: $\dfrac{\overline{X} - \mu_0}{s_{\overline{X}}}$; $\dfrac{5-4}{0.8} = 1.25$. Table lookup equals 0.8944. To find the probability that the well will flow at greater than 5 mcf per day: $1 - 0.8944 = 0.1056$ or 10.6%. (Study Session 3, LOS 9.h)

Economics

33. **B**   Money market equilibrium is achieved when the quantity of money demanded and the quantity of money supplied are equal to each other. This equilibrium generates an equilibrium clearing price (the market interest rate) and a real money supply figure that equates to a level of real GDP. However, at times the money market can be out of equilibrium, just as any other market can be out of equilibrium. At interest rates below 4% (the long-term equilibrium rate), the quantity of money demanded exceeds the quantity of money supplied, creating excess demand for money. Investors will want to hold more money at below equilibrium rates, so they will sell bonds to obtain the needed extra cash. In other words, when the price of money is low, lenders will be unwilling to supply as much money. As they sell more bonds, the prices of bonds fall, and interest rates start to move back towards the 4% equilibrium. (Study Session 6, LOS 24.h)

34. **A**   Reducing taxes is expansionary fiscal policy, and should lead to an increase in aggregate demand. Lowering the reserve requirement is expansionary monetary policy, which should increase the money supply and also lead to an increase in aggregate demand. If aggregate demand increases with no change in the long-run aggregate supply curve, inflation will result. When the money supply grows rapidly (a logical result of the lower reserve requirement), aggregate demand will increase, but inflation will be high. (Study Session 5, LOS 23.c)

35. **C**   When a 10% price subsidy is offered by the Egyptian government for every kilo of cotton produced by the Egyptian farmer, the farmers will supply a greater level of cotton than before the subsidy, when the cotton market was in equilibrium. In the case of a 10% price increase the quantity supplied of cotton will become greater than the quantity demanded. Thus, the marginal social cost of production of cotton will be greater than the marginal social benefit (i.e., what the market is willing to pay) and a surplus of cotton will develop in the market. Surpluses or shortages indicate markets that are out of equilibrium or are inefficient. (Study Session 4, LOS 14.e)

36. **B**   Firms in monopolistic competition maximize economic profits by producing where MC equals MR, and by charging the price at which that quantity meets the demand curve. The statement in answer choice B applies to firms in oligopoly. All other statements are associated with monopolistic competition. (Study Session 5, LOS 20.b)

37. **A**   With the Osobright personal lines, the market has been described by Lopez as having low elasticity of supply and high elasticity of demand. In this case there are many substitutes for the Osobright mouthwash and toothpaste. Therefore, if Wigwam tries to raise the price of Osobright, it will lose a proportional amount of business. Wigwam is stuck paying the tax in the case of the Osobright personal lines. However, in the case of Mabtex, Lopez has described the market as having low elasticity of demand and high elasticity of supply characteristics. In this case, because Mabtex is in demand by consumers, as shown by a low elasticity demand curve, a shift to the left of the highly elastic supply curve will result in a higher market price, with the increase borne by the consumer. (Study Session 4, LOS 15.c)

38. **B**   A simple rule is to produce units that would add more to revenue than cost. Since the Munich plant is generating revenues greater than costs and the Paris plant is not, the CFO should increase output at the Munich plant and reduce output at the Paris plant. While there is a possibility that the Paris plant could lower marginal costs by increasing output, the problem does not give enough information to support this answer choice. (Study Session 5, LOS 18.b)

---

39. **C** The cross elasticity of demand for goods that are complements is negative because their relationship is inverse—an increase in the price of one would tend to decrease the quantity demanded of the other. The cross elasticity of demand for substitute goods is positive—an increase in the price of one would tend to increase the quantity demanded of the other. (Study Session 4, LOS 13.a)

40. **B** A firm in a monopoly position will reduce output to where MC = MR, which will increase price, decrease consumer surplus, and increase producer surplus. A marginal cost pricing strategy refers to regulation which requires a firm to set price equal to marginal cost. (Study Session 5, LOS 19.b)

41. **C** Cost-push inflation works as follows: decreased aggregate supply (caused by increased costs of labor or raw materials) causes an increase in the price level. If the central bank responds by increasing the money supply, aggregate demand increases, causing another increase in the price level. Demand-pull inflation works as follows: increased aggregate demand (caused by increased government spending, exports, or quantity of money) causes an increase in the price level, which causes a decrease in unemployment followed by an increase in money wage rates, which causes short-run aggregate supply to decrease, resulting in another increase in the price level. (Study Session 6, LOS 25.b)

42. **C** Johnson is incorrect about the change in exchange rates. A decrease in his country's interest rates relative to those in other countries reduces the yields on investments in his country, and causes his country's currency to depreciate. (Study Session 6, LOS 27.c)

43. **A** Monopolists charge the profit maximizing price; there is no maximum price. A reduction in output and increase in price under monopoly decrease consumer surplus and welfare compared to perfect competition. A monopoly may have lower costs than several competitive suppliers (natural monopoly). (Study Session 5, LOS 19.d)

44. **B** As production levels increase, there are more units to absorb fixed costs, so AFC declines. Marginal costs will increase due to the law of diminishing returns. (Study Session 4, LOS 17.c)

Financial Reporting and Analysis

45. **C** The supplementary schedule to the financials will detail a company's various business segments. (Study Session 7, LOS 29.c)

46. **C** Assets = Liabilities + Contributed capital + Beginning retained earnings + Revenues − Expenses − Dividends. Assets = 350 + 175 + 125 + 400 − 300 − 10 = 740. (Study Session 7, LOS 30.c)

47. **A** The Sarbanes-Oxley act created the Public Company Accounting Oversight Board (PCAOB) to oversee auditors. The SEC oversees the PCAOB and carries out the requirements of the Sarbanes-Oxley act. (Study Session 7, LOS 31.b)

48. **B** Howard Company should use the lesser of the useful life or legal life (10 years).

    $30 million/10 years = $3 million.

    Intangible assets that have an indefinite life are not amortized.

    (Study Session 8, LOS 32.d)

49. **C**   straight line = 1,500,000 − 200,000 = 1,300,000 / 15 = 86,666

    depreciation rate = 86,666 / 1,300,000 = 0.0666667

    double declining rate = 2 × 0.0666667 = 0.1333334

    double declining depreciation = 0.1333334 × 1,500,000 = 200,000 (Study Session 8, LOS 32.e)

50. **B**   U.S. GAAP requires retrospective restatement of financial statements for all fiscal periods shown in the company's financial report. (Study Session 8, LOS 32.g)

51. **B**   Comprehensive income includes all changes in equity except for transactions with shareholders. All of the transactions listed are included in comprehensive income except the reacquisition of treasury shares, dividends paid and stock issued to shareholders. (Study Session 8, LOS 32.l)

52. **C**   Accrued expenses are expenses incurred but not yet paid or recorded at the statement date. Wage expense should have been debited and the corresponding liability (wages payable) credited. Without this accrual entry, net income and owners' equity were overstated, while liabilities were understated. (Study Session 8, LOS 33.c)

53. **A**   Seller financing is considered a noncash transaction. Accordingly, Wichita's 2008 operating, investing, and financing activities are unaffected on the cash flow statement. (Study Session 8, LOS 34.a)

54. **B**

Net income	$142.00
+ depreciation	100.00
+ change in WC	120.00
= cash flow from operations	362.00
− net capital expenditures	(48.00)
Free cash flow	314.00
÷ shares outstanding	40.00
Free cash flow per share	$7.85

(Study Session 8, LOS 34.i)

55. **B**   Income manipulation through changes in purchasing practices is one problem with LIFO. LIFO overstates COGS when prices are rising and understates COGS when prices are declining. When prices are rising, LIFO inventory costing leads to understated inventory values. (Study Session 9, LOS 35.e)

56. **A**   As compared to FIFO, LIFO will result in higher COGS and lower ending inventory. Higher COGS will result in lower taxable income and, thus, lower income tax expense. Lower inventory will result in lower working capital (current assets − current liabilities). LIFO will result in higher inventory turnover since COGS is higher and ending inventory is lower. The inventory method has no effect on the quick ratio. (Study Session 9, LOS 35.e)

57. **C** When interest is capitalized, the expenditure is reported as an investing outflow. When expensed immediately, the expenditure is reported as an operating outflow. Thus, CFO is higher and CFI is lower when costs are capitalized. Capitalizing construction costs will result in higher fixed assets; thus, fixed asset turnover is lower (higher denominator). Construction interest is not reported as interest expense. Instead, interest, along with the other capitalized construction costs, is allocated to the income statement as depreciation expense. Thus, capitalizing costs will result in a higher interest coverage ratio (lower denominator). (Study Session 9, LOS 36.b)

58. **C** The difference in gross fixed assets and net fixed assets is accumulated depreciation. Accumulated depreciation divided by depreciation expense is equal to the average age. Thus, the average age of SafeNet fixed assets is 4.4 years [(300 gross fixed assets − 80 net fixed assets) / 50 depreciation expense] and the average age of ProTech's fixed assets is 6 years [(520 gross fixed assets − 100 net fixed assets) / 70 depreciation expense]. ProTech's older assets will need to be updated through capital expenditures (a strain on cash flow) sooner than SafeNet. ProTech's average depreciable life (520 gross fixed assets / 70 depreciation expense = 7.4 years) is longer than SafeNet (300 gross fixed assets / 50 depreciation expense = 6.0 years) but ProTech's remaining life (100 net fixed assets / 70 depreciation expense = 1.4 years) is shorter than SafeNet (80 net fixed assets / 50 depreciation expense = 1.6 years). (Study Session 9, LOS 36.e)

59. **C** Gain or loss on sale is equal to the sale proceeds less the book value. Given the loss on sale (from the operating activities of the cash flow statement) and the proceeds from sale (from the investing activities section), we can solve for the book value of $25,000 ($22,000 proceeds − book value = − 3,000). (Study Session 9, LOS 36.h)

60. **A** Since U.S. GAAP prohibits revaluation, no deferred taxes are created. (Study Session 9, LOS 37.j)

61. **B** Valuation allowances occur when the probability of utilizing deferred tax assets is in doubt. If future profitability is questionable, deferred tax assets will go unused and must be reduced in the current period by a valuation allowance. (Study Session 9, LOS 37.g)

62. **B** Barnes' bond offering is issued at a discount (market rate > coupon rate). The amortization of the discount will be added to interest expense, thus making the reported expense greater than the $12 million coupon payment (200 million × 6%). (Study Session 9, LOS 38.a)

63. **B** The bonds were issued (sold) at a discount to par because the market rate at issuance was higher than the bond coupon rate. The price of the bond at issuance is calculated below:
FV = 1000; PMT = 55; i = 7.5%; n = 5; Solve for PV = $919.08.

Therefore, Heritage will record an initial liability of:
5,000 × $919.08 = $4,595,411.51

Due to the amortization of the discount, the balance sheet value of the bonds on January 1, 2009 of the debt liability is: FV = 1000; PMT = 55; i = 7.5%; n = 4; Solve for PV = $933.013475.

On January 1, 2009 Heritage purchased the bonds for 950, for a loss of:
(950 − 933.013475) × 5,000 = $84,932.63.
(Study Session 9, LOS 38.a)

64. **B**   Debt should be increased by the present value of the future payments. Six payments of $200 million discounted at 5.47% is approximately equal to $1 billion. N = 6; i = 5.47; PMT = 200; FV = 0; solve for PV = $1,000.057. (Study Session 9, LOS 38.i)

65. **B**   Using the original DuPont equation, ROE is equal to Net profit margin × Asset turnover × Leverage. Net profit margin is equal to 5.9% (354 / 6,000). Asset turnover is equal to 1.5 (6,000 / 4,000). Thus, ROE is equal to 17.7% (5.9% × 1.5 × 2). (Study Session 10, LOS 39.e)

66. **C**   The relationship between earnings and stock price (known as the P/E ratio) is used to measure a company's valuation. Common-size analysis is useful in comparing a firm's financial statements over time. Total assets and revenues are 100%. Common-size analysis is also useful in comparing financial statements across industries. (Study Session 10, LOS 39.g)

67. **C**   Planter's high inventory level would lead to a lower inventory turnover ratio relative to its peers. (Study Session 10, LOS 40.g)

68. **B**   Repurchasing stock to offset the dilutive effects of stock options can require a substantial amount of the company's cash flow. Usually more stock options are exercised as the company's stock price rises, so to offset any dilution, greater cash flow is required to repurchase the company's shares. While the tax benefits of stock options are a source of operating cash flow, the buyback of shares to offset the dilution effect is classified as a financing outflow on the cash flow statement. (Study Session 10, LOS 41)

69. **B**

EBIT before adjustment	3,172.00
Plus: rent expense	341.00
Minus: depreciation (1,078 / 8)	134.75
Adjusted EBIT	3,378.25

Interest expense before adjustment	374.00
Plus: interest on lease (1,078 × 0.08)	86.24
Adjusted interest expense	460.24

Adjusted interest coverage ratio = 3,378.25 / 460.24 = 7.34 (Study Session 10, LOS 42.e)

70. **C**   Both U.S. GAAP and IFRS standards consider goodwill an unidentifiable intangible asset. Goodwill is capitalized and tested for impairment annually. U.S. GAAP standards do require the equity method be used to account for joint ventures. However, IFRS standards allow the use of either the equity method or the proportionate consolidation method to account for joint ventures. (Study Session 10, LOS 43.a)

71. **B**   A sunk cost is any cost already incurred (e.g., the R&D expenditure in this case), while an opportunity cost is the value of an asset being used in a project (i.e., the empty building already owned by the company) in its next best use. Conventional cash flow assumes cash flows will move from negative to positive (i.e., one sign change), while nonconventional cash flows move from negative to positive, back to negative, then back to positive (i.e. two or more sign changes). (Study Session 11, LOS 44.b)

72. **C**   When a capital budget is limited, the available funds should be allocated among projects that are expected to increase the value of the firm by the greatest amount. The increase in firm value can be measured by the project's NPV. The firm should calculate the NPV of each project and find the mix that maximizes the increase in firm value and does not exceed the funds available for investment. (Study Session 11, LOS 44.c)

73. **B**   An NPV profile is a plot of the relationship between the NPV (expected value added) of a project and the cost of capital used to discount future cash flows. (Study Session 11, LOS 44.e)

74. **A**   By definition, the market has a beta equal to one. Thus, the market beta cannot increase or decrease. It is nonsensical to suggest an increase in the market beta would lead to an increase in the market risk premium. The dividend discount model is defined as follows:

$$r_{market} = \frac{D_1}{P_0} + g$$

Thus, the return on the market is a function of the dividend yield and the growth rate of dividends. As either of these factors increases, the return on the market increases. Holding the risk-free rate constant, as the return on the market increases, the market risk premium (defined as the market return less the risk-free rate) increases. (Study Session 11, LOS 45.h)

75. **B**   The break point at which new debt will increase the marginal cost of capital is calculated as $3 million (the level of debt when the cost will change) divided by the percent of debt in the capital structure (30%). Break point = $3 million / 0.3 = $10 million in total new capital. Selections A and C are incorrect; those are the maximum levels of new debt and new equity that could be issued before a change in the costs. (Study Session 11, LOS 45.k)

76. **A**   The quick ratio is often a better indicator of liquidity than the current ratio because the assets used in the ratio are the most liquid. The quick ratio includes cash, marketable securities and accounts receivable. These assets may be more immediately available to pay current liabilities as compared to inventory, which is included in the current ratio. Even though Company X's current ratio declined in year 2, there was considerable improvement in the quick ratio, indicating an improving trend in liquidity versus Company Y. (Study Session 11, LOS 46.a)

77. **C**   The industry inventory turnover rates can be calculated by dividing 365 by the number of days of inventory for each of the years given. Year 1: 365 / 50 = 7.3x. Year 2: 365 / 49 = 7.4x. Year 3: 365 / 48 = 7.6x. The company's number of days of inventory can be calculated by dividing 365 by the inventory turnover rate for each of the years given. Year 1: 365 / 8.3 = 44. Year 2: 365 / 8.1 = 45.1. Year 3: 365 / 7.6 = 48. Decreases in inventory turnover rates are unfavorable trends because goods on hand are translated into sales more slowly. The company's turnover rate had been above the industry average in year 1. In year 3, the rate had declined to the industry average. (Study Session 11, LOS 46.f)

78. **C**   Harris is correct in viewing Logan's code of ethics as part of the company's risk management policies. Harris is also correct that meeting every other year is not frequent enough to effectively audit and improve governance policies for the company. (Study Session 11, LOS 48.e)

Portfolio Management

79. **B** Pollard desires a portfolio with less risk. Therefore, Pollard's risk aversion (disdain for risk) has increased. To determine the new feasible range of expected returns, note that the efficient frontier is plotted with expected return on the vertical axis and standard deviation on the horizontal axis. The shape of the Markowitz efficient frontier is a curve with slope that is always positive, but decreasing for portfolios of higher risk. Therefore, rates of return increase only slightly as more risk is considered, and fall more dramatically as less risk is considered. Moving back down the efficient frontier along its steeper (lower) portion implies that the decrease in standard deviation from 15% to 10% will be associated with more than a 5 percentage point drop in expected return. Stated mathematically, the shape of the efficient frontier implies that the return-to-risk ratio will decrease as Pollard considers efficient portfolios with either more *or* less risk. The original ratio of return-to-risk equals 1 (15% divided by 15%). The ratio will drop below 1 as Pollard's new portfolio slides down the efficient frontier. Therefore a 5 percentage point drop in standard deviation will be associated with more than a 5 percentage point drop in expected return. (Study Session 12, LOS 50.f)

80. **A** All portfolios on the CML include the same tangency portfolio of risky assets, except the intercept (all invested in risk-free asset). The tangency portfolio contains none of the risk-free asset. Portfolios on the CML are efficient (well-diversified) and have no unsystematic risk. (Study Session 12, LOS 51.b,c)

81. **A** Using the CAPM, the required return for any stock equals:

$$k = RFR + \beta[E(R_m) - RFR]$$

Cayman: $k = 0.05 + 1(0.12 - 0.05) = 12.0\%$. Northerland's forecast return (12.0%) *equals* Cayman's required return (12.0%). According to Northerland's forecast, the Cayman stock is *properly valued*.

Bonaire: $k = 0.05 + 1.5(0.12 - 0.05) = 15.5\%$. Northerland's forecast return (16.3%) *exceeds* Bonaire's required return (15.5%). According to Northerland's forecast, the Bonaire stock is *undervalued*.

Lucia: $k = 0.05 + 2(0.12 - 0.05) = 19.0\%$. Northerland's forecast return (18.2%) is *less than* Lucia's required return (19.0%). According to Northerland's forecast, the Lucia stock is *overvalued*. (Study Session 12, LOS 51.e)

82. **B** The equation for the capital asset pricing model is:

$$E(R_i) = R_F + \beta_i[E(R_m) - R_F]$$

The beta measures the sensitivity of the stock's returns to changes in the returns on the market portfolio, and is a standardized measure of the stock's systematic or non-diversifiable risk. As indicated by the CAPM equation, the expected return for any stock is related to its beta. In contrast, unsystematic risk does not affect the CAPM expected return. Therefore, according to the CAPM, expected returns are identical for assets with identical betas. Stock X has identical systematic risk but greater unsystematic risk than Stock Y, resulting in greater total risk (standard deviation). (Study Session 12, LOS 51.d)

83. **C** Realizing the large capital gains from the stock portfolio and the tax treatment of the bond interest will be the most important issues. (Study Session 12, LOS 49.d)

84. **A** Risk averse does not mean minimizing or eliminating risk, only preferring the lower risk investment of two alternative investments with the same expected return. (Study Session 12, LOS 50.a)

Asset Valuation

85. **C** Book value per share = $54 million shareholder equity / 6 million shares = $9/share. P/BV = $18/9 = 2.0. (Study Session 14, LOS 59.b)

86. **B** A short seller owes to the lender any dividends declared on the shorted stock. The short seller does not receive any dividends to reinvest! (Study Session 13, LOS 52.f)

87. **A** Both attributes are correct. (Study Session 13, LOS 52.a)

88. **C** The bond universe is very broad, which makes it difficult to create an index to accurately measure them. (Study Session 13, LOS 53.b)

89. **C** The implied dividend growth rate g = Retention Rate × ROE.
RR = 1 – dividend payout ratio = 1 – ($34 million / $85 million) = 1 – 0.40 = 0.60.

ROE = net profit margin × asset turnover × financial leverage.

Since net profit margin = net income/sales = $85 million / $680 million = 0.125,

ROE = 0.125 × 0.9 × 1.25 = 0.140625.

Thus g = 0.60 × 0.140625 = 0.0844 or 8.4%. (Study Session 14, LOS 56.f)

90. **C** As the expected dividend payout ratio decreases, the value of P_0/E_1 decreases (not increases). The expected (P_0/E_1) ratio is: $\frac{P_0}{E_1} = \frac{D_1/E_1}{k-g}$. Holding other factors constant, decreasing the dividend payout ratio (D_1/E_1) in the numerator, leads to a decrease in P_0/E_1. The other answers are correct. (Study Session 14, LOS 56.d)

91. **A** $D_1 = 0.5 \times (1.15) = 0.575$
$D_2 = 0.575 \times (1.15) = 0.661$
$D_3 = 0.661 \times (1.15) = 0.760$

$$g = 0.1 \times \left(1 - \frac{0.5}{2.50}\right) = 0.08$$

$$P_3 = \frac{0.76 \times 1.08}{0.1 - 0.08} = \frac{0.821}{0.02} = 41.05$$

$$V = \frac{0.575}{1.10} + \frac{0.661}{(1.10)^2} + \frac{0.760 + 41.05}{(1.10)^3} = 32.48$$

$32.48 < $35.00, so George should not buy the stock. (Study Session 14, LOS 56.c)

92. **A** Net income = $380 million × 12% = $45.6 million

Cash flow = Net income + Depreciation & amortization = 45.6 + 44 = $89.6 million.

Cash flow per share = Cash flow / Number of shares = 89.6 million / 31 million = $2.890

P/CF ratio = Price / CF per share = 20.50 / 2.890 = 7.09 (Study Session 14, LOS 59.b)

93. **B**   A company with major acquisitions may change the nature of its business so that historical information is not as relevant to the investment decision making process. The only ratio to adjust for the impact of the major acquisition, which changed the nature of the business, is the price-to-forward earnings ratio. The other ratios could provide information if the appropriate adjustments are made. (Study Session 14, LOS 59.a)

94. **B**   The low P/E ratio study is a test of the semi-strong form of the EMH. The research is one of a number of anomalies that do not fit the EMH. Academic research on mutual funds supports the strong form of the EMH. (Study Session 13, LOS 54.b)

95. **B**   Statement 1 is correct. There is a cost to rapidly processing information. The investor must believe their efforts will cover this cost and provide them an adequate return. Statement 2 is incorrect. The *higher* the cost of trading, the greater the likelihood financial assets will remain mispriced for a longer period of time. (Study Session 13, LOS 55.a)

96. **B**   D1 = 1.50

D2 = 3.00

D3 = 4.50

g = 0.06

required return = RFR + $\beta[R_m - RFR]$

required return = $0.02 + 1.3[0.08 - 0.02] = 0.098$

$$P_3 = \frac{4.50 \times 1.06}{0.098 - 0.06} = \frac{4.77}{0.038} = 125.53$$

$$V = \frac{1.50}{1.098} + \frac{3.00}{(1.098)^2} + \frac{4.50 + 125.53}{(1.098)^3} = 102.08$$

(Study Session 14, LOS 56.c)

97. **C**   Deferred-coupon bonds carry coupons, but the initial coupon payments are deferred for some period. The coupon payments accrue, at a compound rate, over the deferral period and are paid as a lump sum at the end of that period. After the initial deferment period has passed, these bonds pay regular coupon interest for the rest of the life of the issue (i.e., until the maturity date). Zero coupon bonds do not pay periodic interest. A step-up note has a coupon rate that increases on one or more specified dates during the note's life. (Study Session 15, LOS 60.b)

98. **C**   This bond was issued with seven years to maturity. Treasury issues with a maturity greater than one year and less than ten years are considered Treasury notes. Treasury bills have a maturity less than one year, while Treasury bonds have a maturity ten years or greater. Securities issued in previous auctions and trading in the secondary market are known as off-the-run issues. (Study Session 15, LOS 62.b)

99. **B**   Lower duration will reduce your exposure to rising yields; higher convexity will enhance returns in either a falling or rising yield environment. Therefore, Bond B provides the most protection from the rising interest rates. (Study Session 16, LOS 66.b,c)

100. **C**   Credit enhancement mechanisms and special purpose vehicles relate to asset-backed securities. (Study Session 15, LOS 62.i)

101. **A** If the OAS > Z-spread, the option cost is negative, which means that a put option is embedded in the bond, allowing investors to put the bond back to the issuer. A callable bond will have a positive option cost and a Z-spread > OAS. The bond is acceptable for the portfolio since it has no call option. (Study Session 16, LOS 65.g)

102. **C** With stable inflation, the expectations hypothesis would predict a relatively flat curve. The liquidity preference theory would predict upward sloping to offset the increased risk of the longer time horizon. (Study Session 15, LOS 63.c)

103. **B** The bond with the least percentage price change will be the bond with the lowest interest rate risk. Higher coupons or shorter maturities decrease interest rate risk. The bond with only 5 years to maturity will have the lowest interest rate risk. The government bond would have less credit risk, but similar interest rate risk. (Study Session 15, LOS 61.c)

104. **A** If a Treasury security is undervalued based on prevailing Treasury spot rates, its cash flows are priced higher individually (as Treasury STRIPS) than the bond itself. The dealer can earn an arbitrage profit by buying the bond and selling the STRIPS. We do not know whether the bond is undervalued relative to other Treasury securities. (Study Session 16, LOS 64.f)

105. **A** Revenue bonds are riskier than general obligation bonds since they are only backed by the earning power of the facility issuing the bonds. Potential investors require greater compensation due to the higher risk level. Double barreled bonds are backed both by the issuing authority's taxing power and additional revenue sources (i.e., fees or grants). Double barreled bonds are exempt from federal taxes, but are not necessarily exempt from state taxes. (Study Session 15, LOS 62.g)

106. **C** At maturity, either the investor or the company could experience a currency loss or gain. Both the investor and the issuing company are at risk for a potential exchange rate loss. (Study Session 15, LOS 61.l)

107. **B** Bond X = 1000 / 950 = 1.0526; Bond Y = 1000 / 850 = 1.1765

80 / (1.0526) = 76; 1080 / (1.1765) = 917.98

Bond $Z = 76 + 917.98 = 993.98 \approx 995$

The arbitrage-free valuation approach applies time appropriate spot interest rates to each cash flow of the bond. (Study Session 16, LOS 64.f)

108. **B** First calculate the bond's effective duration as follows: (98.2 – 91.41)/(2 × 94.73 × 0.005) = 6.79/0.9473 = 7.17. The change in price would be –7.17 × (–0.0075) × 94.73 = 5.09, for a new price of 94.73 + 5.09 = 99.82. (Study Session 15, LOS 66.d)

109. **C** If Bond A was priced to yield 5.5%, it would trade at a premium and the current yield would be less than 7%. Because Scott's reinvestment rate is below the yield to maturity of 6.25%, her actual return would be below 6.25%. Because Bond A is currently priced at a premium (YTM < coupon), the yield to call would be below the yield to maturity, and the yield to worst would be below 6.25%, even if coupons were reinvested at 6.25%. (Study Session 16, LOS 65.b)

110. **A** Statement 1 is correct. A futures contract is a standardized instrument that is traded on an exchange, unlike a forward contract which is a customized transaction. Statement 2 is incorrect. The forward contract is not marked-to-market. (Study Session 17, LOS 67.b)

111. **A** The maximum profit to a long call position is infinite since the value of the underlying stock can increase indefinitely. However, the maximum profit on a short call position is limited to the premium for which the option is sold. Since an infinite sum is always greater than a finite call premium, the maximum profit on a long call is always greater than the maximum profit on a short call. Ulrich's first statement about call options is therefore correct. A long put position has a breakeven point equal to the strike price less the premium paid for the option. If the put option is at-the-money, the underlying stock price is equal to the strike price. The stock price must decrease by the amount of the premium before the breakeven point is reached. Ulrich stated that the stock must decrease by any amount to break even, which is incorrect. (Study Session 17, LOS 72.a)

112. **B** The intrinsic value of a put is the difference between strike price and stock price if stock price is less than strike price ($80 - 78 = 2$). The loss is equal to the intrinsic value minus the premium paid ($2 - 5 = -3$). (Study Session 17, LOS 70.e)

113. **A** Being long a call has limited downside risk, but an unlimited upside, just as a protective put does. Covered calls have very limited upside potential and a long call-short put position has significant downside risk. (Study Session 17, LOS 72.b)

114. **B** Turner has several ways to terminate the futures contract he holds. Turner may enter into an offsetting position (called a close-out) by taking a long position in a futures contract at a price of $57. This would cause Turner to incur a mark-to-market loss of $5 ($57 - 52$). The loss occurs since the short futures position loses as the futures price rises. Since the mark-to-market feature effectively resets the contract every day, the relevant futures price to calculate the loss is the settlement price from the previous day. Turner could also leave the contract open and deliver the physical commodity to the long position. In this case, he would have to purchase the wheat specified in the contract at a price of $57 and sell it to the long position for $52, generating a $5 loss. (Study Session 17, LOS 69.d)

115. **C** $c_0 = p_0 + S_0 - X / (1 + r)^T$

    where: c_0 = Buy call current value
    p_0 = Buy put current value
    S_0 = Current stock price
    X = Exercise price
    r = Risk-free rate
    T = Time horizon

    $4 = 2.25 + S_0 - [50/(1 + .02)^1]$

    $S_0 = 50.77 \approx 51$

    (Study Session 17, LOS 70.j)

116. **B** Burke's exposure to cotton is long since she already owns the asset and will need to sell it in the market at a future date. Therefore she needs a short forward position to offset her price risk. Thus Anderson has taken the long position in the forward contract. Since the contract is nondeliverable, it will be settled in cash upon the expiration date. At the time of expiration, the market price of cotton is $49 and the contract price is $47. This is a $2 gain to Anderson, the long position who has the obligation to purchase the cotton for $47 but can immediately sell it for $49 in the market. Therefore, Burke owes Anderson $2. It is possible, however, that Burke will not have the funds or may simply refuse to fulfill her side of the contract. Therefore, Anderson has credit risk since there is no guarantee that Burke will pay. (Study Session 17, LOS 68.a)

117. **B**

Proposed Office Building
(under consideration)

Potential gross rental income (PGI)		$324,000
Vacancy and collection loss	7.50%	$24,300
PGI less vacancy and collection loss		$299,700
Taxes and Insurance		$27,000
Other Expenses		$32,000
Total cash expenses (Depreciation is a non-cash expense)		$59,000
NOI		$240,700

NOI (office)/Transaction price (office) =

272,000/1,700,000 =	Cap rate =	16.0%
NOI (Proposed Office Building)/Cap rate =		$1,504,375.00

The property's appraised value is $1,504,375.00. Since the proposed property is an office building, only the transaction data for another office building should be used for comparison. (Study Session 18, LOS 73.f)

118. **B** The markets for distressed securities and venture capital investments tend to be inefficient. (Study Session 18, LOS 73.o)

119. **A** The return statement is correct. However, because hedge funds have unique structures, industry performance measures have less meaning. In addition, hedge funds are not legally required to disclose performance numbers. Hedge funds have produced a good Sharpe ratio. However, a good Sharpe ratio does not mean they are superior investment vehicles. A more complete analysis is required for Garrett's statement to be correct. (Study Session 18, LOS 73.i,l)

120. **C** While limited information is an issue, it is not unique to venture capital projects. Each investment has a lack of information to some degree. (Study Session 18, LOS 73.g)

Exam 3
Afternoon Session Answers

To get valuable feedback on how your score compares to those of other Level 1 candidates, use your Username and Password to gain Online Access at schweser.com and choose the left-hand menu item "Practice Exams Vol. 2."

121. A	151. C	181. B	211. A
122. C	152. B	182. A	212. C
123. C	153. C	183. A	213. A
124. C	154. B	184. C	214. B
125. C	155. B	185. B	215. C
126. A	156. A	186. C	216. A
127. C	157. B	187. B	217. B
128. C	158. B	188. A	218. A
129. C	159. A	189. C	219. C
130. C	160. C	190. A	220. C
131. B	161. B	191. A	221. C
132. C	162. B	192. B	222. B
133. C	163. A	193. C	223. A
134. C	164. C	194. B	224. A
135. B	165. C	195. B	225. A
136. C	166. B	196. A	226. B
137. B	167. A	197. A	227. C
138. B	168. B	198. A	228. C
139. A	169. C	199. A	229. C
140. A	170. C	200. A	230. B
141. B	171. A	201. B	231. B
142. B	172. A	202. C	232. B
143. B	173. B	203. C	233. C
144. A	174. C	204. A	234. C
145. A	175. B	205. B	235. C
146. C	176. A	206. C	236. C
147. B	177. B	207. C	237. C
148. B	178. C	208. A	238. B
149. C	179. C	209. C	239. B
150. B	180. C	210. B	240. A

Exam 3
Afternoon Session Answers

Ethical and Professional Standards

Answers referencing the Standards of Practice are all Study Session 1, LOS 2.a, b.

121. **A** Standard V(A). There is a presumption that the group is experienced, and has a reasonable and adequate basis for making any changes to recommendations. The question states that Girard is confident with his firm's process. As long as the "consensus opinion" has a reasonable and adequate basis, Girard is in full compliance with Standard V(A) – Investment Analysis, Recommendations and Actions – Diligence and Reasonable Basis.

122. **C** Standard III (D). Standard III(D) does not prohibit showing past performance of funds managed at a previous firm as part of a performance track record if accompanied by appropriate disclosures. In this instance, Martin clearly detailed that the performance occurred while he was the senior portfolio manager of Alpha Emerging Markets Fund. He also identified the period of performance. Under the Standards, the only requirement is to present a fair, accurate, complete presentation of results. Use of GIPS is not required.

123. **C** Standard I(B). In accordance with Standard I(B) – Professionalism – Independence and Objectivity, Callahan must only issue recommendations that reflect his own independent judgment. He certainly has the right to refuse to cover the firm under the conditions specified.

124. **C** Standard VII(B). It is acceptable to specify that a candidate has passed a level of the exam, and to state the year, according to Standard VII(B) – Responsibilities as a CFA Institute Member or CFA Candidate – Reference to CFA Institute, the CFA Designation, and the CFA Program. The CFA Mark must never be used as a noun – a member / candidate cannot refer to oneself as "a CFA", but rather as a "CFA charterholder". It is acceptable to state that Wilson completed the examination program in consecutive years, but not to embellish with "special group".

125. **C** Standard II (A). A Member who possesses material nonpublic information must not act or cause others to act upon the information. News of a qualified opinion by a firm's auditor is material. Information is nonpublic until it is available to the general marketplace. It is recommended that Members make reasonable efforts to achieve public dissemination of material non-public information they have become aware of.

126. **A** Standard I(B). According to the Standard, members must maintain independence and objectivity with regard to their professional duties. Members must not accept any gift that may compromise their independence and objectivity. Because Welch has had a long-standing relationship with ORH Brokers, the symphony tickets have relatively small value, and because ORH provides superior execution at competitive commission rates, it is unlikely that the symphony tickets will influence Welch's independence and objectivity. Therefore it is acceptable for Welch to take the tickets without any disclosure. Modest gifts are OK and no disclosure is required.

127. **C** Standard V(B). Russ can make use of her opinions, so long as she distinguishes them from fact. The lawsuit is public information, based on the newspaper quote from the CFO.

128. **C** Standard I(C) – Professionalism: Misrepresentation prohibits plagiarism. Liu violated the Standard because she included quotations from "investment experts" without specific reference to their source. Yang, however, did not violate the Standard because it permits members to use, without acknowledgment, factual information published by recognized financial and statistical reporting services, such as Standard & Poor's.

129. **C** Standard VI(A). According to Standard VI(A) – Conflicts of Interest – Disclosure of Conflicts, members must prominently and clearly disclose to clients, prospects, and their employer, anything that could affect their independence and objectivity or interfere with their duties to those parties. As a beneficial owner of shares in Swift & Company, Roberts has incentive to increase the value of Swift stock for her personal gain, even though she is unaware of the actual amount or value of the trust holdings. This is a potential conflict of interest that must be disclosed to clients and employer.

130. **C** Standard III(A). Although establishing performance measurement benchmarks will fulfill one of the basic requirements of Standard III(C) Duties to Clients – Suitability, it is not one of the recommended procedures for compliance with Standard III(A) Duties to Clients – Loyalty, Prudence and Care.

131. **B** Standard VI(A). Members must make full and fair disclosure of all matters that could reasonably be expected to interfere with their independence or objectivity when dealing with clients. Both actual and potential conflicts of interest must be disclosed. Disclosure of Anthony's new position in ABCO will allow his clients the opportunity to judge Anthony's motives and potential biases for themselves.

132. **C** Standard V(B) Investment Analysis, Recommendations, and Actions – Diligence and Reasonable Basis. Income and growth needs must be weighed against each other, as should risk tolerance and return requirements.

133. **C** Standard VI(C). Members must disclose to their clients any compensation or benefit received for the recommendation of services. Full disclosure should be made in writing and should include the nature and value of the benefit. Clearly the client would recognize the existence of some bias in Lewis' recommendation of another department within Kite Brothers, but disclosure of a compensation arrangement will allow the client to appropriately evaluate that level of bias.

134. **C** Standard I(A). According to Standard I(A) Professionalism - Knowledge of the Law, members who practice in multiple jurisdictions may be subject to various securities law and regulations. A member must adhere to the stricter of either the applicable securities laws and regulations or Code and Standards. Members / candidates must *always* comply with applicable laws / regulations. In situations in which a local law or regulation permits activity (such as insider trading) that is not permitted by CFA Institute Standards, then the member / candidate must obey the more strict. Choice "A" is incorrect – if the local law imposes a higher responsibility, the member / candidate must follow the law. Choice "B" is incorrect – Even if legally permitted, there are cases where CFA Institute Standards may make an activity unacceptable.

135. **B** Standard IV (B). Brenner's actions complied with the conditions specified in Standard IV(B) Duties to Employers – Additional Compensation Arrangements. He notified his employer in writing (e-mail is acceptable) of the terms and conditions of additional compensation arrangement and received permission from his employer. Thus, Brenner did not violate Standard IV(B). Loyalties to other clients may be affected, but it is the employer's duty to properly determine this. Nothing in the Standard specifies that "all parties involved" includes other clients.

136. **C** Standard III (E). It is always best to check with compliance before going forward to the authorities regarding a possible legal violation. CFA Institute recognizes that in some cases there may be an obligation to not "preserve confidentiality" and disclose information as required by law. The activities described are only suspected, and proper care should be taken to not expose her firm to liability if confidential allegations of impropriety are improperly disclosed.

137. **B** Standard III(B). Members and candidates must make all efforts to treat all clients "fairly" but not "equally". Members and candidates can differentiate levels of service to clients as long as it does not disadvantage any clients.

138. **B** Standard V(C) – Investment Analysis, Recommendations, and Actions: Record Retention recommends that in the absence of local regulatory guidance, records should be kept a minimum of seven years.

Quantitative Methods

139. **A** The lognormal distribution confidence intervals are more complicated than for normal distribution. Stock prices do not have to be normally distributed. The two parameters necessary to define a lognormal distribution are mean and standard deviation (variance). (Study Session 3, LOS 9.j)

140. **A** Pollard has committed a type I error, which is rejecting the null hypothesis when it is true. She has not committed a type II error. (Study Session 3, LOS 11.b)

141. **B** Simply add the probabilities associated with the probability function for the categories 1,000, 1,500, and 2,000: 0.2 + 0.2+ 0.2 = 0.6. There is a 60% probability that unit demand will be between 1,000 and 2,000 units. (Study Session 3, LOS 7.c)

142. **B** To calculate the covariance, you first must calculate the expected returns (means) for each stock:

Expected return for A-Marts: $0.35(0.20) + 0.50(0.04) + 0.15(-0.20) = 0.06$

Expected return for Shops R Us: $0.35(0.10) + 0.50(0.02) + 0.15(-0.10) = 0.03$

The covariance is the weighted average of the cross-products:

Covariance $= 0.35(0.20 - 0.06)(0.10 - 0.03) + 0.50(0.04 - 0.06)(0.02 - 0.03) + 0.15(-0.20 - 0.06)(-0.10 - 0.03)$

Covariance $= 0.35(0.14)(0.07) + 0.50(-0.02)(-0.01) + 0.15(-0.26)(-0.13) = 0.0086$ (Study Session 2, LOS 8.j)

143. **B** The money-weighted rate of return is the internal rate of return, which is defined as the interest rate that makes the present value of cash outflows equal to the present value of cash inflows:

PV(cash outflows) = PV(cash inflows)

From the investors' standpoint, there is only one cash outflow in this problem: the original $10 million. There are no further purchases or contributions into the Fund. The cash flows to the investors are $500,000 + $2,000,000 at year 1, and $400,000 + $9,000,000 at year 2. Therefore, the money-weighted return is the value of r that

solves: $10,000,000 = \dfrac{2,500,000}{(1+r)} + \dfrac{9,400,000}{(1+r)^2}$

The money-weighted return (internal rate of return) can be found by using the following functions on the calculator:

CF_0 = −10,000,000
CF_1 = 2,500,000
CF_2 = 9,400,000

Then hit the IRR button to derive 10.256%. (Study Session 2, LOS 6.c)

144. **A** Bayes' formula uses an adjustment factor to update the prior probability (40%). The updating adjustment factor equals the ratio of P(Information given the Event) divided by P(Event), where Information refers to the increase in consumer sentiment, and Event refers to the increase in ROE. The key to the answer is to notice that the updating ratio exceeds 1, and therefore that the updated probability (Bayes probability) must increase. The problem states that P(CS increase given an increase in ROE) = 0.70, and the P(CS increase) = 0.54. Therefore, the updating ratio equals 0.70/0.54 = 1.30 and the Bayes probability P(ROE increase given CS increases) equals 0.40(1.30) = 0.52 = 52%. (Study Session 2, LOS 8.m)

145. **A** Screened stock returns are assumed to follow a normal distribution with a mean equal to 10% and a standard deviation equal to 5%. According to the normal distribution, approximately:

68% of the observations lie within 1 standard deviation of the mean.

95% of the observations lie within 2 standard deviations of the mean.

The probability of losing money can be written: $\Pr(R < 0)$. Notice that a zero percent return lies 2 standard deviations below the mean return: 10% minus 2 × 5%. From the rule above, we know that 95% of the returns lie within 2 standard deviation of the mean, or from 0% to 20%. Therefore, there is a 5% chance that the return will lie either below 0% or above 20%, or by the symmetry property, that there is a 2.5% chance that the return will lie below 0% (probability of a loss). (Study Session 3, LOS 9.g)

146. **C** A null hypothesis is "not rejected" unless the sampled data provide compelling contradictory evidence (i.e., "innocent until proven guilty"). (Study Session 3, LOS 11.a)

147. **B** The confidence interval formula for a sample mean using the z-distribution and the t-distribution are essentially the same except for the reliability factor (i.e., the distribution critical value) used. The two formulas are:

$$\bar{X} \pm z_{a/2}\frac{s}{\sqrt{n}} \qquad \bar{X} \pm t_{a/2}\frac{s}{\sqrt{n}}$$

If the population standard deviation is unknown, but the sample size is large, then the confidence interval can be calculated using the z-distribution. For example the 95% z-critical value is: $z = 1.96$ If the population standard deviation is unknown, then the confidence interval can also be calculated using the t-distribution. This is the preferred method when the sample size is small, but is normally distributed or approximately normally distributed. The t-distribution has fatter tails (i.e., more probability in the tails) which means that the t-statistic is always at least as large as the z-statistic. For example, for the 95% confidence interval with 100 observations; 99 degrees of freedom, $t = 1.98$. However, as the sample size increases, the t-distribution gets closer to the z-distribution. For very large samples, the two distributions will be very similar. However, for a sample of 100 observations, the confidence interval will be smaller if the z-distribution is used. (Study Session 3, LOS 10.j)

148. **B** The efficient markets hypothesis, which holds that all available information is reflected in current security prices, is the major challenge to technical analysis. (Study Session 3, LOS 12.a, b)

149. **C** The F-statistic tests the variances of two normally distributed populations, while chi-square tests the variance of a single normally distributed population. Neither test is robust to violations of underlying assumptions. Both the chi-square distribution and F-distribution are asymmetrical and defined by degrees of freedom. (Study Session 3, LOS 11.f)

150. **B** 500,000 = PV; N = 12; 12,700 = PMT; FV = –2,000,000; CPT → I/Y = 11%. (Study Session 2, LOS 5.d,e)

151. **C** The graph is positively sloped or skewed to the right and Mean > Median > Mode; A negatively sloped graph is skewed to the left and Mean < Median < Mode. (Study Session 2, LOS 7.i)

152. **B** Geometric = $(22/20)^{0.5} - 1 = 0.0488$. (Study Session 2, LOS 7.d)

Economics

153. **C** Domino sold short term securities that would already have been included in their reserve calculation. There is, therefore, no effect on their capacity to make loans. Domino currently has $50 - 41 = \$9$ million in reserves, versus the required amount of $\$50 \times 0.15 = \$7.5$ million. They can make $\$9 - 7.5 = \$1.5$ million in additional loans. (Study Session 6, LOS 24.e)

154. **B** The elasticity of supply is calculated as the ratio of the percentage change in quantity supplied to the percentage change in price, which in this case is calculated as zero. When drawn graphically, a perpendicular supply curve, (i.e., no change in quantity supplied as the price changes) is considered perfectly inelastic. (Study Session 4, LOS 13.a)

155. **B** A permanent increase in industry demand for a product would, in the short-run, increase its price and production. In the long run, as economic profits increase, new firms would enter the market, increase total supply, bring the price to the original level, and bring the industry to equilibrium (ATC= P_0 at q_0). As a lower cost production process is adopted by a few firms, these firms will experience lower costs and higher profits. This lower cost structure for the firms will shift the industry supply curve to the right, causing industry supply to increase and price to decrease. (Study Session 5, LOS 18.d)

156. **A** The utilitarian principle believes in transfer of income from the rich to the poor until the gap is eliminated. Major drawbacks of the principle include ignoring the costs of income transfer and the possibility of shrinking the economic pie. A bigger share of a smaller pie may be smaller than a smaller share of a bigger pie. (Study Session 4, LOS 14.f)

157. **B** All the characteristics of the market for products S and T point to Product S being in an oligopolic industry and Product T being in a monopolistic competitive industry. (Study Session 4, LOS 16.f, g)

158. **B** Two forces determine the shape of the labor supply curve; the income effect and the substitution effect. The substitution effect explains the upward sloping portion of the labor supply curve. As wage rates increase, workers are willing to substitute work for leisure time. At some point, however, workers' incomes are high enough that they are no longer willing to supply additional hours of labor, but would rather spend time enjoying their higher incomes. This is known as the income effect and is the reason the labor supply curve is backward bending. (Study Session= 5, LOS 21.c)

159. **A** All firms maximize profits at the point where marginal revenue equal marginal cost. For a monopolist, this occurs at a lower output level than for a purely competitive firm, because the monopolist has a marginal revenue curve that falls below the demand curve, while the purely competitive firm has a marginal revenue curve that lies along the demand curve. (Study Session 4, LOS 19.b)

160. **C** The reserve requirement is the fraction of deposits a bank cannot lend and is less than one, typically 20%. The maximum deposit expansion multiplier is the inverse of the reserve requirement. The money multiplier is typically less than the maximum deposit expansion multiplier because of currency drain. (Study Session 6, LOS 24.e, f)

161. **B** An increase in the quantity of money at full employment will reduce interest rates in the short run, which would increase short-run aggregate demand. This would cause wage demands to increase, which would reduce short-run aggregate supply. Thus, in the long run, the real GDP will remain unchanged with an increase in price level equal to the percentage increase in the quantity of money. (Study Session 6, LOS 24.h)

162. **B** Aggregate demand is a downward-sloping function of the price level. A change in the price level simply means that aggregate demand changes along the curve, but the aggregate demand curve itself does not shift. The other two statements are correct. (Study Session 5, LOS 23.b)

163. **A** Selling government securities on the open market reduces bank reserves and drives up the federal funds rate. The other two statements are incorrect because the Federal Reserve does not control exchange rates or the prices of government securities, so those are not tools of Federal Reserve policy. (Study Session 6, LOS 27.b)

164. **C** Unemployment due to lacking the necessary skills for a changing job market is called structural unemployment. Gold will likely seek work elsewhere as a bookkeeper; there was no broad economic downturn, she just needs to change locations. This is an example of frictional unemployment. Regulatory unemployment is a made-up term. (Study Session 5, LOS 22.c)

Financial Reporting and Analysis

165. **C** Management prepares the financial statements, not the auditor. Verification of inventory amounts is not a main objective. Auditors selectively verify some items. (Study Session 7, LOS 29.d)

166. **B** The distribution of dividends to shareholders is considered a financing activity (based on U.S. GAAP). Be aware that U.S. GAAP requires all dividends and interest *received* to be treated as an operating activity. (Study Session 7, LOS 30.a)

167. **A** The FIFO method would have reported a higher inventory balance compared to the LIFO method. The higher inventory level would produce a higher working capital balance. (Study Session 8, LOS 32.c)

168. **B** Double declining balance:

$$\text{Depreciation in Year } i = \frac{2}{n} \times (\text{Original cost} - \text{accumulated depreciation})$$

$$\text{Year } 1 = \frac{2}{10}(550,000 - 0) = 110,000$$

$$\text{Year } 2 = \frac{2}{10}(550,000 - 110,000) = 88,000 \qquad \text{(Study Session 8, LOS 32.e)}$$

169. **C** $\left[100,000 \times 2 \times \left(\frac{5}{12}\right)\right] + \left[80,000 \times 2 \times \left(\frac{7}{12}\right)\right] = 176,666$. There are 100,000 shares

outstanding for the first five months of the year and 80,000 shares outstanding for seven months of the year, which must both be multiplied by 2 to reflect the stock split and by the fraction of the year for which the number of shares outstanding is applicable. (Study Session 8, LOS 32.h)

170. **C** Unrealized gains and losses on securities classified as available-for-sale are recorded as increases (gains) or decreases (losses) in other comprehensive income. Unrealized gains and losses on actively traded securities would be reported in the income statement. (Study Session 8, LOS 32.k)

171. **A** Under U.S. GAAP, research and developments costs are not permitted to be recorded as intangible assets. They must be expensed against income as they occur. (Study Session 8, LOS 33.e)

172. **A** Off-balance-sheet financing provides both of the advantages listed. Reported debt would be lower, thus improving financial leverage ratios, and the company could avoid triggering restrictive covenants in loan agreements. (Study Session 8, LOS 33.f)

173. **B** Initially, both an asset and liability equal to the present value of the expected asset retirement costs are added to the firm's balance sheet. As the asset is depreciated over time and the liability grows, equity is decreased. In the third year, the ARO asset still has positive value and net income is reduced, compared to not accounting for the ARO, by both depreciation and accretion (to the liability). Lower net income and greater asset value reduce ROA. (Study Session 9, LOS 36.g)

174. **C** An analyst can use the information in the details of debt repayment schedules in the footnotes and MD&A to determine the timing and amount of future cash outflows necessary for the firm to make scheduled principal payments on its debt. The market value of outstanding debt is not typically included in the disclosures. Balance sheet values of debt and/or market value of debt, together with information about assets, provide information about leverage. (Study Session 9, LOS 38.c)

175. **B** The repayment of long-term debt is reported as a financing activity on the cash flow statement. The conversion and this particular asset acquisition are noncash transactions, which are not reported on the cash flow statement. However, both transactions must be highlighted in the footnotes. (Study Session 8, LOS 34.b)

176. **A** The beginning LIFO reserve was $20 (110 – 90) and the ending LIFO reserve was $25 (125 – 100). The change in the LIFO reserve is equal to the difference in COGS of $5 (25 – 20). FIFO COGS is lower than LIFO COGS during inflation; thus, FIFO COGS is $65 (70 LIFO COGS – 5 change in reserve). (Study Session 9, LOS 35.f)

177. **B** Reductions in the LIFO reserve that are caused by inventory liquidations will require adjustments to the income statement since the COGS will be artificially low. COGS will be understated as a result of the lower historical cost from inventory booked in previous periods. The lower cost inventory will most likely not be an adequate reflection of current inventory costs. (Study Session 9, LOS 35.g)

178. **C** If Padre Inc. overstates salvage values, depreciation expense is *understated*; thus, net income is overstated. Overstated net income will overstate equity; thus, the debt-to-equity is *understated*. Understated depreciation expense will overstate assets; thus, fixed asset turnover and debt-to-assets are *understated*. (Study Session 9, LOS 36.d)

179. **C** Since the fair value of Raider ($400,000) exceeds the carrying value of Raider ($385,000 including goodwill), no impairment exists; thus, no gain or loss is recognized. (Study Session 9, LOS 36.i)

180. **C** The interest income from municipal bonds is a permanent difference; thus, no deferred taxes are created. The different depreciation methods result in temporary differences that are expected to reverse. In the case of depreciation, a deferred tax liability is created. Valuation allowance accounts do not apply to deferred tax liabilities. (Study Session 9, LOS 37.f)

181. **B** Tax depreciation is 200 / 4 = $50; book depreciation is 200 / 5 = $40. Thus, after two years, the carrying value is $120 [200 – (40 × 2 years)] and the tax base is $100 [200 – (50 × 2 years)]. Taxable income is equal to pretax income less the excess tax depreciation or 1,000 – 10 = 990. The deferred tax *liability* at the end of the second year is $8 [120 carrying value – 100 tax base) ×40%]. (Study Session 9, LOS 37.c)

182. **A** Because of the inverse relationship of interest rates and bond prices, ABC would have higher borrowing capacity (lower debt) and greater solvency as compared to DEF. (Study Session 9, LOS 38.d)

183. **A** Capelli should adjust the value of the bonds to reflect the current market conditions. Since the bonds were issued at par, the book value of the bonds is $100,000,000. Due to the increase in yield spread, the appropriate discount rate, based on the Treasury yield of 4.5%, is 4.5 + 450 bp = 9.0; thus, the market value of the bonds is:

FV = $100,000,000
PMT = $5,500,000
i = 9%
n = 3
Solve for PV = $91,140,469

Therefore, Capelli should reduce the book value of the bonds to $91,140,469 from $100,000,000 and increase the book value of equity by $8,859,531. (Study Session 9, LOS 38.d)

184. **C** Debt is unaffected by the use of operating leases, while debt increases with the use of finance leases. The debt to equity ratio is lower using operating leases. Interest expense is unaffected by the use of operating leases, while interest expense increases with the use of finance leases. Interest coverage is generally higher when operating leases are used. A company using operating leases generally has a higher return on assets because of the lower reported asset base. (Study Session 9, LOS 38.g)

185. **B** In a finance lease, the principal portion of the lease payment is reported as an outflow from financing activities. The entire payment on an operating lease is CFO. (Study Session 9, LOS 38.g)

186. **C** Issuing preferred stock will result in greater total capital. As a result, the total debt-to-capital ratio will be lower (higher denominator) as preferred stock is equity, not debt. (Study Session 10, LOS 39.c)

187. **B** Return on common equity is equal to (Net income − Preferred dividends) / Average common equity. Calculate 2008 preferred dividends [$12.5 million × 8% = $1 million]. Calculate 2007 common equity [($3 million common stock + 30 million additional paid-in-capital + $75 million retained earnings − $4 million treasury stock = $104 million]. Calculate 2008 common equity [$4 million common stock + $40 million additional paid-in-capital + $88 million retained earnings − $4 million treasury stock = $128 million]. Calculate average common equity [($104 million 2007 common equity + $128 million 2008 common equity) / 2 = $116 million]. Calculate return on common equity [($14 million 2008 net income − $1 million preferred dividend) / $116 million average common equity = 11.2%]. (Study Session 10, LOS 39.c)

188. **A** ROE can be broken out as:

ROE = Tax burden × Interest burden × EBIT Margin × Asset Turnover × Leverage

Prior Year: 0.15 = 0.60 × 0.80 × 0.26 × 1.06 × Leverage

Current Year: 0.14 = 0.62 × 0.81 × 0.26 × 1.06 × Leverage

Solving the equation for leverage reveals that the measure has decreased from 1.13 in the prior year to 1.01 in the current year. This indicates BVC is using less debt in its capital structure and is the most likely reason the company's ROE has declined.

The company's net profit margin has actually increased.

Net profit margin (Prior Year): $0.60 \times 0.80 \times 0.26 = 0.12$

Net profit margin (Current Year): $0.62 \times 0.81 \times 0.26 = 0.13$

Finally, the company's tax rate has decreased from $0.40 = (1 - 0.60)$ to $0.38 = (1 - 0.62)$. (Study Session 10, LOS 39.e)

189. **C** To determine the credit rating of a company, four broad factors should be evaluated. The factors include: scale/diversification, financial policies (tolerance for leverage), operational efficiency and margin stability. The ratios EBITDA/Interest and total debt/EBITDA relate to the company's financial policies. Average annual revenues relate to the company's scale/diversification. The ratio EBITDA/Average assets relates to the company's operational efficiency. An analysis of margin stability is missing. The factors provided indicate that Clean Corp should have the higher credit rating. Clean Corp generates higher revenues and has higher coverage ratios. This suggests that Clean Corp could better handle a downturn in the economy than Half Company. (Study Session 10, LOS 42.c)

190. **A** Completeness is a factor in reliability, which is one of the four qualitative characteristics. The other qualitative characteristics are comparability, relevance, and understandability. There are many trade-offs made in compiling financial statements (e.g., timely information versus reliable information). Cost versus benefits is a constraint in producing financial statements. (Study Session 7, LOS 31.d)

191. **A** When evaluating the investment merits of projects, only incremental cash flows are relevant. Sunk costs, such as the feasibility study, must be ignored. Relevant cash flows for the project's investment include equipment costs as well as any shipping and installation costs. For the Darvo project, the investment required today is $700,000 = 680,000 + 13,500 + 6,500$. Now that the initial investment is known, we can calculate the profitability index using the following formula:

$$\text{Profitability Index} = \frac{\text{PV of Cash Flows}}{\text{Initial Investment}} = 1 + \frac{\text{NPV}}{\text{Initial Investment}}$$

$$= 1 + \frac{71,746}{700,000} = 1.1025 \approx 1.1$$

To calculate the payback period, we need to first calculate the cumulative cash flows for the project as follows:

	\multicolumn{4}{c}{*Year*}			
	0	1	2	3
Cash Flows	-700,000	675,000	220,000	25,000
Cumulative Cash Flows	-700,000	-25,000	195,000	220,000

The cash flows turn positive between year 1 and year 2 so we know the payback period is between 1 and 2 years. To get a more precise estimate, divide the remaining cash flow necessary to have a zero cumulative balance (i.e., -25,000) and divide by the cash flow in the next year (i.e., 220,000). This gives us $25,000 / 220,000 = 0.11$. The total payback period is then 1.11 years or approximately 1.1 years.

To calculate average accounting rate of return (AAR), we need to know the average net income of the project and the average book value. The average book value is given as $375,000. Average net income is equal to (458,000 + 3,000 − 192,000) / 3 = 89,667. Calculate AAR can be using the following formula:

$$AAR = \frac{\text{Average Net Income}}{\text{Average Book Value}} = \frac{89,667}{375,000} = 23.91\% \approx 23.9\%$$

(Study Session 11, LOS 44.d)

192. **B** There are several problems that arise from using the internal rate of return (IRR) as an investment criterion. For projects with nonconventional cashflows (i.e., cash flows that change signs more than once during the project), there may be zero, one, or more than one IRR. If there is more than one IRR, how do we know which is the right one? There is no way to tell. Another problem involves the scale of the project. For example, a project may require a large investment and have a small IRR while another project may require only a small investment but has a large IRR. If the firm cannot accept both projects, it may be better to accept the larger project if the NPV is greater than that of the smaller project. If a firm has an unlimited capital budget, it can accept all available positive NPV projects. These projects will also have an IRR greater than the firm's cost of capital. In such a scenario (i.e., projects are independent), the IRR investment criterion will not conflict with the NPV criterion and the firm may use either to make investment decisions. (Study Session 11, LOS 44.e)

193. **C** If two companies have the same capital structure (i.e., equal weights of debt and equity) and have the same pre-tax component costs of capital (i.e., equal costs of debt and equity) they will have the same weighted average cost of capital (WACC) only if the companies have the same marginal tax rate. If one company has a higher tax rate, the after-tax cost of debt: $k_d(1 - t)$, will be lower and the WACC: $w_e k_e + w_d k_d(1 - t)$, will be lower as well. Therefore, Beta Corporation has a lower current WACC since it has a higher tax rate. If Alpha's tax rate increases, its after-tax cost of debt will decrease and its WACC will decrease. Changes in the tax rate would not impact the cost of equity for either company. (Study Session 11, LOS 45.b)

194. **B** $P_p = \dfrac{D_p}{r_p} = \dfrac{2.5}{0.0625} = 40.00$ (Study Session 11, LOS 45.g)

195. **B** Since the developing markets being considered for investment have no equity markets, the risk adjustment should be based on bond credit risk measures. The analyst can calculate a risk to reward ratio for a broad sample of countries with credit ratings and an equity market. From this sample a risk to reward ratio is determined for the developing country without an equity market and applied against the country's credit rating to determine the cost of equity. (Study Session 11, LOS 45.j)

196. **A** Net operating cycle is calculated as the number of days of inventory + number of days of receivables − number of days of payables. Company Y's net operating cycles were 33 + 14 − 18 = 29 days in year 1 and 24 + 12 − 20 = 16 days in year 2. A shorter net operating cycle indicates a more liquid company. It is a better measure of liquidity because the whole cycle is included—from purchase of goods to sales and finally the payment for the goods sold. The decline in net operating cycle days in year 2 indicates an improvement in liquidity. For Company X, the net operating cycle for year 2 was 22 + 16 − 20 = 18 days, an increase from year 1, which was 18 + 14 − 19 = 13 days. The number of days in selection B was the operating cycle days, defined as number of days in inventory + number of days in receivables. (Study Session 11, LOS 46.b)

197. **A** The portfolio yield is a weighted average of the yields of the investments that comprise the portfolio. The weights are calculated as the value of each investment relative to the total portfolio value. The bond equivalent yields of the bank investments are given. The U.S. Treasury bill yield calculation (on a bond-equivalent basis) is:

(face value – market value) / market value × 365 / 90.

($1,000,000 – 990,390) / 990,390 × 365 / 90 = 0.0097 × 0.04056 = 3.93%.

The following table shows the weighted average yield calculation.

Investment	Market Value	% of total portfolio	Bond equivalent yield	Weighted Bond yield
Bank Commercial paper	$100,000	7.7%	4.34%	0.34%
Bank certificates of deposit	200,000	15.5%	4.84%	0.75%
Treasury bill	990,390	76.8%	3.93%	3.02%
Total portfolio	**1,290,390**	**1.00**		**4.11%**
Benchmark				4.08%

Selection B is incorrect because the 3.8% discount rate on the treasury bills was used to calculate weighted bond yield. Selection C is incorrect because a money market yield (using 360 days instead of 365 days in the formula) was used in the calculation of weighed bond yield. (Study Session 11, LOS 46.e)

198. **A** Information on takeover provisions is most likely to be found in the company's Articles of Incorporation. The annual proxy statement would only include takeover information that was being voted on at the annual meeting. Information on proposing shareholder initiatives is usually found in the annual proxy statement. Information on board member qualifications is generally found on a company's Web site and in the annual proxy statement. (Study Session 11, LOS 48.g)

Portfolio Management

199. **A** Statement 2 is incorrect. Markowitz's assumptions about the efficient frontier and investor behavior state that investors base investment decisions solely on expected return and risk, not risk alone. The first statement is a correct assumption, that all investments can be represented in a probability distribution of expected returns. (Study Session 12, LOS 50.b)

200. **A** All risky assets are in the market portfolio. T-bills, however, are not risky. (Study Session 12, LOS 51.b)

201. **B** Correlation determines the effect of adding an asset on the risk of the portfolio. Stock B has a negative covariance and thus a negative correlation with the existing portfolio. Since the other stocks have positive correlation, none could provide more diversification benefit than Stock B. (Study Session 12, LOS 50.e)

202. **C** The security market line is a graph of the capital asset pricing model (which assumes zero transactions costs):

$$E(R_i) = R_F + \beta_i[E(R_m) - R_F],$$

where $E(R_i)$ is the required return for asset i.

According to the SML, all combinations of $E(R_i)$ and β_i lie on a line. The starting point (intercept) is the risk-free rate, R_F, and the slope is the market risk premium. $E(R_m) - R_F$. When markets are not in equilibrium, expected (forecast) returns may deviate from required returns. The decision rule is to purchase all assets for which the expected return exceeds the required return (lies above the SML), and to sell all assets for which the expected return is less than the required return (falls below the SML). If transactions costs exist, however, the decision rule must be restated in terms of net returns. For undervalued stocks (purchase recommendations) the decision rule will be followed only if the expected return exceeds the SML required return *plus* the transaction cost percentage. For overvalued stocks (sell recommendations), the decision rule will be followed only if the expected return is less than the SML required return *minus* the transactions cost percentage. Therefore, the SML expands from a line to a band. The width of the band above and below the original SML equals the percentage transactions cost. The slope of the SML does not change. Therefore, the formation of the band is represented by a higher intercept for undervalued stocks (increasing the buy decision intercept) and a lower intercept (decreasing the sell decision intercept) for overvalued stocks. (Study Session 12, LOS 51.d)

203. **C** The covariance equals the product of the correlation and the two standard deviations. The standard deviations for Lumber Providers and Smithson Homebuilders equal 0.40 $\sqrt{0.16}$ and 0.50 $\sqrt{0.25}$, respectively. Therefore, the covariance equals:

covariance = $-0.60 \times (0.40) \times (0.50) = -0.12$ (Study Session 12, LOS 50.d)

204. **A** As stocks are randomly added to a portfolio, unsystematic risk decreases. A well-diversified 20-stock portfolio has little unsystematic risk. (Study Session 12, LOS 51.c)

Asset Valuation

205. **B** A time-series pattern to stock prices or returns is a violation of the weak form EMH. (Study Session 13, LOS 54.a)

206. **C** The semi-strong form of the EMH states that stock prices reflect all publicly available information. Several studies suggest that earnings surprises are not reflected as fast as expected by the semi-strong EMH. (Study Session 13, LOS 54.b)

207. **C** The dividend can be of any size. Suppose it is $1.00.

The price one year ago is P = 1.00 / 0.06 = 16.667

The price today is P = 1.00 / 0.05 = 20.

Kim pays 16.667 one year ago, and receives 20.00 plus a 1.00 dividend today. The rate of return is r = [(20 + 1)/16.667] − 1 = 21/16.667 − 1 = 26%. (Study Session 14, LOS 56.c)

208. **A** Data mining, even if it is not intentional, results from the likelihood that some statistically significant relationships will show up by chance in a large enough number of tests. A test at the 5% significance level of the hypothesis that stock prices are not correlated with a variable will reject about 1 such hypothesis in 20, even when the hypothesis is true. (Study Session 13, LOS 55.c)

209. **C** Statement 3 is from the capital asset pricing model, not the efficient markets hypothesis. The other two statements are correct. The EMH assumes that security prices follow a random walk. In an efficient market, higher transaction costs will penalize returns and offer no incremental benefit. (Study Session 13, LOS 54.c)

210. **B** The first statement is correct. The inaccuracy of risk measurement (the true risk measure is yet to be found) is a major criticism of research related to anomalistic returns of small companies and low price to earnings ratio stocks research. The second statement is incorrect. Although small sample bias is a potential problem of research related to market anomalies, in this case it is not a correct criticism of the research. Both small company and low price to earnings ratio anomalies have been observed over many time periods for large samples of stocks and do not suffer from a small sample bias. (Study Session 13, LOS 55.c)

211. **A** g = ROE × retention rate = [16.68 / 115] × [1 − (7.5 / 16.68)] = 0.145 × (1 − 0.45) = 7.975% = 8.0%. This growth rate represents the rate at which a company can grow its equity using internally generated funds. (Study Session 14, LOS 56.f)

212. **C** Unfortunately, book value can be negative and result in a negative P/B ratio. So Statement 3 is incorrect. The first two statements are correct. A weakness of the P/S ratio is that it does not allow for comparability of different company cost structures. P/CF ratio is more stable than the P/E ratio. (Study Session 14, LOS 59.a)

213. **A** required return = RFR + β [R_m − RFR]

    equity risk premium = [R_m − RFR]

    required return = 0.03 + 1.5 [0.06] = 0.12 (Study Session 14, LOS 56.g)

214. **B** Firm value is largely determined by its earnings power; a key motivation for using the price to earnings ratio. Sales are hard for management to falsify; a key motivation for using the price to sales ratio. Much like sales, cash flows are also difficult for a firm's managers to influence which makes the price to cash flow ratio attractive. Book value is subject to many accounting choices made by management; creating the potential for an unreliable price to book value ratio. (Study Session 14, LOS 59.a)

215. **C** Company X is a growth company, but its stock is overpriced and therefore speculative. Company Y is a cyclical company, but its stock is a defensive stock. (Study Session 14, LOS 58.a)

216. **A** A direct way to get the P/E is $\dfrac{P}{E} = \dfrac{1 - RR}{k - g} = \dfrac{1 - 0.6}{0.1 - 0.05} = 8$.

    You can also get $P_0/E_1 = 8$ by another route. You know $P_0 = D_1 / (r − g)$. Substituting everything except D_1 is $60 = D_1/(0.10 − 0.05)$, so D_1 must be equal to $60(0.05) = 3.00$. The retention rate is 60%, so the dividend payout rate is 40%. $E_1 = D_1 / 0.40 = 3.00 / 0.40 = 7.50$. So $P_0/E_1 = 60 / 7.50 = 8.0x$. (Study Session 14, LOS 58.b)

217. **B** The effective duration is the expected percentage change in price for a 100 bp change in yield. The actual yield change used to calculate the effective duration does not matter. The formula for calculating the effective duration of a bond is:

$$\frac{P_- - P_+}{2 \times P_0 \times \Delta y} = \frac{895.78 - 833.82}{2 \times 864.10 \times 0.0050} \approx 7.2$$

(Study Session 16, LOS 66.d)

218. **A** First we compute the yield to maturity of the bond. PV = –$958.97, FV = $1,000, PMT = ((4.2% × 1000) / 2 =) 21, n = (6 × 2 =)12, solve for i. I = 2.5%, multiply by 2 since it is a semiannual bond to get an annualized yield to maturity of 5.0%. Now compute the price of the bond at using yield one basis point higher, or 5.01%. FV = $1,000, PMT = 21, n = 12, i = (5.01 / 2 =) 2.505, solve for PV. PV = –$958.47. The price changes from $958.97 to $958.47, or $0.50. (Study Session 16, LOS 66.i)

219. **C** $N = 30(15 \times 2); FV = 100; PMT = 0; PV = -30.83; CPT \rightarrow I / Y = 4.00 \times 2 = 8.00$

(Study Session 16, LOS 64.e)

220. **C** Because Bond A has a coupon rate that is below the required yield, it will trade at a discount to par. Bond B, with a coupon rate greater than the required yield, will trade at a premium to par. The fact that both bonds were issued at premiums does not matter, nor does the difference in times to maturity. (Study Session 15, LOS 61.b)

221. **C** A higher interest rate volatility assumption will lead to a lower OAS. The higher volatility will increase the value of the embedded option, thus reducing the spread remaining after adjusting for the option. The Cavalier bond is not affected because it has no embedded options. The adjustable rate is not an option. (Study Session 16, LOS 65.g)

222. **B** Modified duration is most appropriate for bonds that do not have embedded options since such bond's expected cash flows do not change when the yield changes. Effective duration should be used for securities with options (CMOs have a prepayment option). Convexity measures by themselves are not good measures of interest rate risk. (Study Session 16, LOS 66.e)

223. **A** If expected volatility increases, the value of the call option embedded in a callable bond will increase, thus lowering the value of the bond. $P_{callable\ bond} = P_{non\ callable\ bond}$ – call option. Likewise, the value of a put option will increase, increasing the value of the putable bond. $P_{putable\ bond} = P_{non\ putable\ bond}$ + put option. (Study Session 15, LOS 61.n)

224. **A** If the prefunded bonds are supported by an escrowed portfolio of US Treasury securities, they have less credit risk than insured bonds, which would only be backed by a private insurance company, not the US federal government. Either revenue or general obligation bonds can be prefunded. (Study Session 15, LOS 62.g)

225. **A** Comparable on-the-run and off-the-run Treasury issues have different interest rate risks and reinvestment risks. A security with a higher coupon rate will always have higher reinvestment risk than a comparable security with a lower coupon rate. (Study Session 15, LOS 62.b)

226. **B** $(1.04^5 / 1.032^2)^{1/3} - 1 = 4.5\%$ (Study Session 16, LOS 65.h)

227. **C** The CMO redistributes the prepayment risk among the different tranches, but does not eliminate the risk. In fact, the total prepayment risk remains the same with higher prepayment risk for some tranches and lower prepayment risks for other tranches. (Study Session 15, LOS 62.e)

228. **C** Call protection is much more robust than refunding protection. Refunding protection does not provide absolute protection against retirement. (Study Session 15, LOS 60.d)

229. **C** As rates fall, the option becomes more valuable, and the price of Bond X will not appreciate as rapidly as the noncallable Bond Y. The negative convexity of the callable bond will limit its price appreciation potential. (Study Session 15, LOS 61.d)

230. **B** To compute the value of this bond, you must discount each of the cash flows at a different interest rate appropriate for the timing of the cash flow:

$$\frac{40}{(1+0.04)} + \frac{40}{(1+0.045)^2} + \frac{(40+1,000)}{(1+0.0475)^3} = 979.93.$$

(Study Session 16, LOS 65.e)

231. **B** The downside risk of HSD is reduced by the long puts; the upside potential and probability of gains are both reduced by the cost of the puts; the breakeven price is increased by the cost of the puts. The covered call will reduce the breakeven price of CGF but will also reduce upside potential (since the stock will be called away from Walters if the stock price increases above the strike price). (Study Session 17, LOS 72.b)

232. **B** This is the primary role of the clearinghouse. By providing liquidity, the clearinghouse may also help lower transaction costs indirectly, but B is the best answer. (Study Session 17, LOS 69.a)

233. **C** Interest rate swaps can be structured as fixed for floating (one side pays a floating rate while the other pays a fixed rate) or floating for floating (both sides pay a floating rate). The plain vanilla interest rate swap is by definition a fixed for floating swap. Holt has correctly stated these features. If a netting arrangement exists, then there is no exchange of notional principal, and each counterparty has credit risk limited to the net payment due from the other counterparty. By netting, the risk of losing the notional principal is eliminated, thus reducing credit risk for both sides. (Study Session 17, LOS 71.b)

234. **C** $P = C + \left[\dfrac{X}{(1+\text{RFR})^T} \right] + PV_{CF} - S_0$

$$P = 3.50 + \left[\frac{70}{(1+0.053)^{\frac{3}{12}}} \right] + \left(\frac{0.56}{(1+0.053)^{\frac{3}{12}}} \right) - 64 = 9.15$$

(Study Session 17, LOS 70.j)

235. **C** Interest rates have a direct relationship with call options. An investor can effectively leverage a stock purchase either directly by borrowing funds and paying the interest expense or indirectly by purchasing call options and avoiding the interest expense. Thus when interest rates are high, the value of call options increases. Interest rates have an indirect relationship with put options. An investor can sell short a stock now and invest in bonds which will earn interest, or he can use put options which will also leverage the sale but will also forego the interest earnings. Thus, high interest rates decrease put option prices. Using these relationships, we can deduce that the increase in put option prices could have occurred as a result of a decrease in interest rates. Volatility is directly related to the price of all options (put or call). As volatility increases, so does the potential upside and downside prices of the underlying. The increase in the price of MCC call options could have occurred as a result of increased volatility in MCC stock. (Study Session 17, LOS 70.m)

236. **C** A futures contract requires an initial deposit in the margin account, frequently about 10% of the contract value at initiation. The maintenance margin is the level below which a margin call will be issued to the contract holder. Once a margin call is received, the investor must post enough margin to bring the account balance back to the initial level. This amount is called the variation margin. The variation margin is not necessarily equal to the difference between the maintenance margin and the initial margin. In this question, the variation margin is $17,500. This is the amount required to bring the account balance back to $37,500. Therefore, the maintenance margin must be at least $20,000 (= $37,500 – $17,500). Answer C is the only reasonable choice. Note that it is possible for the margin account balance to drop rapidly enough that the maintenance margin level is surpassed by a significant amount. Thus, the variation margin may be an amount greater than the difference between the initial margin and maintenance margin level. (Study Session 17, LOS 69.b)

237. **C**
$$C = S + P - \left[\frac{X}{(1 + RFR)^T} \right]$$

$$C = 33 + 2.75 - \left[\frac{30}{(1 + 0.055)^{\frac{80}{365}}} \right] = 6.1$$

(Study Session 17, LOS 70.j)

238. **B** Compared to closely held private companies, shares in publicly traded companies include a minority interest discount. Since the public shares are liquid, there are no marketability issues. (Study Session 18, LOS 73.n)

239. **B** The legal structure of an ETF is similar to an open-end fund. The remaining statements are correct. (Study Session 18, LOS 73.b)

240. **A** There is no guarantee that the Fund of Funds (i.e. the hedge funds used) will outperform its investment benchmark, but the reason for investing in the Fund of Funds is to decrease risk (correct). The due diligence process will not completely uncover all potential problems. Hedge fund managers are secretive about their operations and investment strategy so transparency is simply not a characteristic of hedge fund investing. An investor cannot be completely assured that all investment risks are uncovered by the due diligence process (incorrect). (Study Session 18, LOS 73.j)

Notes

Notes

Notes

Notes

Notes

Notes

Notes

Notes